348

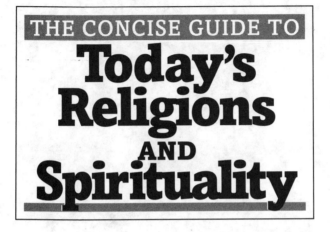

THE CONCISE GUIDE TO
Today's Religions
AND
Spirituality

James K. Walker
with the staff of Watchman Fellowship

HARVEST HOUSE PUBLISHERS

EUGENE, OREGON

Cover by Koechel Peterson & Associates, Minneapolis, Minnesota

Back cover author photo © Sheltons Photography

Cover photo © Photos.com

THE CONCISE GUIDE TO TODAY'S RELIGIONS AND SPIRITUALITY

Copyright © 2007 by Watchman Fellowship, Inc.
Published by Harvest House Publishers
Eugene, Oregon 97402
www.harvesthousepublishers.com

Library of Congress Cataloging-in-Publication Data
Walker, James K.
  The concise guide to today's religions and spirituality / James K. Walker.
      p. cm.
   ISBN-13: 978-0-7369-2011-7 (pbk.)
   ISBN-10: 0-7369-2011-0
 1. Religions—Dictionaries. 2. Cults—Dictionaries. 3. Sects—Dictionaries. I. Title.
   BL31.W35 2007
   200.3—dc22   2006030633

Printed in the United States of America

08 09 10 11 12 13 14 / LB-CF / 12 11 10 9 8 7 6 5 4 3 2

*To my wife, Jimmie, who despite my heavy travel schedule
and long hours of ministry responsibilities, remains
my faithful spouse, biggest supporter, and best friend of 30 years.*

Acknowledgments

This book could not have been written without the dedicated assistance of the great staff at Watchman Fellowship (past and present), who helped with everything from the research, editing, and drafting of additional entries to proofreading and tracking down Web addresses.

I especially want to thank our vice president, Bob Waldrep, whose many hours of hard work were critical to this book.

Other current staff who helped make this book possible include:

Bob Anderson, Pennsylvania director
Laura Arnn, office manager
Phillip Arnn, senior researcher
Brad Blan, director of information technology
Bonnie Bradford, ministry assistant
Preston Condra, associate director
Allan McConnell, executive administrator
Timothy Oliver, Utah director
Rick Sutton, multimedia producer

Former staff members also played an essential role in this book, including:

Jason Barker
Robert Bowman
David Grubbs

In addition, I wish to express my appreciation to Tim Martin, who serves as Illinois director and editor of our *Profile Notebook* (see page 363), and to Debby Frear, who maintains our research library. The *Profile Notebook* and the research library were both very helpful to this project.

I am also very grateful for Nancy Hansen and the Huston Foundation, without whose help and support, this book would have been impossible.

Finally, I want to say a special thanks to David Henke, the founder of Watchman Fellowship, whose kind help and guidance when I was struggling spiritually as a former Mormon was invaluable. His friendship and discipleship also made this book possible.

Foreword

Research for this book began over 20 years ago as a natural outgrowth of my work with Watchman Fellowship, an evangelical Christian organization ministering in the field of alternative spirituality and cults (see page 361 for more information). Since the mid-1980s, my staff and I have visited hundreds of metaphysical bookstores, New Age centers, and used bookstores throughout the country gathering documents and information on alternative faiths and practices. At the same time, scores of friends and supporters of Watchman Fellowship from across the country began sending in news clippings from local media sources reporting on obscure religious sects and controversial spiritual practices.

Through the years, all this data, combined with our ongoing research and writing resources, was cataloged and filed as part of our growing research library, which currently contains over 50,000 files, books, periodicals, and media pieces. Those files became the basis for an internal database we created to assist staff members in research, writing, and answering inquiries. Beginning in the late 1980s, we began publishing portions of that list in newspaper and magazine formats. By the mid-1990s, a scaled-down version of that database, *The Index of Cults and Religions,* was published on our Web site at http://www.watchman.org.

Over the years, many Christians—including ministers and church members—have given us very positive feedback on the index, and have also requested updated and more thorough editions. This book is a significantly expanded version of that online database. It is not exhaustive in that it does not contain information on every religion, doctrine, and practice in America. That would be beyond the scope of any book. What it does attempt to provide is a fairly comprehensive yet reasonably concise guide to every major religious movement in America, including those of evangelical Christianity, along with hundreds of the more obscure faiths, doctrines, and practices.

This book is an extension of our research and, to some degree, a work in progress. Religious groups change over time, and new ones come on the scene, making it necessary to make revisions in future editions. You can help keep our research current with your comments or observations by reaching our staff through our Web site www.watchman.org.

On behalf of the staff of Watchman Fellowship, I want to thank you for choosing this book as part of your library. I hope you find it to be a quick and understandable guide to alternative spirituality—a starting place for understanding other religions. It is our prayer that this book will serve as a catalyst for Christians who desire to earnestly contend for the faith (Jude 3) and speak the truth in love (Ephesians 4:14-15).

—*James K. Walker*

Introduction

The purpose of this book is to provide readers with a handy guide to the diverse landscape of American spirituality. This book contains over 1,700 concise definitions and cross references covering religions, denominations, cults, occult groups, new movements, historical heresies, key leaders, controversial doctrines, practices, and key vocabulary terms.

This book is needed because the face of religion in America is changing. While Christianity and Judaism still rank first and second in numbers of adherents, there are a growing number of other world religions, alternative forms of spirituality, and new religious movements gaining converts. Between 1990 and 2004, Islam and Buddhism grew by an estimated 109 percent and 170 percent respectively in the United States. During the same period, all the religions and denominations classified as "Christian," as a whole, grew by only 5 percent.[1]

There is also widespread interest in the occult as reflected by popular TV programs such as NBC's *Medium*. The drama is reportedly based on the true-life psychic Allison DuBois, who allegedly makes contact with the dead. In 2006, *John Edward Cross Country* was launched on the We network as a sequel to Edward's earlier show, *Crossing Over*, and a best-selling book by the same title featured alleged psychic communication with the dead. CBS has also joined the party with the hit series *Ghost Whisperer*, which stars Jennifer Love Hewitt.

The country's fascination with the occult and witchcraft goes far beyond television programming, reaching into the core beliefs of millions of Americans. A 2003 Harris poll revealed that almost one in three Americans

(31 percent) believe in astrology, an ancient occult divination practice going back to Bible times (Deuteronomy 18:10-12). More telling in the Harris survey is that among Americans ages 25-29, belief in astrology has jumped to an unprecedented 43 percent.[2]

The growing impact of the occult can also be measured by comparing its growth with that of other religions. Based on research conducted at the graduate school of the City University of New York by sociologists Barry A. Kosmin and Seymour P. Lachman, paganism (as represented by Wiccans, pagans, and Druids) now ranks as the seventh-largest organized religion in America, with an estimated 433,267 adherents as of 2004.[3]

Missionary efforts by nontraditional religions are also remarkable. In 2006, the Watchtower Bible and Tract Society reported that 6.7 million Jehovah's Witnesses spent over 1.3 *billion* hours in their door-to-door proclamation.[4] In 2006, the Church of Jesus Christ of Latter-day Saints (LDS) fielded over 56,000 missionaries in 165 countries.[5]

Their massive missionary efforts have paid dividends. Joseph Smith, Jr. founded the LDS church in 1830 with six charter members. They currently have 12.5 million members worldwide with about 5.7 million[6] in the United States, causing some scholars to rank the LDS as the eighth-largest "denomination" in America.[7] The same study positions the Jehovah's Witnesses as the eleventh-largest "denomination." The Watchtower reported that in 2005, 16.6 million people attended their annual Memorial Meal worldwide, with 2.2 million in attendance in the United States.[8]

In addition to large groups, such as the LDS, Jehovah's Witnesses, and Wicca, hundreds of new, much smaller religions are springing up—seemingly on a daily basis. They join an ever-widening stream of American spirituality that includes some groups that promote a host of questionable new doctrines and controversial spiritual practices. This book has been written to provide some basic understanding of much of this phenomena.

An Evangelical Christian Perspective

In the spirit of full disclosure, it is acknowledged that this book is written from a Christian perspective. More specifically, it reflects an evangelical Christian viewpoint as described in the definitions section. While every effort has been made to be factual and accurate, this book is unavoidably flavored by conservative, traditional Christian beliefs about the Bible, sin, salvation, the gospel, and Jesus Christ. This perspective is reflected in the definitions themselves and, in some cases, the decisions that were made as to what subjects and groups should be included.

We believe in religious freedom. Freedom of religion must be cherished and protected. This is my position and the position of Watchman Fellowship. While we believe that all religions should have equal protection, it does not mean that we believe all religions are equally valid from a biblical standpoint. We do not accept the axiom that "all roads lead to heaven." Jesus said that most people take the wrong road, which He described as the "broad" way that takes them to "destruction" (Matthew 7:13). Jesus taught that there is only one road or path to God, saying, "I am the way, the truth, and the life. No man comes to the Father except through Me" (John 14:6).

All religion is an attempt to address spiritual needs. The Bible says that the answer to the spiritual hunger experienced by all humankind is found in a saving relationship with Jesus Christ. It is He who purchased our salvation through His death on the cross, His burial, and His resurrection. The salvation He offers, eternal life, is available only to those who receive it as a gift by grace (undeserved kindness) through faith (complete trust) in the Lord Jesus Christ.

Some General Definitions

The term *cult* is based on the Latin word *cultus,* which is found in English in agrarian terms such as *cultivation* and in the word *culture.* The root is also used in a religious context to refer simply to any system of belief and worship. In a Christian context, the word is used to denote an inauthentic alternative to the Christian faith. That usage can probably be traced to the early twentieth-century with Ernst Troeltsch's *The Social Teaching of the Christian Church,* in which he defined a cult as a mystical religion that appeals to the intelligentsia.[9]

The term *cult* has also evolved in the work of psychologists, sociologists, and anthropologists, who frequently use the word to describe religious structure or belief patterns with meanings (usually nonpejorative) unique to their disciplines.

Another usage for the word *cult* is found in the secular cult-awareness movement—sometimes referred to by critics as the anti-cult movement. The International Cultic Studies Association (ICSA—formerly the American Family Foundation)[10] of Bonita Springs, Florida, is an interdisciplinary network of academicians, professionals, former group members, and families who study and educate the public about religious groups and cults.

Specifically, they provide information about social-psychological influence and control, authoritarianism, and zealotry found in cultic groups, alternative movements, and other environments. They use the word *cult* within the context of the following 10 traits:

1. *Submission to Leadership*—Leaders tend to exert absolute control, frequently portraying themselves as prophets of God (or even God Himself). Such individuals demand submission even if changes or conflicts occur in ideology or behavior.

2. *Polarized Worldview*—Cults usually view the outside world through a paradigm of existential conflict, in which the group must be isolated from the hostile and contaminated world outside.

3. *Emphasizing Emotion over Thought*—Emotions, intuitions, and mystical insights are typically given priority over rational conclusions.

4. *Emotional Manipulation*—Cult leaders frequently manipulate group and interpersonal dynamics to influence responses. (This type of manipulation may be very subtle and take the form of questions or suggestions that evoke emotional responses such as fear, guilt, or a false sense of obligation designed to trigger compliance with the leaders' desires.)

5. *Denigration of Critical Thinking*—Some cults characterize any independent thought as selfish and rational use of intellect as evil.

6. *Restrictive Soteriology*—Salvation, enlightenment, or fulfillment can only be realized in the group.

7. *Situational Ethics*—Any action or behavior is justifiable as long as it furthers the group's goals. The group (or leader) determines absolute truth, which then supersedes all outside juridical laws.

8. *Preeminence of the Group*—The group's concerns typically supersede an individual's goals, needs, aspirations, and concerns. Tremendous pressure is exerted upon individual members to conform to the norms of the group.

9. *Condemnation of Apostates and Critics*—Members are frequently allowed no contact with former members or critics of the group. This prohibition is often even levied against members who make critical comments of the group or its leader.

10. *Isolation from Nonmembers*—Contact with nonmembers, even family, is frequently restricted to proselytic encounters.

Some Christian Definitions

Cult: In addition to the usages mentioned above, mainstream Christians often define a *cult* as a group who presents an inauthentic form of Christianity that seriously deviates from the essential doctrines of classical Christianity. In most cases, the group in question claims to be Christian or compatible with Christianity but the organization's aberrant beliefs concerning central doctrines of the faith result in the group being classified as unorthodox, or cultic. In this sense, the term *cult* primarily has a doctrinal or theological meaning[11] and could be used to describe pseudo-Christian groups or forms of counterfeit Christianity. Most often, Watchman Fellowship uses this theological meaning when using the word *cult*.

For over 20 years at Watchman Fellowship, we have used the following "mathematical formula" to identify four patterns often evident in the cults in terms of theological deviation:

1. ***Addition***—Pseudo-Christian groups often add to Scripture, either by introducing additional works to the canon of Scripture (e.g., the Book of Mormon), receiving additional "revelations" from God (e.g., the apocalyptic revelations of David Koresh), or declaring that the Bible cannot be understood apart from the indispensable literature or teachings of their group (e.g., the reliance of Jehovah's Witnesses upon literature from the Watchtower Society). *See Deuteronomy 4:2; Revelation 22:18.*

2. ***Subtraction***—Pseudo-Christian groups subtract from the humanity of Christ (e.g., the gnostic HERESY) or the deity of Christ, either through an Arian denial of his deity (e.g., the Jehovah's Witnesses) or by claiming that all humans are either gods or united with God (e.g., New Age devotees who attempt to achieve a Christ-consciousness). *See 2 Corinthians 11:3-4.*

3. ***Multiplication***—Pseudo-Christian groups multiply the requirements for salvation, teaching that Christ's atoning work on the

cross and resurrection is not sufficient. Good works, law keeping, and earning favor are also required for one to receive eternal life—rather than salvation by grace through faith in Christ alone (e.g., the sabbatarian groups who require observance of the Jewish Sabbaths, dietary laws, tithing, etc., as preconditions for receiving eternal life). *See Galatians 1:6-8; 2:16.*

4. *Division*—Pseudo-Christian groups often divide their followers' loyalties by teaching that one cannot be loyal to God without being loyal to their leader, group, or organization. This characteristic, sometimes called the "only true church syndrome," leads followers to believe that there is no salvation outside of that organization or leader. This creates *another* "mediator between God and men" besides Jesus. This condition often results in the worst kind of spiritual abuse, as followers feel they must stay and endure whatever the group demands because there is no salvation elsewhere. *See 1 Timothy 2:5.*

Occult: The term *occult* comes from the Latin *occultus,* referring to that which is hidden. In a general sense, the term *occult* can be applied to any attempt to gain supernatural knowledge or power apart from the God of the Bible. The word is generally used to describe secret or mysterious supernatural powers and magical rituals. Occultic groups typically exhibit the following distinctive characteristics:

1. Secret knowledge or wisdom can be attained using techniques that transcend the five human senses.

2. Such techniques usually involve contact with supernatural forces or energies.

3. The goal of obtaining such power is to exercise control over events, humans, or natural forces.

New Age: The New Age is a recent and developing belief system in North America encompassing thousands of autonomous (and sometimes contradictory) beliefs, organizations, and events. Adherents of the New Age often borrow their theology from pantheistic Eastern religions and their practices from nineteenth-century Western spiritualism and occultism. The term *New Age* is used herein as an umbrella term to describe organizations that seem to exhibit one or more of the following beliefs:

1. *Pantheism*—All is one, and all reality is thus part of the whole (monism) and the one is identified as God. Thus the universe (including humanity) is God, which is seen as an impersonal, all-encompassing force.

2. *Reincarnation*—Humans never die, but instead continually develop themselves through a succession of lives.

3. *Reality Manipulation*—Humans can alter or create their own reality or values through a transformed consciousness or altered states of consciousness.

In all cases, our use of words such as *cult, occult,* and *New Age* are merely intended to provide a very basic doctrinal taxonomy. The use of these categories and terms in no way implies that the followers or leaders of these organizations or religions are evil or immoral people. It simply means that such groups promote doctrines or practices that may be considered outside the boundaries of historic, biblical Christianity.

Some Advice for Families

Much of the counseling we do at Watchman Fellowship involves advising Christian families who have had a son or daughter join a new religious movement or alternative faith. If your son is dating a Jehovah's Witness, or your daughter is dabbling in Wicca, or your granddaughter has become a Latter-day Saint, I know how overwhelming that can be. I can remember the strain placed on my relationship with my father when, as a fourth-generation Mormon, I decided to leave the LDS church to become an evangelical Christian. It was devastating. I also know how hard it can be for Christian families to see a loved one leave the faith. It is especially difficult for those families who have a deep and active commitment to traditional Christian faith.

You may have purchased this book in the hopes that it would be a starting place for understanding some of your loved one's beliefs or practices. If so, let me share a few suggestions you may find helpful. First, you may want to refer to our Web site (www.watchman.org). It contains a great deal of free information as well as witnessing resources you can order.

I would also encourage you to do everything possible to maintain the relationship with the family member who has joined an alternative faith. Punishment or ultimatums rarely, if ever, have the desired result. As long as you have an open door of communication, there is a chance for real discussion and resolution. Learn everything you can about the religion or group so that when the Lord opens the door of communication, you will be fully prepared to discuss your concerns. This includes being prepared to address the issues biblically, factually (with the proper documentation), respectfully, and prayerfully. If the opportunity to do this doesn't arise right away, don't become discouraged. I have found that oftentimes, the Lord seems to wait until we are fully prepared before He opens the door for dialogue to take place.

Once you are prepared, you need to be sensitive to the Lord's timing on when and how that discussion should take place. Avoid *ad hominem* attacks against the individual (either the family member or members of the religion). Keep in mind that no one can (or should) be forced to believe anything against his or her will. Instead, you must spend time building a bridge and maintaining the relationship. The Bible says that we are not to quarrel, but "in humility" to "be gentle" in hopes that God will "grant them repentance" (2 Timothy 2:24-26).

Finally, do not forget the power of prayer. Our source of hope and strength in trying times is our trust in the Lord. From before the foundation of the world, He knew you would be facing this challenge. He is still God; He is still in control, He has a plan, and you want to walk willingly with Him wherever that plan may lead. If my staff or I can be of help to you, please let us know. For contact information, see page 361.

A

A-Albionic Consulting and Research, James Daugherty—Ferndale, MI: Also known as the New Paradigms Project. The group's primary agenda involves disseminating a CONSPIRACY THEORY regarding a global power struggle between the British Empire and the Vatican. They also promote other conspiracy theories. Published *The Project* and *Conspiracy Digest* newsletters. Currently publish a *New Paradigms* e-mail list. Web site—http://www.a-albionic.com.

Aaronic Order, Marice Glendenning—Murry, UT: A Mormon splinter group incorporated in 1942 by Glendenning, who was excommunicated by the LDS Church after receiving and publishing revelations later known as the *Levitical Writings*. See CHURCH OF JESUS CHRIST OF LATTER-DAY SAINTS.

Abaddon: (Greek, *Appollyon* = "the destroyer") A demon described in the BIBLE as "the angel of the bottomless pit" (Revelation 9:11). JEHOVAH'S WITNESSES have alternately taught that Abaddon is Jesus Christ and SATAN. See WATCHTOWER BIBLE AND TRACT SOCIETY.

Abaku: Syncretistic religion of the Caribbean and South America. Blends tribal religions of Africa with ROMAN CATHOLICISM. Akabu is particularly influential in the religions of Brazil.

Abbey of Thelema—Old Greenwich, CT: An OCCULT organization practicing ESOTERIC MAGIC, and continuing the teachings of ALEISTER CROWLEY. Web site—http://thelemicmagick.com.

The Abode of the Message: See AEGIS AT THE ABODE OF THE MESSAGE.

Abundant Life United Pentecostal Church—Portland, OR: Part of the United Pentecostal Church, a denomination in the family of APOSTOLIC CHURCHES. Abundant Life UPC, like most Apostolic churches, stresses holiness prohibitions against makeup, jewelry, cutting hair, and television. Publishes *The Apostolic Contender* newsletter. See ONENESS PENTE-COSTALISM.

Academy for Guided Imagery, Martin L. Rossman and David E. Bresler—Mill Valley, CA: Practices physical and psychological healing through ALTERED STATE OF CONSCIOUSNESS, GUIDED IMAGERY, HYPNOSIS, and MAGIC. Web site—http://www.academyforguidedimagery.com.

Academy of Healing Arts, Inc.—Krum, TX: Practices AROMATHERAPY and REFLEXOLOGY. Web site—http://www.academyofhealingarts.info.

Academy of Religion and Psychical Research—Evanston, IL: Organization founded in 1972 as an academic affiliate of SPIRITUAL FRONTIERS FELLOWSHIP to explore PSYCHIC occurrences and metaphysical experiences while evaluating the growing interest in OCCULT phenomena in Christian churches. In 2005 the name was changed to ACADEMY OF SPIRITUALITY AND PARANORMAL STUDIES, Inc. Web site—http://www.lightlink.com/arpr. See SPIRITUALISM; DIVINATION.

Academy of Spirituality and Paranormal Studies—Bloomfield CT: See ACADEMY OF RELIGION AND PSYCHICAL RESEARCH.

Acappella: A contemporary CHRISTIAN music group formed by Keith Lancaster in 1982. Named for their purely *a cappella* (voices only) music, this is by far the most popular group to emerge from the CHURCHES OF CHRIST, which forbids musical instruments in worship. Web site—http://www.acappella.org. See CHURCHES OF CHRIST.

Achievers' Group Corporation—Orlando, FL: Teaches that humans can live to 150 and more by ingesting Achiever's Choice, capsules containing a 200-1 formula of aloe vera and psycnogenol. See HOLISTIC HEALING.

Acoustic Brain Research, Tom Kenyon: Kenyon teaches that humans can attain higher levels of existence through achieving an ALTERED STATE OF CONSCIOUSNESS and learning to vibrate inner sound at a higher rate through their CHAKRAS.

Activated: A monthly subscription-based magazine with links to THE FAMILY (CHILDREN OF GOD). See ACTIVATED MINISTRIES.

Activated Ministries—Escondido, CA: A charitable foundation and licensed distributor of AURORA PRODUCTION AG products worldwide, including the magazine *ACTIVATED*. Web site—http://www.activatedmin istries.org. See THE FAMILY (CHILDREN OF GOD).

Actualism: NEW AGE, PANENTHEISTIC teaching that humanity is divine and united with the Mother-Father-Creator God. See CHRIST CONSCIOUSNESS.

Acupressure: See ACUPUNCTURE.

Acupuncture: Chinese system of healing that uses needles or hand pressure (acupressure) to balance the YIN AND YANG energies in the body by opening blocked MERIDIANS (apexes in the pathways). Once the CHAKRAS (key points or intersections) are open, the energy (CHI) can then flow through the body, bringing all things into harmony. While some limited physical effects (mostly anesthetic) can be attributed to this practice, these effects have scientific, physiological explanations totally unrelated to the theories of TAOISM. See HOLISTIC HEALTH. For further research, a four-page Watchman Fellowship Profile is available (see page 363). Web site—http://www.watchman.org/notebook.

Acuto Center for Renewal and Prayer—Wichita, KS: Named after the town where Maria de Mattias, founder of the Sisters of the Adorers of the Blood of Christ, began her work in 1834. Combines ROMAN CATHOLICISM with Eastern MYSTICISM and NATIVE AMERICAN SPIRITUALITY.

Adams, Dennis—Mount Shasta, CA: A NEW AGE teacher who proclaims that humanity is God. Web site—http://www.dennisadamsseminars.com.

Adelphi Organization, Richard Kieninger (1927–2002)—Dallas, TX: Promotes NEW AGE teachings on ATLANTIS, KARMA, and the seven planes of existence. The group believes a secret organization of saints called The Brotherhoods is using the United States as a launching pad for establishing a paradisiacal world. Kieninger established a utopian community called Adelphi. Web site—http://www.adelphi.com. See STELLE GROUP.

Adeptco, Chuck McDonald—Omaha, NE: McDonald practices YOGA, working with CRYSTALS, REINCARNATION, KARMA, and the teachings of the KABBALAH.

Adi Da, aka Bubba Free John, aka Da Free John: Born Franklin Jones, teaches a variation of *Advaita Vedanta,* or radical MONISM. Adi Da claims to be the one God, BRAHMA, and ATMAN. Former members accuse Adi Da of sexually abusing his female members. Web site—http://www.adidam.org. See SPIRITUAL ABUSE.

Adler, Margo: A witch affiliated with the Covenant of the Goddess, the second-largest coven in the United States. Adler wrote the highly influential book *Drawing Down the Moon.* Adler is also a correspondent for National Public Radio and serves as the host of NPR's *Justice Talking.* See GODDESS; WICCA.

Adoptionism: See DYNAMIC MONARCHIANISM.

Advanced Neuro Dynamics, Tad James—Honolulu, HI: Practices NEURO-LINGUISTIC PROGRAMMING (NLP) to help humans contact their higher self. James also teaches huna, the native Hawaiian religion and created Time Line Therapy, a process that allegedly enables a person to work through past negative experiences and produce positive behavioral change in minutes, making it faster than Brief Therapy. Web site—http://www.tadjames.com.

Advanced Organization of Los Angeles (AOLA): Promotes the philosophy of the CHURCH OF SCIENTOLOGY.

Advanced Systems, Inc.: See ZEN MASTER RAMA.

Advanced Training Institute International (ATII): See GOTHARD, BILL.

Advent Christian Church—Charlotte, NC: Teaches that the HOLY SPIRIT emanates from God, and that humans do not have souls. Not affiliated with the SEVENTH-DAY ADVENTIST CHURCH or the CHRISTIAN CHURCH (DISCIPLES OF CHRIST).

Adventism/Adventist: See SECOND ADVENT MOVEMENT.

Adventures in Enlightenment: Founded in 1986. See COLE-WHITTAKER, TERRY.

Advice Line: See FOUNDATION FOR HUMAN UNDERSTANDING.

AEgis at the Abode of the Message, Pir Vilayat Inayat Khan—New Lebanon, NY: Now known as THE ABODE OF THE MESSAGE. A syncretistic NEW AGE group that combines SUFISM, ALCHEMY, DOWSING, and MEDITATION to lead to "inner attunement." AEgis also uses the sweat lodge that is integral to much of NATIVE AMERICAN SPIRITUALITY. Web site—http://www.theabode.net.

Aesthetic Realism Foundation, Eli Seigel (1902–1978)—New York: The Aesthetic Realism Foundation advances Seigel's teaching that happiness can be achieved through the harmony of opposites—e.g., realizing and accepting that the world is both beautiful and horrific. Educators have criticized the foundation after public school teachers in New York introduced the philosophy into high school English, biology, and art courses. Web site—http://www.aestheticrealism.org.

Aetherius Society, Dr. George King (1919–1997): NEW AGE group that contacts the GREAT WHITE BROTHERHOOD and ASCENDED MASTERS, as well as UFOs, while practicing CLAIRVOYANCE, ALCHEMY, the OCCULT SECRETS of JESUS, and MANTRAS to align KARMA and escape REINCARNATION. Web site—http://www.aetherius.org.

Affective Education: Also called value-free, or non-directive, education. Influenced by the philosophy of Carl Rogers, affective education programs attempt to facilitate the emotional development of children in order to enhance the learning process, particularly focusing on self-esteem. This contrasts with traditional educational paradigms that focus on cognitive, or intellectual, practices such as reading, writing, and arithmetic. Affective education has become particularly influential in drug awareness programs for youth.

African Hebrew Israelites of Jerusalem, Ben Ammi Ben Israel (Ben Carter)—Dimona, Israel: Carter claims that while in Chicago in 1966, the angel Gabriel came to him in a vision and told him the Israelites among African Americans were to return to the Promised Land and establish the kingdom of God. The next year some 30-40 (the number varies, with the group listing it as 350) African Americans from Chicago left with him, traveling first to West Africa. In 1969 they entered Israel as immigrants. Their immigrant status was revoked in 1971; however, they remained steadfast, with upwards of 2,500 members living in the desert until they were granted permanent resident status in 2003. They adhere to many of the Old Testament laws, holy days, and practices, and they keep a vegetarian diet and are polygamous. Web site—http://www.kingdomofyah.com. See BLACK HEBREWS.

African Methodist Episcopal Church (AME)—Nashville, TN: A denomination of PROTESTANTISM with roots in METHODISM. The church grew out of the Free African Society that was formed in 1787 as a reaction to slavery and racism. In the 1990s, the church reported 7,000 congregations worldwide with over 2 million members. Web site—http://www.ame-church.com. See METHODISM.

African Orthodox Church: The spiritual arm of Marcus Garvey's Universal Negro Improvement Association. The church claims to be a member of the Eastern Catholic Church. A bishop in the church ordained Franzo Wayne King, founder of the ST. JOHN COLTRANE AFRICAN ORTHODOX CHURCH. See RASTAFARIANISM; ROMAN CATHOLICISM.

Agasha Temple of Wisdom, Inc., William Eisen—Los Angeles, CA: Proclaims the universal consciousness of God as taught by the ASCENDED MASTERS. Knowledge of such ESOTERIC practices as PYRAMIDOLOGY is gained through REINCARNATION.

Agastiyar, Sage Agastiyar: An Indian astrologist who lived in the eleventh-century B.C., Sage Agastiyar and his disciples allegedly wrote down the future of every person who will ever live. Current disciples of Agastiyar utilize ASTROLOGY to determine the sins committed in previous lives, as well as sins that will be committed in the future, prescribing the penance that must be performed in order to escape the cycle of REINCARNATION.

Aggressive Christianity Mission Training Corps, Major Generals James and Deborah Green—Berino, NM: An anti-ecclesiastical organization that claims that anyone who supports a centralized government or denomination is affiliated with the Antichrist. Salvation can only be found outside church and governmental systems.

Agni Yoga Society, Nicholas and Helena Roerich—New York, NY: The Roerichs started the society in 1920 to promote Agni YOGA, a NEW AGE ideology in which the Hierarchy of Light—similar to the ASCENDED MASTERS—provides guidance to humanity in being transformed by the "fiery energy" of consciousness and directed thought. Web site—http://www.agniyoga.org.

Agnosticism: From the Greek *a* ("no") and *gnosis* ("to know")—the belief that the truth of religious claims concerning the existence of God is inherently unknowable. Some agnostics believe that the knowledge of God's existence is theoretically possible but not part of their personal experience. Thus, they would allow for the possibility of God's existence. Other agnostics see the concept of God as unknowable and incoherent, leading to functional ATHEISM.

Agon Buddhism: Sect of BUDDHISM. Uses the *Agon Sutras* as scriptures.

Agyeman, Jaramogi Abebe: See PAN AFRICAN ORTHODOX CHRISTIAN CHURCH.

Ahabah Asah Prophetic Ministries: See GATEKEEPERS.

Ahmadiyya Movement: An ISLAMic organization that claims that the SECOND COMING of Christ was fulfilled by the birth of the founder, Ahmad, in Qadian, India. Web site—http://www.ahmadiyya.org.

AION: NEW AGE group that practices GODDESS worship, MAGIC, and the reading of RUNES.

Air Land Emergency Response Teams (ALERT): See GOTHARD, BILL.

Akashic Records: THEOSOPHICAL term designating an alleged library that exists on the astral plane containing all the thoughts, actions, and events of mankind. Mystics, through ALTERED STATES OF CONSCIOUS-NESS, tune in to this library for information.

Alamo Christian Foundation, Tony Alamo—Alma, AR: Tony Alamo, leader of this group, has been imprisoned for alleged illegal activities. The foundation teaches that traditional CHRISTIANITY is dead. Former fol-lowers have reported deplorable living conditions, MIND CONTROL, and slave labor. Operates Music Square Church in Tennessee and Holiness Tabernacle in Dyer, Arkansas. End Times Book is the publishing arm for the organization. Web site—http://www.alamoministries.com.

Alan Shawn Feinstein Associates—Cranston, RI: UFO contactee. The Alan Shawn Feinstein Foundation is currently dedicated to humanitarian causes. In the 1980s, however, the group's efforts revolved around attempts to establish PSYCHIC contact with extraterrestrials. Web site—http://www.feinsteinfoundation.com.

Alchemy: In its original, literal meaning, theories and experiments involving the transmutation (dissolving and combining) of base metals to form gold though chemical and/or OCCULT and supernatural processes. Today the term carries the meaning of a mystical transformation in NEW AGE con-sciousness through various mystical techniques.

Alchemy Institute, David Quigley—Santa Rosa, CA: Founded in 1984. Pro-vides training in hypnotherapy using alchemical hypnotherapy developed by Quigley. Uses inner guides, ALTERED STATES OF CONSCIOUSNESS, ALCHEMY, Gestalt, and SHAMANISM to heal a person's higher self. Also uses the names Alchemy Institute of Hypnosis and Alchemy Institute of Healing Arts. Web site—http://www.alchemyinstitute.com.

Alcoholics Anonymous (A.A.): Founded in 1935 by Bill Wilson, the 12-step therapy program for people suffering from alcoholism has inspired numerous other programs. Steps two and three involve believing that there is a Power greater than the person, and then turning one's life over to that Power. Some Christians criticize A.A. for being pluralistic by encouraging personal devotion to non-Christian deities and religions. Web site—http://www.alcoholics-anonymous.org.

Aleph: See AUM SHINRIKYO.

Aleph: Alliance for Jewish Renewal, Rabbi Zalman Schachter-Shalomi—Philadelphia, PA: Combines Chassidic JUDAISM, NATIVE AMERICAN SPIRITUALITY, Eastern MYSTICISM, *A COURSE IN MIRACLES,* and NEW AGE practices. Emphasizes combining syncretistic spirituality and psychology. Web site—http://www.aleph.org.

Aletheia Psycho-Physical Foundation, Jack Schwarz—Ashland, OR: Schwarz conducts NEW AGE seminars on the inner self, paraconsciousness, MEDITATION, and VISUALIZATION. Web site—http://www.holisticu.org.

Alexander, Greta: Alexander was a psychic who, through her use of NEW AGE practices such as CLAIRVOYANCE and ASTRAL PROJECTION, claimed to have solved hundreds of police cases. Alexander died from cancer in 1998.

Allah: The MONOTHEISTIC deity of ISLAM.

Allegro, John: Author and founder of THE SACRED MUSHROOM AND THE CROSS.

All Hallow's Eve: See HALLOWEEN.

All Life Forms, James David Harman—Lykens, PA: Harman denies the deity of JESUS CHRIST, claiming that causing any harm or discomfort to another living being earns damnation. His theology seems to have developed following the death of his son.

All-One-God-Faith, Emanuel H. Bronner (1908–97)—Escondido, CA: Sells Dr. Bronner's Magic Soap, which claims to clean both body and soul. The soap is widely available in health-food stores. Bronner teaches that God, who is continually recreating Himself, desires all nations and religions to unite in an "All-One-God-Faith" on Spaceship Earth. This unification will come about through following 13 precepts and 20 directives revealed to Bronner by God. Web site—http://www.drbronner.com/index.html. See PROCESS THEOLOGY.

All Souls Unitarian Church, John Wolf—Tulsa, OK: Though retired, Wolf remains active in Unitarian circles. The current pastor is Rev. Marlin Lavanhar. Web site—http://www.allsoulschurch.org. See UNITARIAN-UNIVERSALISM.

All Ways Free—Madison, WI: NEW AGE periodical.

Alpha and Omega Christian Foundation, Grigore Sbarcea—Berowra Heights, Australia: The leader of the group is a former member of the WORLDWIDE CHURCH OF GOD, although he now openly rejects both that organization and ARMSTRONGISM. The foundation rejects the immortality of the soul, the existence of heaven and hell, and all organized churches. They also teach that Christians can equal Jesus in power and status, and that the APOCALYPSE will begin when the Pope visits Jerusalem. The WORLDWIDE CHURCH OF GOD officially links the group with GARNER TED ARMSTRONG.

Alphabiotic New Life Center—Dallas, TX: Conducts NEW AGE seminars on each person's divine being and practices YOGA and CHANNELING (with particular emphasis on RAMTHA). Web site—http://alphabiotics. biz.

Alpha-Omega—Laoag, Philippines: Believed that former president Ferdinand Marcos, who died September 28, 1989, would be resurrected and proclaimed a god on September 7, 1993. Despite their failed prophecy, the group continues its activities in the Philippine Islands.

Alphasonics International, Drs. Lee and Joyce Shulman—Santa Fe, NM: A company specializing in tapes with subliminal content. Web site—http://www.alphasonics.com. See HYPNOSIS.

Altered States of Consciousness: The term for TRANCES entered through such practices as HYPNOSIS, MEDITATION, drugs (including hallucinogenics), and GUIDED IMAGERY. It also refers to a state of being in which one allows the subconscious to take control. Entering an altered state of consciousness may heighten one's vulnerability to suggestion or susceptibility to deception.

Alternative Medicine: See HOLISTIC HEALTH.

Amalgamated Flying Saucer Clubs of America, Gabriel Green (1924–2001)—Los Angeles, CA: Founded in 1959, the Amalgamated Flying Saucer Clubs (AFSCA) grew out of the Los Angeles Interplanetary Study Groups, which were also formed by Green. Believes that beings from other planets visit and are in contact with people of Earth and that some of them are the people of Earth's ancestors. In 1960 Green briefly ran for president of the United States before withdrawing to support John F. Kennedy, whom he claims, along with his brother Robert Kennedy, was a member and supporter of the AFSCA. Web site—www.flyingsaucers11.friendpages.com.

Ambassador Church of God—London, England: A WORLDWIDE CHURCH OF GOD splinter group.

Ambassadors for Christ—Tustin, CA: See WATCHTOWER BIBLE AND TRACT SOCIETY for similar theological perspective.

Ambassador University—Big Sandy, TX: Now-defunct liberal arts and religious institution founded by HERBERT ARMSTRONG. See ARMSTRONGISM.

Ameba—San Francisco, CA: A NEO-PAGAN group promoting the teachings of ALEISTER CROWLEY and Celtic rituals.

AME Church: See AFRICAN METHODIST EPISCOPAL CHURCH.

American Academy of Dissident Sciences, Vladimir Terziski, Al Bielek—Los Angeles, CA: Studying a wide array of CONSPIRACY THEORIES, the academy focuses on MIND CONTROL, UFOs, and the ILLUMINATI. Terziski, a Bulgarian physicist, believes that during WWII the Germans were using alien technology to build UFOs and had established a base on the moon. Bielek claims to have been part of the PHILADELPHIA EXPERIMENT and that he and his brother jumped off the USS Eldridge and were transported into the future.

Americana Leadership College, Inc.—Osceola, IA: Teaches such NEW AGE and OCCULT practices as TRANCE healing, working as a MEDIUM, and achieving SELF-REALIZATION through dreams. Web site—http://www.alcworld.com.

American Association of Ayurvedic Medicine—Fairfield, IA: HOLISTIC medical association founded by DEEPAK CHOPRA while he followed the MAHARISHI MAHESH YOGI. See AYURVEDIC MEDICINE; TRANSCENDENTAL MEDITATION.

American Association of Naturopathic Physicians—Seattle, WA: Society for professionals involved in HOLISTIC HEALING. Publishes *The Naturopathic Physician* newsletter. Web site—http://www.naturopathic.org.

American Association of Non-Denominational Christian Schools: Educational group affiliated with the ALAMO CHRISTIAN FOUNDATION.

American Atheists, Inc., Madalyn Murray O'Hair (1919–95)—Austin, TX: Advocates strict separation of church and state, and actively opposes Christian influence on society. Publishes *American Atheist* magazine. Web site—http://www.atheists.org. See MURRAY O'HAIR, MADALYN.

American Baptist Association—Texarkana, TX: A fellowship of independent BAPTIST CHURCHES formed in 1905 as the General Association of Baptists in the United States of America. In 1924, churches from Oklahoma and the Baptist Missionary Association of Texas joined the association and the current name was adopted. The churches hold to Landmarkism, the belief that only those churches with the correct Baptist distinctives are legitimate churches. While true Christians may be members of other churches, all non-Baptist churches are seen as merely religious gatherings or societies. There are about 300,000 members in approximately 2,000 affiliated churches. Web site—http://www.abaptist.org. See BAPTIST CHURCHES.

American Baptist Churches USA—Valley Forge, PA: A denomination of PROTESTANTISM with 1.5 million members in 5,800 congregations. In 1845, the denomination, called then the Northern Baptist Convention, split with the SOUTHERN BAPTIST CONVENTION over slavery. Web site—http://www.abc-usa.org. See BAPTIST CHURCHES.

American Buddhist Society, Robert E. Dickhoff—New York: Combines TIBETAN BUDDHISM, teachings about UFOs, FREEMASONRY, and ALCHEMY. His 1959 book *Agharta* contends that the earth was originally populated by martians who created the first humans and retreated to two subterranean cities with their human associates when attacked by the reptilian inhabitants of Venus. Dickhoff calls himself "The Maitreyamantaka." See MAITREYA.

American Christian Press—New Knoxville, OH: See THE WAY, INTERNATIONAL.

American College of Nutripathy, Gary Martin—Scottsdale, AZ: Operated during the 1980s offering nonaccredited degrees. Taught IRIDOLOGY, REFLEXOLOGY, ACUPRESSURE, HOMEOPATHY, and other forms of alternative medicine. Many "graduates" are active today offering alternative medical care. See HOLISTIC HEALING.

American Constitution Committee: Political organization of the Unification Church founded in 1987 by SUN MYUNG MOON. See HOLY SPIRIT ASSOCIATION FOR THE UNIFICATION OF WORLD CHRISTIANITY.

American Cosmic Solar Research Center, Gene Savoy—Reno, NV: Founded in 1957, an early project of SAVOY's, teaching a form of MYSTICISM allegedly based on the Great School of Mystics of the Andean Plateaus. Uses an ESOTERIC system called "the Process" to generate physical and chemical rejuvenation in initiates. Web site—http://www.genesavoy.org. See JAMILIAN UNIVERSITY OF THE ORDAINED.

American Educational Music Publications, David-Lucas Burge—Fairfield, IA: Utilizes the techniques of TRANSCENDENTAL MEDITATION to develop relative (i.e., perfect) pitch in musicians. Web site—http://www.perfectpitch.com.

American Family Foundation (AFF): See INTERNATIONAL CULTIC STUDIES ASSOCIATION.

American Fellowship Services: Splinter group of THE WAY, INTERNATIONAL.

American Foundation for the Science of Creative Intelligence: A branch of TRANSCENDENTAL MEDITATION.

American Gnostic Church, Daeva Ares Animo—Corpus Christi, TX: An OCCULT group teaching PAGANISM, Egyptian secrets, KABBALAH, the Satanic rituals of ANTON LAVEY, and the gnostic mass. Web site—http://www.americangnosticchurch.com. See CHURCH OF SATAN.

American Holistic Nurses Association—Amherst, MA: The association trains medical nurses to use THERAPEUTIC TOUCH and MEDITATION with patients. Web site—http://www.ahna.org.

American Humanist Association—Washington, DC: America's oldest and largest organization (110 local chapters and affiliates) promoting humanism as a system of ethics and values that are maintained without a belief in a God or an afterlife. Publishes *The Humanist.* Web site—http://www.americanhumanist.org. See SECULAR HUMANISM; ATHEISM; AGNOSTICISM.

American Imagery Institute, Anees A. Sheikh—Milwaukee, WI: Teaches such NEW AGE practices as VISUALIZATION and ASTRAL PROJECTION.

American Interfaith Institute—Philadelphia, PA: An ecumenical organization teaching that no religion is superior to another. Web site—http://www.americaninterfaith.org. See UNIVERSALISM.

American (International) Babaji Yoga Sangam, Yogi S.A.A. Ramaiah—New York, NY: Established in 1952 as a vehicle through which the "immortal" Kriya Babaji could communicate with his followers throughout the world. Teaches HINDU philosophy and KRIYA YOGA. Web site—http://www.kriyayoga.org.

American Pie and the Armageddon Bible Prophecy, Roy Taylor: Believes pop song "American Pie" prophesies the destruction of America, and was foretold in the Song of Moses in Deuteronomy 32. Web site—http://roy-taylorministries.com. See APOCALYPSE.

American Scientific Technical Research Organization, Jack Katchmar— Royal Oak, MI: Conditionally predicted that World War III would occur in 1977. Taught cosmic awareness, claimed that God speaks today through Paul Shockley. See AQUARIAN CHURCH OF UNIVERSAL SCIENCE.

American Society for Psychical Research, Simon Newcomb—New York, NY: Studies and promotes ESP, ASTRAL PROJECTION, MEDIUMS, PARAPSYCHOLOGY, and TELEKINESIS. Web site—http://www.aspr.com.

American Society of Alternative Therapists—Rockport, MA: A professional society for practitioners of HOLISTIC HEALING. Web site—http://www.asat.org.

American Study Group—UT: Defunct Mormon sect that used the BOOK OF MORMON and the teachings of Mormon leaders to speculate on end-time events and the end of the world. See CHURCH OF JESUS CHRIST OF LATTER-DAY SAINTS; APOCALYPSE.

American Temple, Michael Whitney—Portland, OR: A "fourth wave" ESOTERIC and mystical order led by "patriarch" Michael Whitney reviving the doctrines of the now defunct HOLY ORDER OF MANS. Web site—http://www.americantemple.org.

American Vegan Society—Malaga, NJ: The society teaches Ahimsa, which is Sanskrit for nonkilling. They believe that avoiding all animal products will increase the alignment of KARMA and lead to global peace. Publishes *Out of the Jungle* newsletter. Web site—http://www.americanvegan.org. See HINDUISM.

American West Publishers—Tehachapi, CA: NEW AGE publisher that focuses on UFOs and the cosmic laws of balance. Publishes the *Phoenix Journal.*

American World Patriarchates, Uladyslau Ryzy-Ryski (1925–78)—Shrub Oak, NY: Independent church established by Ryzy-Ryski through his consecration into the American Orthodox Catholic Church (AOCC). He continued to lead the American World Patriarchates (AWP) even after being excommunicated from the AOCC by Archbishop Walter Propheta in 1972. His brother, Emigidius J. Ryzy, became the leader of the AWP at Uladyslau's death. The Patriarchates claim to be both Orthodox and Catholic, but reject both the patriarchs of Eastern Orthodoxy and the papacy. As of 1997 the church reported 19,457 members, 17 congregations, and 54 priests in the United States. Web site—http://members.aol.com/AmWorldPat. See ORTHODOX CHRISTIANITY; ROMAN CATHOLIC CHURCH.

American Zen Center: While primarily practicing ZEN BUDDHISM, the center also teaches SUFISM and SHAMANISM.

Americans for the Constitution—Anchorage, AK: A defunct group that advocated the Christian militia movement and publicly supported the Montana Freemen. Published *Connecting the Dots* newsletter.

America's Promise Ministries—Sandpoint, ID: The organization primarily promotes the Christian militia movement. Web site—http://www.amprom.org.

Amish: Religious communities of separate fellowships found in North America that separate themselves from mainstream culture and government and reject the use of technology, such as electricity and automobiles. Known for their plain dress and language, Pennsylvania Dutch (a dialect of German), the movement got its name from Jacob Amman (1656–1730), a MENNONITE who sought to reform that movement by insisting on the practice of strict SHUNNING. Historically the movement developed out of the Swiss Brethren of the Radical Reformation. Unlike Old Order Amish, New Order Amish and Beachy Amish allow the use of technology. See MENNONITE; REFORMATION.

AMOM: See ANCIENT MYSTIC ORDER OF MALCHIZEDEK.

AMOOKOS (Arcane Magikal Order of the Knights of Shambhala), SHRI GURUDEV MAHENDRANATH: An OCCULT organization that teaches MAGIC and some HINDUISM (particularly TANTRA) that was to be comprised of the most highly developed Naths. See INTERNA-TIONAL NATH ORDER.

Amritanandamayi—San Ramon, CA: Mata Amritanandamayi (aka Amma), meaning "Mother of Immortal Bliss," follows mainstream HINDUISM, and includes a *darshan* (vision/meeting) that emphasizes hugging and blessing those who meet with her. Claims that MANTRAS can be taken from, and used in, all religions. Her work has been acclaimed by NEW AGE teacher Jack Kornfield. Web site—http://www.amma.org.

Amulet: An OCCULT object considered magical that can protect or spiritually empower the owner. Objects may include rings, stones, gems, drawings, or written words. See TALISMAN; MAGICK.

Ananael—Ellsworth, ME: See BROTHERHOOD OF SETH.

Ananda Marga: A HINDU sect, founded in Jamalpur, India in 1955 by Prabhat Ranjan Sarkar (also known as Shrii Shrii Ánandamúrti). The group focuses on Hindu deities and teaches MEDITATION and YOGA. *Ananda Marga* is Sanskrit for "path of bliss." The sect has branches in over 160 countries. Web site—http://www.anandamarga.org. See PROUT.

Ananda, Swami Kriyananda (J. Donald Walters)—Nevada City, CA: Founded in 1968, Ananda offers seminars teaching MEDITATION, YOGA, and other HINDU practices. Swami Kriyananda claims to be the direct successor to PARAMHANSA YOGANANDA. Web site—http://www.ananda.org.

Anchor of Golden Light, Dorothy and Henry Leon—Grants Pass, OR: The Leons focus on a wide array of NEW AGE teachings, including UFOs, AS-CENDED MASTERS, KABBALAH, ALCHEMY, and NUMEROLOGY. Guidance is given to the Leons by extraterrestrials who protect the earth with a large fleet of spaceships. They publish the *Anchor of Golden Light* newsletter.

Ancient Mystic Order of Malchizedek, Malachi Z. York (AMOM, Nu-waubians, the Nubian Nation of Moors, Right Knowledge): A UFO group whose leader (aka Dwight York) claims to be from the nineteenth galaxy called Illyuwn. A 1993 FBI report has surfaced calling the group a "front for a wide range of criminal activity, including arson, welfare fraud and extortion." York's group has also operated under other names and organizations including Nubian Islaamic [sic] Hebrew Mission and the Ansaaru Allah Community (an ISLAMic sect with doctrines similar to NATION OF ISLAM), and the Original Tents of Kedar. Unofficial Web site—http://www.netropolis.net/moorish/default.htm.

Ancient Wisdom Connection—N. Myrtle Beach, SC: A NEW AGE group that promotes CHANNELING, NUMEROLOGY, and belief in "Lord Sananda," who is an incarnation of JESUS.

Anderson, Neil: A former associate professor at Talbot School of Theology, founder of Freedom In Christ Ministries, and author of a number of books, including his best-selling *Bondage Breaker.* Anderson is a well-known individual in EVANGELICAL CHRISTIANITY who uses a "Truth Encounter" methodology to help Christians who are thought to be influenced (and not possessed) by demons.

Andrews, Joel: Andrews CHANNELS music to heal people, animals, and plants. He also practices CLAIRVOYANCE, MEDITATION, and PAST LIFE REGRESSION. Web site—http://www.kspace.com/andrews. See REINCARNATION; NEW AGE MUSIC. Web site—http://www.harpofgold.com.

Angelic Outreach, Bob and Nan Murray—Portland, OR: The Murrays teach that relationships involve exercising mastery and sovereignty through manifesting individual and collective divinity. See CHRIST CONSCIOUSNESS; KARMA.

Angels: Supernatural, nonhuman beings created by God. Angels worship God and serve as His messengers. The angels who rebelled against God are called DEMONS. The angelology currently popular in the NEW AGE movement has no biblical support. Instead, much of the reported interaction between people and angels in popular literature seems much closer to the practice of CHANNELING. See SATAN.

Angels on Assignment, **Ronald Buck:** Published in 1979, *Angels on Assignment* describes Buck's alleged encounters with ANGELS (including the archangel Michael) and God. Some Christians have criticized the book for confusing the role of the HOLY SPIRIT, claiming that CHRIST did not die physically, and minimizing the importance of evangelism.

Anglican Churches: An expression of PROTESTANTISM from the Latin term *Anglicana* ("English"), noting the connection to the Church of England. Some U.S. churches are part of the more liberal Anglican Communion, an association of churches that are in full communion with the Church of England and the Archbishop of Canterbury. Others, such as the Anglican Catholic Church and the Anglican Province of Christ the King, are part of the Continuing Anglican Movement and are much more conservative.

Anglo-Israelism: See BRITISH ISRAELISM.

Animal Magnetism: See MESMERISM.

Animism: The idea that all things in the universe are inherently invested with a life force, soul, or mind. This belief is an important component of many primitive religions, the OCCULT, and SPIRITISM.

Annihilationism: Taught by most ADVENTIST groups, including the JEHOVAH'S WITNESSES, this doctrine denies the conscious, eternal punishment of the lost. Instead, humans who do not receive eternal life will be destroyed and cease to exist. See SECOND ADVENT MOVEMENT.

Announce the Lord—Irving, TX: Predicts that CHRIST will return by 2007.

Anointed Class: See LITTLE FLOCK.

Answers Research and Education, Bud Cocherell—San Jose, CA: An organization teaching that humanity's destiny is for each individual to become a god. A key practice for attaining divinity involves keeping the Old Testament festivals. See SABBATARIANISM.

Anthroposophical Society, Rudolf Steiner—Chicago, IL: A highly influential OCCULT organization founded in the early part of the twentieth-century by Rudolf Steiner. Anthrosophy includes teachings on KARMA, MEDITATION, ATLANTIS, and REINCARNATION. Web site—http://www.anthroposophy.org.

Anthroposophic Press—Hudson, NY: Independent organization that publishes the works of Rudolf Steiner and other anthroposophical authors. Web site—http://www.anthropress.org.

Anthroposophic Society, Rudolf Steiner—Hudson, NY: Similar to the Chicago organization (above). The two organizations may be affiliated.

AOTCOOO "Yah"—Jackson, TN: A militant organization that combines CHRISTIANITY with an anti-United Nations agenda.

Apocalypse: Also called Armageddon. From the Greek word *apokalypsis,* meaning "revelation, disclosure, or unveiling," the term *apocalypse,* in the BIBLE, refers to the summation of human history through God's direct judgment upon the world. Central in biblical apocalyptic literature is the book of Revelation. A common feature of many pseudo-Christian groups is their attempts to predict the date of the apocalypse. For examples of groups that have erroneously predicted the timing of the apocalypse, see CHURCH OF THE LIVING STONE MISSION FOR THE COMING DAYS; SECOND ADVENT MOVEMENT; WATCHTOWER BIBLE AND TRACT SOCIETY.

Apocrypha/Apocryphal (or singular, Apocryphon): From the Greek term that means "hidden away," these are books of questioned or uncertain authenticity that failed to be included in the BIBLE (e.g., they are non-canonical). The term can be used of books that are known to be inauthentic or forgeries (called pseudepigrapha) or of books that have historical value but do not measure up to the level of inspiration required for Scripture. The Catholic Apocrypha or Deuterocanonicals are seven books that are accepted as scriptural by ROMAN CATHOLICISM but not by PROTESTANTISM. They include the books of Tobit, Judith, Wisdom, Ecclesiasticus, Baruch, and First and Second Maccabees, and additions to Esther and Daniel. See BIBLE.

Apocryphon of John (The Secret Book of John): One of the GNOSTIC GOSPELS dating to the late second century A.D. recovered in Nag Hammadi, Egypt in 1945. Considered to be an example of New Testament APOCRYPHA, the book recounts the postresurrection reappearing of JESUS CHRIST to the APOSTLES John and Peter to share secret doctrines.

Apologetics: From the Greek word *apologia* ("defense of a position"), the field of study involving a systematic defense of a position or worldview. CHRISTIAN apologetics involves a logical, coherent, consistent defense of Christian doctrine. That may include positive apologetics (reasons the Christian faith is true) and negative apologetics (reasons an opposing worldview or doctrine cannot be true).

Apologia, Rich Poll—Colorado Springs, CO: A Christian APOLOGETICS ministry founded in 1995 that defends the beliefs of EVANGELICAL CHRISTIANITY by providing relevant religious research and information on culture, non-Christian religions, sects, cults, and spiritual trends. The organization maintains a moderated discussion board, AR-TALK, and produces the *Apologia Report,* a helpful weekly e-mail update that reviews and summarizes numerous magazines, journals, and news publications that relate to religious apologetics. The group is a member of EVANGELICAL MINISTRIES TO NEW RELIGIONS (EMNR). Web site—http://apologia.gospelcom.net.

Apologist: From the Greek word *apologia* ("defense of a position"). One who puts forth evidence in favor of a doctrine or belief and refutes conflicting truth-claims. See APOLOGETICS.

Apostasy: From the Greek word *apostasis,* meaning "rebellion," and the Latin word *apostasia,* meaning "abandonment," the term *apostasy* refers to a renunciation of the Christian faith. The label *apostate* is applied to former JEHOVAH'S WITNESSES, who are shunned by all Witnesses in good standing. See SHUNNING; WATCHTOWER BIBLE AND TRACT SOCIETY.

Apostle: From the Greek word *apostolos,* meaning "messenger," the term *apostle* refers to those leaders of the early Christian church who were chosen by Jesus. The criteria for being an apostle was 1) the individual was personally chosen by CHRIST; and 2) the individual must have personally seen Christ. Today, leaders in a number of churches, especially some that are part of the PENTECOSTAL MOVEMENT, use the title. It is also claimed by the 12 senior leaders of THE CHURCH OF JESUS CHRIST OF LATTER-DAY SAINTS.

Apostolic Churches: A branch of Pentecostalism that can trace its roots back to two specific Pentecostal revivals in the early part of the twentieth-century:

the Azusa Street revival in Los Angeles, and the "Apostolic Faith" revival of Charles Parham in Kansas. Both groups helped to birth the PENTE-COSTAL MOVEMENT as a whole and emphasize standard Pentecostal distinctives (e.g., GLOSSOLALIA, the gift of "prophecy," etc.) that are still taught today in most Apostolic Churches. Many (but not all) Pentecostal churches that claim to be Apostolic are adherents to ONENESS PENTE-COSTALISM. See UNITED PENTECOSTAL CHURCH.

Apostolic Church of God 7th Day—Langley, British Columbia: See CHURCH OF GOD SEVENTH DAY.

Apostolic Overcoming Holiness of God, Inc.—Birmingham, AL: Part of the APOSTOLIC CHURCHES, the group stresses the oneness of God while accepting the triune being of the Godhead. Salvation includes baptism, tarrying to receive the HOLY SPIRIT, and holiness. They publish *The People's Mouthpiece* magazine.

Apostolic Prophetic Voice—Dayton, OH: The group predicted that God would destroy the United States in one day by 2000. Publishes the *Apostolic Prophetic Voice Newsletter.*

Apostolic United Brethren, Owen A. Allred—Bluffdale, UT: A polygamous Mormon sect. Membership exceeds 5,000, with United Order communities in several cities in Utah and locations in Montana, Arizona, Missouri, and Wyoming. A community of 1000 in Pinesdale, Montana, is affiliated with the group. Allred died in 2005 and was succeeded by Second Elder J. Lamoine Jenson. See THE CHURCH OF JESUS CHRIST OF LATTER-DAY SAINTS.

Applegate Christian Fellowship, Jon Courson—Jacksonville, OR: See CALVARY CHAPEL.

Applewhite, Marshall: See HEAVEN'S GATE.

Applied Kinesiology: A NEW AGE diagnostic technique sometimes called "muscle testing." Patients often hold health care products (vitamins, herbs, etc.) in their hand while the practitioner pulls or "tests" the reciprocal strength in the finger, arm, etc. to determine the effectiveness or dosage of the remedy. See HOLISTIC HEALTH.

Aquarian Academy, Robert E. Birdsong—Eureka, CA: Jesus is only an avatar of the Cosmic Christ. The GREAT WHITE BROTHERHOOD OF LIGHT teaches that man's purpose is to reach the transcendental plane and be released from the wheel of fate. The group practices ASTRAL PROJECTION and MEDITATION. See ASCENDED MASTERS.

Aquarian Church of Universal Service, Paul Shockley—Portland, OR: NEW AGE church that teaches cosmic awareness. Shockley claims to be an interpreter for this awareness. See CHANNELING.

The Aquarian Conspiracy, **MARILYN FERGUSON:** Published in 1980 and still a strong seller, the book is generally recognized as being a NEW AGE blueprint for cultural transformation that did much to encourage the growth of NEW AGE spirituality throughout the 1980s.

Aquarian Educational Group, Torkom Saraydarian (1917–97)—Sedona, AZ: The group combines HINDUISM and the NEW AGE. Saraydarian's teachings focus on ASTROLOGY, moon festivals, using the *BHAGAVAD-GITA,* and understanding that JESUS was only an avatar. Publishes the *Fiery Synthesis* magazine. After Torkom's death in 1997, his wife Joann succeeded him as president of the institute, which is now known as the Saraydarian Institute. Web site—http://www.saraydarian.org.

Aquarian Foundation, Keith Milton—Seattle, WA: A NEW AGE organization teaching THEOSOPHY, SPIRITISM, YOGA, and UNIVERSALISM. Web site—http://aquarianfoundation.org.

Aquarian Gospel, **Levi H. Dowling:** An APOCRYPHAL NEW AGE story, supposedly based on the AKASHIC RECORDS.

Aquarian Minyan, Rabbi Zalman Schachter-Shalomi—Berkeley, CA: Started out of a month-long KABBALAH workshop in 1974. A NEW AGE group that combines JUDAISM, YOGA, and MYSTICISM. Affiliated with ALEPH. Web site—http://www.aquarianminyan.org.

Aquarian Perspectives Interplanetary Mission—Montgomery, AL: Part of the UFO theological family and headed by individuals who call themselves Moi-RA and RA-Ja Dove the Aquarian Star Shepherds, members receive messages from a group known as Futron and the Rainbow Star Legionnaires.

The revelations teach that the kingdom of God is present in each individual. Web site—http://www.stardoves.com.

Aquarian Research Foundation, Art Rosenblum—Philadelphia, PA: Advocates practicing natural birth control based on astrological charts. Publishes *Green Revolution Magazine* and *Aquarian Research Foundation Newsletter.* Web site—http://www.aquarian.cjb.net. See ASTROLOGY.

Aquarian Tabernacle Church, Pete "Pathfinder" Davis—Index, WA: A NEO-PAGAN church engaging in the worship of "Mother Earth" and the GODDESS. The church also celebrates sun and moon festivals and practices MAGIC. Publishes the *Panegyria* newsletter. Founded in 1976, it has grown into an umbrella organization for many affiliated PAGAN groups. Web site—http://www.aquatabch.org.

Arcana Workshop—Manhattan Beach, CA: Continuing the teachings of ALICE BAILEY, this group teaches MEDITATION, the "Great Invocation," and the celebration of moon festivals. Publishes the *Thoughtline* newsletter. Web site—http://www.meditationtraining.org. See ARCANE SCHOOL.

Arcane School, ALICE BAILEY: Established in 1923. An OCCULT organization connected with LUCIS TRUST, formerly Lucifer Trust, offering correspondence courses in the rudimentary teachings of ALICE BAILEY. The Arcane School's teachings are similar to those of THEOSOPHY. Publishes *The Beacon Magazine.* Web site—http://www.lucistrust.org.

Arcline Publications—Berkeley, CA: A NEW AGE publisher that focuses on HOLISTIC HEALING.

Area 51: A military base located 90 miles north of Las Vegas, Nevada, that was the location for testing the U-2 aircraft in the 1950s. In 1989, Bob Lazar claimed to have worked with UFOs at Papoose Lake (south of Area 51). Later CONSPIRACY THEORIES allege that the site is the location of top-secret UFO testing that is being kept concealed by the government.

Arete Truth Center, Paul Lachlan Peck—Las Vegas, NV: A NEW AGE center teaching the use of METAPHYSICS to balance the body, mind, and spirit. Peck is not related to M. SCOTT PECK. Web site—http://www. paullpeck.com.

Arguelles, Jose: See HARMONIC CONVERGENCE.

Arian Conditionalist Newsletter—Sunnyvale, CA: Examines the relationship of JEHOVAH'S WITNESSES to ADVENTIST denominations. See SECOND ADVENT MOVEMENT; WATCHTOWER BIBLE AND TRACT SOCIETY.

Arianism: The doctrines of ARIUS, the fourth-century HERETIC, whose teaching concerning CHRIST was rejected in A.D. 325 at the COUNCIL OF NICEA. Arianism denies the deity of Christ by teaching Christ and God the Father were not of the same substance (Greek *homoousios*—"same essence"), but rather, of similar substance (Greek *homoiousios*—"similar essence"). Thus, Christ (the Word) was not God in the same way the Father is God. Jesus, therefore, was a created being and had a beginning (there was a time when He was not). Essentially a form of DYNAMIC MONARCHIANISM, Arianism was rejected as HERESY at the Council of Nicea. Variations of Arianism, however, have continued through the centuries, including in the teachings of the WATCHTOWER BIBLE AND TRACT SOCIETY. See ARIUS; DYNAMIC MONARCHIANISM; COUNCIL OF NICEA.

Arica Institute, Oscar Ichazo—New York: Founded in 1968, a school was established in New York in 1971 after a group of Americans, led by Ichazo, returned from ten months of training in Arica, Chile, where they had traveled to learn to discover the mind by what they call Protoanalysis. This NEW AGE organization teaches the attainment of higher consciousness through MEDITATION, dance, YOGA, KABBALAH, and vegetarianism. The organization unsuccessfully sued Harper & Row publishers in 1991 (and unsuccessfully appealed in 1992) for violation of copyright in publishing a book on ENNEAGRAMS. Web site—http://www.arica.org.

The Arithmetic of God, **Don Kistler**—Kings Mountain, NC: Kistler, in a TRANCE, received the revelation *The Arithmetic of God,* which applies numerological analyses to the prophecies of the Authorized Version (KJV) of the BIBLE. The author is not the same individual who operates the Protestant Soli Deo Gloria Ministries. See NUMEROLOGY.

Arius (A.D. 256–336): A fourth-century HERETIC of Alexandria, Egypt, who denied the deity of CHRIST and taught that He was not eternal.

Arius's teachings, called ARIANISM, were challenged by ATHANASIUS and rejected at the COUNCIL OF NICEA. See ARIANISM; COUNCIL OF NICEA.

Arizona Light—Phoenix, AZ: A NEW AGE periodical.

Arizona Metaphysical Society, Frank Alper—Phoenix, AZ: Founded in 1974, the society was placed under the CHURCH OF TZADDI in 1980. Alper conducts NEW AGE seminars on REBIRTHING, ASTRAL PROJECTION, CHANNELING, KARMA, REINCARNATION, and CRYSTALS.

Arizona Networking News—Scottsdale, AZ: A NEW AGE, HOLISTIC HEALTH periodical. Web site—http://www.aznetnews.com.

Armageddon: See APOCALYPSE.

Armageddon Time Ark Base Operation, O.T. Nodrog—Weslaco, TX: Part of the UFO family, the group channels messages from outer-dimensional forces. They teach that ARMAGEDDON began on September 3, 1966, and that the United States is in violation of numerous universal laws against energy usage. Salvation into the millennial kingdom of Yahsua Hamashiia requires extensive training and purchasing a time ark that can travel in the fourth dimension. See CHANNELING.

Armstrong, Garner Ted (1930–2003): The son of HERBERT W. ARMSTRONG (founder of the WORLDWIDE CHURCH OF GOD). Garner Ted formed his own rival, splinter group in 1978, the CHURCH OF GOD, INTERNATIONAL. He was removed from his leadership position of the CGI in 1996 due to sexual improprieties and founded the GARNER TED ARMSTRONG EVANGELISTIC ASSOCIATION. See ARMSTRONGISM.

Armstrong, Herbert W. (1892–1986): Developed an eclectic doctrinal system known as ARMSTRONGISM and founded the WORLDWIDE CHURCH OF GOD (WCG), which rejected virtually all of his unique beliefs in the decade following his death. Splinter groups of the WCG, however, continue to teach various forms of Armstrong's teachings. See ARMSTRONGISM.

Armstrongism: The doctrines and theories of HERBERT W. ARM-STRONG (1892–1986), who founded the WORLDWIDE CHURCH OF GOD (WCG). These beliefs include a rejection of the essential doctrines of EVANGELICAL CHRISTIANITY, such as the doctrine of the TRINITY, the full deity of Jesus, and the personality of the HOLY SPIRIT. ARMSTRONG taught BRITISH ISRAELISM and believed that worthy humans could eventually "become God as God is God." Salvation was predicated upon observing the Sabbath laws each Saturday, tithing (20-30 percent), keeping the Old Testament feast days and dietary laws. Under the leadership of Armstrong's successors, Joseph W. Tkach and his son Joe Tkach, the WCG has undergone a radical doctrinal transformation. Scores of WCG splinter groups, such as the Global Church of God and the United Church of God, continue to teach various forms of Armstrongism. See SALVATION BY WORKS; SALVATION BY GRACE; GOSPEL; SABBATARIANISM. For further research, a four-page Watchman Fellowship Profile is available (see page 363). Web site—http://www.watchman.org/notebook.

Ar nDraiocht Fein, P.E.I. Bonewits—Nyack, NY: A REFORMED DRUIDS break-off group. Practices DRUIDISM, NEO-PAGANISM, and polytheistic nature worship. Publishes the *News from the Mother Grove* newsletter. Web site—http://www.adf.org. See POLYTHEISM.

Arohn—Burlington, WA: Independent Catholic magazine. Teachings are based on ROSICRUCIANISM and THEOSOPHY. *Arohn* also publishes *A Catechesis for Independent Catholics.* See ROMAN CATHOLICISM.

Aromatherapy: The belief that certain diseases or illnesses can be healed by inhaling scented steam or fragrances. See HOLISTIC HEALTH.

Aromatherapy Seminars—Los Angeles, CA: Holistic healing therapy using oils to heal the psyche. See AROMATHERAPY.

Arthur Findlay College—Essex, Great Britain: An OCCULT college that promotes SPIRITUALISM and CLAIRVOYANCE. Affiliated with the SPIRITUALISTS' NATIONAL UNION. Web site—http://www. arthurfindlaycollege.org.

Arunachala Ashrama, Bhagavan Sri Ramana Maharshi (1879–1950): A HINDU sect. The Maharshi promised his disciples that they could attain enlightenment, or pure advaita, without any change in their lifestyles. He also promised on his deathbed that he would always remain with his disciples. Web sites—http://www.arunachala.org and http://www.ramana-maharshi.org.

Aryan Nations, Richard Girnt Butler (1918–2004)—Hayden Lake, ID: A neo-Nazi paramilitary organization originally formed in 1974 as the political wing of the CHURCH OF JESUS CHRIST-CHRISTIAN. A judgment rendered against the group in a civil lawsuit forced the group to surrender its Hayden Lake compound and to go bankrupt in 2001. This and Butler's death caused different factions to develop, all claiming to be the true Aryan Nations. Two currently remain: one in Lexington, South Carolina, led by August Kreis III, and one in Lincoln, Alabama, which is led by a three-man council and Jonathan Williams, the senior pastor. The Aryan Nations preaches against all non-Caucasian groups. The Order, an Aryan Nations break-off group, killed Alan Berg, a Jewish radio personality, in Denver in 1984. The Aryan Nations received national notice in 1992 when the wife of member Randy Weaver was killed in a shootout with the FBI in Ruby Ridge, Idaho. Web site—http://www.twelvearyannations.com and http://www.aryan-nations.org. See IDENTITY MOVEMENT.

Asatru Folk Assembly—Denair, CA: Formerly the Asatru Free Assembly. A group specializing in northern European PAGANISM, particularly Nordic myth. Asatru worships Odin, Frigga, among other Norse gods, and Nerthus as Mother-Earth. Publishes *The Runestone* newsletter. Web site—http://www.runestone.org. See NEO-PAGANISM; ODINISM.

Ascended Master Teaching Foundation—Mount Shasta, CA: Formed in 1980 by two group leaders of the BRIDGE TO FREEDOM who did not believe the group was acting in accordance with all the desires of the AS-CENDED MASTERS. Part of the I AM family of theology, this OCCULT organization's teachings about the GREAT WHITE BROTHERHOOD are similar to those found in THEOSOPHY. Web site—http://www.ascendedmaster.org.

Ascended Masters: Sometimes called the GREAT WHITE BROTHER-HOOD, teachings about the ascended masters are prominent in both the NEW AGE and OCCULT. Ascended masters are allegedly teachers who once lived on earth but have progressed beyond a human/physical existence and live on an ASTRAL PLANE as nonphysical entities beyond time and space. They can supposedly communicate spiritual truths to humans through CHANNELING and other occult techniques. Ascended masters allegedly include JESUS, BUDDHA, ST. GERMAIN, RAMTHA, MAFU, and others.

Ascended Masters School of Light, Toni Moltzan—Carrollton, TX: NEW AGE group that practices CHANNELING to achieve contact with the ASCENDED MASTERS (including Christ) and unite with the universal consciousness. See A COURSE IN LIGHT; AZ REALITY PUBLISHERS.

Ascension Week Enterprises—Santa Fe, NM: A NEW AGE organization that emphasizes CHANNELING and reaching out to children with New Age programs. A sister company of the World Ascension Network.

ASCENT Foundation, Larry Jensen—Sedona, AZ: This foundation is involved with NEW AGE enlightenment, similar to SILVA MIND CONTROL, EST, and LIFESPRING. Not affiliated with Ascent Foundation of Santa Clara, California.

Asha of Antares—Atlanta, GA: A PSYCHIC MEDIUM who allegedly manipulates energy fields for healing purposes and practices psychic archaeology and space travel. Web site—http://www.ashaofantares.com. See ASTRAL PROJECTION; CHI; PSYCHIC.

Asheville Meditation Center—Asheville, NC: NEW AGE organization that teaches how to achieve a divine nature through transcendence. See CHRIST CONSCIOUSNESS.

As It Is: See PROCESS CHURCH OF THE FINAL JUDGMENT.

Askin Publishers—London, Great Britain: Reprints old OCCULT books.

Assemblies of God: See PENTECOSTAL MOVEMENT.

Assemblies of the Called Out Ones of "Yah," Sam Surratt—Milan, TX: See YAHWEHISM.

Assemblies of Yahweh, Jacob Meyer—Bethel, PA: A SACRED NAME organization. Meyer was raised in the German Baptist Brethren, a church founded by his parents. Meyer founded the Assemblies of Yahweh to assimilate all the disparate Sacred Name groups. Publishes *The Sacred Name Broadcaster* magazine. Web site—http://www.assembliesofyahweh.com. See YAHWEHISM. For further research, a four-page Watchman Fellowship Profile is available (see page 363). Web site—http://www.watchman.org/notebook.

Assembly of God in Christ Jesus, Bill Phillips—Lakewood, OH: A SABBATARIAN group that requires observing all Old Testament laws and teaches BAPTISMAL REGENERATION. Publishes *End of the World Report.* The WORLDWIDE CHURCH OF GOD links the group with GARNER TED ARMSTRONG.

Assembly of Scientific Astrologers, George Cardinal—LeGrosoplin, MO: ESOTERIC ASTROLOGY and horoscope reading. Emphasizes KARMA and REINCARNATION.

Assembly of Yahvah—Winfield, AL: A SACRED NAME organization that has cited Watchtower publications in support of their doctrine. May be affiliated with the Assembly of Yahvah in Emory, Texas. See WATCHTOWER BIBLE AND TRACT SOCIETY; YAHWEHISM.

Assembly of Yahvah, L.D. Snow—Emory, TX: CHURCH OF GOD, SEVENTH DAY break-off group. This SACRED NAME group claims to be the restoration of the Apostolic Organization of the Assembly of Yahvah as it existed under Moses and the Messiah. Has operated missions in India, the Philippines, and Jamaica. Web site—http://assemblyofyahvah.com. See YAHWEHISM.

Assembly of Yahweh—Eaton Rapids, MI: Founded in 1930, perhaps the oldest of the SACRED NAME groups in America. Publishes *The Faith.* Web site—http://www.assemblyofyahweh.com. See SABBATARIANISM; YAHWEHISM.

Assembly of Yahweh—Newark, OH: Teaches that using the SACRED NAME of God is necessary for salvation. See YAHWEHISM.

Assembly of Yahweh (7th Day)—Cisco, TX: SABBATARIAN group that teaches that using the SACRED NAME of God is necessary for salvation. Web site—http://www.halleluyah.org. See YAHWEHISM.

Assembly of YHWH Yoshua—Pueblo, CO: A group that uses the SACRED NAME of God. See YAHWEHISM.

Associated Bible Students—Tustin, CA: WATCHTOWER BIBLE AND TRACT SOCIETY break-off group. Web site—http://www.biblestudents. net. See BIBLE STUDENTS.

Associated Bible Students—Waterbury, CT: WATCHTOWER BIBLE AND TRACT SOCIETY break-off group. Publishes *Associated Bible Students* newsletter. See BIBLE STUDENTS.

Associated Bible Students of Central Ohio—Westerville, OH: WATCH-TOWER BIBLE AND TRACT SOCIETY break-off group. Publishes *End Times Bible Report Quarterly.* Web sites—http://www.biblestudents.org/ absco and http://www.biblestudents.com. See BIBLE STUDENTS.

Associated Bible Students of Jersey City—Jersey City, NJ: WATCH-TOWER BIBLE AND TRACT SOCIETY break-off group. See BIBLE STUDENTS.

Associated Readers of Tarot International (T.A.R.O.T.)—Carbondale, IL: Now defunct, this OCCULT group used TAROT CARDS and practiced rituals they claimed were of Celtic origin. It also served as a certification organization for tarot readers, some of whom still list their certification from T.A.R.O.T. among their credentials.

Associates for Scriptural Knowledge, Ernest L. Martin—Portland, OR: Antidenominational group whose associates study doctrine through a home-study course. Teaches that all people will be saved (although not all will experience the first resurrection and live in Christ's millennial kingdom), and that the name *Yahweh* was removed from the Bible by Jerome. Martin was fired by the Foundation for Biblical Research (a WORLDWIDE CHURCH OF GOD break-off group in Alhambra, CA) in 1984 for espousing these doctrines. Publishes a "restored" Bible called *The Manuscript Version of the Bible,* and *The ASK Communicator.* Web site—http://www.askelm.com. See UNIVERSALISM; SACRED NAME.

Association for Christian Development, Kenneth Westby—Tukwila, WA: Splinter group of WORLDWIDE CHURCH OF GOD. The group has its roots in ARMSTRONGISM, although a 1998 issue of their newsletter made a pejorative reference to ARMSTRONG in an article attacking "HERESY hunters." Publishes the *ACD Newsletter.* Web site—http://www.godward.org.

Association for Past-Life Research and Therapies, Inc.—Riverside, CA: A NEW AGE organization that teaches REINCARNATION and ASTROLOGY. Formed in 1980, the organization changed its name in 2000 to The International Association for Regression Research and Therapies, Inc. (IARRT) to reflect an emphasis on past lives being an energy field that is in the now rather than in the past. Therapeutic techniques revolve around past-life regression. Publishes *Journal of Regression Therapy.* Web site—http://www.iarrt.org. See HYPNOSIS.

Association for Research and Enlightenment, Edgar Cayce—Virginia Beach, VA: Edgar Cayce was an early twentieth-century student of the OCCULT who claimed to receive revelations while in a TRANCE and was known as the "sleeping prophet." His teachings involve PANTHEISM, REINCARNATION, and readings of present and past lives. Web site—http://www.are-cayce.com. For further research, a four-page Watchman Fellowship Profile is available (see page 363). Web site—http://www.watchman.org/notebook.

Association for the Understanding of Man, Ray Stanford—Austin, TX: Incorporated in 1971, a NEW AGE group that practices PSYCHIC readings and CHANNELING while in ALTERED STATES OF CONSCIOUSNESS. Through its PROJECT STARLIGHT INTERNATIONAL, the group also attempts to make contact with and prove the existence of UFOs and extraterrestrial civilizations.

Association of Happiness for All Mankind, Dee Wayne Trammell (Arunachala Ramana) and Elizabeth MacDonald—Asheboro, NC: NEW AGE center for MEDITATION. Follows the teachings of Bhagavan Sri Ramana Maharshi. Web site—http://www.aham.com. See ARUNACHALA ASHRAMA.

Association of Holistic Healing Centers—Virginia Beach, VA: Organization for practitioners of alternative medicine, focusing on energy vibrations. Web site—http://205.180.229.2/othersites/Ahhc/index.html. See HOLISTIC HEALING; THERAPEUTIC TOUCH.

Association of Vineyard Churches, John Wimber—Sugarland, TX: A fellowship of autonomous NONDENOMINATIONAL CHURCHES founded largely on the ministry of John Wimber (1934–1997), a former CALVARY CHAPEL pastor. Wimber's church in Anaheim, California, was disassociated from the Calvary Chapel fellowship over differences concerning spiritual gifts and manifestations. Wimber's emphasis on HOLY SPIRIT healing and power evangelism (reaching the lost through miraculous signs and wonders) was identified by C. Peter Wagner as part of the THIRD WAVE OF THE HOLY SPIRIT and distinct from the earlier CHARISMATIC MOVEMENT. The Vineyard movement drew criticism from more traditional Christians on a number of issues—especially in relationship to the TORONTO BLESSING coming out of the Airport Vineyard Fellowship in Toronto and the KANSAS CITY PROPHETS. Before his death, Wimber distanced himself from what he considered to be excesses and accountability issues with the Toronto revival. In 2000, Berten Waggoner became national director of the association while maintaining his duties as senior pastor of the Vineyard Church of Sugarland, Texas. The independent associated churches maintain a strong commitment to church planting. In 2003, there were over 850 associated churches worldwide. The movement also spawned a successful music publishing company, Vineyard Music. Web site—http://www.vineyardusa.org. See THIRD WAVE OF THE HOLY SPIRIT.

Association Sananda & Sanat Kumara, Inc.—Mount Shasta, CA: NEW AGE organization that teaches CHANNELING in order to develop a person's CHRIST CONSCIOUSNESS.

Associazione Nazionale Pranoterapeuti Sensitivi Italiana—Milano, Italy: An organization that studies the possibilities of developing EXTRASENSORY PERCEPTION using electronic devices. ANPSI sells two ESP-related products: the *Cerebral Regenerator Karnak,* which allegedly develops extrasensory powers through psychobiophysic stimulation, and the *Psychic Sensor Karnak,* which allegedly measures the energy emitted by PSYCHIC HEALERS from a range of 1-5 meters. Web site—http://www.anpsi.it. See HOLISTIC HEALING; PSYCHICS.

Astara, Robert and Evelyn Chaney—Rancho Cucamonga, CA: Founded in 1951, it now claims members in more than 85 countries. A NEW AGE organization through which the Chaneys teach SPIRITISM, CHAKRAS, using the THIRD EYE, and YOGA. Publishes *Voice of Astara*. Web site—http://www.astara.org.

Astor, Lauri: Teaches that, using ASTROLOGY, people can set up a magnetic current through which to fulfill their desires. Astor claims to be a direct descendant of Edward VII.

Astral Projection: NEW AGE/OCCULT method whereby a person's soul can depart the body, travel to various parts of the universe, then re-enter the body. Usually the soul and body are said to be connected at all times by a "cord." Also called out-of-body experiences (OBE).

Astral Travel. See ASTRAL PROJECTION.

Astro Computing Services, Neil Michelsen—San Diego, CA: Teaches ASTROLOGY. Operates ACS Publications, which offers various books, publications, and software programs by astrologers. Web site—http://www.astrocom.com.

Astro Consciousness Institute—Denver, CO: Practices Eastern MYSTICISM and believes that all people can realize their divinity through self-enlightenment. See CHRIST CONSCIOUSNESS.

Astrological Society of America—Montvale, NJ: Also known as the National Parapsychology Center. Features toll-free hotlines for members involving PSYCHIC consultations, TAROT readings, angelology, and the prophecies of Nostradamus. The Better Business Bureau of New York released a consumer alert about the organization in 1996. Publishes *New Directions*. See ASTROLOGY.

Astrology: An ancient fatalistic system of DIVINATION using the position of the planets, moon, and sun in the 12 ZODIAC positions at the moment of one's birth to supernaturally gain hidden OCCULT knowledge. See DIVINATION. For further research, a four-page Watchman Fellowship Profile is available (see page 363). Web site—http://www.watchman.org/notebook.

Astrology and Psychic News—North Hollywood, CA: NEW AGE periodical published by the California Astrology Association. Web site—http://www. psychicstories.com.

Astro-Soul: Closely follows the teachings of Francisco Coll and practices CHANNELING, ESP, CLAIRVOYANCE, and ASTRAL PROJECTION. Affiliated with the INNER PEACE MOVEMENT.

Athame: In MAGICK, a ceremonial two-edged knife or dagger, usually with a black handle, that is used in WICCA rituals.

Athanasius (A.D. 298–373): The Bishop of Alexandria, who defended the ORTHODOX position of the deity of CHRIST against a HERETIC named ARIUS at the COUNCIL OF NICEA. In addition, his list of New Testament books may be the earliest existing canon naming the same 27 books of the New Testament that appear in today's Bibles. See COUNCIL OF NICEA.

Atheism: From Greek *a* ("no") and *theos* ("God"), the belief that there is no supreme being or God. See SECULAR HUMANISM; AGNOSTICISM.

Atlantic Institute of Aromatherapy—Tampa, FL: Offers seminars in AROMATHERAPY and HOLISTIC HEALING. Web site—http://www. atlanticinstitute.com.

Atlantic Pagan Council: Association of East Coast pagans. Members are involved in such practices as MAGIC and observing moon festivals. Publishes the *Atlantic Pagan Council Amateur Publishers' Association* newsletter. See PAGANISM.

Atlantis: A mythical island/continent said to have sunk beneath the ocean. Purported to have been a highly advanced civilization. Many NEW AGE devotees channel former inhabitants of Atlantis. See CHANNELING; RAMTHA.

ATLAS Communities: ATLAS is an acronym for Authentic Teaching, Learning, and Assessment for all Students, an education program developed by educators at Brown, Harvard, and Yale universities. The communities are alternative schools focusing on metaphysical questions. The level of achievement attained by students is used by instructors to determine the representative standard for excellence for each individual class. The ATLAS program is part of the NEW AMERICAN SCHOOLS network. Web site—http://www.atlascommunities.org. See AFFECTIVE EDUCATION.

Atman: A term used in HINDUISM that refers to the eternal or real self and sometimes refers to the universal life principle.

At-one-ment: Term used by several MIND SCIENCE or NEW THOUGHT religions (such as CHRISTIAN SCIENCE) in reference to the unity of the minds of man and God demonstrated by Christ. See FIRST CHURCH OF CHRIST, SCIENTIST.

At the Gate—Columbus, OH: Singles network for individuals involved with social causes and alternative religions.

Audrey Cohen College—New York, NY: Named after an educator who integrated scholastic education with ethical enculturation, this network consists of primary schools orienting education from five perspectives: purpose, values and ethics, self and others, systems, and skills. The college focuses on undergraduate education while also offering K-12 curricula distributed through the network. See AFFECTIVE EDUCATION.

Aum Shinrikyo (aka Aum Supreme Truth), Shoko Asahara—Tokyo, Japan: *Aum* (a MANTRA) *Shinri Kyo* ("Supreme Truth") is the apocalyptic Buddhist sect suspected of masterminding the 1995 subway nerve gas murders in Japan. Police raiding CULT compounds discovered stockpiles of nerve gas and the basic ingredients of biological warfare. Sect leaders have been charged with, and found guilty of, abduction and "murder preparation." One of these, Aum leader Chizuo Matsumoto (called Shoko Asahara), predicted the end of the world between 1997 and 2000. The DALAI LAMA, the leader of TIBETAN BUDDHISM, has denied Aum claims that Asahara was ever his disciple. At its height, the sect had about $29 million in assets and 10,000 disciples in Japan and 30,000 in Russia. The sect has followers in other countries, including the United States and Australia. The group currently goes by the name Aleph. See BUDDHISM. For further research, a four-page Watchman Fellowship Profile is available (see page 363). Web site—http://www.watchman.org/notebook.

Aum Supreme Truth: See AUM SHINRIKYO.

Aura: A subtle light or energy field said to surround people or objects. Mystics explain that the color of the aura can help reveal a person's emotional and intellectual moods. The aura is a focal point for many individuals claiming PSYCHIC powers.

Auras: The belief held by some metaphysical teachers and proponents of NEW AGE spirituality that psychic energies, spiritual fields, or electromagnetic forces radiate from humans (or all living things). Allegedly, these normally invisible energy fields can sometimes be viewed as multicolored emanations or halos by those who are psychically gifted or are specially trained. Some practitioners claim to be able to read or diagnose physical and spiritual information about their clients through aura readings. See PSYCHIC; NEW AGE.

Aurora Production AG—Zug, Switzerland: Copyright holder for products of THE FAMILY (CHILDREN OF GOD).

Austin Bible Foundation, Carl C. Austin—Whispering Pines, NC: Teachings are derived from Marconianism (a second-century HERESY rejecting the Old Testament) and Manichaeism (a HERESY proclaiming that good and evil are in continual and irreconcilable conflict). The Foundation has its own Bible, *The Christian Bible: Interpreted Edition.* Publishes *The Christian Light.*

Author Services, Inc.: Promotes CHURCH OF SCIENTOLOGY philosophy via the writings of L. Ron Hubbard. Web site—http://www.authorservicesinc.com.

Automatic Writing: A type of writing said to be inspired by the spirit world, in which the writer has no conscious muscular control of his or her hands or arms. Teresa of Avila, a saint and doctor of the church in ROMAN CATHOLICISM, is said to have written many of her works through automatic writing. The practice is found in many OCCULT and NEW AGE groups.

Avalon Concept—Manitou Springs, CO: Teaches NEW AGE feminist spirituality.

The Avalon School of Astrology, David and Fei Cochrane—Gainesville, FL: Founded in 2002, the school trains students to become certified astrologers. Licensed by the state, this school, according to its literature, is one of less than a half-dozen such schools in the United States. Web site—http://www. avalonastrology.com. See ASTROLOGY.

Avanta Network, Virginia Satir (1916–88)—Palo Alto, CA: A NEW AGE network that teaches the Satir Growth Model, in which the phases of human development are controlled by positive and negative energies. The phases are making contact, validating, facilitating awareness, promoting acceptance, making changes, and reinforcing changes. Web site—http:// www.avanta.net.

Avatar: Similar to EST and LIFESPRING, this organization's NEW AGE seminars enable participants to have conscious shift of beliefs. Publishes *Avatar Journal.* See STAR'S EDGE INTERNATIONAL.

Avatars: From the Sanskrit word *avatāra,* which means "descending." In HINDUISM and some forms of NEW AGE spirituality, these are alleged deities or spiritual beings that come down to earth in bodily form to provide wisdom or enlightenment to humans. Similar to ASCENDED MASTERS.

Awake!: A bimonthly magazine published by the WATCHTOWER BIBLE AND TRACT SOCIETY.

Awakenings, Inc.—Prescott, AZ: Distributes books, charts, and computer programs for practicing ASTROLOGY. Web site—http://www.awaken ingsastrology.com.

Awareness Research Foundation, Inc., Helen I. Hoag—Hayesville, NC: The organization started in North Miami, Florida, where Hoag claimed to have had an encounter with a UFO. A NEW AGE organization combining teachings about ASTROLOGY, ATLANTIS, UFOs, ESP, and Lord Sananda. Published a number of books, especially in the late 1960s to early 1990s, relating to UFOs and METAPHYSICS.

Axil Press—Seattle, WA: Neo-pagan publisher. See NEO-PAGANISM.

Ayurvedic Institute—Albuquerque, NM: Offers products for practicing ayurveda. Web site—http://www.ayurveda.com. See AYURVEDIC MEDICINE; HOLISTIC HEALING.

Ayurvedic Lifestyle Center, Pearl Miller Laperla—Reno, NV: Established in 1991. Teaches Eastern MYSTICISM, MEDITATION, and homeopathic medicine. Web site—http://lotusvideoproductions.com. See AYURVEDIC MEDICINE; HOLISTIC HEALING.

Ayurvedic Medicine: Promoted by MAHARISHI MAHESH YOGI and DEEPAK CHOPRA. Teaches the balancing of vibrational centers for health through diet, exercise, herbs, and purification procedures. See CHAKRAS; HOLISTIC HEALING; TRANSCENDENTAL MEDITATION.

AZ Reality Publishers, TONI MOLTZAN—Keller, TX: NEW AGE publishing company formed in 2004 to publish the books authored by ANTOINETTE (TONI) MOLTZAN. Web site for Toni Moltzan—http://www.courseinlight.net.

B

Baba, Sathya Sai: Sai Baba was born November 23, 1926 in Puttaparthi in southern India. In 1940, at age 13, he declared, "I am Sai Baba," which means "divine mother and father." Sai Baba claims that he is the REINCAR-NATION of Shirdi Sai Baba, an Indian holy man who died in 1918. Sai Baba prophesies that he will "die" at the age of 96 in 2021 and reincarnate a year later as Prema Sai Baba (*Prema* means "love"). He claims this "triple incarnation" (as Shirdi , Sathya, and Prema Sai Baba) is referred to in the UPANISHADS. Sai Baba's millions of followers consider him to be a full avatar—i.e., a spiritual teacher of the stature of KRISHNA, BUDDHA, or JESUS. Sai Baba claims to have established over 1,200 Sathya Sai Baba centers in 137 countries. Web site—http://www.sathyasai.org. See HIN-DUISM; MEDITATION; KUNDALINI YOGA.

The Bahá'í Faith, Bahá'ulláh: A syncretistic sect of ISLAM that has evolved into a major independent religion with approximately five million believers worldwide. Baha'is teach that Moses, BUDDHA, KRISHNA, JESUS, MUHAMMAD, Zoroaster, and others formed a succession of divine messengers. A nineteenth-century Persian teacher, the Báb (or Gate), pre-dicted the coming of Bahá'u'lláh, the most recent messenger and founder of Baha'i. The movement's goals involve establishing a new global order of sexual equality, a one-world economic system to eliminate poverty, and a one-world religion. Web site—http://www.bahai.org. For further research, a four-page Watchman Fellowship Profile is available (see page 363). Web site—http://www.watchman.org/notebook.

Bailey, Alice: An early twentieth-century leader in THEOSOPHY who was heavily influenced by MADAME BLAVATSKY and allegedly received messages from an ASCENDED MASTER named Master KH (Koot Hoomi). She formed a number of organizations to help spread her philosophies, including World Goodwill, ARCANE SCHOOL, and LUCIS TRUST. Web site—http://www.alicebailey.org. For further research, a four-page Watchman Fellowship Profile is available (see page 363). Web site—http://www.watchman.org/notebook.

Baker, Greg: An Australian computer programmer who maintains an online collection of prophecies called *The PROBABLE Pages.* The site contains a "Hall of Fame" (listing correct predictions) and a "Hall of Shame" (listing a much longer list of incorrect predictions). Web site—http://www.ifost. org.au/~gregb.

Bak Learning Center—Crestone, CO: A NEW AGE organization that promotes physical and emotional healing through self-awareness. References to receiving energy transmissions to remove energy blocked at the cellular level is similar to the emphasis many HOLISTIC HEALING practitioners place on CHI.

Balaamism: A term used in some FUNDAMENTALIST CHRISTIAN circles for APOSTASY. Refers to the false prophet Balaam, who attempted to curse Israel but instead was used by God to bless the nation (Numbers 22–24).

Baltimore School of Massage—Baltimore, MD: Part of the STEINER EDUCATION GROUP. In addition to standard massage techniques and body movement, the school teaches polarity work—i.e., refining the relationship between mind and body for maximizing energy flow. Web site—http://www.bsom.com. See HOLISTIC HEALING.

Banner Ministries—Great Britain: Charismatic Christian APOLOGETICS ministry that focuses on the WORD-FAITH MOVEMENT. Publishes an alleged prophecy given in 1997 by David Noakes that God is beginning to judge and punish the leaders and members of the Word-Faith Movement. Web site—http://www.intotruth.org.

Baptism: From the Greek verb *baptizo* (Matthew 28:19), the Christian ordinance symbolizing the cleansing of sin and identification with Christ's death, burial, and resurrection. Doctrinal differences concerning water baptism include the mode (sprinkling, immersing, etc.) and participants (infants versus believers only). In addition to baptism by water, New Testament references to baptism include the baptism of the HOLY SPIRIT (Acts 1:5). Some groups believe that water baptism is a requirement for salvation in addition to faith in Christ. PROTESTANTISM and EVANGELICAL CHRISTIANITY traditionally hold to salvation by grace through faith alone and see baptism as an ordinance, sign, or symbol and not as a saving work per se. See BAPTISMAL REGENERATION.

Baptismal Regeneration: The belief that salvation or eternal life is conditioned upon water baptism. Most groups teaching this doctrine also add that a proper mode (immersion or sprinkling) and a proper minister (one authorized by the organization) is necessary. This has been historically seen by PROTESTANTISM as teaching a form of works salvation, which was repudiated by the REFORMATION and is rejected today by FUNDAMENTALIST and EVANGELICAL CHRISTIANITY on the basis of Ephesians 2:8-10. See SALVATION BY WORKS; SALVATION BY GRACE; GOSPEL.

Baptism for the Dead: Practice of the LDS church based on an unusual interpretation of 1 Corinthians 15:29, whereby living members are baptized by proxy for people who have died without knowing the LDS gospel. If the dead accept the LDS gospel while in spirit prison, they can potentially have access to full salvation or godhood (EXALTATION). This ceremony is performed only in a Mormon temple. See CHURCH OF JESUS CHRIST OF LATTER-DAY SAINTS; BAPTISMAL REGENERATION; BAPTISM.

Baptist Bible Fellowship International (BBFI)—Springfield, MO: A fellowship of like-minded INDEPENDENT BAPTIST CHURCHES that support missionaries and education. Web site—http://www.bbfi.org. See BAPTIST CHURCHES; FUNDAMENTALIST CHRISTIANITY.

Baptist Churches: Baptist churches are expressions of PROTESTANTISM that are generally classified as EVANGELICAL CHRISTIANITY. In addition to standard evangelical beliefs, most place an emphasis on baptism by immersion for believers only, congregational rule, and the autonomy of each local church. Modern Baptist churches find their roots in the REFORMATION (particularly some of the Anabaptist distinctives) and the English

Puritan movement. In 2004, an estimated 47.7 million adults identified their religion as Baptist. Baptist groups include: 1) THE SOUTHERN BAPTIST CONVENTION (the largest group, with over 16 million members), 2) THE AMERICAN BAPTIST CHURCHES USA, 3) NATIONAL BAPTIST CONVENTION, 4) PROGRESSIVE NATIONAL BAPTIST CONVENTION, 5) CONSERVATIVE BAPTIST ASSOCIATION OF AMERICA, 6) AMERICAN BAPTIST ASSOCIATION, 7) GENERAL ASSOCIATION OF REGULAR BAPTIST CHURCHES, 8) NATIONAL ASSOCIATION OF FREE WILL BAPTISTS, 9) PRIMITIVE BAPTISTS, and 10) INDEPENDENT BAPTIST CHURCHES.

Barbara Brennan School of Healing—East Hampton, NY: A NEW AGE institution teaching HOLISTIC HEALING and THERAPEUTIC TOUCH. Offers a four-year certification program in professional healing science training. Brennan wrote *Hands of Light: A Guide to Healing Through the Human Energy Field* and *Light Emerging: The Journey of Personal Healing.* Web site—http://www.barbarabrennan.com.

Barnabas Ministries—Farmington Hills, MI: An independent organization that distributes resources that promote SABBATARIANISM. Web site—http://www.biblestudy.org.

***The Barnes Review,* Willis Carto**—Washington, DC: Named after Harry Elmer Barnes, a WWI historian and revisionist, the *Review* was founded in 1994 and promotes numerous anti-Communist CONSPIRACY THEORIES. Its claims of ethnic differences and its occasional references to ostensibly biblical values may suggest an affinity to the Christian IDENTITY MOVEMENT. Web site—http://www.barnesreview.com.

Barr, K.E.: Opposes the activities of the AD2000 and Beyond movement, a nondenominational Protestant organization that intended to evangelize the world by the year 2000. Barr alleges that the primary leaders of AD 2000 (e.g., BILLY GRAHAM, JAMES DOBSON, and the late BILL BRIGHT, etc.) are supporters of the NEW AGE and advocate a one-world religion. Barr self-published the booklet *Unholy Alliances 2000.*

Barsana Dham, H.D. Swami Prakashanand Saraswati—Austin, TX: Established in 1990. This Hindu community is part of JAGADGURU KRIPALU PARISHAT. Web site—http://www.barsanadham.org. See HINDUISM.

Bartsch, Leo: Claims a UFO revealed to him that the "mark of the beast" mentioned in Revelation 13:16-17 is the glorification of humanity. This mark will be revealed following the resurrection of the dead.

Basic Bible Church of America—Order of Almighty God—Madison, WI: An organization that offers mail-order ordinations. The church, denied tax-exempt status in 1977, was assessed $7,819 in back taxes and penalties in 1992 for failing to pay property taxes from 1978–1983. The U.S. Department of Justice cites a scheme by this church as an example of tax fraud in its 1994 *Criminal Tax Manual.*

Bastyr College—Seattle, WA: Founded in 1978 as the John Bastyr College of Naturopathic Medicine, the school is a fully accredited institution for education in HOLISTIC HEALING. Critics allege that the accreditation committee included an individual who was convicted of attempting to sell a bogus medical degree and another person who received two of his three degrees from diploma mills. Web site—http://www.bastyr.edu.

Bawa Muhayiaddeen Fellowship, Bawa Muhayiaddeen—Philadelphia, PA: A sect of SUFISM, the fellowship follows the teachings of Bawa Muhayiaddeen, who syncretistically derives his doctrine from HINDUISM, CHRISTIANITY, ISLAM, and the indigenous fire religions of Sri Lanka. Web site—http://www.bmf.org.

Bear Tribe Medicine Society, Sun Bear (1929–92)—Mobile, AL: Sun Bear was an Ojibaway medicine man who authored a number of books promoting harmonious relationship of all peoples with one another and Mother Earth. After his death, Wabun Wind served briefly as the chief of the tribe and was succeeded by Wind Daughter in 1996. The organization teaches NATIVE AMERICAN SPIRITUALITY and HOLISTIC HEALING. Publishes *Wildfire* newsletter.

The Beatles: A highly influential rock'n'roll group from the 1960s. Their involvement, beginning in 1966, with TRANSCENDENTAL MEDI-TATION (which was later repudiated by both George Harrison—who subsequently became involved with the INTERNATIONAL SOCIETY FOR KRISHNA CONSCIOUSNESS and recorded his hit single "My Sweet Lord" as a devotion to Lord KRISHNA—and John Lennon) is widely credited with the popular success of Eastern religions in the United States.

Believers and Overcomers Church—Queen Creek, AZ: Promotes CONSPIRACY THEORIES involving communists, the Internal Revenue Service, the New World Order, ROMAN CATHOLICISM, and JUDAISM.

Believers International—Tucson, AZ: Republishes WILLIAM BRANHAM's teachings and publishes *Believer's News.* Web site—http://www.biblebelievers.org. See BRANHAMISM.

Believer's Voice of Victory—Fort Worth, TX: See COPELAND, KENNETH.

Bell, Art: Popular late-night radio talk show host. While his *Coast to Coast AM* weeknight broadcast and *Dreamland* weekend broadcast focus on a wide array of NEW AGE and OCCULT issues, as well as many CONSPIRACY THEORIES, one of the most common subjects discussed by program guests is UFOs. Bell has retired and returned to the program a number of times since 1998. Currently he hosts the show on a semi-retired basis. Web site—http://www.coasttocoastam.com.

Bell, Don—Palm Beach, FL: Promotes CONSPIRACY THEORIES involving the New World Order, ROMAN CATHOLICISM, and JUDAISM. Published *Don Bell Reports* from the 1950s into the early 1990s. These are still referred to by those who hold to CONSPIRACY THEORIES. Some of the *Reports* can be viewed online. Web site—http://www.americandeception.com.

Benevolent Mother, Park Soon-ja: A pseudo-Christian CULT lead by Soon-ja, who was called Benevolent Mother by her followers. After preaching the imminence of the end of the world, Soon-ja and 32 followers committed suicide in Seoul, Korea, on August 28, 1987.

Benjamine, Elbert: See CHURCH OF LIGHT.

Berachah Church, Robert B. Thieme, Jr.—Houston, TX: A nondenominational Christian church formed in 1935 and pastored by the controversial Bible teacher, Robert B. Thieme, Jr. from 1950 to 2003. He was then succeeded by his son, Robert B. Thieme, III. The teachings of the elder Thieme, a retired lieutenant colonel, are propagated worldwide through the free distribution of over 11,000 hours of recorded sermons. His unique jargon, illustrations, and biblical interpretations have drawn fire from a number of former members and critics. Controversial teachings include his belief that Christ's spiritual death alone (and not the physical death or literal blood of CHRIST) was given in payment for man's sin. He also has been criticized for his doctrine of "right pastor-teacher," which allows for only one correct pastor for each Christian. Christians cannot grow spiritually through personal study or from other teachers but only by being under the authority of that one right pastor. Web site—http://www.berachah.org.

Berean Bible Society, C.R. Stam—Germantown, WI: Teaches that the Great Commission, water baptism, and the teachings of Jesus were intended only for the early church. The society claims that only Acts 28:9 through the book of Revelation is valid for the modern church. Publishes the *Berean Searchlight*. Web site—http://www.bereanbiblesociety.org.

Berean Committee for an Open Bible, P. Norman Carlson—Salida, CO: Teaches that the Great Commission and communion were intended only for the early church. Quoting Ephesians 4:5, the committee teaches that water baptism was replaced by being baptized by one Spirit. The committee also claims that the teachings of Paul supplant the teachings of the Gospels.

Bermuda Triangle: Geographically, the Triangle composes the southwestern quadrant of the North Atlantic, with apexes in Bermuda, Puerto Rico, and in the Gulf of Mexico west of Florida. Some people involved in the OC-CULT and UFO studies believe the Triangle is a supernaturally dangerous area, with many ships and airplanes disappearing in the Triangle all through the twentieth-century.

Bernard, David: A well-known JESUS ONLY writer and speaker. See ONENESS PENTECOSTALISM.

Berry, Thomas: A former monk of ROMAN CATHOLICISM and later a cultural historian, Berry calls for a "New Story" for the universe. Berry teaches that humans should reinvent themselves as a species, changing their genetic coding so they can recover their relatedness to the earth. See NEW AGE.

Besant, Annie: Successor to MADAME BLAVATSKY, who proclaimed KRISHNAMURTI as the MESSIAH (Krishnamurti later renounced the role). See THEOSOPHY.

Beth El Shaddai, Dick Amos—Plano, TX: Teaches DUAL COVENANT theology (i.e., that there are separate covenants for Jews and Gentiles), and denies that Jesus is God. Claims that the New Testament cannot be understood without a knowledge of the Dead Sea Scrolls. Also teaches that religious Jews can be saved through observing Jewish law. See JUDAISM; SALVATION BY WORKS.

Beth HaShem, Jacob Hawkins—Odessa, TX: A SACRED NAME and SABBATARIAN group, Beth HaShem keeps Old Testament feasts and laws for salvation. Hawkins, who died in 1991, was the brother of Yisayl Hawkins of the HOUSE OF YAHWEH. Publishes *The Prophetic Watchman* newsletter.

Beth HaShem, Shmuel Ben Aharon—Woodburn, IN: A SACRED NAME group that believes there are two texts to the BIBLE. The "black text," which contains the lower frequencies of revelation, contains the narrative stories of the sins of the people. The "white text," which consists of the passages relating to life in Mashiyach, is also the spiritual reading of the text that results in the transmission of "Light Nature" or spiritual energy to the reader. Web site—http://www.bethashem.org.

Bhagavad-Gita: Meaning "Song of the Lord," this text of scripture is used by HINDUS and Hare Krishnas. See INTERNATIONAL SOCIETY FOR KRISHNA CONSCIOUSNESS.

Bhagwan Shree Rajneesh: See OSHO.

Bhakti Yoga: A type of YOGA or spiritual exercise involving devotion to a GURU. The YOGI directs unconditional love to the guru, who in turn prescribes MANTRAs, VISUALIZATION, etc., to facilitate the spiritual development of the yogi. The practice is central to the INTERNATIONAL SOCIETY FOR KRISHNA CONSCIOUSNESS.

Bible: Considered scripture by CHRISTIANITY. Consists of the Jewish scriptures (TANAKH), called the Old Testament, and the Christian scriptures, called the New Testament. The Old Testament is made up of 39 books originally written in Hebrew and Aramaic. The New Testament is a compilation of 27 books originally written in Greek during the first century. In all, the books of the Bible were written by over 40 different writers over about a 1,500-year period. Evangelical Christians believe that the Bible came from God through the following process: 1) revelation: God chose to reveal truth to His people; 2) inspiration (God-breathed): the Spirit of God moved on the biblical writers to write scripture using their own words in such a way that the product was exactly what God intended to communicate without error (2 Timothy 3:16-17); 3) autographs: the first or original copy of the written scripture written by the biblical writers (none of which are still extant); 4) manuscripts: handwritten copies derived from the original autographs, of which there are thousands; 5) textual criticism: the process of comparing manuscripts to eliminate copyists' errors; 6) canonicity: the process of discovering which books should be included in the Bible and eliminating the non-inspired APOCRYPHA and inauthentic books; 7) translation: the faithful conversion of the texts from the ancient Hebrew, Aramaic, and Greek into modern languages.

Bible Believers, Inc.: See BRANHAM, WILLIAM.

Bible Church Movement: Independent congregations of EVANGELICAL CHRISTIANITY, many of which have ties to Dallas Theological Seminary (DTS). A leading example is Fellowship Bible Church North founded in 1972 by Gene Getz, a professor at DTS and director of the Center for Church Renewal. Web site—http://www.fbcnorth.org. See EVANGELICAL CHRISTIANITY.

***Bible Code,* Michael Drosnin:** Best-selling 1997 book teaches that prophecies are hidden in a complex network of letters and words within the Old Testament. Drosnin claims that he attempted to warn Israeli leader Yitzak Rabin of his impending assassination based on a prediction he claims is in the biblical code. See NUMEROLOGY; KABBALAH.

Bible Research Association—Baltimore, MD: Similar in theology to the WATCHTOWER BIBLE AND TRACT SOCIETY. Teaches that Jesus was created, denies the immortal soul and the existence of hell, and teaches that the HOLY SPIRIT is only the power of God.

Bible Sabbath Association—Gillette, WY: A SABBATARIAN association consisting of members of the SEVENTH-DAY ADVENTISTS, followers of ARMSTRONGISM, and other sabbatarian groups. Publishes *The Sabbath Sentinel.* Web site—http://www.biblestudy.org.

The Bible Speaks: See GREATER GRACE WORLD OUTREACH.

Bible Students Congregation of New Brunswick—Edison, NJ: WATCHTOWER BIBLE AND TRACT SOCIETY break-off group. Their Web site contains an extensive amount of the group's literature. Web site—http://bible411.com.

Bible Students: Various semiautonomous groups that broke off from the WATCHTOWER BIBLE AND TRACT SOCIETY after Joseph Rutherford took control of the organization in 1916-17. The groups reprint the early writings of Watchtower founder CHARLES TAZE RUSSELL, including the six-volume *Studies in the Scriptures.* Groups across the country go under various names (i.e., Fort Worth Bible Students or Chicago Bible Students, etc.). Web site—http://www.biblestudents.net.

Bible Studies Fellowship—San Diego, CA: WATCHTOWER BIBLE AND TRACT SOCIETY break-off group. Also called Faithbuilders Fellowship. Now known as the Bible Students of San Diego. *Note: This group is not affiliated with BIBLE STUDY FELLOWSHIP, INTERNATIONAL (BSF), headquartered in San Antonio, Texas.*

Bible Study Association—Eugene, OR: SACRED NAME, SABBATARIAN group emphasizing the observance of the Jewish festivals.

Bible Study, Charles and Yvonne Svitlik—Waterbury, CT: Denies the TRINITY and the deity of CHRIST.

Bible Study Fellowship, International (BSF)—San Antonio, TX: An organization of EVANGELICAL CHRISTIANITY founded in the mid-1900s by A. Wetherell Johnson, a former missionary to China. Focused on encouraging and facilitating small-group BIBLE studies, there are about 1,000 BSF classes in over 30 countries. Web site—http://www.bsfinternational.org.

Bible Talks: Home and campus group studies sponsored by the INTER-NATIONAL CHURCH OF CHRIST.

Bible Way Church of Our Lord Jesus Christ World Wide: Founded in 1957 by Smallwood E. Williams, the Bible Way Church is now a de-nomination of 300 congregations. The church denies the doctrine of the TRINITY, teaching the JESUS ONLY doctrine. Web site—http://www. biblewaychurch.org. See ONENESS PENTECOSTALISM; MODALISM; SALVATION BY WORKS.

Bible Way Publications—Fort Lauderdale, FL: Break-off group from the WATCHTOWER BIBLE AND TRACT SOCIETY. In the past they also called themselves Jehovah's Witnesses, the name by which the members of the Watchtower Society are commonly known. Publishes *Neighborhood Bible Study.*

Biblical Church of God—Santa Cruz, CA: WORLDWIDE CHURCH OF GOD splinter group. See ARMSTRONGISM.

Biblical Errancy, **Dennis McKinsey**—Springfield, OH: Newsletter focusing on alleged biblical errors, contradictions, and fallacies. Web site—http:// members.aol.com/ckbloomfld.

Biblical Research Centers: Regional centers for THE WAY INTERNA-TIONAL.

Bickle, Mike: See KANSAS CITY PROPHETS.

Bigfoot: Also known as Sasquatch, Bigfoot is allegedly an ape-like creature that has reportedly been spotted in the northwestern United States and southwestern Canada since the eighteenth-century. Dr. Grover Krantz (1931–2002), who served as professor of anthropology at Washington State University, was one of the foremost experts on Bigfoot. The Bigfoot Field Researchers Organization Web site—http://www.bfro.net.

Billy Graham Evangelistic Association (BGEA), Billy Graham—Charlotte, NC: An outreach organization promoting EVANGELICAL CHRISTI-ANITY founded in 1950 to promote the preaching and evangelistic crusades (now called festivals) of the BAPTIST evangelist Billy Graham. In 2001,

Graham's son Franklin became president of BGEA. Since 1979, Franklin Graham has also served as president of Samaritan's Purse, an international relief organization headquartered in Boone, North Carolina. BGEA has a worldwide impact with international offices in seven countries, large evangelistic festivals, and television and radio ministries. Publishes *Decision* magazine and owns Worldwide Pictures. Web site—http://www. billygraham.org. See GRAHAM, BILLY.

Bio-Energetic Synchronization Techniques (BEST): NEW AGE practice in CHIROPRACTIC MEDICINE in which sensory nerve adjustments are said to cause the brain to improve its normal motor impulse to muscles, glands, and tissues. See HOLISTIC HEALING.

Bioenergy: NEW AGE practice of healing, in which life-energy is balanced by opening blocked MERIDIANS. See HOLISTIC HEALING.

Biofeedback: The use of EEG (electroencephalographic) feedback instruments to monitor brain waves and skin resistance with the goal of the modification of brain waves. Participants can learn to control heart rates or generate brain wave activity (alpha, beta, and delta) to induce ALTERED STATES OF CONSCIOUSNESS, enhancing the capacity for relaxation or to induce meditative states and physiological control similar to that of a YOGI, or ZEN master.

Bio-Magnetics: A NEW AGE practice involving realigning the magnetic fields allegedly surrounding the body. See CHI; HOLISTIC HEALING.

BioPsciences Institute (BPI), Martin Bulgerin—Minneapolis, MN: Established in 1987. Practices ASTROLOGY, as well as using "flower essences" and vibrational energies to balance individuals' energy fields. Bulgerin is active in the endeavor to convince the Minnesota legislature to recognize HOLISTIC HEALING. Web site: http://www2.bitstream.net/~bunlion/bpi/index.html.

Biorhythms: The theory that three cycles are initiated at birth: a physical cycle of 23 days, emotional cycle of 28 days, and an intellectual cycle of 33 days. Charting these biorhythmic cycles allegedly allows individuals to determine when they will be most capable of performing certain tasks.

Bio/Tech News—Portland, OR: Promotes HOLISTIC HEALING practices and products. Web site—http://www.biotechnews.com.

Black Christian Nationalist Movement. See PAN AFRICAN ORTHODOX CHRISTIAN CHURCH.

Black Hebrews: A number of sects who refer to themselves, or are identified, as Black Hebrews. Though the beliefs may vary greatly from group to group, they hold a common belief that the Jews were originally black or that there was a black tribe of Israelites of which they are descendants. For example, according to Yahweh Ben Yahweh, they are the African descendants of the ten lost tribes of Israel. Black Hebrews is also a name that some have used to describe such groups as the NATION OF YAHWEH, the AFRICAN HEBREW ISRAELITES OF JERUSALEM, and the ISRAELITE NATION WORLDWIDE MINISTRIES, though the groups may not use the term themselves.

Black Mass: An OCCULT ceremony, usually performed by Satanists, often involving the desecration of Christian symbols or a ritual reversal of the Roman Catholic mass. Blood and raw flesh (human or animal) are occasionally consumed, and ritual sex is performed. While the practice is common fare for movies and novels, the ceremony is in reality somewhat rare.

Black Moon Publishing—Cincinnati, OH: OCCULT book publisher.

Black Muslim: See NATION OF ISLAM.

Black Panthers Party: A largely defunct movement, founded in 1966 by Bobby Seale, intended to protect African-Americans from police brutality and other forms of abuse and discrimination. Members frequently engaged in armed conflicts with police. A small group claiming to be a revival of the Black Panthers has been seen at some gatherings involving African-American issues.

Blavatsky, Helena Petrovna (1831–91): Known as Madame Blavatsky, this Ukrainian-born PSYCHIC was an important nineteenth-century occultist with alleged powers of LEVITATION, MATERIALIZATION, TELEPATHY, and CLAIRVOYANCE. She cofounded the influential THEOSOPHICAL SOCIETY in 1875. Her works include *Isis Unveiled*

(1877), *The Secret Doctrine* (1888), *The Voice of the Silence* (1889), *The Key to Theosophy* (1889), and a 15-volume collection of articles titled *The Collected Writings of H.P. Blavatsky.* See OCCULT; THEOSOPHY; PSYCHIC.

Blue Dolphin Publishing—Nevada City, CA: NEW AGE publishing company and product retailer. Web site—http://www.bluedolphinpub lishing.com.

Blue Lotus—Wilmot, WI: Company selling NEW AGE and HOLISTIC HEALING products.

Blue Mountain Center of Meditation, Eknath Easwaran—Petaluma, CA: A NEW AGE retreat center that teaches HINDUISM, MEDITA-TION, and uses the *BHAGAVAD-GITA.* Operates the Nilgiri Press. Web site—http://www.easwaran.org.

Blue Mountain Center, Verna V. Aridon Yater—Colorardo Springs, CO: A NEW AGE retreat center that promotes spiritual healing through NA-TIVE AMERICAN SPIRITUALITY, CHANNELING, PAST LIFE REGRESSION, and the use of CRYSTALS. Web site—http://www.blue mountaincenter.com.

Blue Rose Ministry, Robert Short—Cornville, AZ: Short claims to have had several contacts with extraterrestrials, beginning in 1952. Through CHANNELING, he receives messages from UFOs and the space brothers. Publishes the *Solar Space-Letter.* He has written two books of his channeled messages, *Out of the Stars* and *Master of the Rose* (2004).

Blue Star, Inc., Mary Elizabeth Thunder—West Point, TX: Also known as Church of the Blue Star. Founded in 1988 to share the teachings of Thunder and her spiritual teachers. The church has ordained some 50 ministers in states throughout the United States. It operates out of Thunder-Horse Ranch, a NEW AGE "spiritual university" that engages in a wide variety of spiritualities from NATIVE AMERICAN to TIBETAN BUDDHISM and CHANNELING. Thunder believes that all paths lead to the Creator. Web site—http://www.marythunder.com.

B'nei Noach (alternate spelling B'nai Noach): Translated as "Sons of Noah," the term refers to the rabbinic belief that Gentiles must keep the seven universal laws given to Noah (i.e., forbidding idolatry, blasphemy, murder, theft, and eating the limb of a living animal; regulating sexual relations; and establishing courts of law). Also known as Noahides, the movement is widespread and involved a number of organizations. In some cases it is DUAL COVENANT, teaching that Jesus is not the Savior of the Jews. Other groups hold that JESUS was not the MESSIAH for the Jews or the Gentiles. For one example of this theology, see JONES, VENDYL. Web site—http://www.bneinoach.org.

Bo: One of the names used by Marshall Applewhite. See HEAVEN'S GATE.

Bodhi Tree Bookstore—Los Angeles, CA: NEW AGE bookstore offering resources and lectures on BUDDHISM, METAPHYSICS, and HOLISTIC HEALING. Web site—http://www.bodhitree.com.

Body & Soul: Started in 1974 as *New Age Journal, Body & Soul* covers such topics as FEMINISM, environmentalism, alternative education and business practices, HOLISTIC HEALTH, and alternative spiritualities. Though now part of Martha Stewart Living Omnimedia, Inc., it maintains some of its NEW AGE roots, particularly in its self-healing section and promotion of ANDREW WEIL. Web site—http://www.bodyandsoulmag.com. See HOLISTIC HEALTH.

Body Therapy Institute, Rick Rosen—Siler City, NC: Founded in 1983 as the Bodyworks School of Massage Therapy. The name was changed in 1989. The institute trains massage therapists and incorporates "energy balancing" into its practices. Includes continuing education presenters in a variety of Eastern massage techniques and AROMATHERAPY and REFLEXOLOGY. Web site—http://www.massage.net. See HOLISTIC HEALTH.

Bohemian Grove—Monte Rio, CA: Owned by the Bohemian Club, a private men's club formed in 1872, the Grove is an exclusive retreat for influential males, including a number of U.S. presidents. The Bohemian Club is popularly used in CONSPIRACY THEORIES surrounding who really controls the U.S. and world governments. A number of news stories in the 1980s claimed that club activities included OCCULT-like rituals and sexual orgies.

Bohica Concepts—Randle, WA: A retailer that offers antigovernment resources, many involving an allegedly Christian basis for antigovernment activities.

The Bondage Breaker: See ANDERSON, NEIL.

Bongo: An interdisciplinary educational course for public schools intended to enhance the creative abilities of students through ALTERED STATES OF CONSCIOUSNESS.

Bonnelle, Brother Harry—Wenatchee, WA: Claims that a battalion of UFOs are setting up an intergalactic command center over eastern Washington state. Potential inductees are contacted by a smiling pink alien named Bee Dee Bee Dee Caw Caw Guy-A. Bonnelle obtains much of his information by practicing ASTROLOGY.

Bookmark—Santa Clarita, CA: CHRISTIAN SCIENCE splinter group. Republishes works by early Christian Scientists, and maintains a listing of independent Christian Science practitioners. Web site—http://www.thebookmark.com.

Book of Changes: See I CHING.

Book of Mormon: One of the scriptures or standard works of the CHURCH OF JESUS CHRIST OF LATTER-DAY SAINTS (LDS) and many other Mormon splinter groups. LDS church founder, the prophet JOSEPH SMITH, JR., allegedly translated the book from ancient golden plates that were recovered near his home in Palmyra, New York, in the Hill Cumorah. Smith said that the plates were engraved in "Reformed Egyptian Hieroglyphics," which he was able to translate into English by "the gift and power of God." The Book of Mormon was published in 1830 and tells the story of a Jewish man named Lehi and his descendants, who arrived in Central America by boat from Jerusalem about 600 B.C. Lehi's descendants later divided into two warring factions: the Nephites and the Lamanites. The book ends about 1000 years later with the complete destruction of the Nephites in A.D. 421, leaving only the Lamanites, who became "principal ancestors of the American Indians." Critics have noted that DNA evidence uniformly shows that Native Americans are descended from Northeast Asians and not Israelites. Unlike the BIBLE, none of the coins described in the Book of

Mormon (Alma 11) or any of the large, fortified cities named in it have ever been found or identified. Anthropologists have also noted that horses were not introduced to the New World until after 1492; thus, horses described in the Book of Mormon (Alma 18:9-10,12) could not have existed there between 600 B.C. and A.D. 421. The Book of Mormon is available online at http://scriptures.lds.org/bm/contents. See CHURCH OF JESUS CHRIST OF LATTER-DAY SAINTS.

Borderland Science Research Foundation, Meade Layne (1883–1961)— Garberville, CA: Founded in 1945 by Layne to study the PARANORMAL, the foundation studies such NEW AGE elements as ALCHEMY, DOWSING, UFOs, and ASTROLOGY. Publishes *The Journal of Borderland Research*. Web site—http://www.borderlands.com.

Born Again: Biblical term used to describe regeneration (John 3:3-7). The term has been given a wide range of meanings. Some NEW AGE followers teach that the term was Christ's reference to REINCARNATION or REBIRTHING. Churches that lean toward BAPTISMAL REGENERA-TION tend to interpret the phrase to be a reference to water baptism. EVANGELICAL and FUNDAMENTALIST Christians believe that Jesus was speaking of a spiritual event effected by God through the HOLY SPIRIT to restore a sinful, fallen human to right relationship with Him. See GOSPEL.

Born to Win: See CHRISTIAN EDUCATIONAL MINISTRIES.

Borysenko, Joan: A practitioner in the mind-body movement, Borysenko claims that people can achieve spontaneous healing. Author of *Minding the Body, Mending the Mind*. Web site—http://joanborysenko.com. See NEW AGE; HOLISTIC HEALING.

Boston Church of Christ: The former name of the INTERNATIONAL CHURCHES OF CHRIST, it remains one of the largest churches in the group.

Bottom Line/Personal—Boulder, CO: NEW AGE publication promoting financial success and personal health through enhanced personal awareness. Web site—http://www.bottomlinepersonal.com.

Bradshaw, John: Prominent NEW AGE teacher and author of *Healing the Inner Child*. Web site—http://www.bradshawcassettes.com.

Bragg, Paul: Bragg allegedly recovered from tuberculosis at 16, climbed the Matterhorn at 70, and claimed to be the founder of the health food store industry. Bragg and his wife started Bragg Live Foods, a health and fitness company. Web site—http://www.bragg.com. See HOLISTIC HEALING.

Brahma: The creator and first member of the triad of Hindu demigods, including SHIVA and VISHNU. See HINDUISM.

Brahma Kumaris World Spiritual Organization—Tampa, FL: An organization teaching RAJA YOGA, a form of MEDITATION for communicating with the Supreme Being. The organization operates the Brahma Kumaris World Spiritual University, which allegedly has 2000 branches in 60 countries. Web site—http://www.bkwsu.com.

Brainbeau, J.C.: George E. Lemon, an American soldier who suffered a head injury in Africa during World War II, changed his name to J.C. Brainbeau at the age of 72. Brainbeau, until his death in 1992, published a wave of classified advertisements calling for a four-way peace plan and a 50/50 split of world wealth and labor. In addition to publishing such classified advertisements, Lemon (using his real name) also distributed business cards with the name *Century Apex* and his message.

Brain-Mind Expansion: See JOHN-DAVID LEARNING INSTITUTE and WHOLE BRAIN LEARNING INSTITUTE.

Brainspeak: See WHOLE BRAIN LEARNING INSTITUTE.

Brain Sync, Kelly Howell—Ashland, OR: A NEW AGE business that sells packages featuring audio recordings that allegedly match your brain frequency and enhance bodily transformation at the cellular level. Web site—http://www.brainsync.com. See HOLISTIC HEALING.

Brainwashing: Forced indoctrination through various techniques that may cause a subject to abandon basic political, social, or religious ideas or beliefs and replace those ideals with a contrasting belief system. A translation of a

Chinese word *xinao, brainwashing* became a popular term to describe the phenomena of radical change in behavior and core beliefs that took place in some prisoners of war held in Chinese camps in the mid-twentieth-century. In a more general sense, the word is sometimes used to describe any form of persuasion, perceived to be unethical, that results in a radical and negative change in personality. See LIFTON, ROBERT; MIND CONTROL.

Branch Davidians, Benjamin Roden: Splinter group of the Seventh-day Adventist Church. David Koresh (aka Vernon Howell) was leader from 1984 to 1993. He and many of his most devout followers were killed when their headquarters near Waco, Texas was destroyed by fire in 1993 during a government raid. Taught knowledge of the seven seals of the book of Revelation brought salvation. Many followers still believe Koresh's messianic claims and expect him to soon be resurrected.

Branch of Jerusalem—Tulsa, OK: A SABBATARIAN and SACRED NAME group.

Branhamism, William Branham—Jeffersonville, IN: A JESUS ONLY Pentecostal preacher who claimed he received healing and prophetic powers from an angel. Denied the doctrine of the TRINITY and rejected other Pentecostal and traditional Christian churches. A significant Web site dedicated to Branhamism is at http://www.biblebelievers.org. See MODALISM, PENTECOSTALISM, SERPENT SEED. For further research, a four-page Watchman Fellowship Profile is available (see page 363). Web site—http://www.watchman.org/notebook.

Branham Tabernacle: See BRANHAMISM.

Branham, William: See BRANHAMISM.

Bread of Life Internet Ministry—Fletcher, NC: An independent SEVENTH-DAY ADVENTIST APOLOGETICS and evangelism ministry. Promotes the prophetic teachings of Ellen G. White, as well as more recent ADVENTIST teachers A.T. Jones and E.J. Waggoner. Web site—http://www.sdabol.org.

The Brethren Church—Ashland, OH: A movement of Anabaptist PROTESTANTISM that traces its history to Schwarzenau, Germany in 1708. Web site—http://www.brethrenchurch.org. See BRETHREN, ALEXANDER MACK.

The Brethren, Alexander Mack (1679–1735): A number of Brethren groups can be traced back to a movement of Anabaptist PROTESTANTISM formed in Schwarzenau, Germany in 1708. Also known as the Dunkers and German Baptist Brethren, the movement was formed out of the Radical Pietist movement when Mack and other leaders became convicted that full obedience to Christ required BAPTISM, communion, and discipline. Beginning in the 1880s, a number of schisms led to the formation of other groups, including the Old German Baptist Brethren Church, the Brethren Church, and the Church of the Brethren. A split in 1939 formed the Grace Brethren and the Ashland Brethren. Several Brethren groups are not historically related to Mack, including the PLYMOUTH BRETHREN, UNITED BRETHREN, and the BRETHREN, JIM ROBERTS.

The Brethren, Jim Roberts: Also known as the Garbage Eaters, the group follows the teachings of Brother Evangelist Roberts. The group requires renouncing both family and worldly possessions in order to earn salvation. Members travel nomadically, earning their nickname because of their practice of eating discarded food. Families of members claim that Roberts hides their relatives, moving the individuals to avoid familial contact. *Note: This group is not affiliated with the Church of the Brethren, an Anabaptist denomination.* See SALVATION BY WORKS. For further research, a four-page Watchman Fellowship Profile is available (see page 363). Web site—http://www.watchman.org/notebook.

Bridge to Freedom, Geraldine Innocente: Founded in 1952 by Innocente, who claimed to be the "twin flame" of ASCENDED MASTER El Morya, the organization was part of the I AM MOVEMENT founded by Guy Ballard. The organization taught that humans must develop their CHRIST CONSCIOUSNESS and become one with the I AM presence. An early member of the group was MARK PROPHET, founder of the CHURCH UNIVERSAL AND TRIUMPHANT. See FOUNDATION FOR HIGHER SPIRITUAL LEARNING.

Brigade of Light, Marian Starnes—Cedar Mountain, NC: A NEW AGE church. In 1992 the Terra Nova Center was established as a nondenominational retreat and the legal name for the entity became Terra Nova Center of the Brigade of Light, Inc. Starnes teaches that humans can attain peace and enlightenment by accessing the energy of the Divine Mother resident in each human. According to Starnes, the Divine Mother, using the name Alorah, was projected onto the Earth during the time of LEMURIA (over 100,000 years ago) to help humans celebrate light and sound. Web site—http://www.terranovacenter.com.

Bright, Bill (1921–2003): See CAMPUS CRUSADE FOR CHRIST INTERNATIONAL.

Bright Dawn Home Spread, Richard Brandon—Plymouth, WI: A Zen Buddhist retreat center. From 1977–99 the center was High Wind Foundation, a 128-acre ecological village focusing on sustainable living based upon harmony between humanity and nature. Web site—http://www. awakenedone.org. See ZEN BUDDHISM.

Brilliant Star: A BAHÁ'Í FAITH periodical designed for children.

Brinkley, Dannion: As chronicled in his best-seller *Saved by the Light,* Brinkley allegedly underwent a NEAR-DEATH EXPERIENCE after being struck by lightning. Brinkley teaches people to perform "life reviews" to enhance their perception of life and death and find their life missions. He operates a hospice organization called Compassion in Action/The Twilight Brigade. Web site—http://www.dannion.com. See PAST LIFE REGRESSION.

British Israelism (Anglo-Israelism/Israelitism): The doctrine that the true identity of modern Israel (or the ten lost tribes) is Britain and (sometimes) the British colonies (i.e., America). According to this doctrine, the monarchs of England sit on the throne of David. In more extreme forms, Israel is identified with a particular race—usually white Anglo-Saxon, Germanic, and Scandinavian peoples. Opposing versions of this doctrine teach that blacks are God's chosen people Israel. See ARMSTRONGISM, IDENTITY MOVEMENT, BLACK HEBREWS.

Bromley, David: A sociologist who researches alternative religions. Critics have alleged that he is an APOLOGIST for some cultic groups, particularly after it was revealed that some of his research has been funded by the Rev. SUN MYUNG MOON. Web site—http://www.people.vcu.

edu/~dbromley. See HOLY SPIRIT ASSOCIATION FOR THE UNIFI-CATION OF WORLD CHRISTIANITY.

Brooke, Anthony: Prominent NEW AGE scholar affiliated with the SPIRI-TUAL FRONTIERS FELLOWSHIP and Operation Peace Through Unity. Web sites—http://www.angelfire.com/journal/brooke2000/index.html and http://www.peacethroughunity.info.

Brotherhood, aka Broederbond—Johannesburg, South Africa: Founded in 1918. A secret fraternity, operating as a political party, that worked to establish the supremacy of the racial and cultural South African Afrikaner population. Membership in the Brotherhood was restricted to Protestants, and those who spoke English were prohibited from joining. After a movement toward greater racial and cultural tolerance, the organization changed its name in the 1990s to Afrikanerbond. Web site—http://www.afrikaner bond.co.za/welcome.php?pg=7.

Brotherhood and Order of the Pleroma, Richard Duc de Palatine—Sherman Oaks, CA: Teaches the "Arcane Discipline," a gnostic philosophy that God and man are the same being. See GNOSTICISM; PANTHEISM.

Brotherhood of Eternal Truth—New Albany, IN: A NEW AGE organization that teaches that God infuses all creation. Humans are to communicate with their "Higher God-Self" through practicing SPIRITUALISM, AS-TROLOGY, CHANNELING, MAGIC, and PAST LIFE REGRESSION. The Brotherhood is also known as Center of Light and Life. See PANEN-THEISM.

Brotherhood of Light: See GREAT WHITE BROTHERHOOD.

Brotherhood of Seth—Ellsworth, ME: Established in the mid 1980s by a small OCCULT order known as O.R. for the purpose of practicing ho-mosexual or homophilic magic that follows the teachings of ALEISTER CROWLEY. The first Magister was Frater Z. Another founding member, Zen Ananael Sibsi, served as the interim director following Frater Z's departure. Dark Appollo 69 became the new Magister in 1989 and served in that role until the group dissolved in 1995. See MAGICK.

Brotherhood of the Cross and Star, Olumba Olumba Obu—Calabar, Nigeria: Teaches that humans preexisted with God before being born, and that all people will be saved. In 1991 Obu's son, also named Olumba Olumba Obu, was declared the spiritual head of the church. In 2000 he was declared to be the reincarnated Christ, the begotten of God most high. Denies the existence of SATAN and HELL. The Brotherhood has local contacts, called Bethels, in the United States. Web site—http://www.ooo-bcs.org. See UNIVERSALISM.

Brotherhood of the Followers of the Present Jesus, Ann and Peter Meyer—San Diego, CA: NEW AGE group that teaches individuals can experience perfect health and fulfillment by contacting the Christ-Self through CHANNELING and ALCHEMY. Publishes *The Pink Books* series of monographs. See CHRIST CONSCIOUSNESS.

Brotherhood of the White Temple, Inc., M. Doreal—Mount Shasta, CA: Formed in 1930. An ESOTERIC group that combines both NEW AGE and OCCULT teachings. Doreal is known for teaching the three planes of existence, including understanding the BUDDHIST legend of Shamballa, to refer to entrance to the extra-dimensional GREAT WHITE LODGE, which is accessible far beneath the Himalayas. See UFOs. Web site—http://www.bwtemple.org.

Brother Julius, aka Julius Schacknow: Brother Julius, who died in 1996, proclaimed himself in the 1960s to be the REINCARNATION of JESUS CHRIST, and then in the 1970s to be God. Julius's ex-wife, Joanne Sweetman, was known by followers as "the HOLY SPIRIT," and her husband Paul was known as the "chief apostle." Julius's multimillion-dollar real estate and construction empire collapsed in the late 1980s.

Brown, Dan: See *DA VINCI CODE.*

Browne, Mary T.: Popular PSYCHIC counselor and author who teaches that people must learn to deal with karmic situations. See KARMA.

Browne, Sylvia: Popular PSYCHIC and best-selling author. Born Sylvia Celeste Shoemaker, Browne has made numerous appearances on television, including *Larry King Live* and the *Montell Williams Show.* Her books include *Light a Candle* (2006), *Contacting Your Spirit Guides* (2005), *Secrets*

& Mysteries of the World (2005), and *Life on the Other Side* (2001), which gives her description of heaven. Critics have pointed to her legal problems (a 1988 bankruptcy and a 1992 grand larceny fraud conviction) and numerous false predictions as evidence of her spiritual deception. False prophecies include her predictions that Bill Bradley would win the 2000 U.S. presidential election, that Michael Jackson would be found guilty of child molestation in his 2005 trial, and that a cure for breast cancer would be discovered by 1999. Browne, a former ROMAN CATHOLIC, formed a church in 1996, the Society of Novus Spiritus, in Campbell, California. See PSYCHIC; SOCIETY OF NOVUS SPIRITUS.

Brown, Rebecca, aka Ruth Bailey: Widely accepted within the DELIVER-ANCE MINISTRIES movement, Brown teaches that Christians can be possessed by DEMONS. Her books detail alleged encounters with SATAN, witches, and members of the OCCULT. Her teachings regarding persons possessing a natural body and a spirit body are influenced by GNOSTI-CISM. Brown, a former MD, had her medical license revoked in Indiana in 1984. Web site—http://www.harvestwarriors.com.

Bruderhof Communities: Also known as the Society of Brothers and Hutterian Brethren, the Bruderhof began in Germany in the 1920s as a communal society based upon the sixteenth-century German Anabaptist movement. They support their community through Children's Playthings (children's toys) and Rifton Equipment (for the disabled). Critics allege that the Bruderhof exercise inappropriate control over members through such practices as SHUNNING. They operate Plough Press and publish *The Plough* magazine. Web site—http://www.bruderhof.org.

Bubba Free John: See ADI DA.

Bucke, Richard Maurice (1837–1902): Taught that all humans are guided by an immortal, invisible Master. He authored a number of books and his last, *Cosmic Consciousness* (1901), is still in print today and continues to have an influence. See ASCENDED MASTERS.

Buddha: Siddhartha Gautama Buddha ("enlightened one") was born about 560 B.C. in northeastern India and, according to legend, received spiritual enlightenment through MEDITATION. During his lifetime, his spiritual insights and teachings became a major alternative to HINDUISM throughout India. Diverse versions of his teachings can be found worldwide today. See BUDDHISM.

Buddha's Universal Church—San Francisco, CA: Similar to BUDDHISM in theology. Web site—http://www.bucsf.org.

Buddhism: World religion based on the spiritual teachings of Siddhartha Gautama BUDDHA (563–483 B.C.). There are a number of versions or sects of Buddhism generally teaching paths to NIRVANA (enlightenment or bliss) though the four noble truths (recognizing existence and source of suffering) and the eightfold path (correct understanding, behavior, and MEDITATION). Some variations of Buddhism include traditional Theravada schools of India, Mahayana Buddhism (which became very popular in China and Japan), and Tibetan Buddhism (Lamaism) in Tibet. Two more recent forms that have had great influence in America are ZEN and Nichiren Shoshu Buddhism. See ZEN BUDDHISM; NICHIREN SHOSHU OF AMERICA; TIBETAN BUDDHISM.

Builders, Norman Paulsen—Oasis, NV: Paulsen learned a MEDITATION technique from PARAMAHANSA YOGANANDA that enabled him to achieve his CHRIST CONSCIOUSNESS. Followers attempt to pursue 12 virtues and eight paths that will lead to enlightenment. See NEW AGE; SELF-REALIZATION FELLOWSHIP.

Builders of the Adytum, Ltd., Paul Foster Case—Los Angeles, CA: An OCCULT group that practices ASTROLOGY, ALCHEMY, and utilizes KABBALAH and TAROT CARDS for guidance. Professes to follow the Mystery School tradition. Web site—http://www.bota.org. See ROSICRUCIANISM.

Builders of the Nation—Garland, TX: A fraternal order attempting to rediscover and transmit the ancient ESOTERIC knowledge allegedly destroyed by Christian churches during the Renaissance. See FREEMASONRY; ROSICRUCIANISM.

Burgess, Patricia: Burgess was allegedly erroneously convinced by psychiatrists that she was a satanic high priestess who both underwent and subjected her children to ritual abuse. Her case was important, as it brought a high level of publicity to the issue of repressed memories when she filed suit against her former psychiatrist and was ultimately awarded $10.6 million in a settlement with a Chicago hospital. See SATANISM.

Burmester, Helen S.: Author of *The Seven Rays Made Visual,* a pictorial introduction to the teachings of ALICE A. BAILEY. See ARCANE SCHOOL.

Burnham, Sophy: Popular NEW AGE author and lecturer. Her Web site describes her as an intuitive or MEDIUM, a REIKI master and spiritual director. She has written extensively on ANGELS and has been a frequent guest on the *OPRAH WINFREY Show.* Her teachings include such NEW AGE beliefs and practices as all religions are true, REINCARNATION, and MEDITATION. Web site—http://www.sophyburnham.com.

Burning Man Festival—Black Rock Desert, NV: An annual festival celebrating anarchic and nonconformist lifestyles, including NEO-PAGANISM and the NEW AGE. The name comes from an event at the culmination of the festival, in which a large wooden man is burned by the crowd. The "burn" resembles a ritual described by Roman historians, in which the Celtic Gauls burned live humans inside a giant man-shaped wicker figure (the "Wicker Man"). However, the founder of the Burning Man Festival, Larry Harvey, claims not to have known about this ancient Celtic rite, asserting instead that the burning man represents "radical self expression." Web site—http://www.burningman.com.

Butterworth, Eric: A NEW AGE business teacher who claims that physical, emotional, and financial success can be achieved by opening one's spirit to the flow of universal energy. Among Butterworth's books is the best-selling *Spiritual Economics.* Web site—http://www.ericbutterworth.com. See CHI.

Buzzworm: A NEW AGE/environmental periodical. The magazine filed for Chapter 11 bankruptcy in 1994.

C

C.O.B.U.: See CHURCH OF BIBLE UNDERSTANDING.

Cabalah: See KABBALAH.

Caelum Moor—Arlington, TX: Private park (now closed) containing menhirs (large upright stones) similar to those found at STONEHENGE. Newspaper reports claim trespassers have used the site for NEO-PAGAN ceremonies.

Cain, Paul: See KANSAS CITY PROPHETS.

California Institute of Integral Studies, Dr. Haridas Chaudhuri (d. 1975)— San Francisco, CA: Founded in 1968 as the educational arm of CULTURAL INTEGRATION FELLOWSHIP, it became a separate entity in 1974. A fully accredited NEW AGE school that teaches students to holistically unite philosophy, psychology, and spirituality, the courses focus on integrating Eastern religious practices and doctrine into western medical practices. In 2006 the school reported an enrollment of 1005 (75 percent being female) and a core faculty of 55. Web site—http://www.ciis.edu. See HOLISTIC HEALING.

Calvary Chapel, Chuck Smith—Costa Mesa, CA: A fellowship of autonomous NONDENOMINATIONAL CHURCHES affiliated with Calvary Chapel of Costa Mesa, California, founded in 1965 by pastor Chuck Smith (b. 1927), a former FOURSQUARE CHURCH minister. Independent churches in accord with Calvary Chapel distinctives are allowed to use the name Calvary Chapel if they agree to be associated together under the

Calvary Chapel Outreach Fellowship for the purposes of "fellowship, encouragement, and accountability." Calvary Chapels are known to be conservative in their theology with an emphasis on evangelism. As of 2006, there were about 1,100 affiliated churches worldwide. Some do not use the name Calvary Chapel, such as Harvest Christian Fellowship in Riverside, California, founded by Greg Laurie; Applegate Christian Fellowship in Jacksonville, Oregon, founded by Jon Courson; and Horizon Christian Fellowship in San Diego, California, pastored by Mike MacIntosh. Web site—http://www.calvarychapel.com. See EVANGELICAL CHRISTIANITY.

Cambrian Episcopal Church of the Grail—Moscow, ID: A gnostic group claiming to be descended from the Celtic church established by James, the leader of the early church in Jerusalem, and thus superior to CHRISTIANITY in general. The group claims that the Grail family of earth reflects the Godkind family in heaven, and that Jesus was married and procreated. Publishes the *Cambrian Pesher* newsletter. Web site—http://www.grailchurch.org. See GNOSTICISM.

Campbell, Alexander: See THE RESTORATION MOVEMENT.

Campbell, Joseph (1904–87): Best known for his book and PBS series with BILL MOYERS, *The Power of Myth,* which teaches all religions are based on common mythological themes. His work was heavily influenced by the psychology of Carl Jung, who taught that all people share a collective unconscious dominated by archetypes (inherited images and symbols that influence our thoughts and actions). Web site—http://www.jcf.org.

Camping, Harold: Predicted that the APOCALYPSE would occur in 1994. In 2002 Camping, claiming that the church age had ended because organized churches had become apostate, called for Christians to leave their churches and gather in small home fellowships. In his 2005 book *Time Has an End: A Biblical History of the World 11,013 B.C.–2011 A.D.,* Camping redefines 1994 as the second jubilee (rather than the APOCALYPSE). Camping's new probable date for the end is the year 2011. He promotes his beliefs through the FAMILY RADIO WORLDWIDE NETWORK, of which he is president. Web site—http://worldwide.familyradio.org/zusa/english/connect/bio/haroldcamping_bio.html. See FALSE PROPHECY.

Campus Crusade for Christ International, Bill Bright—Orlando, FL: A nondenominational organization of EVANGELICAL CHRISTIANITY consisting of over 60 different ministries operating in 190 countries. Bill Bright (1921–2003) founded the organization in 1951 as a student ministry on the campus of UCLA. In 2001, Steve Douglass was chosen to succeed Bright. Web site—http://www.ccci.org.

CAN: See CULT AWARENESS NETWORK.

Canadian College of Acupuncture and Oriental Medicine, Wee Chong Tan—Victoria, BC: Founded in 1985 as the School of Traditional Chinese Medicine, the name was changed when a nonprofit, The East West Medical Society, was formed to take control of it. The College received official charity status in 2000 and teaches traditional Chinese medical practices. Web site—http://www.ccaom.com. See HOLISTIC HEALING; TAOISM.

Canfield, Jack: NEW AGE education author whose work centers on enhancing the self-esteem of individuals. Canfield developed public school curricula using VISUALIZATION. He is best known for his *Chicken Soup for the Soul* series of inspirational books. Web site—http://www.jackcanfield.com.

Cantillation Research Foundation: See LIFE ENERGY FOUNDATION.

Capps, Charles: Popular WORD-FAITH teacher and founder of Charles Capps Ministries in England, Arkansas. Capps claims that each person determines his future by how effectively he speaks things into existence. He has written a number of Word-Faith books teaching this, including the best-seller *The Tongue, a Creative Force.* He also has a nationally syndicated radio and television program, *Concepts of Faith.* Web site—http://www.charlescappsministries.org. See WORD-FAITH MOVEMENT.

Capra, Fritjof: A physicist who teaches that all of life is interconnected and thus all things share a set of common properties and system of organization. Capra is best known for emphasizing the ways in which BUDDHISM, HINDUISM, and TAOISM can be used to provide a basis for modern science. His works include *The Tao of Physics, The Web of Life,* and *The Hidden Connections.* Web site—http://www.fritjofcapra.net.

CARP: See COLLEGIATE ASSOCIATION FOR THE RESEARCH OF PRINCIPLES.

Castaneda, Carlos: Author of *The Teachings of Don Juan* series. His writings were instrumental in popularizing NATIVE AMERICAN SPIRITUALITY and SHAMANISM, the hallucinogenic drug peyote, as well as the NEW AGE and OCCULT. Castaneda, who died in 1998, was accused by his wife and others of inventing the SHAMAN Don Juan. CLEARGREEN, INCORPORATED, Castaneda's last publisher, promotes his works online at http://www.castaneda.com.

Catechism of Light: NEW AGE book written by Evangeline, who practiced CHANNELING to communicate with ASCENDED MASTERS and other "Beings from the Inner Level of Heavenly Bliss." Evangeline taught that the goal of all humans is to be absorbed into the Great Central Sun. See PANTHEISM.

Cathedral of Divine Abundance, Prince Alexius Bassey—London: Bassey taught that all religions share a universal kinship. He wanted to build a retreat center containing a synagogue, mosque, HINDU temple, and a Christian church. He also claimed that the goal of human life is to experience tremendous physical, emotional, and financial abundance, and that JESUS CHRIST was financially rich.

Catholic Answers, Karl Keating—El Cajon, CA: An APOLOGETICS ministry founded in 1979 to promote conversion to and to defend the doctrines and practices of ROMAN CATHOLICISM. The group publishes a magazine, *This Rock,* and produces a radio program, *Catholic Answers Live.* Web site—http://www.catholic.com. See ROMAN CATHOLICISM.

Catholic Apostolic Church of Antioch—**Malabar Rite, Herman Adrian Spruit**—Santa Fe, NM: The church is an independent group that combines NEW AGE MYSTICISM with ROMAN CATHOLICISM. The group teaches PANTHEISM, CHRIST CONSCIOUSNESS, and REINCARNA-TION. The church operates the SOPHIA DIVINITY SCHOOL, which offers home courses. The church is a major force behind the Federation of Independent Catholic & Orthodox Bishops, although not all members of the FICOB share the church's gnostic theology. Web site—http://www. churchofantioch.org. See GNOSTICISM.

Catholicism: See ROMAN CATHOLICISM.

CAUSA Foundation: Political organization of Rev. SUN MYUNG MOON. Web site—http://www.causainternational.org. See HOLY SPIRIT ASSOCI-ATION FOR THE UNIFICATION OF WORLD CHRISTIANITY.

Cayce, Edgar: See ASSOCIATION FOR RESEARCH AND ENLIGHT-ENMENT.

Celestial Church of Christ, Samuel Bilehou Joseph Oshoffa—Ikeja, Lagos State, Nigeria: Founded in 1947, the group requires the observance of numerous rules and obligations for salvation, including purifying homes after baptism, being anointed three years after baptism, participating in church services, tithing, and observing the church's moral code. Web site—http://www.celestialchurch.com. See SALVATION BY WORKS.

The Celestine Prophecy: A best-selling NEW AGE book by JAMES RED-FIELD that teaches enlightenment through the fictional Nine Insights contained in secret manuscripts written by Mayan natives in the jungles of Peru. The Nine Insights focus on synchronicity: seemingly coincidental events occur so that individuals, influenced by the life vision they adopted when reincarnated, can work towards global awareness. Web site—http://www.celestinevision.com. See REINCARNATION; PANTHEISM.

Celtic Christianity: From Roman emperor Claudius's invasion in A.D. 43 until the withdrawal of the Roman legions in A.D. 410, Britain (modern-day England and Wales) was under Roman control and, like the rest of the empire, became strongly Christianized. In A.D. 433, Saint Patrick under-took a mission to Ireland, establishing there a strong Christian presence. After the Anglo-Saxons invaded in the mid-fifth-century, Celtic control of Britain was eventually broken, and pagans occupied the formerly Christian territory. This conquest isolated the remaining Celtic Christians of Wales and Ireland, leading Celtic Christianity to develop small differences from its continental counterpart. Distinctive traits of Celtic Christianity include a great appreciation for God's revelation in the created world, use of mon-asteries as the centers of Christian community, and a different method for calculating the date for Easter. Differences in practice within the Celtic church were gradually eradicated during the Middle Ages as the Roman papacy asserted its authority over Ireland. Modern groups that claim to revive Celtic Christianity are frequently a mixture of PROTESTANTISM and ROMAN CATHOLICISM, with few legitimate ties to the early Celtic church. Nonetheless, these groups should not be confused with NEO-PAGAN groups that also claim to be Celtic.

Celticism, Celts: The Celts were a group of related tribes whose territory extended throughout Europe early in the first millennium A.D., but who are most commonly associated with the British Isles. The Celts worshipped local deities (frequently associated with nature), who were often served by a priestly class of DRUIDS. Human sacrifice was reportedly important to Druidic religion, though little remains of specific Celtic beliefs and practices outside of the works of Roman historians. Modern neo-pagans frequently claim to be Celtic, although the modern beliefs and practices bear little resemblance to ancient Celticism. See NEO-PAGANISM.

Center for Action and Contemplation, Fr. Richard Rohr—Albuquerque, NM: An ecumenical Catholic organization that promotes world peace and social service ministries. The center also runs the M.A.L.Es (Males As Learners and Elders) program for male spirituality. Activities include YOGA, ENNEAGRAM, and LIBERATION THEOLOGY workshops. Web site— http://www.cacradicalgrace.org. See ROMAN CATHOLICISM.

Center for Creative Living, Dr. Marilyn Hall—San Diego, CA: A NEW THOUGHT church. Web site—http://www.thecenterforcreativeliving.org.

The Center for Health Sciences—Cambridge, MA: See THE INSTITUTE FOR THE STUDY OF HUMAN KNOWLEDGE.

Center for Inquiry Transnational, Paul Kurtz—Amherst, NY: Encourages critical investigation of PARANORMAL claims and nontraditional sciences. It began in 1991 as a joint project of the COMMITTEE FOR THE SCIENTIFIC INVESTIGATION OF CLAIMS OF THE PARANORMAL and the COUNCIL FOR SECULAR HUMANISM, which are now affiliate organizations. Publishes *Free Inquiry* and *Philo*. Web site—http://www. centerforinquiry.net. See CHURCH OF FREETHOUGHT; SECULAR HUMANISM.

Center for Mind-Body Medicine, James S. Gordon, MD—Washington, DC: Founded in 1991. NEW AGE organization that promotes HOLISTIC

HEALING through such practices as BIOFEEDBACK, CREATIVE VISUALIZATION, HYPNOSIS, and PROGRESSIVE RELAXATION. Web site—http://www.cmbm.org.

Center for Spiritual Awareness, Roy Eugene Davis—Lakemont, GA: Incorporated in 1964 as a nonsectarian, nonprofit organization. Davis, who claims to be a direct disciple of PARAMAHANSA YOGANANDA, teaches achieving ENLIGHTENMENT through developing one's COSMIC CONSCIOUSNESS. Web site—http://www.csa-davis.org.

Center for Studies on New Religions (CESNUR)—Torino, Italy: Established in 1988, the center functions as a network of scholars and a forum for research and collaboration of studies related to new religious movements and minority religions—mostly from a secular or academic perspective. A major purpose of the organization is to defend new religions by correcting "inaccurate information" disseminated to the media by the "anti-cult movement" (groups such as INTERNATIONAL CULTIC STUDIES ASSOCIATION and the original CULT AWARENESS NETWORK). The managing director is Massimo Introvigne, and its U.S. center is located at the Institute for the Study of American Religion in Santa Barbara, California, which was founded by J. Gordon Melton. CESNUR, like Melton, has drawn criticism from some who see it as an organization of "cult apologists" because of its alleged defense of the teachings or practices of some alternative faiths and new religions. Web site—http://www.cesnur.org. See MELTON, J. GORDON.

Center for Studies on New Religions, Massimo Introvigne—Torino, Italy: Established in 1988. Introvigne studies new and alternative religious groups. He and his work, which is frequently highly supportive of new religions, are often used by alternative religious groups to support their activities when pursuing governmental recognition. Web site—http://www.cesnur.org.

The Center for the Improvement of Human Functioning, Inc., Hugh D. Riordan, MD—Wichita, KS: Founded in 1975. Also known as Bright Spot for Health, the center is a HOLISTIC HEALING facility with a focus on nutritional medicine and biochemistry for conditions that are not responding to conventional medical treatment. Web site—http://www.brightspot.org.

Centering/Contemplative Prayer: Popularized in the mid 1970s at St. Joseph's Abbey in Spencer, Massachusetts, as a result of the studies and practices of trappist monks WILLIAM MENINGER, THOMAS KEATING, and BASIL PENNINGTON. Critics of centering often point to its roots in, or similarities with, the MEDITATION practices of Eastern religions, such as BUDDHISM, HINDUISM, and TM (TRANSCENDENTAL MEDITATION). These common practices/elements include sitting, emptying one's mind of directed thoughts (or mental activity), looking inward, and utilizing a MANTRA (or focused thought) to keep the mind from thinking or wandering. Even Keating notes the commonality, stating, "Is there something that we can do to prepare ourselves for the gift of contemplation instead of waiting for God to do everything? My acquaintance with Eastern methods of meditation has convinced me that there is. There are ways of calming the mind in the spiritual disciplines of both East and West that can help to lay the groundwork for contemplative prayer."[12] Though the centering prayer movement began within ROMAN CATHOLICISM, it is not without non- Roman Catholic devotees such as popular authors BRENNAN MANNING (a former Roman Catholic monk) and RICHARD FOSTER (a QUAKER), who promote centering/contemplative prayer in their writings. For further research, a four-page Watchman Fellowship Profile is available (see page 363). Web site—http://www.watchman.org/notebook.

Centerpointe Research Institute, Bill Harris and Wes Wait—Beaverton, OR: Started in 1989, this company sells *Holosync* audiocassettes, which allegedly use audio technology in conjunction with music and environmental sounds to subliminally enhance the listener's MEDITATION, and thus the person's self-awareness and personal fulfillment. Web site—http://www. centerpointe.com. See NEW AGE, HOLISTIC HEALING.

The Centers for Apologetics Research (C/FAR), Paul Carden—San Juan Capistrano, CA: An international APOLOGETICS ministry that defends EVANGELICAL CHRISTIANITY from heretical doctrines of religious cults and aberrant theology. The organization specializes in training and equipping national APOLOGISTS in Eastern Europe, Latin America, Africa, and other mission fields. They provide resources and Web sites in numerous languages and have a presence in Russia, Ukraine, Hungary, Romania, Mexico, Brazil, and Ethiopia. Web site—http://www.thecenters. org.

Century Apex—Youngstown, OH: See BRAINBEAU, J.C.

Cerinthus: A late first-century or early second-century HERETIC who taught that JESUS was the natural son of Joseph and Mary. He believed that Jesus was simply a man who received the CHRIST spirit at His baptism until that spirit departed at His crucifixion. Like the EBIONITES, Cerinthus denied the deity of Jesus and the TRINITY. His teachings are sometimes called Cerinthian gnosticism because his view of creation was GNOSTIC (a lesser deity or demigod made the physical universe).

Cesar—San Antonio, TX: An OCCULT spell worker who claims to specialize in legal matters and who practices WITCHCRAFT and VOODOO. Cesar also claims to be an assistant to PAPA JIM.

CESNUR: See CENTER FOR STUDIES ON NEW RELIGIONS.

Chakras: PSYCHIC centers, or trigger points, of *PRANA* (the life force) located in seven specific areas of the body. Reciting the MANTRA associated with each chakra will allow the KUNDALINI energy to rise from the base of the spine to the sahasrara chakra at the crown of the head. Some HOLISTIC HEALING practitioners use CRYSTALS and herbs to enhance the energy flow through the chakras. See HINDUISM; NEW AGE.

Champaign Church of Christ—Champaign, IL: A local church of the INTERNATIONAL CHURCHES OF CHRIST. The church was banned from proselytizing on the campus of the University of Illinois.

Channeling: Similar to the OCCULT practice of SPIRITUALISM, channeling (also called trance channeling) is a NEW AGE practice whereby spirit beings, ASCENDED MASTERS, deceased humans, or animal spirits allegedly communicate important messages by temporarily entering the body and controlling the voice of a host (channel or MEDIUM). The message conveyed by many channelers is that humans are divine, a basic tenet of PANTHEISM. Famous channelers include J.Z. KNIGHT and PENNY TORRES. See NECROMANCY. For further research, a four-page Watchman Fellowship Profile is available (see page 363). Web site—http://www.watchman.org/notebook.

Chaos Magick: Chaos (also spelled kaos) is an OCCULT movement oriented in an egocentric worldview. Many practitioners ascribe the founding of chaos magick to Peter Carroll's efforts in the 1970s to blend beliefs and practices of GOLDEN DAWN, THELEMA, TAOISM, and TIBETAN BUDDHISM. Chaos is entirely syncretistic and eclectic; practitioners develop their own magickal practices and OCCULT laws. In contrast to other ESOTERIC movements, chaos magicians generally eschew any idea of leadership and apprenticeship, and frequently even claim that magick cannot be taught but can only be learned through individual and independent experience. See MAGICK.

Chapel Hill Harvester Church—Decatur, GA: See PAULK, BISHOP EARL

Charismatic Movement: From the Greek word *charisma* ("gift"), this movement is characterized by a renewed interest in the gifts of the HOLY SPIRIT, such as SPEAKING IN TONGUES, prophecy, miracles, and healing. The phenomena began in the 1960s within PROTESTANTISM (including mainline denominations) and EVANGELICAL CHRISTIANITY as an effort to bring renewal into established churches. While some Charismatic Christians can be found within most traditional churches, including the ROMAN CATHOLIC Church, in most cases, the movement was unable to effect widespread change on whole churches or denominations. Eventually most Charismatic Christians left their old churches to form their own independent churches or to join churches with roots in the PENTECOSTAL MOVEMENT. By the 1980s, some Charismatic Christians were drawn to what C. Peter Wagner called the THIRD WAVE OF THE HOLY SPIRIT and controversial developments such as the WORD-FAITH MOVEMENT, which was popularized by ROBERT TILTON and others. Beginning in the 1990s, the TORONTO BLESSING and HOLY LAUGHTER revivals brought a new wave of manifestations but also drew additional concerns and criticisms from more traditional EVANGELICALS and PENTECOSTALS.

Cheetham, John: See GREAT LAKES SOCIETY FOR BIBLICAL RESEARCH.

Chen Tao, Hon-ming Chen (Also called The Right Way, God's Salvation Church, and God Saves the Earth Flying Saucer Foundation): Apocalyptic

Taiwanese UFO group that drew international media attention when it predicted that God would descend to their headquarters (at that time located in Garland, Texas) in a flying saucer on March 31, 1998. In June 1999, Teacher Chen predicted that God, leading American and Taiwanese ancestors and flying 12,000-year-old American airplanes, would drop neutron bombs on China. Publishes *Practical Evidence and Study of the World of God and Buddha* and *God's Descending in Clouds (Flying Saucers) on Earth to Save People*. For further research, a four-page Watchman Fellowship Profile is available (see page 363). Web site—http://www.watchman.org/notebook.

Chen, Hon-ming: See CHEN TAO.

Chi: The invisible energy or force that is alleged to make up the universe and flow through all living things via MERIDIANS or CHAKRAS. Some HOLISTIC HEALING practitioners attempt to heal patients by clearing blockages in the MERIDIANS so that the chi can flow unimpeded. See TAOISM; YIN AND YANG; ACUPUNCTURE.

Chicago Bible Students—Chicago, IL: The largest and best-known of the independent groups of BIBLE STUDENTS in the United States, which broke off from the WATCHTOWER BIBLE AND TRACT SOCIETY after Joseph Rutherford took control of the organization. The group reprints the early writings of Watchtower founder CHARLES TAZE RUSSELL, including *Divine Plan of the Ages*. Web site—http://www.chicagobible.org.

Chi Gong: A HOLISTIC HEALING practice of positioning one's body in specific postures that are said to enhance the flow of CHI to joints, muscles, and internal organs.

Chick Publications, Jack T. Chick—Chino, CA: Controversial publisher of tracts and other evangelistic materials. Publications oriented toward ROMAN CATHOLICISM, such as *The Death Cookie*, are widely criticized for their inaccuracies and demonizing of Roman Catholics. Publishes *Battle Cry* newsletter. Web site—http://www.chick.com.

Children of God: See THE FAMILY (CHILDREN OF GOD).

Chinmaya Mission, Swami Chinmayananda (d. 1993): Founded in Bombay, India, in 1953 by devotees of Swami Chinmayananda, the mission teaches Vedanta BUDDHISM, focusing on "Gita Guidance" using the *BHAGAVAD-GITA.* The mission is divided into local centers. Web site— http://www.chinmayamission.org.

Chinmoy, Sri: A NEW AGE teacher who promotes a philosophy based on HINDUISM and MEDITATION. Chinmoy claims that devotees can facilitate world peace through music, literature, art, and running marathons. Web site—http://www.srichinmoy.org.

Chinook Learning Community, Fritz and Vivienne Hull—Clinton, WA: Established in 1972, this NEW AGE organization teaches NATIVE AMER-ICAN SPIRITUALITY, shamanistic studies, and MEDITATION. Despite being called a community, the majority of the group lives in varying locations on Whidbey Island in Puget Sound. In 1995 Chinook was assimilated into a new organization started by the Hulls, the WHIDBEY INSTITUTE.

Chiromancy: See PALMISTRY.

Chiropractic medicine: A HOLISTIC HEALING practice whereby practitioners use a form of manipulative therapy to treat musculoskeletal problems. While many chiropractors are not engaging in alternative religious activities via their practice, critics claim that some chiropractors engage in chiropractic medicine in accordance with the Taoist principle of facilitating the flow of CHI. See TAOISM.

The Choice Experience, Jerry Stocking—Chetek, WI: Stocking and his followers practice NEURO-LINGUISTIC PROGRAMMING and HYP-NOSIS to achieve full human potential. Through his book *Cognitive Harmony: An Adventure in Mental Fitness,* Stocking teaches that a person's success in life is limited only by self-created emotional and psychological impediments. Stocking publishes his works through the self-owned Moose Ear Press. Web site—http://www.jerrystocking.com.

Chopra, Deepak: A former follower of the MAHARISHI MAHESH YOGI, Chopra teaches the HOLISTIC HEALING practice of AYURVEDIC MEDICINE. Chopra is best known for his "Seven Spiritual Laws," which revolve around the belief that humans are part of the "field of pure potentiality" and thus can create their own reality, including health and wealth. He runs the Chopra Center at La Costa Resort and Spa in Carlsbad, CA.

Web site—http://www.chopra.com. See PANTHEISM; TRANSCEN-
DENTAL MEDITATION. For further research, a four-page Watchman
Fellowship Profile is available (see page 363). Web site—http://www.
watchman.org/notebook.

Christ: Based on the Greek term meaning "anointed one," equivalent to
the Hebrew term translated "MESSIAH." Generally used of one who has
been anointed with oil or set apart for a specific mission. Specifically used
to speak of the promised Messiah/Savior of Israel and the world. Christians
believe this to be Jesus of Nazareth, who died to atone for human sin.
ORTHODOX CHRISTIANITY professes that JESUS Christ was God
incarnate (in human flesh) and as the second person of the TRINITY is
both fully God and fully man. He was crucified in the early first century, was
buried, rose bodily from the dead, and ascended back into heaven. Christians
also believe in the SECOND COMING of Christ. Other religions believe
in a succession of Christ figures through history, sometimes including Jesus,
who were great teachers. NEW AGE groups sometimes understand the term
Christ as a reference to the pantheistic deity found in all humanity. Thus,
Jesus was conscious of His deity, and others can have this same CHRIST
CONSCIOUSNESS by realizing that they, too, are divine beings. Other
religious leaders have historically claimed to hold the office or ministry
of Christ, including Rev. SUN MYUNG MOON. Biblical warnings are
given for "false christs" (Mark 13:22). Scripture also speaks of an Antichrist
and antichrists who attempt to stand against or in place of the true Christ
(1 John 2:18). See JESUS; TRINITY.

Christadelphians, John Thomas: Christadelphians reject the TRINITY,
teaching instead that JESUS Christ is a created being, and that the HOLY
SPIRIT is the power of God. The group also rejects the immortality of the
soul, and thus rejects the ideas of heaven and hell. It has several splinter
groups. Publishes *The Christadelphian, The Christadelphian Tidings of the
Kingdom of God, The Bible Magazine, Faith Alive,* and *Lookout.* Web site—
http://www.christadelphia.org. For further research, a four-page Watchman
Fellowship Profile is available (see page 363). Web site—http://www.
watchman.org/notebook.

Christ Consciousness: Some NEW AGE and OCCULT teachers see a
distinction between the human man JESUS and the Christ idea or spiritual
concept. Jesus, they believe, was a mere man who developed a realization

that everything is divine (PANTHEISM) and thus He too was part of the cosmic divine. This realization is often seen as more experiential than cognitive. Thus, Jesus is seen as a man who had a consciousness (self-awareness) of His own divinity. By following His example, everyone can develop a similar awareness or self-realization of his or her own deity or Christ consciousness. See NEW AGE; CHRIST.

Christ Family, Charles McHugh: McHugh, aka Lightning Amen, claims to be the incarnation of JESUS CHRIST. Followers dress in robes (foregoing shoes and leather) and practice vegetarianism.

Christian Biblical Church of God, Fred Coulter—Hollister, CA: Coulter resigned from the WORLDWIDE CHURCH OF GOD (See ARMSTRONGISM) in 1979 and established this church. They teach SALVATION BY WORKS through SABBATARIANISM and observing the Ten Commandments. They also deny the TRINITY by teaching that the Father and Son are members of the God family, while the HOLY SPIRIT is the power of the Father. Web site—http://www.cbcg.org.

Christian Broadcasting Network (CBN)—Virginia Beach, VA: A worldwide television and radio ministry promoting EVANGELICAL CHRISTIANITY founded by PAT ROBERTSON in 1961. The network portion of the ministry was sold to the Fox network and eventually to Disney, becoming the ABC Family Channel. The original CBN continues to have a significant influence in the United States and internationally as a production and distribution organization for Christian programs such as the *700 Club*. Web site—http://www.cbn.com. See ROBERTSON, PAT.

Christian Church (Disciples of Christ): See THE RESTORATION MOVEMENT.

Christian Church of God—Amarillo, TX: Teaches SABBATARIANISM. The church annually celebrates the Feast of Tabernacles at a different city in the United States. Web site—http://www.christianchurchofgod.org.

Christian Churches of God: A SABBATARIAN group based in Canberra, Australia and Rockton, Ontario, Canada. Like other Sabbatarian groups, the Christian Churches deny the TRINITY by teaching that JESUS CHRIST was created by the Father, and that the HOLY SPIRIT is the power of the Father. Web site—http://www.logon.org.

Christian Community Churches, Inc., Robert Bristow: Bristow teaches SALVATION BY WORKS, referring to churches that teach SALVATION BY GRACE as "the Judas church." Bristow is strongly opposed to EVAN-GELICAL CHRISTIANITY, and particularly to the Chicago-based Willow Creek Community Church and Moody Bible Institute. Web site—http://www.cccinc-7candlesticks.org.

Christian Community: A movement for religious renewal based on teach-ings of RUDOLF STEINER. There are some 350 congregations worldwide, 12 of which are in North America. The first American congregation was established in New York in 1948. See ANTHROSOPHICAL SOCIETY for theological similarities. Web site—www.thechristiancommunity.org.

Christian Defense League—Mandeville, LA: A white supremacist group at-tempting to expose the New World Order and worldwide Jewish conspiracy. Claims that the Holocaust is a myth. Operates Sons of Liberty Books and publishes *The CDL Report.* Web site—http://www.cdlreport.com.

Christian Educational Ministries, Ronald L. Dart—Whitehouse, TX: Founded in 1995. Continues the teachings of HERBERT W. ARM-STRONG. CEM claims that it is not a church, but rather is a service ministry that provides resources for other churches. Over the years it has been able to secure broadcast time for its radio program, *Born to Win,* on a number of Christian radio stations. Web site—http://www.borntowin. net. See ARMSTRONGISM.

Christian Faith Center—Seattle, WA: See TREAT, CASEY.

Christian Forum Research Foundation—Grand Rapids, MI: A Seventh-day Adventist organization that focuses on religious persecution. Publishes *Christians in Crisis.* See SEVENTH-DAY ADVENTIST CHURCH.

Christian Foundation—Canyon County, CA: See ALAMO CHRISTIAN FOUNDATION.

Christian Identity: A loose movement of racist groups adhering to a form of BRITISH ISRAELISM. Identity adherents believe that people of western European descent are the ten tribes of Israel, whereas Jews are the descendents of SATAN and non-Caucasians are a different species descended from pre-Adamic races. See SERPENT SEED. For further research, a four-page Watchman Fellowship Profile is available (see page 363). Web site—http:// www.watchman.org/notebook.

Christian Israelite Church: Founded by John Wroe in England in 1822, the primary bodies of the church are now based in Australia, principally in Sydney, Melbourne, Singleton, and Terrigal. The church teaches BRITISH ISRAELISM. Web site—http://www.cichurch.asn.au. See SERPENT SEED.

Christian Millennial Fellowship—Hampton, NJ: A WATCHTOWER BIBLE AND TRACT SOCIETY splinter group. The fellowship is the leading church in a small organization called FREE BIBLE STUDENTS. Publishes *The New Creation.* Web site—http://www.cmfellowship.org.

Christian Prosperity Theology: See WORD-FAITH MOVEMENT.

Christian Research Institute (CRI), Walter Martin—Charlotte, NC: An APOLOGETICS ministry of EVANGELICAL CHRISTIANITY founded in 1960 by Walter R. Martin (1928–89) focusing mostly on countering CULTS and doctrinal HERESY. Martin began a syndicated radio program, *The Bible Answer Man,* and launched a newsletter that later became the *Christian Research Journal.* His best-known book, *The Kingdom of the Cults,* has sold about 750,000 copies. After Martin's death in 1989, Hendrik "Hank" Hanegraaff became the president of CRI and host of the radio program. Web site—www.equip.org.

Christian Science: See CHURCH OF CHRIST, SCIENTIST.

Christianity, Jesus Christ: Major world religion developed in the first century A.D. based on the belief that Jesus of Nazareth was the promised MESSIAH of Israel. Followers, called Christians, were initially viewed as a sect of JUDAISM. It quickly developed as a separate religion when the relatively small minority of Jewish followers was supplemented by non-Jewish converts and, through a strong missionary emphasis, Christianity became a diverse worldwide movement. Their scripture is the BIBLE, which contains the Jewish Scriptures (Old Testament) and the Christian Scriptures (New Testament). Except for cults, aberrant sects, and the liberal fringe, those who claim to be Christians have historically believed the following: There is only one true God eternally revealed in three distinct persons—the Father, the Son, and the HOLY SPIRIT; that humans are sinners who (without the grace of God received through faith in Christ) are eternally lost; and that Jesus is God in the flesh who died on the cross and rose from the dead as the only and sufficient payment for the sins of humanity. See JESUS; GOSPEL; BORN AGAIN; FUNDAMENTALIST CHRISTIANITY; EVANGELICAL CHRISTIANITY; PROTESTANTISM; ORTHODOX CHRISTIANITY; ROMAN CATHOLICISM; LIBERAL CHRISTI-ANITY; SALVATION BY GRACE; SALVATION BY WORKS; CULT.

Christianity Today: A magazine of EVANGELICAL CHRISTIANITY founded in 1956 by the well-known evangelist Billy Graham with Carl F. H. Henry serving as the first editor. The parent company, Christianity Today International, operates a number of Web sites and publishes about a dozen affiliated periodicals, including *Leadership Journal* and *Books & Culture.* Web site—http://www.christianitytoday.com.

Christ Light Community, Gilbert and June Holloway—Deming, NM: Project the Holloways developed in the mid-1960s on a parcel of land donated to the NEW AGE CHURCH OF TRUTH by an elderly woman who had been told in a dream to give them the land. A church building, manse, and several apartments for out-of-state members would be built on the land, which was known as the Land of Enchantment.

Christ Savior Brotherhood: Formed in 1988 by former members of the HOLY ORDER OF MANS. Vincent Rossi, successor to HOOM founder Earl Brighton, became interested in ORTHODOX CHRISTIANITY in 1983. Following the guidance of Herman Podmoshensky, a defrocked Russian Orthodox priest, Rossi and the Brotherhood entered a pseudo-Orthodox group led by Pangratios Vrionis. Vrionis was himself defrocked by the Greek Orthodox archdiocese in 1968 at the same time he was accused of child molestation (for which he pleaded guilty in 1970, and again pleaded guilty to new charges in 2003). The Brotherhood left Vrionis's church in 1999, and in 2000, 21 parishes and eight monastic groups entered different jurisdictions of the ORTHODOX CHURCH.

Christ United Church: See REVEREND IKE.

Christ Universal Temple, Johnnie Colemon—Chicago, IL: A NEW THOUGHT church. Colemon was previously affiliated with the UNITY SCHOOL OF CHRISTIANITY. The church teaches that people can attain their highest good by listening to the "'still small voice' within us." It runs the Universal Foundation for Better Living, an umbrella organization of approximately 20 affiliated churches. One of these, UNDERSTANDING PRINCIPLES FOR BETTER LIVING, is pastored by actress DELLA REESE, who starred in the hit television series *Touched by an Angel* and was mentored by Colemon. Publishes *Daily Inspiration for Better Living.* Web site—http://www.cutemple.org. See NEW AGE.

Christ's Gospel Fellowship, Karl F. Schott—Spokane, WA: Schott teaches CHRISTIAN IDENTITY and BRITISH ISRAELISM. The group widely distributes a map that allegedly proves that the ten tribes of Israel migrated to western Europe and eventually established a new Israel in the United States. Publishes *The Pathfinder.*

Christward Ministry, Flower and Lawrence Newhouse—Escondido, CA: Founded in 1940, a NEW AGE organization that teaches GUIDED MEDITATION and emphasizes the work of ANGELS to guide us to the CHRIST. The ministry offers retreats and classes at its facility, Questhaven Retreat. Publishes *Life at Questhaven.* Web site—http://www.questhaven.org.

Chuang-tzu: See TAOISM.

The Church, Jim Roberts: See BRETHREN, JIM ROBERTS.

Church and Coven of Y Tylwyth Teg—Smyrna, GA: A NEO-PAGAN group, established in 1967, that allegedly practices the Welsh tradition of WITCHCRAFT. Like most WICCA groups, the church focuses on rituals involving nature and celestial cycles. It was priest-led by Rhuddlwm Gawr until 2003, when Lady Cerridwen became high priestess. Web site—http://www.ytylwythteg.org.

Churches of Christ: The independent Churches of Christ movement developed from the early nineteenth-century RESTORATION MOVEMENT of Alexander Campbell, Walter Scott, and Barton W. Stone. While the goal of the Restoration movement was the unification of CHRISTIANITY, the movement splintered into many groups and denominations—foremost of which are the Churches of Christ and the mainline Disciples of Christ (Christian Church). A number of influential churches of Christ are very EVANGELICAL in their theology with an emphasis on SALVATION BY GRACE (such as Max Lucado's Oak Hills Church, formerly Oak Hills Church of Christ, in San Antonio, Texas). Most Churches of Christ, however, differ from traditional PROTESTANT theology in two key areas. First, many members of the Churches of Christ maintain that water baptism and the observance of other commandments (rather than grace through faith in JESUS CHRIST alone) are a requirement of salvation. Second, some members also believe that today's Churches of Christ are the only true churches on earth and that they can literally trace their history to the first-century church in Jerusalem. Most of these churches are also distinct in their rejection of all musical instruments in favor of *a cappella* (voices only) music. While the Churches of Christ do not have an official Web site, a significant unofficial site is http://www.church-of-christ. org. See BAPTISMAL REGENERATION; SALVATION BY GRACE; SALVATION BY WORKS.

Churchlight Publishing Association—Colorado Springs, CO: Founded in 1979. Follows the teachings of HERBERT W. ARMSTRONG. Publishes SABBATARIAN booklets and pamphlets. Web site—http://www.church-light.net. See ARMSTRONGISM.

Church of All Worlds, Otter Zell—Berkeley, CA: Organized in 1970, it grew out of a group of friends who began meeting in 1962 after being influenced by the science fiction novel *Stranger in a Strange Land* by Robert Heinlein. The church is actually named after the church in the book. This NEO-PAGAN group promotes OCCULT practices, GAIA (the church spells the name *Gaea*) worship, sacred sex, and PAGANISM. It includes a practice they call water sharing, in which participants drink water and recognize the divine being in one another. Publishes the *Green Egg* periodical for adults and *How About Magic* for children. Web site—http://www.caw.org.

Church of Bible Understanding, Stewart Traill: Started in 1971, it was first known as Forever Family. This controversial network of churches, headquartered in New York, historically has been charged with SPIRITUAL ABUSE due to LEGALISM, undue influence, and control mechanisms.

During its peak in the 1970s there were estimated to be over 1,500 members in fellowship houses. Currently there are less than 100. Web site—www.cbuhaiti.org. See LEGALISM; SPIRITUAL ABUSE.

Church of Christ: See CHURCHES OF CHRIST.

Church of E Yada di Shi-ite, MARK PROBERT (d. 1969)—Mountain View, CA: PROBERT channeled Yada, an ASCENDED MASTER who first lived 500,000 years ago. Yada's messages revolved around freeing oneself from the cycle of REINCARNATION. Probert published Yada's messages through two organizations: Mark Probert Educational Foundation and Mark Probert's Kethra E'Da (Teachers of Light). Lectures and channeled messages by Proberts are still available. Web site—http://teachers-of-light.com.

Church of Christ Jesus: See INTERNATIONAL CHURCHES OF CHRIST.

Church of Christ, Otto Fetting—Independence, MO: A splinter group of THE CHURCH OF JESUS CHRIST OF LATTER-DAY SAINTS. The church refers to itself as The Church with the Elijah Message, referring to the alleged appearance of John the Baptist to Fetting from 1927–33. Publishes *The Voice of Joy* newsletter. Web site—http://www.elijahmessage.com.

Church of Christ, Scientist, Mary Baker Eddy—Boston, MA: The Christian Science church teaches that the idea of the TRINITY is polytheistic, and that the Godhead is composed of God the Father-Mother, Christ the spiritual idea of Sonship, and the Holy Ghost is the Divine Science or Christian Science. They make a distinction between JESUS the man and Christ the Divine Idea: Jesus simply possessed and demonstrated the Christ Idea or Consciousness to a greater extent than other humans. Sin, sickness, and death are all illusions and thus can be cured through right thinking. *SCIENCE AND HEALTH WITH KEY TO THE SCRIPTURES* is their primary text. Many current NEW AGE teachings can find their historical roots in the Christian Science and NEW THOUGHT movements. Publishes *The Christian Science Monitor* newspaper and the periodicals *Herald of Christian Science* and *The Christian Science Sentinel.* Web site—http://www.tfccs.com. See MIND SCIENCE, QUIMBY, PHINEAS P. For further research, a four-page Watchman Fellowship Profile is available (see page 363). Web site—http://www.watchman.org/notebook.

Church of Christ, Temple Lot, Granville Hedrick—Independence, MO: A splinter group of THE CHURCH OF JESUS CHRIST OF LATTER-DAY SAINTS, formed in 1863. Web site—http://www.churchofchrist-tl.org.

Church of Christ with the Elijah Message—Greenwood, MO: A 1998 splinter group from Otto Fetting's group of the same name.

Church of England: See ANGLICAN CHURCHES.

Church of Freethought: A social organization for atheists that provides opportunities for socializing, community service, and social support offered by theistic churches. There is not an official Freethought Web site; nonetheless, many sites for local Freethought churches link to http://www.freethought. org and http://www.infidels.org.

Church of Gaia—Boulder, CO: Also known as the Foundation for Gaian Studies and the Gaian Contemplative Community, this NEW AGE organization promotes earth-centered spiritual practice. The church emphasizes NATIVE AMERICAN SPIRITUALITY, particularly the medicine wheel, peace pipe, and VISION QUEST. Web site—http://www.gaianstudies. org.

Church of God—Reisterstown, MD: Follows the teachings of HERBERT W. ARMSTRONG. Publishes *Baltimore Church of God Bulletin.* See ARMSTRONGISM.

Church of God, 7th Day—Meridian, ID: A SABBATARIAN group that practices BAPTISMAL REGENERATION and teaches ANNIHILATIONISM and SOUL SLEEP. Web site—http://www.meridianchurch. org.

Church of God (7th Day)—Salem, WV: An anti-Trinitarian group that teaches SABBATARIANISM and BAPTISMAL REGENERATION. The church also forbids eating pork, thus observing one of the primary dietary laws of JUDAISM. The church operates the Church of God Publishing House and publishes *The Advocate of Truth* and *The Sabbath Bulletin.* Web site—http://hometown.aol.com/cogsevday.

Church of God—Cleveland, TN: See PENTECOSTAL MOVEMENT.

Church of God (Seventh Day)—Denver, CO: The church began in Iowa and Michigan in 1860. Originally part of the SECOND ADVENT MOVEMENT, the founders of the church separated from the group that became the SEVENTH-DAY ADVENTISTS over the validity of Ellen G. White's prophecies. Like most other Adventists, the church teaches SABBATARIANISM. Publishes *Bible Advocate.* Web site—http://www.cog7.org.

Church of God and True Holiness, Robert Carr—Raleigh, NC: Critics allege that the church practices slavery and mind control. Carr was sentenced to ten years in prison in 1980 for allegedly taking paychecks, food stamps, and welfare checks from members.

Church of God, an International Community, David Hulme—Pasadena, CA: Follows the teachings of HERBERT W. ARMSTRONG. After leaving the WCG, Hulme helped found the UNITED CHURCH OF GOD—AN INTERNATIONAL ASSOCIATION, but left that group in 1998 over a conflict concerning Hulme's television program. Web site—http://www.church-of-god.org. See ARMSTRONGISM.

Church of God Evangelistic Association, David J. Smith—Waxahachie, TX: Follows the teachings of HERBERT W. ARMSTRONG. Publishes *Newswatch Magazine* and *Newswatch* radio and television programs. Web site—http://www.newswatchmagazine.org. See ARMSTRONGISM.

Church of God, Faith of Abraham—Wenatchee, WA: A WATCHTOWER BIBLE AND TRACT SOCIETY splinter group. The church is a member of the CHURCH OF GOD GENERAL CONFERENCE. Publishes *Notes for Bible Students* newsletter. Web site—http://www.faithofabraham.org.

Church of God, Gary Liebold and Don Roth: A PHILADELPHIA CHURCH OF GOD splinter group. Liebold's congregation is located in Seminole, Florida, and Roth's congregation is located in Hustisford, Wisconsin. Through its Web site the group engages in outreach to South America. Web site—http://www.t-cog.org. See ARMSTRONGISM.

Church of God General Conference—Morrow, GA: An anti-Trinitarian group founded in Philadelphia in 1888 as the Church of God of the Abrahamic Faith. Many of the conference's current members are former JEHOVAH'S WITNESSES. The conference teaches ANNIHILATIONISM and BAPTISMAL REGENERATION. Publishes *The Restitution Herald.* Web site—http://www.abc-coggc.org. *Note: This group is not affiliated with the Church of God General Conference of Atlanta, GA.*

The Church of God in Christ, Mennonite, John Holdeman—Moundridge, KS: A controversial offshoot of the more traditional Mennonite Church (within PROTESTANTISM) founded on the teachings of the sixteenth-century Dutch Anabaptist Menno Simons. In the 1850s Holdeman formed his own movement, claiming to be called by God to cleanse the Mennonites in general and CHRISTIANITY as a whole. Holdeman's followers teach that Christ was not fully a human being and only appeared to have a body of human flesh—a position similar to the ancient HERESY of DOCETISM. Former members allege that the movement fosters LEGALISM, SALVATION BY WORKS, and SHUNNING. Current active membership is believed to be about 20,000. The church publishes a biweekly periodical *Messenger of Truth.* Web sites—http://www.holdemanmennonite. com; http://www.cogicm.org. For further research, a four-page Watchman Fellowship Profile is available (see page 363). Web site—http://www. watchman.org/notebook.

Church of God, International—Tyler, TX: GARNER TED ARMSTRONG broke away from the WORLDWIDE CHURCH OF GOD and formed this rival group in 1978 after a conflict with his father, HERBERT W. ARMSTRONG. Despite this conflict, the church teaches a form of ARMSTRONGISM. Armstrong later stepped down from his top leadership position amidst allegations of sexual misconduct and litigation. Publishes the *International News* and *Twentieth-century Watch* periodicals. Web site— http://www.cgi.org.

Church of God, in Truth, James Russell—Corona, CA: Formed in 1993 by a group that had left the WORLDWIDE CHURCH OF GOD after its departure from the teachings of ARMSTRONGISM. A SABBATARIAN group. The church claims that JUDAISM is not the religion of the Old Testament. Publishes *Prove All Things.* Web site—http://www.postpone ments.com.

Church of God of Jessamine—Nicholasville, KY: A CHURCH OF GOD, INTERNATIONAL splinter group. The church teaches SABBATARIANISM. See ARMSTRONGISM.

Church of God Outreach Ministries: A CHURCH OF GOD, INTERNA-TIONAL splinter group. The ministries create resources for independent church groups. Publishes *Fountain of Life, New Horizons, CGOM Newsletter,* and the *Bible Basics* study series. Web site—http://www.cogm.org. See ARMSTRONGISM.

Church of God Philadelphia Era, David Fraser—Pasadena, CA: Follows the teachings of HERBERT W. ARMSTRONG. Publishes *Proclaim Liberty* magazine. See ARMSTRONGISM.

Church of God Southern Missouri—West Plains, MO: An affiliate of the GARNER TED ARMSTRONG EVANGELISTIC ASSOCIATION. The church follows a variation of ARMSTRONGISM. Web site—http://mem bers.tripod.com/~icgwp.

Church of God, John Trescott—Anadarko, OK: Follows the teachings of HERBERT W. ARMSTRONG. Publishes *Light of Truth Newsletter.* See ARMSTRONGISM.

Church of God, Paul Royer—Sonoma, CA: Follows the teachings of HERBERT W. ARMSTRONG. See ARMSTRONGISM.

Church of God, Sabbath Day—Springdale, AR: The church distrib-utes reprints of writings by HERBERT W. ARMSTRONG. See ARMSTRONGISM.

Church of God, Seventh Day—Caldwell, ID: A SABBATARIAN group that practices BAPTISMAL REGENERATION. Publishes *The Herald of Truth* newsletter.

Church of God, the Eternal, Raymond C. Cole—Eugene, OR: Follows the teachings of HERBERT W. ARMSTRONG. Web site—http://www.cogeternal.org. See ARMSTRONGISM.

Church of God's Truth—Corona, CA: Follows the teachings of HERBERT W. ARMSTRONG. The church strongly encourages a reunion of groups that were formerly part of the WORLDWIDE CHURCH OF GOD through its manifesto, *Church Reunification through Reorganization.*

Church of Hakeem, Hakeem Abdul Rasheed—Oakland, CA: Rasheed (aka Clifton Jones) taught how the god within makes people rich. Members allegedly paid money to join the church with the promise that, upon receiving sufficient new members, the original members would receive 400 times their investment. Rasheed was convicted in 1979 on six counts of fraud; his yacht and $921,208 in bank accounts were seized to satisfy his tax liability.

Church of Israel, Dan Gayman—Schell City, MO: A CHRISTIAN IDENTITY group. Publishes *The Watchman*. Web site—http://watch manoutreach.com.

Church of Jesus Christ-Christian, Wesley Swift—Hayden Lake, ID: Founded in 1946. Two groups currently claim to be the true Church of Jesus Christ-Christian, the church for the ARYAN NATIONS. Web sites—http://www.twelvearyannations.com and http://www.aryan-nations. org. See IDENTITY MOVEMENT.

Church of Jesus Christ of Latter-day Saints, Joseph Smith, Jr.—Salt Lake City, UT (Latter-day Saints, LDS, Mormon Church, Mormonism): The LDS Church was organized on April 6, 1830, in Fayette, New York, with six charter members by JOSEPH SMITH, JR. (1805–44). The foundation of the movement can be traced to the first vision that Smith reported to have experienced in 1820. In the vision, JESUS CHRIST told Smith that true CHRISTIANITY ceased to exist shortly after the first century and that all the creeds and doctrines of contemporary Christian churches were corrupt. Smith learned that he had been chosen to restore the only true church on the face of the earth. After Smith was killed in 1844, the majority of Latter-day Saints followed Brigham Young, who became the second prophet, to Salt Lake City, Utah. Many of the teachings of the church under Smith and Young were controversial—particularly the doctrine of POLYTHEISM (Abraham 4) and the practice of polygamy, known as the "plural marriage" or "plural wives" doctrine (D&C 132). After Young's death the fourth prophet, Wilford Woodruff, repealed the doctrine of polygamy (although a number of fundamentalist splinter groups such as the FUNDAMENTALIST CHURCH OF JESUS CHRIST OF LATTER-DAY SAINTS continue to practice polygamy). The LDS church accepts four books, known as the Standard Works, as scripture: The BIBLE (King James Version), the BOOK OF MORMON, DOCTRINE & COVENANTS

(D&C), and the PEARL OF GREAT PRICE. The LDS Church teaches that before becoming God, our heavenly Father was once a man on another planet who progressed to EXALTATION and became the God of this earth. He and his wife, our "Heavenly Mother," procreated billions of spirit children who eventually were born on earth as human beings. Those men and women who are obedient to their heavenly Father's commandments have the potential of eventually becoming like their heavenly Parents—gods and goddesses of their own earths. Their gospel, known as "the law of eternal progression," teaches EXALTATION, a doctrine summarized by the famous couplet of their fifth prophet, Lorenzo Snow: "As man now is, God once was; as God now is, man may be." It promotes SALVATION BY WORKS, teaching that full salvation depends upon personal obedience to "the laws and ordinances of the gospel." In 2006, the church reported 12.5 million members (5.7 million in the United States) and 56,000 missionaries in 165 countries. Publishes *Church News* and *Ensign, New Era, Friend,* and *Liahona* magazines. Web site—http://www.lds.org. For further research, a four-page Watchman Fellowship Profile is available (see page 363). Web site—http://www.watchman.org/notebook.

Church of Light, Benjamine P. Williams (1882–1951)—Brea, CA: Williams changed his name to Elbert Benjamine when he began publicizing the BROTHERHOOD OF LIGHT Lessons. He used the pen name C.C. Zain in writing the 21 courses of the Brotherhood of Light Lessons, which he began in 1914 and completed in 1934. In 1932 he incorporated the Church of Light with his wife, Elizabeth Benjamine, and Fred Skinner. Associated with the BROTHERHOOD OF LIGHT, the church rejects heaven and hell, and instead teaches that atonement is to be found in each person's own spiritual path. The church teaches that God's laws can be understood through the study of ASTROLOGY and TAROT CARDS. Web site—http://www.light.org. See UNIVERSALISM.

Church of Metaphysical Christianity, Russell and Dorothy Flexer—Sarasota, FL: Founded in 1958 by the Flexers, who had been formerly associated with the Spiritualist Episcopal Church, the church is a NEW AGE organization which teaches that JESUS is an ASCENDED MASTER, and that creation occurs through vibrations. The goal was to make the church a national organization of like-minded churches. The Flexers also founded the SHRINE OF THE MASTER CHURCH in Sarasota. Publishes *Messenger* magazine.

Church of Pan—Foster, RI: The church was founded in 1971 by Kenneth Walker in order to marry two individuals who wanted to be naked when married. The church teaches PANTHEISM and practices nudism, claiming that nudity celebrates the body that is part of nature. See REINCARNATION.

Church of Perfect Liberty: Founded in 1912 by Tokumitsu Kanada, a Shinto priest, Perfect Liberty (known by followers as PL) is a Japan-based sect with a small number of churches in the United States. PL teaches that humans are a manifestation of God and the point of existence is to live an artistic life in which the ego is sublimated in the pursuit of perfect mental freedom. Among the works that members must perform in order to attain enlightenment include engaging in physical work for PL and wearing rings or AMULETS that were blessed by the Oshieoya (Father of the Teachings, also called the Patriarch). Web site—http://web.perfect-liberty.or.jp. See SHINTOISM.

Church of Religious Science: See UNITED CHURCH OF RELIGIOUS SCIENCE.

Church of Satan, Anton Szandor LaVey (1930–97)—New York, NY: Founded in 1966 by Anton LaVey, who believed that other organized religions suppressed the natural pursuit of pleasure. The goal of the church, therefore, is to pursue the gratification of physical and psychological desires. Adhering to the nontheistic conception of SATANISM, the OCCULT rituals practiced by the church involve neither animal nor human sacrifice. The church instead practices three types of rituals through engagement in BLACK MASSES or satanic magic: sexual rituals to fulfill desires, compassionate rituals to help one another, and destructive rituals that serve as channels for anger and hate. Publications include the *Satanic Bible*. Web site—http://www.churchofsatan.com. For further research, a four-page Watchman Fellowship Profile is available (see page 363). Web site—http://www.watchman.org/notebook.

Church of Scientology, L. Ron Hubbard: Founded in the early 1950s by science fiction writer Lafayette Ron Hubbard (1911–86) as a religion that developed out of the controversial mental health theories published in his 1950 book *Dianetics: The Modern Science of Mental Health*. Scientology teaches that humans are immortal spiritual beings called *thetans* who have existed for millions of years progressing through countless lifetimes in a process similar to REINCARNATION. Human happiness and full potential is blocked by "engrams" (past moments of pain or trauma received during periods of unconsciousness or diminished awareness). Engrams can also be caused from events during previous lives. Engrams are stored in what Hubbard called the "Reactive Mind" and can act to influence the person in the present by bypassing analytical thought or volition—a process that is the ultimate cause of many mental disorders and physical problems. These engrams can be "cleared" through a process called *auditing,* which often involves a briefcase-size electronics device called an *E-Meter* (a galvanic skin response detector). Using the E-Meter, a trained auditor can identify engrams and clear them using the principles of Dianetics and Scientology. When all engrams have been removed, the person being audited is declared "cleared." Through auditing and other Hubbard technology (teachings), humans can potentially operate at a higher spiritual level, eventually superseding the supposed limitations of the physical universe of MEST (Matter, Energy, Space, and Time). Total freedom and human potential, however, can only be reached through advanced Scientology technology known as Operating Thetan (OT) courses (Levels I–VIII). OT courses involve the advanced technique of solo auditing and can last for years and, in some cases, can cost over $100,000. Hubbard's principles and technologies are also advanced through WISE (World Institute of Scientology Enterprises), affiliated business management companies such as Sterling Management Systems, the drug prevention program Narconon, and in public schools through the Way to Happiness program. The writings and recorded spoken words of L. Ron Hubbard (contained in over 500,000 pages of writings and over 3,000 tape-recorded lectures) constitute the scriptures of the religion and extreme efforts are undertaken to assure that they are protected and not altered in any way. Scientology publishes several magazines, including *Advance, High Winds,* and *Source,* and several newspapers and newsletters, including *The Auditor, Tech News, KSW News,* and the *FSM Newsletter.* Scientology has long been involved in ongoing battles with the news media, government agencies, and critics who have charged the church with abuse and illegal activities. The church claims that most of that conflict is in the past and strongly denies the bulk of the allegations, including those published in a *Time* magazine cover story "Scientology: The Thriving Cult of Greed and Power" (May 6, 1991). In 2005 the church reported membership of 10 million in 150 countries. Web site—http://www.scientology.org. For further research, a four-page Watchman Fellowship Profile is available (see page 363). Web site—http://www.watchman.org/notebook.

Church of Seven Arrows, George Dew—Wheatridge, CO: Founded in 1975, this is a congregation of the UNIVERSAL LIFE CHURCH. Dew teaches NATIVE AMERICAN SPIRITUALITY and SHAMANISM. The church also offers materials for learning MAGIC and studying Jungian archetypes. Publishes the *Thunderbow II* newsletter.

Church of the Blue Star: See BLUE STAR, INC.

Church of the Brethren—Elgin, IL: A movement of Anabaptist PROT-ESTANTISM that traces its history to Schwarzenau, Germany in 1708. Web site—http://www.brethren.org. See BRETHREN, ALEXANDER MACK.

Church of the Creator, Ben Klassen—Otto, NC: See WORLD CHURCH OF THE CREATOR.

Church of the Creator, Grace Marama URI—Ashland, OR: A NEW AGE group founded in 1969 as Grace House Prayer Ministry after URI, in an altered state of consciousness, was ordained into the Order, Brotherhood, and Priesthood of Melchizedek by the archangel Michael. In the mid-1970s the name was changed to Church of the Creator. The group teaches that members should develop their CHRIST CONSCIOUSNESS and uplift humanity through the vibrational energy of the Feminine Principle. URI teaches that Jesus Christ is the lifestream of Michael, and that the HOLY SPIRIT is the Divine Mother. In 1973-74 the Cross released KARMA and allowed members to experience the New Birth. Web site—http://www. churchofthecreator.org.

Church of the Eternal Source—Burbank, CA: An OCCULT federation of temples that practice ancient Egyptian religion. The emphasis is on working out ma'at (i.e., KARMA) by becoming priests and priestesses of Egyptian deities. See POLYTHEISM.

Church of the Final Judgment: See PROCESS CHURCH OF THE FINAL JUDGMENT.

Church of the Great God, John Ritenbaugh—Charlotte, NC: Follows the teachings of HERBERT W. ARMSTRONG. Publishes *Forerunner: Preparing Christians for the Kingdom of God.* Web site—http://www.cgg.org. See ARMSTRONGISM.

Church of the Holy Water—Irrigon, OR: Founded in 1993 by Bill Nelson to unite Columbia Basin irrigators against water controls imposed by the Oregon Water Resources Department. Nelson claimed that water is a "sacrament" in an attempt to allow irrigators to claim a freedom-of-religion exemption from water usage restrictions.

Church of the Living Stone Mission for the Coming Days, Bang-ik Ha—Seoul, Korea: Predicted JESUS CHRIST would return on October 28, 1992. See FALSE PROPHECY.

Church of the Lukumi Babalu Aye, Carmen Pia—Hialeah, FL: A SANTERIA church. Founded in 1974 by Pia, her husband, Raul Rodriguez, and Ernesto and Fernando Pichardo. The church won a landmark lawsuit against the city of Hialeah in 1993 when the U.S. Supreme Court unanimously ruled that it is legal for the church—and thus setting the precedent for all priests of SANTERIA—to practice animal sacrifice in their religious ceremonies. Web site—http://www.church-of-the-lukumi.org.

Church of the Most High Goddess, Mary Ellen Tracy—Los Angeles, CA: A NEW AGE religious group that, allegedly reviving ancient Egyptian religion, teaches salvation through sexual relations, sometimes known as HIEROS GAMOS. In 1990 Tracy, a former member of THE CHURCH OF JESUS CHRIST OF LATTER-DAY SAINTS, was convicted of prostitution. Tracy goes by the name Sabrina Aset. Web site—http://www.goddess.org.

Church of the Movement of Spiritual Inner Awareness: See MOVEMENT OF SPIRITUAL INNER AWARENESS.

Church of the Nazarene—Kansas City, MO: A denomination of PROTESTANTISM with roots in METHODISM. The church was founded in 1908 by the union of several existing Holiness denominations. In 2006, there were 14,000 churches worldwide with over 1.5 million members. Web site—http://www.nazarene.org. See EVANGELICAL CHRISTIANITY.

Church of the New Jerusalem: See SWEDENBORG FOUNDATION.

Church of the Subgenius, J.R. "Bob" Dobbs—Cleveland Heights, OH: Founded in 1980 by Ivan Stang as a parody of traditional religious groups. The church refers to itself as an inherently bogus religion that will tell you that you are superior to other people. The logo for the church, a smiling man—said to be "Bob"—holding a pipe between his teeth, has become a well-recognized icon on the Internet. Produces the *Hour of Slack* radio program. Web site—http://www.subgenius.com.

Church of Tzaddi, Amy Krees—Ellijay, GA: Founded in 1964 in California when Krees, who was preparing to become a minister in the UNITY CHURCH, said she was given a revelation from God that she was to start her own church that was open to all based on their common relationship to the divine, regardless of their beliefs. Teaches development of PSYCHIC and spiritual centers to reach oneness consciousness (see NEW AGE). Practices and beliefs include ASTRAL PROJECTION, CHANNELING, KARMA, UFOs, and REINCARNATION. Web site—http://www.tzaddi.org.

Church of Unlimited Devotion: A defunct group who worshipped Jerry Garcia of the rock'n'roll band The Grateful Dead and believed Garcia's guitar was a channel for God. The group, who followed The Grateful Dead's tours, were also known as The Spinners because of their engagement in the SUFI practice of whirling.

Church Universal and Triumphant, Mark and Elizabeth Clare Prophet—Corwin Springs, MT: An offshoot of the I AM MOVEMENT, CUT was incorporated in 1974 by Elizabeth Clare Prophet as part of the SUMMIT LIGHTHOUSE. Elizabeth—known in the group as Guru Ma—took over CUT following Mark's death in 1973, but withdrew from leadership in 1999 after being diagnosed with Alzheimer's in 1998. Since 2005 the organization has been led by a board of directors with two presidents. In its heyday, under Prophet's leadership, the organization had a staff of over 700; now it is less than 100. CUT teaches members to realize their CHRIST CONSCIOUSNESS, thereby being united with the ASCENDED MASTERS. A person's soul undergoes REINCARNATION until it reunites with the Christ Self. Publishes messages received from the Ascended Masters through CHANNELING in *Pearls of Wisdom.* Web site—http://www.tsl.org/AboutUs/TheMysticalPath.asp. For further research, a four-page

Watchman Fellowship Profile is available (see page 363). Web site—http://www.watchman.org/notebook.

Cipher Manuscripts: See GOLDEN DAWN.

Circle of Light, Cassandra Anaya: Anaya claims to be a PSYCHIC counselor whose practice consists of reading a client's vibrational energy. Anaya receives further information by CHANNELING three ANGELS: Metatron, Uriel, and Yannie. Web site—http://www.circle-of-light.com.

Circle Sanctuary, Selena Fox—Madison, WI: A NEO-PAGAN group founded in 1974. Circle emphasizes nature-based spirituality and is active in interfaith dialogue. The group also maintains the Circle Sanctuary Nature Preserve in southwest Wisconsin. Publishes *Circle Magazine* and *Circle Sanctuary Newsletter* as well as the *Circle Guide to Pagan Groups,* a listing of hundreds of pagan groups and resources. Web site—http://www.circlesanctuary.org.

Circles of Life, Dorothy Espiau—Sedona, AZ: Part of Espiau's International Success Institute, Circles of Life is a system developed by Espiau that uses a process of "integration" to successfully set and achieve goals. Espiau's Geotran™ system enters a numeric-geometric code into key points in the egg-shaped energy field surrounding each person, allegedly integrating unused energy pathways to fulfill the intention of the individual. Web site—http://www.geotran.com.

Circles of Light—Kauai, HI: An online magazine promoting ASTROLOGY and other NEW AGE practices. Web site—http://www.circlesoflight.com.

Clairaudience: A popular form of SPIRITUALISM involving the alleged ability to hear, in a manner beyond natural explanation, PARANORMAL phenomena such as GHOSTS or SPIRIT GUIDES.

Clairvoyance: The supposed ability to supernaturally "see" psychic information, including historical or future events or other phenomena that cannot be discerned naturally through the five senses. See PSYCHIC; EXTRA-SENSORY PERCEPTION (ESP); DIVINATION; OCCULT.

Cleage, Jr., Albert B.: See PAN AFRICAN ORTHODOX CHRISTIAN CHURCH.

Coast to Coast AM: See BELL, ART.

Cognitive Dissonance: A mental, emotional, or psychological state that results from attempting to hold two totally incompatible beliefs or opposing attitudes at the same time. See DOUBLE BIND.

Cold Reading: A technique sometimes used by PSYCHICS in order to appear to gain supernatural OCCULT knowledge about their clients. The technique involves providing vague information using generalities while carefully watching the client for subtle clues in voice fluctuations, body language, or facial expressions. See WARM READING; HOT READING.

Colemon, Johnnie: See CHRIST UNIVERSAL TEMPLE.

Cole-Whittaker, Terry: A popular NEW AGE teacher who emphasizes the power of positive thinking for achieving success in life. Her teachings are influenced by HINDUISM and her publications include books and CDs on REINCARNATION and AYURVEDIC MEDICINE. Cole-Whittaker operates the educational foundation Adventures in Enlightenment as well as the International Institute of Sacred Knowledge, which works to bridge Eastern and Western spiritualities. Her books include *What You Think of Me Is None of My Business* and *Every Saint Has a Past, Every Sinner a Future.* Web site—http://www.terrycolewhittaker.com.

College of Divine Metaphysics, Dr. Joseph Perry Green—Glendora, CA: Organized in 1918, the correspondence college offers unaccredited doctorates in METAPHYSICS and divinity. Web site—http://www.di vinemetaphysics.org.

Collegiate Association for the Research of Principles (CARP): CARP is the college and university outreach of Rev. SUN MYUNG MOON's Unification Church. Web site—http://www.worldcarp.org. See HOLY SPIRIT ASSOCIATION FOR THE UNIFICATION OF WORLD CHRISTIANITY.

Committee for the Scientific Investigation of Claims of the Paranormal (CSICOP): See COMMITTEE FOR SKEPTICAL INQUIRY (CSI).

Committee for Skeptical Inquiry (CSI)—Amherst, NY: Founded in 1976 as the Committee for the Scientific Investigation of Claims of the Paranormal (CSICOP) to investigate paranormal and fringe science claims from a scientific point of view and to disseminate the findings. The name was changed in 2006 out of concern that the word *paranormal* was causing the committee to be mistaken as a group promoting the paranormal as opposed to investigating it. The committee generally approaches all spirituality from an ATHEIST or AGNOSTIC worldview. Its founding members include Carl Sagan, Isaac Asimov, Phillip Klass, JAMES RANDI, and current chairman Paul Kurtz. Publishes *Skeptical Inquirer.* Web site—http://www.csicop.org. See THE JAMES RANDI EDUCATIONAL FOUNDATION.

Common Boundary—Chevy Chase, MD: Defunct NEW AGE periodical.

Common Ground Cafe: Coffee shops in numerous communities operated by the followers of Elbert Spriggs. Web site—http://www.commonground cafe.com. See THE TWELVE TRIBES.

Communal Society: A group of people who live together and have given ownership of most or all their private property to the group for the benefit of the whole. The group is often held together by a common ideology that forms an extended family. This community can, in some cases, function as a substitute for a traditional family unit based on kinship. Communal societies are often formed to create a utopian community based on the ideals of the group. When the ideal of the group is a spiritual one, the term *religious communism* is sometimes used. As biblical examples of religious communism, Acts 2:44-45 and 4:32-35 are sometimes cited. Most Christians, however, interpret the circumstances in Acts as a unique response to an urgent situation and not as a prescription or command for typical Christian life. Critics have also claimed that communal living may make one more vulnerable to SPIRITUAL ABUSE because of increased dependency on the group and MILIEU CONTROL.

Communion Letter: A defunct periodical that focused on UFOs and was published by WHITLEY STRIEBER.

Community Chapel, Don Barnett—Seattle, WA: Essentially a Pentecostal church, Community Chapel began to disintegrate in 1979 when all authority was taken by Barnett and the church leadership. In the early 1980s the church became involved in DELIVERANCE MINISTRIES activities, and in the mid 1980s the church focused on "spiritual connections," in which members (typically not married to each other) would dance together and caress during worship services. The elders wrested control of the church from Barnett in 1988. The original church is reported to now have 100 members (from a high of over 3000 in the 1980s). See SPIRITUAL ABUSE.

Community of Christ, Joseph Smith, III—Independence, MO: In 2001, the community changed its name from the well-known Reorganized Church of Jesus Christ of Latter-day Saints to Community of Christ. This group is the largest splinter group of THE CHURCH OF JESUS CHRIST OF LATTER-DAY SAINTS (LDS) founded by JOSEPH SMITH, JR. The community was officially formed as the Reorganized Church of Jesus Christ of Latter-day Saints when Joseph Smith, III (son of the LDS church founder) agreed to lead the founding group of 300 members, who rejected Joseph Smith, Jr.'s institution of polygamy and Brigham Young's leadership. The community has slightly different versions of the BOOK OF MORMON and DOCTRINE & COVENANTS. The community, however, rejects the PEARL OF GREAT PRICE as well as such distinctive LDS beliefs as the doctrine of EXALTATION. Publishes *Herald* magazine and *Face to Face* journal. Web site—http://www.cofchrist.org. For further research, a four-page Watchman Fellowship Profile is available (see page 363). Web site—http://www.watchman.org/notebook.

Concepts of Faith: See CAPPS, CHARLES.

Concept Therapy Institute—San Antonio, TX: A NEW AGE theory developed by Thurman Fleet in 1931, concept therapy involves eradicating illness through natural laws that govern the mind, body, and soul. Through learning the Wisdom of the Ages, the participant can achieve health, peace, and eternal wisdom. Web site—http://www.concept-therapy.org.

Concerned Christians, Monte Kim Miller—Denver, CO: Ironically begun in the early 1980s as a Christian ministry that exposes cults and false teachings, Miller's organization began to take on cult-like characteristics in later years. Becoming increasingly controversial and bizarre, Miller's group drew national media attention in 1998: More than 50 followers disappeared from the Denver area after Miller predicted the APOCALYPSE was to begin and that Denver was to be destroyed by an earthquake on October 10. Miller, who claims to be one of the two end-time prophets mentioned in Revelation chapter 11 in the Bible, published *Report from Concerned Christians* and *Take Heed Update*. Miller also produced *Our Foundation* radio program. *Note: This group in not connected with Concerned Christians, the Mesa, Arizona-based evangelical Christian outreach to Mormons headed by Jim and Judy Robertson.)* Web site—http://www.kimmillerconcernedchristians.com. For further research, a four-page Watchman Fellowship Profile is available (see page 363). Web site—http://www.watchman.org/notebook.

Confucianism, Chiu King (King Fu-tzu—anglicized as Confucius—"Kung the Master"): A world religion based on the teachings of Chiu King, who, according to tradition, was born in Lu, China about 550 B.C. Chiu King promoted peace and social harmony through the traditions of the ancestors, focusing on a comprehensive societal ethic governing all relationships and particularly the individual's duty to others. The central texts of Confucianism are the Five Classics—the most notable of which is the *I CHING*, or *Book of Changes*—and the Four Books, which include the sayings of Chiu King and the teachings of his disciple and grandson.

Congregational Churches: In most cases churches of PROTESTANT and EVANGELICAL CHRISTIANITY that practice a congregational form of church government in which each church is independent and each member of the church has an equal vote in church decisions. Alternative forms of church government include Episcopal governance (bishop rule) and Presbyterian governance (elder rule).

Congregation of God—San Jose, CA: See ANSWERS RESEARCH AND EDUCATION.

Congregation of God Seventh Day, John Pinkston—Kennesaw, GA: Follows the teachings of HERBERT W. ARMSTRONG. Publishes *The Herald* magazine and produces the *Watch America* radio program. Web site—http://www.watchamerica.com. See ARMSTRONGISM.

Congregation of the Firstborn, Raymond Glenn (d. 2002)—Grapeland, TX: Formed in a house church in the early 1970s, this is a COMMUNAL group living in individual homes on a 50-acre property in east Texas. The congregation holds services and Bible studies on a daily basis, and mandates SABBATARIANISM and observing the Jewish festivals. The group also denies the deity of Christ. Web site—http://www.firstbornchristiancom munity.com.

Conscious Development of Body, Mind, and Soul: See HOFFMAN, TERI.

Conscious Living Foundation, Tim Lowenstein—Drain, OR: Using the principles of BIOFEEDBACK, Lowenstein developed "holographic music" cassettes that allegedly create feelings of peace or mental clarity as well as inspiring dreams and mental IMAGERY. The foundation also sells such stress-related products as a mood card/stress card and "Biodots" that change colors based on a person's emotions, as well as a stress thermometer. Web site—http://www.cliving.org.

Conservative Baptist Association of America—Longmont, CO: A fellowship of regional Baptist associations consisting of 1,200 churches. Web site—http://www.cbamerica.org. See BAPTIST CHURCHES.

Conspiracy Theory: The belief that an event and the subsequent results can only be explained as the plans and work of a secret and powerful group of individuals or an organization, such as a government or a church. This is not to say that a group never conspires to accomplish a goal in secret, but rather, the term *conspiracy theory* is more popularly used to describe those theories that typically cut against the grain of logic, reason, and the evidence present. Some popular conspiracy theories include subjects such as UFOs, AREA 51, John F. Kennedy's assassination, the death of Elvis, and stories surrounding the HOLY GRAIL. These theories have been popularized in the entertainment industry through such television shows and films as *The X Files, Roswell, Signs, Men in Black,* and Oliver Stone's *JFK.*

Constellation, Elton Powers—Dallas, TX: A NEW AGE bookstore.

Cooneyites: Unofficially named after Edward Cooney, one of a group of itinerant Irish preachers in the late nineteenth–early twentieth centuries. Also known by such names as Go Preachers, No Name Church, and Two by Twos, and officially registered in the United States as Christian Conventions.

The name *Two by Twos* comes from their practice of working in pairs in an itinerant proselytic ministry. They hold their services in private homes and disavow the TRINITY, believing that Jesus was created and that the HOLY SPIRIT is God's power.

Copeland, Kenneth: Probably the most popular WORD-FAITH televangelist/teacher today and viewed by many in the WORD-FAITH MOVEMENT as the heir of KENNETH HAGIN as the voice of the movement. He and his wife, Gloria, oversee Kenneth Copeland Ministries and its nationally syndicated television program, *Believer's Voice of Victory.* Web site—http://www.kcm.org. See WORD-FAITH MOVEMENT.

The Coptic Church: See ORTHODOX CHURCH.

Cornerstone, Jim Rector—Texarkana, TX: Founded in 1991. Follows the teachings of HERBERT W. ARMSTRONG. Publishes *Cornerstone.* Web site—http://www.cornerstonepublication.com. See also ARMSTRONGISM.

Cosmerism: A mixture of CHRISTIANITY and BUDDHISM that emphasizes love, empathy, compassion, and the activation of good and nonviolent knowledge. The central scripture is the *Book of Cosmer.*

Cosmic Awareness Communications—Olympia, WA: In 1962, Ralph Duby began CHANNELING the Universal Consciousness he claims spoke through JESUS, the BUDDHA, KRISHNA, MUHAMMAD, and other persons. Operates the Aquarian Church of Universal Service. Web site—http://www.transactual.com/cac. See NEW AGE.

Council for Secular Humanism—Amherst, NY: Established to promote the advancement of SECULAR HUMANISM. As part of this, it engages in critical examination of religious and supernatural claims. Publishes *Free Inquiry,* the leading humanist magazine in the world. Web site—http://www.secularhumanism.org.

Council of Nicea: An important ecumenical council that was held in A.D. 325 at Nicea (modern Iznik, Turkey) and called by the Roman emperor Constantine primarily to settle a theological dispute created by the teachings of ARIUS. The critical issue was the question of the nature of CHRIST and especially His full deity (the doctrine that JESUS is fully God). ATHANA-SIUS argued against ARIANISM and for the traditional ORTHODOX position that Jesus was of the same substance as the Father (Greek *homo-ousios*—"same essence") and thus fully God—"true God from true God." The resulting document, called the Nicene Creed, reaffirmed the Orthodox view of Christ, stating that He was "begotten, not made," and including the language that He was "of the same substance as the Father." Over 300 bishops attended the council, and all but two signed the Nicene Creed. The Second Council of Nicea was held in 787, in which attendees debated the veneration of icons. See ARIANISM; ATHANASIUS; TRINITY.

Council of the Magickal Arts—Austin, TX: Founded in 1980, this neo-pagan group practices WITCHCRAFT and MAGICK. It claims to have over 900 members as of 2006. Produces the online publication *The Accord.* Web site—http://www.magickal-arts.org. See NEO-PAGANISM.

A Course in Light, Toni Moltzan—Keller, TX: Series of NEW AGE lessons from TONI MOLTZAN to develop inner peace and spiritual advance-ment. Beliefs and practices include CHANNELING, MEDITATION, ASCENDED MASTERS, CHAKRAS, PSYCHIC READINGS, and REINCARNATION. Web site—http://www.courseinlight.net. See AZ REALITY PUBLISHERS.

A Course in Miracles, **Helen Schucman:** Written from 1965–75, the *Course* is a 500,000-word text Schucman—at the time an associate professor of medical psychology at Columbia University—received through dictation from a being who identified himself as Jesus. Dr. William Thetford assisted Schucman and helped birth a loosely organized but widespread movement of followers as the book sold over 1.5 million copies in 15 languages. Ac-cording to this Jesus, the world is an illusion, and humans who develop their CHRIST CONSCIOUSNESS will realize that they are in heaven. A key point of the *Course* is arguing that death is illusory, for by doing so, the *Course* attempts to prove that sin itself is an illusion. One of the most popular teachers of the *Course* is MARIANNE WILLIAMSON. Web site—http://www.acim.org. See NEW AGE. For further research, a four-page Watchman Fellowship Profile is available (see page 363). Web site—http://www.watchman.org/notebook.

Coven Gardens—Boulder, CO: A store that sells resources for practice of WICCA and the OCCULT.

Covey, Stephen R.: Popular author and speaker on enhancing personal effectiveness at home and work. His best-known book, *The 7 Habits of Highly Effective People,* emphasizes the importance of acting with fairness, honesty, and dignity. Covey is one of the founders of FranklinCovey, which provides effectiveness training and productivity tools. Critics note the influence of THE CHURCH OF JESUS CHRIST OF LATTER-DAY SAINTS and NEW AGE teachings on Covey's presentation of how to live a successful life. Web site—http://www.stephencovey.com.

Creme, Benjamin: See SHARE INTERNATIONAL.

Crenshaw Christian Center—Los Angeles, CA: See PRICE, FREDERICK K.C.

Crop Circles: Geometric patterns in crop fields that are attributed by people involved in the NEW AGE and OCCULT to UFOs, ANGELS, and other PARANORMAL or supernatural sources. Individuals who accept a supernatural origin for crop circles claim that the sites, located primarily in Great Britain but also seen in other areas, emit strong electrical currents. Scientists believe that the circles may result from such natural phenomena as wind currents or are created as hoaxes. A significant Web site advocating the supernatural origin of crop circles is http://www.cropcircleresearch.com.

Crossroads Church of Christ: A traditional CHURCH OF CHRIST in Gainesville, Florida that developed a highly controversial SHEPHERDING/discipleship program under Chuck Lucas. That movement spread through other churches and eventually broke away from the traditional Churches of Christ and, under the leadership of Kip McKean, became a worldwide movement called the BOSTON CHURCH OF CHRIST. After the headquarters was relocated to Los Angeles, the movement was renamed INTERNATIONAL CHURCHES OF CHRIST.

Crouch, Paul and Jan: Founders of the Trinity Broadcasting Network (TBN), the world's largest religious television network. Critics point out that while the network does offer a diversity of programming, much of the teaching and preaching that is aired is of the WORD-FAITH variety, reflecting the personal beliefs of its founders. Web site—http://www.tbn. org. See WORD-FAITH MOVEMENT.

Crowley, Aleister: An English MAGICIAN and occultist. Crowley (1875–1974) was known for sex magick, homosexual rituals, and a fascination with drugs, blood, and torture. He headed the British branch of the ORDO TEMPLI ORIENTIS and founded the ABBEY OF THELEMA at Cefalu in Sicily. He is the author of *Diary of a Drug Fiend* and *Magick in Theory and Practice.* The THELEMIC ORDER OF THE GOLDEN DAWN operates a Web site called the Aleister Crowley Foundation at http://www. thelemicknights.org/acfhome.html. See MAGICK; OCCULT.

Crusade of Innocence: Believed to be a splinter of the PROCESS CHURCH OF THE FINAL JUDGMENT.

Crystals: Many individuals involved in the NEW AGE believe gems—and, in particular, crystals—emit or conduct vibrational energy that opens CHAKRAS and promotes healing. Some also believe that the energy from crystals can bring wealth and good fortune.

CSICOP: See COMMITTEE FOR SCIENTIFIC INVESTIGATION OF CLAIMS OF THE PARANORMAL.

Cthulhu Mythos: Also known as the Lovecraft Mythos, a cosmology and pantheon based upon the fantastic horror stories of pulp author H.P. Lovecraft (1890–1937). While Lovecraft was an atheist who emphatically rejected belief in any spiritual or religious reality, his stories often contained magical, PARANORMAL elements. Prominent among these is the notion of secret cults worshipping ancient alien gods, sometimes known as the Great Old Ones. Cthulhu, a squid-headed monster with bat-like wings, is a prominent Great Old One. Lovecraft also invented the *Necronomicon,* a fictional book of OCCULT lore purportedly written by an insane Arab poet, Abdul al-Hazred. Due to the popularity of Lovecraft's works, several editions of faux *Necronomicon*s have been published and many practitioners of NEO-PAGANISM and the occult have built Lovecraft's mythology into their own rituals. Some occult-inclined Lovecraft enthusiasts have claimed that Lovecraft was himself an OCCULT adept, but biographical evidence, including Lovecraft's copious personal correspondence, indicates that Lovecraft was a confirmed skeptic throughout his life.

Cult: See the "Christian Definitions" section of the introduction.

Cult Awareness Network (CAN): Headed by Cynthia Kisser and based in Chicago, Illinois, this was once the largest secular CULTwatch organization or anticult group in America. From 1991–96, CAN was the defendant in a large number of civil lawsuits. In 1995, a successful lawsuit by Jason Scott against several individuals and groups—including CAN—resulted in CAN filing for bankruptcy. In 1996, CAN's name, logo, and phone number were sold to the law firm which for years represented the CHURCH OF SCIENTOLOGY. In 1999, the files previously owned by CAN were turned over to the Church of Scientology in a legal settlement. The organization currently uses the name the New Cult Awareness Network and actively supports new religious movements. Web site—http://www.cultawareness network.org. See CULT.

Cult of Confession: One of eight criteria of MIND CONTROL according to ROBERT LIFTON's theory of THOUGHT REFORM. According to Lifton, the cult of confession is a system that requires members to disclose to their leaders or superiors the personal thoughts, attitudes, and actions that do not conform to the group's ideals. This practice diminishes healthy personal boundaries and privacy and may facilitate additional abuses. See BRAINWASHING.

Cultural Integration Fellowship, Dr. Haridas Chaudhuri (d. 1975)—San Francisco, CA: Founded in 1951. Its creation was inspired by the Integral YOGA of Sri Aurobindo (See MATAGIRI SRI AUROBINDO CENTER, INC.). Dr. Frederic Spielberg of Stanford University was seeking to bring a philosopher from the East that could bridge the gap between West and East. He invited Chaudhuri to be that person at the recommendation of Aurobindo. Since Chaudhuri's death the organization has been led by his widow, Bina Chaudhuri. Teaches universality of all religions, HINDUISM, BUDDHISM, and MEDITATION. See CALIFORNIA INSTITUTE OF INTEGRAL STUDIES.

Cumorah Books—Independence, MO: Affiliated with the more conservative RESTORATION BRANCHES of the COMMUNITY OF CHRIST. Publishes *Restoration Voice.* Web site—http://www.restorationvoice.org.

D

Daily Word: A monthly publication of the UNITY SCHOOL OF CHRISTIANITY. Web site—http://www.dailyword.com.

Dalai Lama: Tezin Gyatso, the fourteenth Dalai Lama, is believed by Tibetan Buddhists to be a manifestation of the Bodhisattva of compassion. In 1959 he was forced into exile by the government of China, which has occupied Tibet since 1950. He is currently head of the Tibetan government in exile, headquartered in Dharamsala, India. He was awarded the Nobel Peace Prize in 1989. Immensely popular in the West, the Dalai Lama is arguably the most popular teacher of BUDDHISM. Web site for the Tibetan government in exile—http://www.tibet.com. See TIBETAN BUDDHISM.

Dallas Fellowship Society, Inc.—Arlington, TX: A local study group of the URANTIA BOOK FELLOWSHIP. Published *The Circles*. Possibly defunct. See *THE URANTIA BOOK.*

Dart, Ronald (Ron) L.: Web site—http://www.rondart.com. See CHRISTIAN EDUCATIONAL MINISTRIES.

Davera Mission Church—Korea: See CHURCH OF THE LIVING STONE MISSION FOR THE COMING DAYS.

David, John, Learning Institute: See JOHN-DAVID LEARNING INSTITUTE.

David, Moses: Also known as King David. A pseudonym for David Berg, the late founder of THE FAMILY (CHILDREN OF GOD).

The Da Vinci Code, **Dan Brown:** Popular and controversial mystery novel published in 2003 and released as a movie in 2006, directed by Ron Howard and starring Tom Hanks. The book remained on best-seller lists for more than two years, selling over 40 million copies worldwide during that time. The controversy stemmed from the fact that the author, while acknowledging the book was a work of fiction, maintained all information pertaining to historical places, data, and practices is accurate. In promotional interviews Brown would also attest to the historicity of the book, even stating that he began researching his book as a skeptic but became a believer in the theories in it about "Mary Magdalene and holy blood, and all that" (*ABC Primetime,* 11/11/03). In responding to litigation filed over the book, Brown stated that his characters sometimes spoke for him or reflected his experiences and that he hoped the novel would cause people to "discuss the important topics of faith, religion, and history." The book's claims include: 1) The BIBLE is a fabrication of men, while the GNOSTIC GOSPELS are the true scriptures; 2) JESUS CHRIST was not God but just a man; 3) Jesus came to restore GODDESS worship through being married to Mary Magdalene (who is the HOLY GRAIL) and through restoring the practice of HIEROS GAMOS. Other controversial elements of the book include Brown's use of CONSPIRACY THEORY: the OPUS DEI strives to hide the truth about Magdalene, while the PRIORY OF SION tries to protect the truth of the Holy Grail. Brown claims the priory's leadership has included many famous historical figures, including Leonardo da Vinci, whom Brown claims depicted Mary Magdalene as the Holy Grail in his painting of the Last Supper. Brown readily admits that some of his supporting documentation comes from such books as *HOLY BLOOD, HOLY GRAIL* and the *TEMPLAR REVELATION,* which are among the books named in the *Da Vinci Code* as being written by important "historians." Web site—http://www.danbrown.com. For further research, a four-page Watchman Fellowship Profile is available (see page 363). Web site—http://www.watchman.org/notebook.

Dawn Bible Students—East Rutherford, NJ: One of the original splinter groups formed after Joseph Rutherford assumed leadership of the WATCHTOWER BIBLE AND TRACT SOCIETY.

Dayspring Resources, Leonie Rosenstiel—Albuquerque, NM: Specializes in HOLISTIC HEALTH. Rosenstiel has written several books about REIKI (universal life energy). See NEW AGE.

DayStar Television Network, Markus and Joni Lamb—Dallas, TX: A worldwide television network promoting EVANGELICAL CHRISTI-ANITY that broadcasts on cable and satellite in addition to the television stations it owns or operates in more than 40 U.S. cities. The network has a potential viewing audience of 128 million U.S. viewers, and its satellite signal reaches over 200 countries. It is the second-largest Christian television network behind the TRINITY BROADCASTING NETWORK (TBN). The Lambs, who founded the network, host the popular daily program *Celebration.* Web site—http://www.daystar.com.

de Mello, Anthony: An Indian-born Jesuit priest who combined teachings from CHRISTIANITY, HINDUISM, and BUDDHISM. De Mello's works include *One Minute Wisdom, One Minute Nonsense, Wellsprings: A Book of Spiritual Exercises,* and *Walking on Water.* In 1998—over a decade after his death—the Vatican's Congregation for the Doctrine of Faith denounced de Mello's writings, warning of dangers contained in his works, including a denial of objective morality and the claim that all religions, including Christianity, are obstacles to truth. See NEW AGE; ROMAN CATHOLICISM.

Deliverance Ministries: Organizations and individuals involved in battling the influence of DEMONS. The movement began to gain popularity in the United States in the mid-1970s in the wake of the popular movie, *The Exorcist* (1973), and the controversial book *Pigs in the Parlor* (1973) by Frank and Ida Mae Hammond. In most cases, the focus of such ministries involves the EXORCISM of DEMON-possessed (or demonized) Christians. This has created controversy amongst believers who question the appropriateness of exorcising Christians and debate whether true Christians can be demonized or demon-possessed. Critics have also noted that for many deliverance ministries the participants seem to become more dependent over time. Participants are constantly repossessed, requiring new rounds of deliverance on a weekly basis. See EXORCISM.

Delphi Schools—Sheridan, OR: A network of Delphian boarding schools that uses Heron Curriculum—which incorporates the teachings of L. Ron Hubbard—in its curricula for elementary through high school. Web site—http://www.delphian.org. See CHURCH OF SCIENTOLOGY.

Delphi University and Spiritual Center, Patricia Hayes and Marshall Smith—McCaysville, GA: In 1963, Patricia Hayes started the Patricia Hayes School of Inner Sense Development to offer training in METAPHYSICS. Following the 1971 death of MEDIUM Arthur Ford (founder of the SPIRITUAL FRONTIERS FELLOWSHIP), Hayes started the Arthur Ford International Academy of Mediumship in 1974—allegedly after Ford appeared to her in a vision—to offer professional training to mediums. In 1983, Hayes also started the RoHun Institute to offer credentialed training in the practice of ROHUN. While the initial Delphi was started by Hayes in 1974, the current Delphi University—with the aforementioned programs as schools within the university—was created by Hayes and Smith in 1985. Web site—http://www.delphi-center.com. See NEW AGE.

Demand for Purity: One of eight criteria of MIND CONTROL according to ROBERT LIFTON'S theory of THOUGHT REFORM. The Demand for Purity is an environment of blame and guilt based on an impossible ideal of human behavior or perfection. This shame-based culture punishes failure and can even subtly train members to punish themselves for their inability to live up to the group's ideals or standards. See LIFTON, ROBERT; MIND CONTROL; BRAINWASHING; CULT.

Demons: In modern usage, a demon is an evil spirit. The word derives from the Greek *daimon,* which refers to a (usually) inhuman spirit being inferior to the gods, which may be benevolent or wicked. However, in orthodox Christian theology, demons are fallen ANGELS under the direction of SATAN who seek to destroy God's purpose and people. Demons are spiritual beings (Ephesians 6:12), are organized, and have supernatural power and knowledge (Matthew 12:24; Revelation 16:14), can possess humans and animals (Luke 8:2; Mark 5:13), and can teach false doctrine (1 Timothy 4:1). Many other religions of the world also profess a belief in evil spiritual beings, often referred to in English texts by the word *demon.*

Denver, John: Prominent folk singer who promoted EST, YOGA, TRANSCENDENTAL MEDITATION, and the WINDSTAR FOUNDATION before his death in 1997. Web site—http://www.johndenver.com. See NEW AGE.

Deprogram: An attempt to dissuade an individual from religious or ideological convictions believed to be harmful through a concentrated (usually two- to three-day) counseling procedure designed to produce a sudden "snapping out." Deprogramming was developed in the 1970s by Ted Patrick and others as a way to rescue family members who were perceived to have undergone negative personality change after joining destructive cults. Often presented as an antidote for BRAINWASHING, some deprogrammers rationalized the unethical use of force and coercion to rescue victims by illegally holding individuals against their will (abduction or "snatching") in a process known as "involuntary" deprogramming. See BRAINWASHING; MIND CONTROL; EXIT COUNSELING.

Deseret Book: An LDS book publisher and chain of Mormon bookstores owned by the Church of Jesus Christ of Latter-day Saints. Divisions include Bookcraft, Eagle Gate, Shadow Mountain, and Excel Entertainment, which produces video and music products. Web site—http://deseretbook.com. See CHURCH OF JESUS CHRIST OF LATTER-DAY SAINTS.

Deuterocanonicals: Seven books considered canonical (part of the BIBLE) by ROMAN CATHOLICISM but not by PROTESTANTISM. See APOCRYPHA; BIBLE; ROMAN CATHOLICISM.

Devil: See SATAN.

Dianetics: See CHURCH OF SCIENTOLOGY.

Di Mambro, Joseph: See ORDER OF THE SOLAR TEMPLE.

Disciples of Christ (Christian Church): See THE RESTORATION MOVEMENT.

Disfellowshipping: See SHUNNING.

Dispensing of Existence: One of eight criteria of mind control according to ROBERT LIFTON'S theory of THOUGHT REFORM. In this component of thought reform, the organization's dogma determines whether or not other groups or individuals have the right to exist. All alternative belief systems or organizations are therefore considered illegitimate. In extreme cases this mindset can promote violence or murder. See LIFTON, ROBERT; MIND CONTROL; BRAINWASHING.

Divination: In Christian theology, the attempt to supernaturally gain hidden knowledge, usually about the future, through means separate from the God of the BIBLE (Ezekiel 21:22-25; Acts 16:16). Physical objects are often used in the process, such as the hand (PALMISTRY), the stars (ASTROLOGY), TAROT CARDS, or sticks (*I CHING*). See OCCULT.

Divine Light Mission: The former organization headed by Maharaji, who, as a teenage GURU in the 1970s, proclaimed himself to be an incarnation of God. Maharaji taught a four-step process of MEDITATION that involved ritual movements of the hands around the eyes and ears, as well as the tongue (which, according to some former members, was supposed to taste "nectar" from the back of the throat). The central event in the history of the organization was Millennium 1973, held in the Astrodome in Houston, Texas. While the event received significant media attention, the debt it incurred—combined with Maharaji's later marriage to a follower—led to a dramatic loss in membership. The organization has developed into the modern ELAN VITAL.

Divine Science—Washington, DC: The theological system of a small NEW AGE denomination with beliefs similar to those of CHRISTIAN SCIENCE. God is the One Presence containing all wisdom, power, and substance, and the development of right thinking will therefore enable the believer to experience the unity of all things. The most famous member was Emmet Fox. Web site—http://www.divinescience.org. See PANTHEISM; FIRST CHURCH OF CHRIST, SCIENTIST.

Dixon, Jeane: Dixon (1918–97) was a PSYCHIC who was credited with predicting that John F. Kennedy would be assassinated. Her numerous failed prophecies include predicting World War III would begin in 1958, a cure for cancer would be discovered in 1967, and world peace by 2000. See FALSE PROPHECY.

Docetism: From the Greek word *dokeo* ("to seem or appear"). A doctrine held in early GNOSTICISM that JESUS was not truly human but only appeared to have a real, physical body. Based on their belief that matter is evil and spirit is good, Docetists believed that Jesus was God and therefore pure spirit (good) and could not have had a physical body of evil matter. Likewise, the suffering, crucifixion, and death of Christ were viewed as illusions. Christ only *seemed* to die on the cross.

Doctrine & Covenants (D&C): One of the scriptures or Standard Works of THE CHURCH OF JESUS CHRIST OF LATTER-DAY SAINTS and other Mormon splinter groups. Originally it was a compilation of two works. The first part, the doctrine section, consisted of the *Lectures on Faith,* first written in 1834 as part of a curriculum for the School of the Prophets in Kirtland, Ohio. The second part, or covenants, was originally published by the LDS church in 1833 as The *Book of Commandments* in Independence, Missouri. The *Book of Commandments* was essentially a record of the prophecies and revelations received by the LDS prophet JOSEPH SMITH, JR. When D&C was compiled in 1835, Smith's revelations underwent significant redaction. Eighty-six years later, in the 1921 edition (and all subsequent editions), the doctrine section (the *Lectures on Faith*) was removed from the D&C, leaving only part two, the covenants portion. Critics have speculated that the *Lectures on Faith* were "decanonized" after serving as scripture for over 80 years because of blatant contradictions with other LDS scripture. Most notable is Lecture Five, which states there are only two personages in the Godhead (the Father and the Son) and that the Father is a "personage of Spirit" in contrast to the Son, who is "a personage of tabernacle, made or fashioned like unto man." See CHURCH OF JESUS CHRIST OF LATTER-DAY SAINTS.

Doctrine Over Person: One of eight criteria of Mind Control according to ROBERT LIFTON'S theory of THOUGHT REFORM. In a cultic system the ideas and doctrines of the leader and organization overrule the personal experiences, conscience, and integrity of the individual. See LIFTON, ROBERT; MIND CONTROL; BRAINWASHING.

Dollar, Creflo: Popular WORD-FAITH teacher and founder/senior pastor of World Changers Church in College Park, Georgia. His organization also operates an extensive radio and television ministry promoting the prosperity message. Web sites—http://www.worldchangers.org/ and http://www.cre flodollarministries.org. See WORD-FAITH MOVEMENT.

Donate Car for Charity—Spring Valley, CA: A nonprofit charity functioning as part of the FAMILY CARE FOUNDATION (FCF) with alleged ties to THE FAMILY (CHILDREN OF GOD). Web site—http://www.donate-car-for-charity.com. See THE FAMILY (CHILDREN OF GOD).

The Door Christian Fellowship Churches, Wayman Mitchell: Formerly the Potter's House (a name still used in some congregations). Started by Mitchell in Prescott, Arizona in 1970, the fellowship has grown into an organization of hundreds of churches. Critics allege that Mitchell, through what the churches call "discipleship," engages in MIND CONTROL and SPIRITUAL ABUSE. Web sites—http://www.cfmusa.org and http://www.worldcfm.com.

Dorene Publishing—Arlington, TX: Publishing company specializing in OCCULT, MAGIC, and PAGAN books and memorabilia. Some publications date back to the 1930s.

Double Bind: A mental or psychological dilemma caused when a person receives conflicting messages or "truths" from a single source, leaving them unsure of the appropriate response to an issue. See COGNITIVE DISSONANCE.

Dowsing: A form of DIVINATION using a forked rod, a bent wire, or a pendulum. Dowsing is most popularly known as a method of locating underground water, but it is also used to locate people, objects, or substances and to diagnose illnesses.

Dragonfly Media—Brooklyn, NY: Dragonfly publishes magazines in Los Angeles, San Francisco, Seattle, Vancouver, B.C., and Chicago. These magazines focus on HOLISTIC HEALTH, alternative spiritualities, environmentalism, and social justice issues. Web site—http://www.dragonflymedia.com.

Druidism: See DRUIDS.

Druids: The priestly caste of the ancient Celtic people of France and the British Isles. Druids preserved oral history and law and officiated pagan religious practices. Little is known of what druidism actually taught, outside of occasional outsider descriptions of Celtic religion in Roman histories; the actual tenets and practices of druidism remain the object of academic and amateur speculation. Many NEO-PAGANISM groups claim to be druidic orders. See OCCULT; HALLOWEEN; PAGANISM.

Dual Covenant: The belief that the New Testament (or covenant) applies to Gentiles (non-Jews) only. JESUS CHRIST is therefore not the Savior of the Jewish people, and they should thus relate to God through the earlier Old Testament or Abrahamic Covenant. A similar doctrine, called the Plural Covenant theory, emphasizes other covenants in addition to these two major systems.

Dualism: An understanding of reality as existing in two opposite extremes. Metaphysical dualism sees the universe as existing in two contrary (and sometimes conflicting) realities—mind and matter, or spirit and physical, or YIN AND YANG. Ethical dualism posits a conflict between universal good and an equal and opposite force of universal evil (for instance, the belief that God and SATAN are equal and opposite beings).

DuBois, Allison: An Arizona-based PSYCHIC and author whose life story is the basis of the NBC television drama *MEDIUM*. DuBois also serves as the research consultant for the show. DeBois's 2004 best-selling book, *Don't Kiss Them Goodbye,* was followed by *We Are Their Heaven: Why the Dead Never Leave Us.* Web site—http://www.allisondubois.com. See MEDIUM; PSYCHIC; NECROMANCY; OCCULT.

Dungeons & Dragons, Gary Gygax (D&D): The first and most popular FANTASY ROLE PLAYING GAME (FRPG). D&D developed out of miniatures wargaming when Gygax adapted the rules for mass army-scale combat to individual small-scale combat and introduced narrative-driven game scenarios. In building a fictional setting for early D&D, Gygax drew inspiration from popular fantasy fiction, including the *Lord of the Rings* trilogy (J.R.R. Tolkien) and the Conan the Barbarian stories (Robert Howard). The typical concerns about FRPGs are often directed at D&D. Web site—http://www.wizards.com/default.asp?x=dnd/welcome. Web site for Wizards of the Coast, the game's publisher—http://www.wizards.com.

Duplantis, Jesse: Popular WORD-FAITH televangelist and teacher. Operates Jesse Duplantis Ministries out of New Orleans, Louisiana. He has a nationally syndicated television program and regularly speaks in conferences throughout the world. Web site—http://www.jdm.org. See WORD-FAITH MOVEMENT.

Dyer, Wayne: A popular NEW AGE writer and motivational speaker on business applications and personal transformation. His teaching is heavily influenced by BUDDHISM, emphasizing the need for nonattachment and quieting one's mind. His books include *Your Erroneous Zones, Your Sacred Self,* and *Pulling Your Own Strings.* Web site—http://www.waynedyerbooks. com.

Dynamic Monarchianism: Also called *adoptionism,* dynamic MONAR-CHIANISM was a late-second-century HERESY that denied the full deity of Christ by claiming that JESUS was God only in the sense that He had a powerful, divine influence (in Greek, *dynamis*) resting on His human person. Christ was therefore not divine until He was adopted by God (either at His baptism, when the HOLY SPIRIT descended upon Him, or at His ascension). One form of this HERESY is ARIANISM. See MONARCHIANISM; ARIANISM.

E

Eadie, Betty: A NEW AGE author of best-sellers *Embraced by the Light, The Awakening Heart,* and *The Ripple Effect.* Eadie claims to have died, gone to heaven, and then returned to share a series of spiritual laws that will bring the peace of God. In the past, Eadie claimed to be an active member of THE CHURCH OF JESUS CHRIST OF LATTER-DAY SAINTS, and critics have noted that Mormon doctrines strongly influence the spirituality expressed in her books. Web site—http://www.embracedbythelight.com.

Earth Church of Amargi—Dania, FL: A NEW AGE group that emphasizes WITCHCRAFT and worshipping earth as the mother. See NEO-PAGANISM.

Eastern Orthodox Church: See ORTHODOX CHURCH.

Ebionite Jewish Community, Shemayah Phillips: Claims to be the modern-day successor of the first-century EBIONITES. Phillips was a disillusioned Christian who briefly joined the ASSEMBLIES OF YAHWEH in 1985 before becoming an Ebionite. In 1995 he began an online community. This SACRED NAME movement denies CHRIST's deity, rejects the doctrine of the TRINITY, and views the APOSTLE Paul as a false teacher. Web site—http://www.ebionite.org.

Ebionites: From the Hebrew term *ebyonim* ("poor ones"). A heretical first-century movement that seemed to blend doctrines from JUDAISM and CHRISTIANITY. Followers denied the deity of CHRIST and the doctrine of the TRINITY. The movement is thought to have died out sometime around A.D. 500, but the EBIONITE JEWISH COMMUNITY claims to be the modern successor of the original Ebionite doctrines and practices.

Ebon, Martin: See SPIRITUAL FRONTIERS FELLOWSHIP.

Ecclesia Athletic Association, Eldridge Broussard, Jr.—Clackamas, OR: A pseudoreligious group that moved from 70-100 followers from Los Angeles to a "promised land" in rural Oregon. Children were forced to perform in arduous athletic exhibitions to attract corporate financial sponsorship. Authorities intervened in 1988 after Broussard's daughter was beaten to death. Three followers were convicted of manslaughter. Broussard himself died shortly after a 30-count indictment was handed down by a federal grand jury in 1991, and seven additional followers pleaded guilty to slavery.

Eckankar, Paul Twitchell: Begun in 1965, Eckankar teaches that the person's eternal soul is on a journey to realizing its identity as God. This process can be accelerated by contacting the ECK, or Divine Spirit, and following the leadership of the Mahanta, or Living ECK Master. Eckankar promises that followers can visit one of the 11 worlds through soul travel (which differs from ASTRAL PROJECTION in that travel is not limited to the astral plane) and dreams. Every soul is connected to God through the ECK Current, which consists of an inner sound (which may be heard in music or nature) and an inner light that can be seen in MEDITATION. Web site—http://www.eckankar.org. See NEW AGE. For further research, a four-page Watchman Fellowship Profile is available (see page 363). Web site—http://www.watchman.org/notebook.

Eddy, Mary Baker: See FIRST CHURCH OF CHRIST, SCIENTIST.

Edward, John: Perhaps America's most prominent PSYCHIC, Edward specializes in allegedly "crossing over" to make contact with the dead (NECROMANCY). Born John Edward McGee, Jr. to a mother heavily involved in the OCCULT, Edward's popular television program, *Crossing Over,* became the number one program on the Sci-Fi Network before being syndicated nationwide on broadcast television in 2001. In 2006, a new program was launched on the We (Women's Entertainment) network, titled *John Edward Cross Country.* Both programs feature Edward making contact with the deceased friends and relatives of his on-air guests using techniques that appear similar to COLD READING. His popular books include *Crossing*

Over, Final Beginnings, One Last Time, Practical Praying, and *After Life.* Web site—www.johnedward.net. See PSYCHIC; NECROMANCY; OCCULT. For further research, a four-page Watchman Fellowship Profile is available (see page 363). Web site—http://www.watchman.org/notebook.

Edwards, Bishop Luke: See REACH, INC.

Effective Learning Systems—Edina, MN: Offers subliminal tapes that train individuals in deep relaxation and VISUALIZATION. Web site—http://www.efflearn.com.

Eikerenkoetter, Frederick: See REVEREND IKE.

Elan Vital, Maharaji—Malibu, CA: A continuation of Maharaji's DIVINE LIGHT MISSION, which promoted his teaching that he was an incarnation of God, as well as a four-step process of MEDITATION. Elan Vital itself is the media arm of Maharaji's current activities. Affiliated with Elan Vital is the Prem Rawat Foundation (Prem Rawat is Maharaji's name). Web site—http://www.elanvital.org.

Elemis Spa: Part of STEINER LEISURE. Offers a variety of massage treatments including AROMATHERAPY and a Well-Being Massage that includes CHAKRA Balancing. Web site—http://www.elemis.com. See HOLISTIC HEALING.

Elihu Books and Media: See STAFFORD, GREG.

E-Meter: See CHURCH OF SCIENTOLOGY.

Emmanuel, J. David Davis—Athens, TN: A B'NEI NOACH teacher. Publishes *The Gap* newsletter. The Web site for the Emmanuel Study Center is at http://www.noach.com/emmanuel.

Enneagram: The roots of the enneagram are unknown, with researchers claiming to find elements of the enneagram in sources as diverse as Greek philosophy, SUFISM, and the KABBALAH. The enneagram itself is a diagram of a circle with nine equidistant points, with lines inside the circle connecting various points. Each of the points represents a personality type (i.e., Reformer, Helper, Enthusiast, etc.), with the goal being better understanding the way each person unconsciously perceives and experiences the world. Many critics claim the enneagram is an occultic system that is incompatible with CHRISTIANITY. See OCCULT.

Epiphany Bible Students Association—Mount Dora, FL: A splinter of the LAYMEN'S HOME MISSIONARY MOVEMENT. Publishes the *Epiphany Bible Students* newsletter.

Episcopalian Churches: In most cases churches of PROTESTANTISM that practice an Episcopalian form of church government, in which each congregation and the clergy are under the authority of and in communion with the bishop of the churches. Alternative forms of church government include Congregational governance (member rule) and Presbyterian governance (elder rule). Almost all Episcopal churches in the United States are Anglican and, in most cases, are in communion with the Archbishop of Canterbury. See ANGLICAN CHURCHES.

Erhard, Warner: See EST.

Esalen Institute—Big Sur, CA: Founded in 1962, Esalen is one of the original and foremost organizations to merge Eastern and Western spiritualities to tap into the human potential and has been associated with such prominent figures as Aldous Huxley, JOSEPH CAMPBELL, and Alan Ginsberg. Esalen offers workshops in such practices and spiritualities as MEDITATION, YOGA, KABBALAH, and BUDDHISM. See HUMAN POTENTIAL MOVEMENT. Web site—http://www.esalen.org.

Esoteric: Esotericism refers to the secret teachings and practices of a religious group that are known only by those initiated into the group. See GNOSTICISM; OCCULT.

Esoteric Order of Dagon: The antagonists of H.P. LOVECRAFT's story "The Shadow over Innsmouth," the order is a cult in the fictional town of Innsmouth, Massachusetts, which worships a gigantic aquatic entity called Dagon. According to the story, the order is in league with a fish-like race called the Deep Ones, who live in a reef at the mouth of Innsmouth's harbor. A group of Lovecraft fans have created a Web site at http://www.esotericorderofdagon.tk. See CTHULHU MYTHOS.

ESP: See EXTRASENSORY PERCEPTION.

ESPress, Inc.—Washington, DC: See NATIONAL SPIRITUAL SCIENCE CENTER.

ES Press Magazine, The—North Fort Myers, FL: Online NEW AGE magazine. Web site—http://www.theespress.com.

ESPress Publishers, Inc: Defunct NEW AGE book publisher. Not to be confused with the online THE ES PRESS MAGAZINE.

Essene Gospels of Peace, Edmond Bordeaux Szekely: Allegedly translated by Szekely in the 1920s from scrolls dated approximately A.D. 300, the Essene Gospels of Peace presents Jesus as a raw-food vegetarian who taught that peace is the key to all wisdom. The Essene Gospels are promoted largely by NEW AGE practitioners. One Web site publishing the Essene Gospels is http://www.essene.com/GospelOfPeace. See GNOSTICISM.

Essene Order of Light—Patagonia, AZ: Trains preachers, priests, and priestesses for the TREE OF LIFE FOUNDATION.

Essential Christian Education: See HOMESTEAD HERITAGE.

est, Warner Erhard (aka John Paul Rosenberg): Personal transformation seminar promising individual growth, business management skills, and stress reduction. Through large group awareness training meetings in hotels and conference centers around the world, Erhard and his disciples sought to help their students to "get *it*"—in essence, to achieve enlightenment. Personal responsibility and virtually limitless human possibilities were promoted through slogans such as, "You're god in your universe. You caused it." Many early participants reported strenuous emotional—and, for some, physical—strain from the 60-hour sessions and confrontational tenor of the seminar. According to published reports, Erhard incorporated elements from a variety of religions, including ZEN BUDDHISM and SCIENTOLOGY, into est. Controversy surrounded the movement including charges of tax evasion. A *60 Minutes* television report aired in 1991 accused Erhard of spousal abuse and included the accusation of incest by several of his daughters (one of whom later recanted). In the midst of mounting troubles, Erhard decided to leave the United States. The seminar and organization have undergone numerous transformations and name changes through the years. Est was discontinued and replaced with The Forum, and in 1991, Werner Erhard and Associates (WE&A) was dissolved. In its place, Landmark Education was incorporated, with Erhard's brother, Harry Rosenberg, serving as CEO and overseeing the current seminar, which is called Landmark Forum. In addition, a number of other est-like transformational/encounter seminars are currently conducted by organizations not connected with Erhard but using some of his basic ideologies and methodologies. See HUMAN POTENTIAL MOVEMENT. Web site—http://www.landmarkeducation.com.

Eupsychia Institute for Well-Being—Austin, TX: Founded by Jacquelyn Small in 1975, Eupsychia claims mental problems and addictions are the pangs from the birth of a new consciousness. The process for developing this new consciousness includes such practices as GUIDED IMAGERY, MEDITATION, YOGA, and CHAKRA clearing. Web site—http://www. eupsychiainc.com. See NEW AGE.

Evangelical Christianity: *Evangelical* (from the Greek word that translates to "good news" or "GOSPEL") generally means a focus on the essentials of the Christian gospel. The term is generally used to describe all Christians or churches that hold to or give heavy emphasis to specific conservative beliefs. These include the authority and infallibility of the BIBLE, the nature of God (sovereign, holy, compassionate, personal, etc.), the sinful and fallen state of humanity, and SALVATION BY GRACE through faith in the death, burial, and resurrection of Christ as the only means of salvation. More specifically, the term has come to be more closely identified with a widespread transdenominational shift toward more conservative Christian doctrine—a shift that developed after World War II. See CHRISTIANITY; FUNDA-MENTALIST CHRISTIANITY; PROTESTANTISM; GOSPEL.

Evangelical Free Church of America (EFCA)—Minneapolis, MN: A denomination of PROTESTANTISM formed in 1950 by the merger of the Norwegian-Danish Evangelical Free Church Association and the Swedish Evangelical Free Church. In 2006 there were 1,300 autonomous churches in association with the EFCA ministering in 45 countries. Web site—http:// www.efca.org. See EVANGELICAL CHRISTIANITY.

Evangelical Friends International: See RELIGIOUS SOCIETY OF FRIENDS.

Evangelical Lutheran Church in America (ELCA)—Chicago, IL: A denomination of PROTESTANTISM based on LUTHERANISM that was formed in 1988 by the merger of three churches: the Lutheran Church in America, the American Lutheran Church, and the Association of Evangelical Lutheran Churches. ELCA is the largest Lutheran denomination in the United States (almost 5 million members in over 10,000 churches) and it is considered to be somewhat more liberal than most other Lutheran denominations in the country. The ELCA is in full communion with ANGLICAN CHURCHES that conform to the Anglican Communion. Web site—http://www.elca.org. See LUTHERANISM; REFORMATION; PROTESTANTISM.

Evangelical Ministries to New Religions (EMNR): Formed in 1982, EMNR is a "consortium of Christians in North America, seeking to help people distinguish authentic from in-authentic Christianity and strengthen evangelical Christian ministries to new religionists and cultists." Ministries that are associated with EMNR provide research and outreach in the field of new religious movements and agree to conform to a written standard of ethical and doctrinal guidelines. Currently about 50 organizations and individuals are associated with EMNR, including WATCHMAN FELLOWSHIP, Institute for Religious Research, Centers for Apologetics Research, Mormonism Research Ministry, Midwest Christian Outreach, New England Institute of Religious Research, and Evidence Ministries. Web site:—http://www.emnr.org.

Every Nation Churches—Brentwood, TN: An organization of Christian churches formed by Rice Broocks, Steve Murrell, and Phil Bonasso in 1994 as Morning Star International and renamed in 2004. The movement, which focuses on campus ministry, church planting, and training, has been associated with the NEW APOSTOLIC REFORMATION. It is not affiliated with Rick Joyner's MORNINGSTAR MINISTRIES. Web site—http://www.everynation.org. See THIRD WAVE OF THE HOLY SPIRIT.

Evidence Ministries, Keith & Becky Walker—San Antonio, TX: A Christian APOLOGETICS ministry that defends the beliefs of EVANGELICAL CHRISTIANITY and examines the competing religious claims of the CHURCH OF JESUS CHRIST OF LATTER-DAY SAINTS and the WATCHTOWER BIBLE AND TRACT SOCIETY in light of the BIBLE. The organization is a member of EVANGELICAL MINISTRIES TO NEW RELIGIONS (EMNR). Web site—http://www.evidenceministries.org.

Evolutionary Kingdom Level Above Human—Richardson, TX: An early name of Marshall Applewhite's UFO CULT. See HEAVEN'S GATE.

Exaltation: This is the concept for the highest form of salvation in the Mormon Church. It means to become a god, procreate throughout all eternity, and rule over one's offspring. See CHURCH OF JESUS CHRIST OF LATTER-DAY SAINTS.

Exit Counseling: Also called THOUGHT REFORM consulting. A noncoercive technique designed to help rescue members of religions or cults that are considered false, harmful, or dangerous. The program usually involves a two- to three-day voluntary counseling session emphasizing education and dialogue, often with a licensed mental health professional, a former member of the group, and a specialist on CULT dynamics. The approach stresses true personal and religious freedom in the context of providing additional information and full disclosure, which helps facilitate more informed decision-making. Family counseling and intervention techniques may also be incorporated. See DEPROGRAM.

Exorcism: The practice of casting out DEMONS from possessed humans or animals. Exorcism is practiced in many religions—usually through ceremony or ritual. Biblical examples include Mark 5:1-13; 9:17-29.

Extrasensory Perception (ESP): The alleged ability to receive knowledge or acquire information apart from the five senses. This can take place in either a conscious or unconscious state. Although it has yet to be successfully validated or independently verified in a controlled environment, according to many proponents, ESP is supposedly based on natural but latent powers of the mind. Others view ESP as a supernatural spiritual gift similar to the abilities to do PSYCHIC readings or TELEPATHY.

F

FAIR: See FOUNDATION FOR APOLOGETIC INFORMATION RESEARCH.

Faith Assembly Church, Raymond Jackson—Jeffersonville, IN: Jackson was a follower of WILLIAM BRANHAM from 1952–55, but in 1955 left Branham to start Faith Assembly. Publishes *The Contender.* Web site—http://www.fachurch.org. See BRANHAMISM.

Faithbuilders Fellowship—San Diego, CA: Theology is similar to that of the WATCHTOWER BIBLE AND TRACT SOCIETY. Kenneth Allen hosts a library of Faithbuilders Fellowship materials on his Web site at http://www.auburn.edu/~allenkc/fbf/fbfmenu.html.

Faithful Word, **Ed and Cindy Burson**—Longview, TX: Online version of an earlier periodical published in the 1980s by the Bursons. While influenced by the teachings of HERBERT W. ARMSTRONG, a significant difference is that the Bursons teach that individuals who receive the HOLY SPIRIT become members of the true church regardless of where they attend services. See ARMSTRONGISM.

Faith Temple, Rosemary "Mama" Cosby—Salt Lake City, UT: One of the APOSTOLIC CHURCHES. Before her death in 1997, Cosby was reported to have claimed to be the MESSIAH. The group later split between followers of Cosby's husband and daughter.

False Memory Syndrome (FMS): The theory that the human mind can experience vivid recollections of events that never actually happened. Recent evidence suggests that some techniques used in RECOVERED MEMORY THERAPY can result in FMS when a therapist inadvertently "plants" false recollections in the minds of patients. FMS may also provide a partial explanation for various reports of UFO sightings, alien abduction stories, and the recollection of vivid memories of past lives via REINCARNATION. Some people are perhaps more vulnerable to FMS when placed in an ALTERED STATE OF CONSCIOUSNESS or under HYPNOSIS. In a TRANCElike state, the subject may be very susceptible to suggestion. See RECOVERED MEMORY THERAPY.

False Prophecy: A false prophecy is, in the most general sense, any teaching by a prophet that is not true. Specifically, it is a prediction of a specific event that fails to occur by the given date. The BIBLE teaches that an individual who gives even one false prophecy is not a legitimate spiritual leader and should not be followed (Deuteronomy 13:1-5; 18:20-22).

Falun Gong, Li Hongzhi (Chinese "Practice of the Wheel of Law"): a controversial Chinese religion (aka Falun Dafa, "Great Law of the Wheel of Law") introduced to the public around 1992 by Li Hongzhi, a former military police officer with the Chinese military (now a U.S. citizen living in Brooklyn, New York). The religion, which has been suppressed by the Beijing government since 1999, promotes Li's spiritual teachings and five sets of MEDITATION exercises involving slow, gentle movements. Practitioners seek physical and spiritual transformation through personal discipline and character refinement. Falun Gong supporters have estimated as many as 100 million followers in 60 countries, including about 70 million in the People's Republic of China. Web site—http://clearwisdom.net.

The Family, Charles Manson: The followers of Charles Manson, some of whom were convicted for the 1969 murders of Sharon Tate and Leno and Rosemary LaBianca. Manson is serving a life sentence for the murders, as are Charles Watson, Susan Atkins, Leslie Van Houten, and Patricia Krenwinkel. Other Manson family members have been jailed for other offenses, including murder. The Manson Family is not related to THE FAMILY (CHILDREN OF GOD).

The Family (Children of God), David Berg: Started by Berg (1919–94) in 1968, and called early in its history the Children of God (still the name by which the group is best known), the Family encouraged becoming a "revolutionary" for Jesus by abandoning all outside elements and living in communal colonies. Berg taught that Christ was conceived as a result of sexual union between the angel Gabriel and the VIRGIN MARY and that JESUS obeyed the "law of love" in part by having sexual relations with his female followers, including Mary, her sister Martha, and Mary Magdalene. The movement began as a much more orthodox group called Teens for Christ. After developing a sexual relationship with his secretary, Karen Zerby, Berg explained that God had revealed that he was to leave his first wife, Jane Miller (Mother Eve), for Zerby. The Family is best known for FLIRTY FISHING, or engaging in sexual practices to attract converts and reinforce group life (the group claims to have abandoned this practice, although former members allege that it continues within the group's inner circles). Recent statistics by the group puts full-time and fellow members at just over 11,200 in over 100 countries, including about 4,000 children. They operate a number of ministries and charities including AURORA PRODUCTION AG, HEAVEN'S MAGIC, ACTIVATED MINISTRIES, Sunnyside Up Entertainment, The Family Singers, Teaching Education and More (TEAM) Foundation, and Kidzvids International. They also have alleged ties to FAMILY CARE FOUNDATION (FCF) and DONATE CAR FOR CHARITY. Karen Zerby and her husband Steven Douglas Kelly (aka Christopher Smith and "King Peter") have been the leaders of the group since the death of Berg in 1994. In 1997, Zerby (aka Maria David, Maria Berg, and Queen Maria) had her name legally changed to Katherine Rianna Smith. Publishes *Activated* magazine. Web site—http://www.thefamily.org. For further research, a four-page Watchman Fellowship Profile is available (see page 363). Web site—http://www.watchman.org/notebook.

Family Care Foundation (FCF), Grant Cameron Montgomery—Dulzura, CA: A charitable organization with revenues of about $3 million with alleged ties to THE FAMILY (CHILDREN OF GOD). Montgomery is the former "prime minister" of The Family. Both FCF and The Family denied any connection despite published reports linking the two (*San Francisco Chronicle*, February 2, 2005). Web site—http://www.familycare.org. See THE FAMILY (CHILDREN OF GOD).

The Family of Love: See THE FAMILY (CHILDREN OF GOD).

Family Radio Worldwide Network (Family Stations, Inc.): A worldwide broadcasting network founded by HAROLD CAMPING in 1958, which is broadcast via satellite on over 50 stations nationwide and by shortwave around the world in 11 languages. The network became a source of controversy when its president, HAROLD CAMPING, made false predictions about the end of the world and declared that organized churches had become apostate. *Note: This network is not affiliated with the similar-sounding American Family Radio, a conservative Christian network headed by Don Wildmon.* Web site—http://www.familyradio.com. See CAMPING, HAROLD. For further research, a four-page Watchman Fellowship Profile is available (see page 363). Web site—http://www.watchman.org/notebook.

Family Stations, Inc.: See FAMILY RADIO WORLDWIDE NETWORK; CAMPING, HAROLD.

Fantasy Role-Playing Game (FRPG): A major subgenre of role-playing game. In a role-playing game, players control hero characters in an open-ended adventure story that is mediated and narrated by a storyteller or referee known as a game master (GM). FRPGs, like the fantasy genre of fiction that inspired them, have drawn criticism due to the violent content in many of the adventure scenarios. Also, many games (as is true with fantasy fiction) contain a MAGIC or PARANORMAL element that some critics consider dangerously close to the OCCULT. See DUNGEONS & DRAGONS.

FARMS: See FOUNDATION FOR ANCIENT RESEARCH AND MORMON STUDIES.

The Farm, Stephen Gaskin—Summertown, TN: An organization that promotes a sustainable agricultural lifestyle. Many members live in a communal collective called The Second Foundation. The Farm actively encourages HOLISTIC HEALTH and supports a wide array of religious perspectives. Web site—http://www.thefarm.org.

Farrakhan, Louis: See NATION OF ISLAM.

Fate Magazine—Lakeville, MN: Examines a wide variety of PARANORMAL experiences, UFOs, and PSYCHICS. Web site—http://www.fatemag.com.

Fellowship for Spiritual Understanding, Marcus Bach—Palos Verdes Estates, CA: Bach (1901–95) was a professor at the University of Iowa School of Religion from 1945–64 and started the Fellowship for Spiritual Under-standing in 1964 to promote MIND SCIENCE. Bach was active in both RELIGIOUS SCIENCE and UNITY SCHOOL OF CHRISTIANITY circles. His collection, including his periodical *Outreach,* is maintained at Brigham Young University, the flagship school for THE CHURCH OF JESUS CHRIST OF LATTER-DAY SAINTS. Web site—http://www.lib.byu.edu/spc/bach.

Fellowship of Isis—Enniscorthy, Ireland: A panreligious organization that promotes the worship of Isis as the goddess of all humans. The fellowship also promotes general GODDESS worship. Web site—http://www.fellowshipofisis.com. See PAGANISM.

Fellowship of the Inner Light, Paul Solomon—Virginia Beach, VA: A NEW AGE group founded in 1972 that promotes universal spiritual studies. The Fellowship combines such elements as YOGA, CHRISTIANITY, and *A COURSE IN MIRACLES.* Solomon (1939–94) channeled a group of entities who called themselves The Source. Web site—http://groups.hamptonroads.com/Fellowship. A follower of Solomon maintains another Web site at http://www.wisdomofsolomon.com. See CHANNELING.

Feminism: See RADICAL FEMINISM.

Feng Shui (pronounced *fung schway*): The ancient Chinese practice of placing and arranging objects in space in accord with certain religious beliefs (including ASTROLOGY, YIN AND YANG, and spiritual energy called CHI) that will allegedly result in either favorable or unfavorable effects. Practitioners claim to be able to bring harmony, awareness, and prosperity to an office or home through techniques said to increase spiritual energy, reduce negative power, and balance the yin and yang. The practice has grown tremendously in the United States during the last decade with a swelling number of interior decorators and architects offering Fung Shui services. There are several schools of Fung Shui theory. They include the Compass School (using the eight points of the *lo pan* compass), Form School (using the shape of the surrounding land with four compass points corresponding with four animals), Black Hat School (traditional Feng Shui blended with TIBETAN BUDDHISM, TAOISM, and TANTRA), and Flying Star School (an advanced school that also considers the "birth chart" [construction date] of the building in relationship with nine "flying stars" or energies).

Feraferia, Lady Svetlana—Nevada City, CA: Svetlana promotes PAGANISM and GODDESS worship. Web site—http://www.phaedrus.dds.nl/fera.htm.

Ferguson, Marilyn: A popular NEW AGE lecturer and author of several books, including the best-seller *THE AQUARIAN CONSPIRACY.* From 1975 to 1995 she was the editor of the *Brain/Mind Bulletin,* a publication that addressed developments in brain and consciousness research and in the fields of psychology and education. She has been a member of the Association of Humanistic Psychology and the Association of Transpersonal Psychology and has served on the board of directors for the INSTITUTE OF NOETIC SCIENCE.

Fifth Epochal Fellowship: The name used in the late 1980s and early 1990s by the URANTIA BOOK FELLOWSHIP.

Findhorn Foundation—Moray, Scotland: Founded in 1962 by Peter and Eileen Caddy and Dorothy Maclean, Findhorn was established in accordance with what the Caddys and Maclean believed to be inner divine guidance to engage in a lifestyle of following God's will in an environment that is harmonious with nature. In the early 1970s, DAVID SPANGLER lived in the community, teaching members to engage in a holistic spiritual lifestyle. The Findhorn Foundation exists to promote this vision of holistic life through individuals and businesses. Web site—http://www.findhorn.org. See NEW AGE.

Firewalking Institute of Research and Education, Tony Burkan—Twain Harte, CA: An institute begun in 1979 that uses walking over a bed of hot coals to help individuals and corporate groups overcome low self-esteem, depression, phobias, and psychosomatic disorders. Web site—http://www.firewalking.com. See HOLISTIC HEALTH.

First Demonic Church, Efrem Del Gatto—Italy: A small group practicing SATANISM.

First Presleyterian Church of Elvis the Divine—Bethlehem, PA: Begun in 1988 as a marketing ploy or parody by Farndu and Karl Edwards, the church spoofs traditional religions and cults by "worshipping" Elvis Presley in weekly services held on the Internet and, at one time, in the campus chapel of Lehigh University in Bethlehem, Pennsylvania. Web site—http://www.geocities.com/presleyterian_church.

First Temple of the Craft of W.I.C.A.—Berwyn, IL: Founded in 1972, the temple is one of the oldest legally recognized churches practicing WICCA.

First World Conclave of Light: A gathering in San Diego, California sponsored by the UNARIUS ACADEMY OF SCIENCE.

First Zen Institute of America—New York, NY: Promotes the Rinzai school of ZEN BUDDHISM. Publishes the *Zen Notes* newsletter. Web site—http://www.firstzen.org/index.html.

Fitch, Joseph: See SPIRITUAL FRONTIERS FELLOWSHIP.

Flag Service Organization—Clearwater, FL: A retreat center for members of the CHURCH OF SCIENTOLOGY. Web site—http://www.scientology-fso.org.

Flirty Fishing: Also known by the abbreviation FFing, this is the practice in THE FAMILY (CHILDREN OF GOD) of engaging in sexual encounters to attract converts and reinforce group life. The Family claims to have abandoned this practice, although former members allege that it continues within the group's inner circles.

Florida College of Natural Health: Part of the STEINER EDUCATION GROUP. In addition to offering more traditional massages such as sports and medical the group offers training in Eastern massage techniques, including: Shiatsu, REFLEXOLOGY, and AROMATHERAPY. See STEINER EDUCATION GROUP; HOLISTIC HEALING.

Flying Saucer Information Center, Laura Mundo—Pasadena, MD: Founded in 1954, the center functions as a clearinghouse for information about UFOs. The group believes aliens are benevolent and act to protect humans from atmospheric disturbances.

Followers of Christ Church, Walter T. White—Oregon City, OR: Legalistic sect that practices SHUNNING, holds to a strict faith-healing doctrine, and refuses to allow medical treatment for followers and their children. The state medical examiner has claimed that the death rate for children of members is 26 times higher than that of the general population. See LEGALISM; SHUNNING.

Ford, Arthur: See SPIRITUAL FRONTIERS FELLOWSHIP.

Forever Family: Former name for the CHURCH OF BIBLE UNDER-STANDING.

Form Criticism: An approach to biblical scholarship that studies the texts according to what is called their *prehistory:* the oral and written stages through which they allegedly passed until they were finalized in the versions canonized as Scripture. According to form critics, the biblical writers were not so much authors as they were collectors and editors of religious stories and beliefs; the forms in which the biblical narratives are recorded therefore reflect the *Sitz im Leben,* or social situation, in which they were written. When applied to the Gospels, for example, such form critics as Rudolph Bultmann (and, more recently, the members of the Jesus Seminar) maintain that the New Testament accounts about Jesus were influenced—and, in many cases, modified—by the social and theological concerns and perspectives of the early church. Bible scholars from within EVANGELICAL CHRISTIANITY and other conservative traditions generally reject the excesses of form criticism, asserting that while it is necessary to understand the historical situation in which a text was written, the biblical records are both historically and theologically accurate. See LITERARY CRITICISM.

Fortunetelling: An attempt to predict the future using alleged supernatural powers. See DIVINATION.

Fort Worth Bible Students—Fort Worth, TX: A splinter group of the WATCHTOWER BIBLE AND TRACT SOCIETY. Publishes *The Divine Plan Journal.* Web site—http://www.divineplan.org. See BIBLE STU-DENTS.

The Forum: See EST.

Foster, Richard: A QUAKER author, pastor, and lecturer. He has written on a wide array of Christian issues and practices, including prayer. Though he is a proponent of CENTERING/CONTEMPLATIVE PRAYER, he also recognizes it to be dangerous for the uninitiated. In his book *Prayer: Finding the Heart's True Home,* he writes, "I need to give a word of warning...[it] is not for the novice...we are not all equally ready to listen to 'God's speech in His wondrous, terrible, gentle, loving, all-embracing silence.'" He adds this further precaution: "In the silent contemplation of God we are entering deeply into the spiritual realm, and there is such a thing as supernatural guidance that is not divine guidance." Web site—http://www.renovare.org. See RELIGIOUS SOCIETY OF FRIENDS.

Foundation Church of Divine Truth, James E. Padgett—Washington, DC: From 1914–23, PSYCHIC James E. Padgett allegedly channeled messages from JESUS CHRIST and the 12 APOSTLES. These messages claimed that souls can escape REINCARNATION by coming into possession of God's divine essence. The purpose of existence is to achieve the "new birth of soul"—i.e., achieve union with God in His true nature. Central teachings are contained in *Angelic Revelations of Divine Truth, Volumes One and Two.* Web site—http://www.fcdt.org. See CHANNELING; FOUNDATION CHURCH OF THE NEW BIRTH; PANTHEISM.

Foundation Church of the Millennium: A splinter group of the PROCESS CHURCH OF THE FINAL JUDGMENT.

Foundation Church of the New Birth—Washington, D.C.: Accepts the channeled messages received by James E. Padgett. Central scripture is the four-volume *True Gospel Revealed Anew by Jesus.* Web site—http://www.divinelove.org. See FOUNDATION CHURCH OF DIVINE TRUTH; PANTHEISM.

Foundation Faith: Also called the Foundation Faith of God, this was another name for the FOUNDATION CHURCH OF THE MILLENNIUM. See PROCESS CHURCH OF THE FINAL JUDGMENT.

Foundation for Ancient Research and Mormon Studies (FARMS)— Provo, UT: An association of Latter-day Saint scholars at Brigham Young

University's Neal A. Maxwell Institute for Religious Scholarship. The organization's members serve as APOLOGISTS for the CHURCH OF JESUS CHRIST OF LATTER-DAY SAINTS; they defend LDS scripture and doctrines from critics. Web site—http://farms.byu.edu. See FOUNDATION FOR APOLOGETIC INFORMATION RESEARCH (FAIR); SCHOLARLY & HISTORICAL INFORMATION EXCHANGE FOR LATTER-DAY SAINTS (SHIELDS).

Foundation for Apologetic Information Research (FAIR)—Mesa, AZ: A nonprofit organization founded in 1997 and staffed by volunteer Latter-day Saint APOLOGISTS dedicated to providing reasoned answers to public criticisms of LDS doctrine, beliefs, and practices. Scott Gordon serves as president. Web site—http://www.fairlds.org. See FOUNDATION FOR ANCIENT RESEARCH AND MORMON STUDIES (FARMS); SCHOLARLY & HISTORICAL INFORMATION EXCHANGE FOR LATTER-DAY SAINTS (SHIELDS).

Foundation for Conscious Evolution, Barbara Marx Hubbard—Santa Barbara, CA: Hubbard began writing in the 1960s about the spiritual, social, and scientific evolution of humanity. Hubbard asserts that by raising the level of human consciousness, we can become co-creators with the Spirit of a deeper pattern of universal design. Web site—http://www.evolve.org. See NEW AGE.

Foundation for Higher Spiritual Learning—Moorestown, N.J.: The name of BRIDGE TO FREEDOM since 1979. The group follows the theosophical teachings of Guy Ballard. See I AM MOVEMENT.

Foundation for Human Understanding, Roy Masters (born Reuben Obermeister)—Grants Pass, OR: Masters was born in London and moved to South Africa at the age of 18 to apprentice in the diamond trade. While there he continued to develop his interest in HYPNOSIS. In 1949 he came to America, eventually settling in Houston, where he established the Institute for Hypnosis. During that time the American Medical Association pressed charges against him for practicing medicine without a license. Later he moved to Los Angeles and began a syndicated radio program, now known as *Advice Line,* in 1960. In 1963 he founded the Foundation for Human Understanding. Masters claims that his use of hypnosis is to show that it is dangerous. He teaches that there is a hypnotic influence in the world negatively affecting people (causing worries, fears, lack of confidence, etc.) and that people must learn to "dehypnotize" themselves. This is done through Masters' meditation exercise Be Still and Know. Though born to a Jewish family, Masters professes to be a Christian and maintains that his teachings are in line with the BIBLE. Acknowledging that many label him as NEW AGE, he has taken strides to try and address this as incorrect on his Web site and through an open letter to churches, written in 1992. Web site—http://www.fhu.com.

Foundation for Inner Peace: See *A COURSE IN MIRACLES.*

Foundation for Shamanic Studies, Michael Harner—Norwalk, CT: Harner established the foundation in 1985 to study and transmit knowledge about SHAMANISM. Harner claims to have been initiated in Upper Amazonian shamanism, and promotes shamanic practices as a means of healing. Web site—http://www.shamanism.org. See NATIVE AMERICAN SPIRITU-ALITY.

Foundation for the Future, Peter Bloch—Silver Spring, MD: A NEW AGE organization, started in 1987, that teaches "power MEDITATION" and other techniques for maximizing human potential.

Foundation of Revelation, Siva Kalpa—San Francisco, CA: Founded in 1969, the foundation teaches that all things can be reintegrated through the power of YOGA. See NEW AGE; PANTHEISM.

Foursquare Church: See PENTECOSTAL MOVEMENT.

Fourth Way, George I. Gurdjieff and Peter D. Ouspensky: Gurdjieff (1866–1949) taught that human life is spent in a "waking sleep" in which humans automatically respond to external stimuli. This sleep can be transcended only through extensive inner work, which is done both privately and in the presence of a group being taught by a spiritual teacher. Human potential is based on developing consciousness, conscience, and sensation. Gurdjieff's most famous pupil was P.D. Ouspensky (1848–1947), who expanded upon Gurdjieff's system and taught that inner work consists of self-observation, self-remembering, external consideration, verification, and valuation.

Fox, Kate: See SPIRITUALISM.

Fox, Margarett: See SPIRITUALISM.

Fox, Matthew: A former Dominican priest who was silenced by the Vatican and later defrocked by the Dominican order (he was subsequently received as a priest by the Episcopal Church USA) for his integration of CHRISTIANITY and other religions to awaken the world to the interconnectedness of all things. Fox advocates using such techniques as YOGA and MEDITATION, as well as artistic endeavors, to experience the blessings of PANENTHEISM. Fox's works include *Original Blessing, Creativity,* and *The Reinvention of Work.* Fox is the driving force behind the University of Creation Spirituality. Web site—http://www.matthewfox.org/sys-tmpl/door. See NEW AGE.

Fraternity of the Hidden Light (Fraternitis L.V.X. Occulta)—Castle Rock, CO: The fraternity is an ESOTERIC order that trains initiates in the OCCULT. The fraternity emphasizes studies in the KABBALAH and ASTROLOGY. Web site—http://www.lvx.org.

Free Bible Students: A splinter group from the WATCHTOWER BIBLE AND TRACT SOCIETY. A small organization currently consisting of approximately four congregations and 27 home groups, the group appears to be separate from the larger group of BIBLE STUDENTS. Christian Millennial Fellowship, a Free Bible Student congregation in St. Charles, Illinois, operates a Web site at http://www.cmfellowship.org.

Freeman, Bill and Patsy: Former members of The LOCAL CHURCH movement. They left in 1986 and formed their own meetings first in Scottsdale, Arizona and then in Spokane, Washington. Controversy has followed the couple, with some former members of their small flocks charging them with LEGALISM and SPIRITUAL ABUSE. In 2004, 27 elders of The Local Church wrote an open letter to the Freemans, issuing "a word of strong concern, especially with regard of the practices of interfering with others' marriages...."

Freemasonry: A fraternal order revived in the early eighteenth-century in England loosely based on associations or guilds of stone cutters ("operative" masons). Freemasonry ("speculative" masons) sought to give philosophical, moral, or spiritual meaning to the lodge, tools, and oaths of the stonecutters. Branches of Freemasonry include the Blue Lodge, York Rite, Scottish Rite, and Shriners. Affiliated organizations include the Order of the Eastern Star (for women), the Order of DeMolay (for boys), and Order of Rainbow (for girls). Most modern adherents maintain that the organization is not a religion but a club or fraternity promoting high moral values and good works. They believe, therefore, Freemasonry is compatible with and supplements CHRISTIANITY and other religions. Critics counter that Freemasonry involves secret blood oaths or curses and that the writings of respected early leaders (ALBERT MACKEY, Albert Pike, etc.) are replete with OCCULT philosophy and religious doctrine contrary to Christianity. Despite Freemasonry's promotion and funding of a number of worthwhile philanthropic endeavors (free Shriner children's hospitals, nursing homes, etc.), many Christian individuals and churches have condemned Freemasonry or warned of elements that they believe are contrary to Christianity. These churches include the PRESBYTERIAN CHURCH IN AMERICA, the SOUTHERN BAPTIST CONVENTION, the Episcopal Church, the Christian Reformed Church, the CHURCH OF THE NAZARENE, and the Lutheran Church (Missouri and Wisconsin Synods).

Free Methodist Church: A denomination of PROTESTANTISM with roots in METHODISM founded in 1860 by Benjamin T. Roberts and other former members of the Methodist Episcopal Church. In 2005, there were 1,000 congregations with 76,000 members in the United States and 729,500 members worldwide. Web site—http://www.ame-church.com.

Free Soul, Pete A. Sanders—Sedona, AZ: A NEW AGE organization that trains individuals to engage in PSYCHIC perception and mind/body healing. Sanders holds his seminars in Sedona because the area allegedly contains spiritual vortexes that will facilitate MEDITATION and spiritual growth. Web site—http://www.freesoul.net.

Free Will Baptists: Churches that, unlike most Baptist churches, teach that believers can, by an act of their free will, repudiate their faith in Christ and thus lose their eternal life or salvation. Early leaders include Paul Palmer, who helped launch the movement in the southern United States by organizing the first church in 1727 in North Carolina and Benjamin Randall (1749–1808), who helped launch the work in the north by organizing a church in New Hampshire in 1780. Both men rejected some of the key doctrines of the Regular Baptists (aka Particular Baptists), who have followed the Reformed theology of PRESBYTERIANISM and John Calvin—doctrines such as eternal security and limited atonement. The largest body of Free Will Baptists is the NATIONAL ASSOCIATION OF FREE WILL BAPTISTS. See BAPTIST CHURCHES.

Freewinds Relay Office—Clearwater, FL: Supports the CHURCH OF SCIENTOLOGY Flag Ship Service Organization.

Friends General Conference: See RELIGIOUS SOCIETY OF FRIENDS.

Friends United Meeting: See RELIGIOUS SOCIETY OF FRIENDS.

Full Gospel Interdenominational Church, Inc., Philip P. Saunders (1931–98)—Manchester, CT: Teaches SALVATION BY WORKS and denies the TRINITY, teaching a form of MODALISM. A number of former members have alleged extreme SHEPHERDING. Worldwide Lighthouse Missions, Inc. serves as the international missions outreach for the church, which is now pastored by Eleanor M. Kalinsky. The church has been in existence for about 30 years and hosts an annual pastor's conference. Web site—http://www.fgichurch.org.

Fundamental Church of Jesus Christ of Latter-day Saints (FLDS), John Barlow and Joseph Musser—Colorado City, AZ and Hildale, UT: Begun in 1935 as a fundamentalist Mormon splinter group that broke away from the CHURCH OF JESUS CHRIST OF LATTER-DAY SAINTS (LDS) over the doctrine of polygamy, which had been officially discontinued by the LDS in the 1890s. The FLDS believed the LDS leadership was in APOSTASY and formed their own church that continued to practice polygamy (known as "the Principle") in their community on the border of Utah and Arizona. In 1953, Arizona state authorities conducted a raid on the community (at that time called Short Creek) and arrested hundreds of polygamists on charges of bigamy. In 1986, Rulon Jeffs became the prophet and leader of the FLDS. At the time of his death in 2002, Rulon Jeffs was reported to have 75 wives and more than 60 children. His son Warren Jeffs became the leader of the movement. In 2006 he was a fugitive featured on the FBI's 10 Most Wanted list for alleged sexual assault on a minor. For further research, a four-page Watchman Fellowship Profile is available (see page 363). Web site—http://www.watchman.org/notebook.

Fundamentalist Christianity: Generally a reference to conservative Christians who believe five fundamentals of the faith: the inerrancy of Scripture, the VIRGIN BIRTH of Christ, the substitutionary atonement of Christ, the bodily resurrection of Christ, and the historicity of biblical miracles. More specifically the term is identified with the conservative reaction to LIBERAL CHRISTIANITY in the early twentieth-century. Core beliefs of the movement are virtually identical with EVANGELICAL CHRISTIANITY. Some fundamentalists, however, later distinguished themselves from evangelicals (or neo-evangelicals) whom they saw as too compromising and ecumenical. More recently some have given a negative meaning to the term *fundamentalist,* using it as a synonym for narrow-minded, bigoted, anti-intellectual, or divisive Christians.

G

Gaia: In Greek mythology, Gaia was the earth, who either was the daughter of Chaos or came into being after it. In NEW AGE thought, Gaia is the name for the single organism that is the earth and all life on it. Since all life is part of Gaia, Gaia is to be particularly cherished, and even worshipped. See PANENTHEISM; PANTHEISM.

Gandhi Memorial Center, Swami Premananda—Washington, DC: Founded in 1959 by Premananda, the center educates people about the life and thought of Mahatma Gandhi. The center further promotes the traditional doctrine of HINDUISM of the oneness of life. Publishes *The Gandhi Message*. Web site—http://www.gandhimc.org. See PANTHEISM.

The Garbage Eaters: See BRETHREN, THE.

Garner Ted Armstrong Evangelistic Association—Tyler, TX: Formed in 1996 by Garner Ted Armstrong after he was removed from the leadership of the CHURCH OF GOD, INTERNATIONAL due to sexual improprieties. Armstrong's son, Mark, assumed leadership of the association following Armstrong's death in 2003. Web site—http://www.garnertedarmstrong.ws. See ARMSTRONG, GARNER TED; ARMSTRONGISM.

Gatekeepers, Christopher James Turgeon—Pala, CA: The Gatekeepers were a small CULT formerly called Ahabah Sasah Prophetic Ministries in Everett, Washington. The cult's leader, Turgeon, once claimed to be the prophet Elijah, and allegedly claimed that another member was an incarnation of Moses. In 1998, a police SWAT team served a warrant on the group's five-acre compound located 60 miles north of San Diego and recovered weapons and other stolen property. Later that year, Turgeon and another member (Blaine Alan Applin) murdered former member Daniel Jess. In 2001 Turgeon was sentenced to 50 years in prison, and Applin was sentenced to 39 years.

Gateways Institute, Jonathan Parker—Ojai, CA: A NEW AGE teacher whose subliminal audiotapes promise to cure listeners from smoking and stress and promote wealth and other benefits. According to the now-defunct *Ambassador Report* (which worked to expose ARMSTRONGISM), Parker is in fact Jack Packozdi, a former minister under HERBERT W. ARMSTRONG.

Gawain, Shakti: A popular NEW AGE author and speaker who teaches creative VISUALIZATION, a process of MEDITATION and visualization in which followers use mental IMAGERY and verbal affirmations to unleash the power of their imaginations and create the fulfillment of their desires. Gawain's books include *Creative Visualization, Living in the Light,* and *The Path of Transformation.* Web site—http://www.shaktigawain.com.

Geisler, Norman L.: An influential philosopher and APOLOGIST who defends EVANGELICAL CHRISTIANITY. Geisler earned a PhD in philosophy at Loyola University in Chicago and has authored or coauthored over 60 books and hundreds of articles. He is cofounder and dean at Southern Evangelical Seminary in Charlotte, North Carolina. Web site—http://www.normgeisler.com.

Geller, Uri: A PSYCHIC who is famous for practicing ESP, DOWSING, and, particularly on television, for bending spoons using mindpower. Geller's activities were debunked by JAMES RANDI in Randi's book *The Truth About Uri Geller.* Web site—http://www.uri-geller.com.

General Association of Regular Baptist Churches (GARBC)—Schaumburg, IL: A network of independent BAPTIST CHURCHES that formed in 1932 as an alliance of more conservative and fundamentalist churches that had broken away from the Northern Baptist Convention (now called AMERICAN BAPTIST CONVENTION IN THE USA). As of 1995, the GARBC included over 1,500 churches with about 150,000 members. Web site—http://www.garbc.org.

Geotran: See CIRCLES OF LIFE.

Germain, Saint: See SAINT GERMAIN.

Ghosts: Nonphysical entities or spirit beings, often believed to be the spirits of the dead. See SPIRITUALISM; DEMON; NECROMANCY; OCCULT.

Ghost Whisperer: A popular CBS television drama staring Jennifer Love Hewitt that promotes PSYCHIC manifestation and NECROMANCY. The series was inspired by JAMES VAN PRAAGH, a famous MEDIUM, and Mary Ann Winkowski, who claims to be able to communicate with spirits. Web site—http://www.cbs.com/primetime/ghost_whisperer. See VAN PRAAGH, JAMES; PSYCHIC; OCCULT.

Global Church of God—San Diego, CA: A now-defunct group that followed the teachings of HERBERT W. ARMSTRONG. When the church's leaders and its followers split in 1998 into several different groups, the majority formed the LIVING CHURCH OF GOD. See ARMSTRONGISM.

Global Times: The bimonthly magazine published by the Denmark office for Proutist International. See PROUT.

Globalism: When used in a religious sense, this term most often means to lose all national identity. Mankind must see itself as one world family without the need for distinctions between religions. From this "global" perspective, all religions become true, or the distinctive doctrines of the various religions must be disregarded in an attempt to achieve the new "Global Family" ideal. Globalism is the goal of many NEW AGE systems, but is feared by some Christians who believe that it is the Antichrist who will initiate a global political and religious system.

Glossolalia: From the Greek terms *glossa* ("tongue") and *lalo* ("to speak"), or the ability to "speak in tongues"—that is, to speak in or understand a foreign language without formal training (Acts 2:4-11). In addition, some interpret 1 Corinthians 13:1-3 as referring to a spiritual gift of being able to speak in an unknown, heavenly language used by ANGELS. Glossolalia was an important emphasis of the PENTECOSTAL MOVEMENT that developed in the early twentieth-century and in the CHARISMATIC

MOVEMENT that began in the 1960s. Glossolalia remains an important distinctive of Pentecostal denominations such as the ASSEMBLIES OF GOD and the CHURCH OF GOD (CLEVELAND). A form of glossolalia is also practiced by a number of heretical groups such as the WAY INTERNATIONAL, the UNITED PENTECOSTAL CHURCH, and other variations of ONENESS PENTECOSTALISM.

Gnostic Catholic Church: Also called the Ecclesia Gnostica Catholica, an ecclesiastical aspect of the ORDO TEMPLI ORIENTIS. The group, which was founded in 1907, received its name from ALEISTER CROWLEY.

Gnostic Gospels: A collection of ancient documents dating from the second to the fourth centuries that promoted GNOSTICISM, a rival to ORTHODOX CHRISTIANITY. The majority of the gnostic texts were discovered in 1945 near Nag Hammadi, Egypt, in leather-bound codices (books) written in Coptic (Egyptian) on papyrus. There were 52 texts in all, including the *GOSPEL OF THOMAS,* the *GOSPEL OF PHILLIP,* the *APOCRYPHON OF JOHN,* and the *SOPHIA OF JESUS CHRIST.* A few GNOSTIC texts had been previously discovered at other locations, including the *GOSPEL OF MARY MAGDALENE* and the *GOSPEL OF JUDAS.* Considered APOCRYPHAL, these gnostic writings were never accepted into the New Testament canon as part of the BIBLE for several reasons. Because of their late date (second to fourth centuries), they could not have been written by eyewitnesses of Jesus, or the APOSTLES, or the direct disciples of the apostles. (All 27 books of the New Testament were known to have been written during the first century.) In addition, many of the gnostic gospels contain teachings that contradict the Old Testament, which had already been accepted as Scripture and validated by JESUS. Much of the gnostic writings also contradict accepted New Testament teachings by denying the full humanity and physical death of JESUS Christ on the cross. See GNOSTICISM; BIBLE.

Gnosticism: From the Greek word *gnosis* ("knowledge"), gnostic belief systems maintain that salvation comes through receiving secret, ESOTERIC knowledge. Ancient gnosticism was one of the earliest HERESIES that challenged CHRISTIANITY. While refutations to early forms of first-century gnosticism can be found in the New Testament, gnosticism fully developed as a system and flourished during the second, third, and fourth centuries. Gnosticism was a diverse system of beliefs influenced by Greek philosophy. Gnostic DUALISM held that matter was inherently evil and spirit was good. Thus, the supreme God, which is spirit and good, could not have created the physical universe, which by nature must be evil. Gnostics taught that the ANGELS or some lesser, evil deity known as the demiurge must have created the physical world. In addition, because of their belief that matter was evil, many gnostics taught that JESUS was God but not human. According to them, CHRIST did not come in the flesh (which is refuted in 1 John 1:1; 4:3; 2 John 1:7) because flesh is matter that is evil. Thus, Christ only *appeared* to be human but was really only spirit (DOCETISM). From the late second century through the fourth, gnostics wrote their own scriptures, called GNOSTIC GOSPELS, to compete with the New Testament documents. Most modern-day groups that claim to be gnostic orders also engage in NEW AGE and OCCULT spirituality and practices.

The Gnostic Order of Christ, Timothy Harris—San Jose, CA: An ESOTERIC and mystical order that is reviving the doctrines of the now-defunct HOLY ORDER OF MANS. Web site—http://www.gnosticorderofchrist. net.

God: In general, a religious term to describe a supreme being. In traditional Christian faith, a reference to the holy and eternal Creator of all things, who is the only true deity and eternally exists in three persons: Father, Son, and HOLY SPIRIT. See TRINITY; MONOTHEISM.

Goddess: In its most basic sense, such as in primitive PAGANISM, a goddess is a female deity figure. In popular NEW AGE thought, the goddess is the divine itself (in whatever sense the devotee defines *divine*), which can include the "divine spark" of the "goddess within" (as is commonly taught in New Age PANENTHEISM). Some teachers of RADICAL FEMINISM further teach that the concept of a goddess can be used to counter the oppressive patriarchies of the monotheistic religions. For further research, a four-page Watchman Fellowship Profile is available (see page 363). Web site—http://www.watchman.org/notebook.

God Saves the Earth Flying Saucer Foundation: See CHEN TAO.

God's Eternal Universal Religion, Bhagavan Sri Babajhan-Al-Kahlil— Redondo Beach, CA: A NEW AGE group that teaches all things are God. The Bhagavan (formerly John Lee Douglas) claims to be God's Awakened

One, who has been ordained to end spiritual ignorance and lead Earth to the Age of Divine Pure Truth. While the group uses such Eastern practices and concepts as YOGA and dharma, they deny any direct connection with HINDUISM or any other Eastern religion. Web site—http://www. thefriendsway.com. See PANTHEISM.

God's Salvation Church: See CHEN TAO.

Golden Dawn: aka Hermetic Order of the Golden Dawn. This influential form of Western occultism was founded by William Woodman, Samuel Liddell (aka MacGregor Mathers), and William Westcott, who was also involved with the THEOSOPHICAL SOCIETY. The first lodge, the Isis-Urania Temple, was founded in London in 1888, allegedly based on the teachings of an encrypted document called the *Cipher Manuscripts.* Golden Dawn appears to systematize and harmonize teachings and practices from a wide variety of OCCULT traditions, including elements of FREEMASONRY, ROSICRUCIANISM, ALCHEMY, KABBALAH, ASTROLOGY, and TAROT reading. Perhaps the most famous and influential early member was ALEISTER CROWLEY, who was initiated into THE ORDO TEMPLI ORIENTIS (OTO) in 1910. Another prominent early member was A.E. Waite, best known as a scholar of occult lore and as the designer of the Rider-Waite TAROT deck. Golden Dawn was an important influence on other forms of Western-style occultism and the tradition is continued by many groups today, including the HERMETIC ORDER OF THE GOLDEN DAWN, the THELEMIC ORDER OF THE GOLDEN DAWN, and the ABBEY OF THELEMA. See OCCULT; CROWLEY, ALEISTER; HERMETICISM.

Golden Quest, Hilda Charlton—Lake Hill, NY: Golden Quest is the publisher of the late Hilda Charlton's (d. 1988) books. Charlton taught that a synthesis of world religions, particularly HINDUISM and CHRISTIANITY, led to self-mastery and world peace. Web site—http://www. hildacharlton.com.

Goldstein, Joseph: Became interested in BUDDHISM as a Peace Corp volunteer in Thailand in 1965. He has followed the teachings and practices of Buddhism since 1967 and has been leading MEDITATION retreats since 1974. Cofounder of INSIGHT MEDITATION SOCIETY.

Good Cheer Press—Boulder, CO: A defunct publishing arm of the JESU-SONIAN FOUNDATION. See *THE URANTIA BOOK.*

Good, Joseph: See HATIKVA MINISTRIES.

Gospel: From the Greek term *euangelion* ("good news"), the word *gospel* is used by traditional Christians as a reference to the death, burial, and resurrection of JESUS CHRIST for salvation to those who believe (1 Corinthians 15:1-4). *Gospel* also is used to refer to the four New Testament books containing the life story of Jesus (Matthew, Mark, Luke, and John). In Christian APOLOGETICS the term is also used in contrast with "other gospels," which are false salvation messages that are ultimately "bad news" (2 Corinthians 11:4; Galatians 1:6-9). See JESUS; CHRISTIANITY; BORN AGAIN; SALVATION BY GRACE; SALVATION BY WORKS; CULT.

Gospel of Judas: One of the few GNOSTIC GOSPELS that was not part of the Nag Hammadi collection discovered in 1945. The text was part of the Codex Tchacos discovered in the 1970s at El Minya, Egypt. Considered to be an example of New Testament APOCRYPHA, the book presents Judas Iscariot as the favorite disciple of JESUS and the only one who really understood His message. Rather than the betrayer of CHRIST portrayed in the canonical Gospels (Matthew, Mark, Luke, and John) of the BIBLE, Judas is cast as the hero whom Christ trusted with His secret teachings. In 2006, National Geographic presented a *Gospel of Judas* television special and a corresponding cover story in their magazine. The only extant text of this gospel is a Coptic manuscript believed to date somewhere between the third and fourth centuries. Textural analysis suggests that it may be based on an early Greek original—possibly as old as A.D. 130–180. Nevertheless, its late date would rule out authorship by Judas Iscariot or any other first-century writer.

Gospel of Mary Magdalene: A GNOSTIC GOSPEL discovered in Cairo, Egypt, in 1896. Older fragments of the gospel can be dated as early as the third century A.D. The text, considered to be an example of New Testament APOCRYPHA, seems to place Mary as the head of the disciples after Christ's resurrection. Although it is popularly linked to Mary Magdalene, some 10 pages are missing from the only known copy of the gospel and the name *Magdalene* is not found anywhere in the manuscript. The late date (third century A.D.) would rule out authorship by Magdalene or any other first-century writer.

Gospel of Phillip: One of the GNOSTIC GOSPELS discovered in Nag Hammadi, Egypt, in 1945. The text contains a collection of sayings attributed to JESUS CHRIST. The text is in Coptic (although the original may have been written in Syriac or Greek). Scholars date the text to the second half of the third century A.D. and it is considered to be an example of New Testament APOCRYPHA.

Gospel of Thomas: Part of a collection of writings known as the GNOSTIC GOSPELS. The document is a compilation of some 114 sayings or proverbs attributed to JESUS CHRIST. Portions of the Gospel were originally rediscovered in Oxyrhynchus, Egypt, in 1898. A complete manuscript was also included with the gnostic writings recovered in Nag Hammadi, Egypt, in 1945. While scholars have debated the earliest possible date of the gospel, there are undoubtedly contradictions between it and the four canonical gospels (Matthew, Mark, Luke, and John) of the BIBLE. One example is its apparent attack on women: "Simon Peter said to them, 'Make Mary leave us, for females don't deserve life.' Jesus said, 'Look, I will guide her to make her male, so that she too may become a living spirit resembling you males. For every female who makes herself male will enter the kingdom of Heaven'" (114).

Gothard, Bill (b. 1934)—Oak Brook, IL: A popular FUNDAMENTALIST CHRISTIAN teacher, best known for his teachings on practical Christian living. Most popular in the 1970s and 1980s, Gothard retains a strong worldwide following. Gothard's strict teachings about such issues as diet, birth control, dating, dress, and entertainment are seen by many critics as LEGALISM; his teachings on DEMONS, particularly on demonic strongholds, may be influenced by the DELIVERANCE MINISTRIES movement; in recent years, Gothard has taught a practice called "crying out," a form of POSITIVE CONFESSION. Gothard heads several interrelated ministries: the Institute in Basic Life Principles (IBLP), formerly the Institute in Basic Youth Conflicts (IBYC), which promotes Gothard's basic and advanced seminars; the Advanced Training Institute International (ATII), Gothard's home education organization; and numerous community service-oriented ministries, including programs for juvenile delinquents, prison ministries, and the Air Land Emergency Response Teams (ALERT), a young men's organization that undertakes disaster relief and other humanitarian projects. Web sites—Gothard's personal Web site is at http://www.billgothard.com; IBLP's Web site is at http://iblp.org; ATII's Web site is at http://ati.iblp.org; and the ALERT Web site is at http://www.alertacademy.com.

Grabowski, Laura: A pen name of Laurel Rose Willson (aka Lauren Stratford). See STRATFORD, LAUREN.

Graham, Billy: Popular BAPTIST evangelist who promotes EVANGELICAL CHRISTIANITY through large evangelistic festivals throughout the United States and internationally. See BILLY GRAHAM EVANGELISTIC ASSOCIATION.

Grail Foundation, Abd-ru-shin—Stuttgart, Germany: The foundation exists to promote the teachings of Abd-ru-shin (born Oskar Ernst Bernhardt, 1875–1941), who wrote in *The Grail Message* that there are three Laws of Creation: the Law of Reciprocal Action, the Law of the Attraction of Homogeneous Species, and the Law of Gravitation. The Grail Castle, which exists above creation and is the "temple of God" referred to in the BIBLE, is the source of divine power and peace. Web site—http://www.grailmessage.com.

Grand Canyon Society—Scottsdale, AZ: The Arizona chapter of the URANTIA BOOK FELLOWSHIP. See *THE URANTIA BOOK.*

Greater Grace World Outreach, Carl H. Stevens, Jr.—Baltimore, MD: Formerly The Bible Speaks, which declared bankruptcy in 1987 after being ordered by a court to return the $6.6 million in donations from Besty DovyDenas, which she testified were made as a result of BRAINWASHING. Critics accuse Stevens of claiming that he has a special relationship with CHRIST, and allege that he is authoritarian and abusive. Many relatives of church members claim their loved ones rejected them after joining the church. Greater Grace operates Maryland Bible College and Seminary. Produces *The Grace Hour* radio program. Web site—http://www.ggwo.org. See SHEPHERDING; SPIRITUAL ABUSE.

Great Invocation: A NEW AGE prayer written by ALICE BAILEY in 1937 and circulated by various New Age groups that believe widespread recitation may help initiate a new utopia on earth. See ARCANE SCHOOL.

Great Lakes Society for Biblical Research, John Cheetham: Follows the teachings of HERBERT W. ARMSTRONG. See ARMSTRONGISM.

Great Tomorrow, Nick Bunick—Lake Oswego, OR: Bunick claims that through HYPNOSIS and PAST LIFE REGRESSION, he discovered that in a previous life he was the apostle Paul. He now speaks at Spiritual Symposiums in which he teaches his audience to contact ANGELS, particularly by using the metaphysical power of the number four. Bunick was the focus of the bestselling book *The Messengers* and is the author of *In God's Truth.* See REINCARNATION.

Great White Brotherhood: A group of ASCENDED MASTERS who, similar to the concept of the Bodhisattva in BUDDHISM, do not enter fully into the highest spiritual planes, but instead remain in contact with humanity to facilitate the spiritual progression of humans. See NEW AGE; OCCULT; THEOSOPHY.

Greek Orthodox Church: ORTHODOX CHURCHes that recognize the spiritual preeminence of the Ecumenical Patriarch of the Orthodox Church of Constantinople (Istanbul, Turkey). The Greek Orthodox Archdiocese of America consists of about 1.5 million members in 540 parishes. Web site—http://www.goarch.org. See ORTHODOX CHURCH.

Group for Creative Meditation: See MEDITATION GROUP FOR NEW AGE.

Grove of the Unicorn, Galadriel—Atlanta, GA: A NEO-PAGAN group that celebrates solar and new moon festivals and engages in GODDESS worship. There are seven groups in the Unicorn tradition. Web site—http://www.unicorntrad.org.

Guardian Action International—Deming, NM: Now defunct, numerous copies of Guardian Action publications are available from online booksellers. The group published channelled messages from the Ashtar Command (a group of beings on flying saucers that surrounded the Earth). Some of these publications, such as *Ashtar Command,* warned that the Earth was in immediate danger. See UFOs.

Guided Imagery (aka Directed Fantasy, Mini Vacation): A controversial practice used in many schools and other institutions in which the student or subject is instructed to relax deeply (without falling asleep) while the facilitator takes the subject on an imaginary journey in which calming, restful scenery and events are described. In some cases, these stories include encounters with SPIRIT GUIDEs in the form of animals or supposedly wise friends who communicate important information along the journey. Critics have cautioned that the techniques used in guided imagery are the same as the well-known induction techniques in HYPNOSIS that can produce ALTERED STATES OF CONSCIOUSNESS. In many cases, the stories also contain NEW AGE concepts. See VISUALIZATION.

Guideposts: An inspirational magazine created by the late NORMAN VINCENT PEALE. Web site—http://www.guideposts.org.

Gurdjieff, George I.: See FOURTH WAY.

Guru: A religious teacher in Eastern religious systems (particularly HINDUISM) who gives personal guidance toward enlightenment. In some groups gurus are the focus of devotion and worship.

Guru Dev: The swami (religious master) who was the teacher of Maharishi Mahesh Yogi, founder of TRANSCENDENTAL MEDITATION. See HINDUISM.

H

H2B Company—San Francisco, CA: Short for Healthware 2 Bodycare, H2B manufactures pillows, wrist rests, and sleep masks based on the principles of HOLISTIC HEALTH. Apparently defunct.

Hagin, Kenneth (1917–2003): Recognized by many in the WORD-FAITH MOVEMENT as one of its founders, he was widely known as Dad Hagin. He founded the Rhema Bible Church and the Rhema Bible Training Center, which has trained many Word-Faith pastors/preachers serving in Word-Faith churches throughout the world. He was succeeded by his son, Kenneth Hagin, Jr. Web site—http://www.rhema.org. See WORD-FAITH MOVEMENT.

Halloween: Originally SAMHAIN (pronounced *sow-en*), the celebration on November 1 by the pre-Christian CELTS of the new year. It was believed by the Celtic DRUIDS that the dead would cause panic and destruction among the living unless appeased with an offering (the basis for the modern-day practice of trick or treat). In 835 Pope Gregory IV extended the November 1 Christian observance of the memory of All Saint's (or All Hallowed) to all the Western church, including the traditional Celtic lands of Ireland and Scotland. The observance of the eve of All Hallowed—Halloween—gradually replaced the observance of Samhain. Some practitioners of WITCHCRAFT and NEO-PAGANISM observe a modern derivative of Samhain as a religious observance. See OCCULT. For further research, a four-page Watchman Fellowship Profile is available (see page 363). Web site—http://www.watchman.org/notebook.

Halpern, Steven: A prominent NEW AGE music composer and lecturer. Written works include *Sound Health.* Web site—http://www.stevenhalpern. com.

Hanegraaff, Hendrik "Hank": see CHRISTIAN RESEARCH INSTITUTE (CRI).

Hare Krishna: The opening words to a MANTRA devoted to the Hindu Lord KRISHNA, the phrase is a popular nickname for the INTERNATIONAL SOCIETY FOR KRISHNA CONSCIOUSNESS. See HINDUISM.

Harmonic Convergence: A NEW AGE social, environmental, and personal transformational event formulated by Jose Arguelles based on alleged Mayan prophecies and astrological conjecture. Arguelles promoted a gathering of NEW AGE believers on August 16-17, 1987 at the earth's vortexes (psychic power centers) for MEDITATION and chanting to theoretically usher in a cosmic transformation. Another significant date was December 31, 1987, with a culmination in 2012.

Harr, Brian—Rochester, NY: In the late 1980s, Harr claimed to be the REINCARNATION of JESUS CHRIST. He further claimed that the government allegedly suppressed his identity and had arranged for a coming APOCALYPSE as a result of his existence.

Harris, Timothy: See GNOSTIC ORDER OF CHRIST.

Harvest Christian Fellowship, Greg Laurie—Riverside, CA: See CALVARY CHAPEL.

Hatha Yoga: Translated "Forceful Yoga," Hatha is a YOGA tradition in which posture and breathing are used to access and bring forth the KUNDALINI energy.

Hatikva Ministries, Joseph Good—Nederland, TX: A non-Trinitarian Messianic Jewish organization. Produces *The Promise of the Father* television program. Web site—http://www.hatikva.org.

Haven Ministries, Bill and Terri Honsberger—Centennial, CO: A Christian APOLOGETICS ministry that defends the beliefs of EVANGELICAL CHRISTIANITY and reaches out to followers of NEW AGE spirituality, CULTS, the OCCULT, and non-Christian religions. The organization is a member of EVANGELICAL MINISTRIES TO NEW RELIGIONS (EMNR). Web site—http://www.havenministry.com.

Hawkwind Earth Renewal Cooperative, Charla Hermann and John Tarwater—Valley Head, AL: A 100-acre HOLISTIC HEALTH center that teaches NATIVE AMERICAN SPIRITUALITY. Supported in part by Hermann and Tarwater's Red Queen Body Art tattoo parlor in Chattanooga, Tennessee. Web site—http://xnau.com/rq/hawkwind/hawkwind.html.

Hay House Publishers—Carlsbad, CA: Founded in 1984 by LOUISE L. HAY to self-publish her first two books, Hay House is one of the leading publishers in personal development. Web site—http://www.hayhouse.com. See NEW AGE.

Hay, Louise L.: A popular NEW AGE author and counselor. In the 1970s Hay studied psychosomatic medicine, allegedly putting her findings into practice by healing herself from cancer over a six-month period through positive affirmations and VISUALIZATION. Her works include *Heal Your Body* and *You Can Heal Your Life*. See HAY HOUSE PUBLISHERS.

Health and Wealth Gospel: See WORD-FAITH MOVEMENT.

Healthy, Happy, and Holy, Yogi Bhagan—Espanola, CA: Commonly abbreviated as 3HO, the group uses KUNDALINI YOGA to enable a person to improve physical health and achieve enlightenment. 3HO operates the large Sikhnet Web site. Web site for 3HO—http://www.3ho.org. Web site for Sikhnet—http://www.sikhnet.org. Web site for Yogi Bhajan—http://www.yogibhajan.com. See SIKHISM.

Heart Consciousness Church—Middletown, CA: A NEW AGE church that promotes HINDUISM, New Age spirituality, and NEO-PAGANISM. The church includes the New Age Church of Being. Operates the 1600-acre Harbin Hot Springs and publishes the *Harbin Quarterly Catalog*. Web site—http://www.harbin.org.

Heaven's Gate, Marshall Herff Applewhite and Bonnie Lou Nettles— Rancho Santa Fe, CA: A defunct NEW AGE group that focused on the existence of UFOs. Applewhite (aka Do) and 38 other members committed suicide on March 27, 1997, believing that by leaving their bodies behind they could join the previously deceased Nettles (aka Ti) and other "older members" from "the next level above human" on a UFO allegedly hidden behind the Hale-Bopp comet. The primary text of the group was *How and When Heaven's Gate May Be Entered*. The University of Virginia hosts an archived copy of the Heaven's Gate Web site at http://religiousmovements. lib.virginia.edu/nrms/heavensgate_mirror/index.html. For further research, a four-page Watchman Fellowship Profile is available (see page 363). Web site—http://www.watchman.org/notebook.

Heaven's Magic: Another name for the followers of David Berg, Heaven's Magic produces multicolor children's posters and music. See THE FAMILY (CHILDREN OF GOD).

Hebrew Roots Movement: A great many groups fall in to this general category. The most aberrant deny the doctrine of the TRINITY, reject the deity of CHRIST, and generally view the New Testament as unreliable. Followers are encouraged to rely on Jewish literature (i.e., MISHNAH, MIDRASH, TALMUD, etc.) to understand the New Testament and restore the Hebrew roots of CHRISTIANITY. Some also teach various forms of DUAL COVENANT theology, in which Jews find salvation in the covenant of the Mosaic Law while the Gentiles' covenant consists of observing the Seven Laws of Noah. See B'NEI NOACH.

HERESY: In its most basic meaning, a HERESY is a belief or practice that is contrary to a generally accepted belief or practice. In a more specific religious context, a HERESY is a deviation from the established dogma of a religious group or tradition. In Christian theology, a HERESY is a deliberate denial of revealed truth. Christians traditionally define heresies according to the formula in 2 Peter 2:1: erroneous beliefs (particularly about JESUS CHRIST), taught by false teachers, which are destructive to the Christian faith. Heresies are understood to exclude believers from the revealed truth of CHRISTIANITY, and therefore from salvation. See CULT; GOSPEL.

Heretic: A person who causes a division within a religious group by teaching false doctrine and/or engaging in erroneous practices. See HERESY.

Hermeticism: A form of MAGICK and philosophy said to be derived from ancient Egyptian religion and based on teachings ascribed to Hermes Trismegistus (Greek for "Hermes the Thrice Great"), a combination of the Greek god Hermes and the Egyptian god Thoth. Hermeticism was especially prominent in Europe during the Renaissance, when it was often associated with ALCHEMY. The modern practice appears to promote elements of PANTHEISM and TAOIST DUALISM. See GOLDEN DAWN; ORDO TEMPLI ORIENTIS; MAGICK; OCCULT.

Hermetic Order of the Golden Dawn, Chic Cicero—Effers, FL: Incorporated in 1988 for the purpose of preserving the ritual and tradition of the GOLDEN DAWN. Chic Cicero formerly assisted Israel Regardie, Chief Adept of the Isis-Urania Temple, founded in 1977 in Columbus, Georgia. Web site—http://www.hermeticgoldendawn.org. See GOLDEN DAWN.

Hickey, Marilyn: Popular WORD-FAITH teacher and president/founder of Marilyn Hickey Ministries. She and her husband, Wallace Hickey, are also the founders/pastors of Orchard Road Christian Center in Denver, Colorado. She and her daughter, Sarah Bowling, host a daily, nationally syndicated television program, *Today with Marilyn and Sarah*. Web site—http://www. mhmin.org. See WORD-FAITH MOVEMENT.

Hieros Gamos: Sacred sex, or sacred marriage. The ancient belief and practice that through sacred sex or sacred marriage (sexual relations) one can be brought into contact with their god(s) or have a religious experience, or in some cases, even obtain salvation. Some believe they are having relations with a deity who is being channeled by their female partner. Today, this is practiced especially among PAGAN groups. For example, in WICCA, a form of this is practiced on Beltane (the Celtic May Day festival), when a couple engages in sexual relations that symbolize the union of the god and goddess. See TANTRA.

Higher Source: See HEAVEN'S GATE.

High Wind Association, Lisa and Beldon Paulson—Plymouth, WI: See BRIGHT DAWN HOME SPREAD.

Himalayan International Institute of Yoga Science and Philosophy, Swami Rama—Honesdale, PA: Swami Rama, who died in 1996, founded the Institute to help people achieve health, happiness, and prosperity through YOGA, MEDITATION, HOLISTIC HEALTH, and AYURVEDIC MEDICINE. The institute runs both an extensive mail-order business and a 400-acre center in Pennsylvania. Operates the Himalayan Institute Press. Web site—http://www.himalayaninstitute.org. See HINDUISM; NEW AGE.

Hinduism: This is the third-largest world religion, with about one billion followers as of 2005. There is no main founder of Hinduism, nor is there one central scripture. Initially four books, or *VEDAS* ("knowledge"), were the principal texts: the *Rigveda, Yajurveda, Samaveda,* and *Atharvaved.* Other scriptures were added over time. There are many schools of Hinduism, but some basic beliefs include dharma (personal duties and obligations), SAMSARA (the "running around" of REINCARNATION), KARMA ("to act," which generates the cause and effect cycle) and MOKSHA ("release," or salvation). There are different paths one may choose in Hinduism, including bhakti (devotional service), karma (unselfish acts), jnana (enlightenment and learning), raja (MEDITATION), and the path of belief (ishvara). A central belief of Hinduism is reincarnation, in which the impersonal soul experiences transmigration through hundreds or thousands of birth-and-death cycles governed by karma until it attains moksha, where the impersonal soul is "released" from the cycle. Some forms of Hinduism emphasize the illusion (MAYA) of the physical, material universe. The only true reality is God, which is impersonal. Ultimately everything, therefore (humans, animals, the deities, vegetation, and the earth), is a part of the universal God (PANTHEISM). Some of the underlying presuppositions of this form of Hinduism are incorporated, modified, and expanded upon in the NEW AGE spirituality. See PANTHEISM.

Hinkins, John-Roger: See CHURCH OF THE MOVEMENT OF SPIRITUAL INNER AWARENESS.

Hippocrates Health Institute, Ann Wigmore—West Palm Beach, FL: A NEW AGE medical institute that teaches HOLISTIC HEALTH. Founded by Wigmore in 1956, it is now headed by Brian and Anna Maria Clement. Two of the institute's more distinctive practices are Nutripuncture, which combines intaking small dosages of natural substances with Eastern religious concepts to facilitate the flow of energy through the body's five MERIDIANS, and Tsubotherapy, which uses ACUPUNCTURE and ACUPRESSURE to stimulate the hypothalamus and pituitary. Web site— http://hippocratesinst.org. See CHI.

Hoffman, Teri—Dallas, TX: A NEW AGE teacher believed by many to have practiced MIND CONTROL. Twelve followers or close associates of Hoffman committed suicide or died under unusual circumstances in the late 1970s–1980s. Many left large sums of money to Hoffman or her organization, Conscious Development of Body, Mind, and Soul. In 1993, Hoffman was convicted on ten counts of bankruptcy fraud.

Hohm Community, Lee Lozowick—Tabor, NJ: Lozowick established Hohm Community in 1972 to promulgate the tradition of the Bauls, a sect from the Bengal region of India. While influenced by BUDDHISM, Lozowick claims to hold to no doctrine, but instead promotes spiritual integrity through harmonious relationships and HOLISTIC HEALTH. Lozowick's books, including *The Alchemy of Transformation* and *Living God Blues,* are published by Hohm Press. Web site—http://www.hohmpress.com.

Holiness Tabernacle—Dyer, AR: See ALAMO CHRISTIAN FOUNDATION.

Holistic Health: Frequently simply called *alternative medicine,* the holistic view of health care focuses on the whole self (body, mind, and spirit) and natural or spiritual cures. Some holistic health remedies and assumptions (i.e., a focus on wellness and prevention) are well within the Christian worldview and are scientifically valid. Much within this movement, however, is based on pantheistic concepts, NEW AGE concepts of VISUALIZATION, and Eastern religious beliefs such as Chinese TAOISM (YIN AND YANG). Most questionable are holistic practices that have no valid physiological explanation or valid scientific proof to validate them, such as APPLIED KINESIOLOGY, REFLEXOLOGY, and IRIDOLOGY.

Hollyhock, Rex Weyler—Cortes Island, BC: A NEW AGE retreat center that offers programs in NATIVE AMERICAN SPIRITUALITY, BUDDHISM, YOGA, MEDITATION, and HOLISTIC HEALTH. Web site—http://www.hollyhock.bc.ca.

Holy Bible Recovery Version: A study BIBLE by WITNESS LEE that's distributed by LIVING STREAM MINISTRY, the publishing arm of THE LOCAL CHURCH. Lee's Bible contains a massive amount of study notes that support the doctrines and interpretations of Lee's movement, which is sometimes referred to as the Lord's Recovery. Critics have pointed to Lee's study note on "a synagogue of Satan" found in Revelation 2:9 as an example of The Local Church's critical stance against believers outside their movement. Lee's footnote explains, "Roman Catholicism and Protestantism, as well as Judaism, all fall into this category, having become an organization of Satan as his tool to damage God's economy." Web site—http://www.recoveryversion.org.

Holy Blood, Holy Grail, **Michael Baigent, Richard Leigh, and Henry Lincoln:** Controversial book published in 1982 in which the authors claimed to present evidence to support the theory that JESUS was married and fathered a child through whom His bloodline continues today. Pierre Plantard's PRIORY OF SION strongly influenced the authors' representations. There was a renewed interest in the book after it was cited as one of the source materials for the *DA VINCI CODE,* making it a best-seller.

Holy Body of the Coming Jesus Christ Mission in New York: See CHURCH OF THE LIVING STONE MISSION FOR THE COMING DAYS.

Holy Grail: aka Sangreal, Sankgreal. The object of the spiritual quest of King Arthur's knights of the Round Table. The earliest appearance of the Grail is in the twelfth-century French chivalric romance *Perceval;* Grail romances soon became one of the most popular genres of chivalric romance. While in *Perceval* the Grail is simply a serving platter, many later romances merged the Grail story with legends of the cup of the Last Supper: the Grail became the cup of CHRIST, brought from Palestine to Britain by Joseph of Arimathea. Grail romances describe the adventures of a knight or knights searching for the Grail. These adventures are frequently allegories of salvation history and other theological concepts. In the Grail romances, those who achieve the quest are not the strongest warriors, but rather, those who have pure hearts and holy conduct. For this reason, the powerful Lancelot fails because of his sin of adultery, while the chaste Galahad succeeds. The Grail is also an icon in modern pop culture, particularly in the 1975 spoof *Monty Python and the Holy Grail* and Steven Spielberg's 1989 film *Indiana Jones and the Last Crusade.* More outlandish speculations about the Grail have been popularized by the 2003 novel *The DA VINCI CODE,* in which the Grail is Mary Magdalene and the object of GODDESS worship.

Holyland: see REACH, INC.

Holy Laughter: A phenomena that accompanies the TORONTO BLESSING and the ministry of evangelist RODNEY HOWARD-BROWNE, in which worshipers spontaneously break out in uncontrollable laughter purportedly while under the influence of the HOLY SPIRIT. Other manifestations can include the appearance of drunkenness, being slain in the Spirit, TRANCE-like states, and the manifestation of animal sounds such as barking like dogs or roaring like lions. See TORONTO BLESSING.

Holy Order of MANS (HOOM), Earl W. Blighton: A monastic NEW AGE group that practiced ESOTERIC, mystical religion that blended biblical themes with REINCARNATION and other concepts from Eastern religions and the OCCULT. Blighton, an ex-engineer who was once fined for practicing medicine without a license, began the order in 1968. MANS was an acronym for a phrase revealed only to initiates. After advancing through the order, men reached the status of Brown Brother of the Holy Light while women became an Immaculate Sister of Mary for Missionary Training. After the death of Blighton, the group underwent radical changes. In 1983 the majority of followers became interested in ORTHODOX CHRISTIANITY, and in 1988 formed CHRIST THE SAVIOR BROTHERHOOD. Several competing groups later formed, each claiming to preserve Blighton's original purpose and message. They include The Gnostic Order of Christ, Science of Man, and the AMERICAN TEMPLE. A Web site dedicated to HOOM can be found at http://www.holyorderofmans.org.

HOLY SPIRIT: In ORTHODOX expressions of CHRISTIANITY, the third person of the TRINITY. The HOLY SPIRIT is seen as being personal (*He,* not *it*) and fully God (when Ananias and Sapphira lied to the HOLY SPIRIT, they lied to God—Acts 5:3-4). In the King James Version (KJV) BIBLE, usually referred to as the Holy Ghost. See TRINITY.

HOLY SPIRIT Association for the Unification of World Christianity, Sun Myung Moon—New York, NY: Moon claims that on Easter morning in 1936 he saw JESUS, who told Moon that he was to restore God's perfect kingdom and be the SECOND COMING of Christ (Moon claims to have later communicated with Moses, BUDDHA, and others). Moon started a church in 1946, which in 1954 became the Unification Church. Moon spent 13 months in prison in 1984–85 for underreporting his taxes. In 2002, the Unification Church announced that a council in heaven of all the great religious and political leaders of history proclaimed Moon to be the savior of humanity. The Unification Church is explicitly anti-Trinitarian, claiming that God is a polarity of masculine and feminine aspects, Jesus is merely an image of God, and the HOLY SPIRIT is simply God's redemptive activity. Moon further teaches that Jesus failed in His mission to save humanity because He failed to marry, thereby necessitating Moon's salvific work as the head of his "Perfect Family." The Unification Church operates over 200 front organizations and owns *The Washington Times* and United Press International. Moon's *Divine Principle* is considered a scriptural work by the church. Web site—http://www.unification.org. For further research, a four-page Watchman Fellowship Profile is available (see page 363). Web site—http://www.watchman.org/notebook.

Homeopathy: A HOLISTIC HEALTH practice developed in the late seventeenth-early eighteenth centuries by Christian Friedrich Samuel Hahnemann. Homeopathy is rooted in the Law of Similars (*similia similibus curantur,* or "like cures like"): Health is restored by administering small doses of medicines that, in larger doses, would create symptoms similar to those currently experienced by the patient. The National Center for Homeopathy, publishers of *Homeopathy Today,* have a Web site at http://www.homeopathic.org.

Homestead Heritage, Blair Adams—Elm Mott, TX: Formerly Koinonia Communities, Emmaus Fellowship. Teaches MODALISM and a multilevel form of SALVATION BY WORKS. Leaders have also claimed their authority is that of "Jesus coming in the flesh." A number of former members have alleged SPIRITUAL ABUSE and SHEPHERDING. The movement is known for its large, picturesque farm and crafts center. Thousands attend the group's annual public fairs, and the group was positively portrayed in a feature article in *Christianity Today* (February 2005). They also produce homeschool curricula under their publishing subsidiaries Essential Christian Education and Truth Forum. Web site—http://www.homesteadheritage.com.

Honolulu Church of Light, Fred Sterling—Honolulu, HI: Began as the Inward Healing Center in 1995 and was established as a Church in 1996. A NEW AGE group that teaches each person is a light particle from God and is called to evolve into the Truth of Oneness. Sterling, who also goes by the name Kahu, is a SHAMAN and MEDIUM who channels Kirael. Web sites—http://www.kirael.com and http://www.inward.com. See PANTHEISM.

Horizon Christian Fellowship, Mike MacIntosh—San Diego, CA: See CALVARY CHAPEL.

Horoscope: See ASTROLOGY.

Horus/Maat Lodge: An OCCULT group founded in 1979 that traces its roots to ALEISTER CROWLEY and works to promote occultic teaching without submission to authoritarian leadership. Ancient Egyptian religious philosophies are central to the doctrines of the lodge. At this time, the lodge exists almost entirely on the Internet. Web site—http://www.horusmaat. com. See NEO-PAGANISM.

Hot Reading: A technique sometimes used by PSYCHICS in order to appear to gain supernatural OCCULT knowledge about their clients. The technique involves using confidants or employees of the PSYCHIC who are planted in the audience as shills. The PSYCHIC seems to have miraculous knowledge of the audience member who is actually in collusion with the psychic. See COLD READING; WARM READING.

House of David, Benjamin Purnell—Benton Harbor, MI: Also known as Seventh Church at the Latter-Day. Founded in 1902, the House of David was a communal group which taught BRITISH ISRAELISM. Purnell, who died in 1927, claimed to be the seventh (and last) angelic messenger of God; his wife, Mary Purnell, later claimed to be a co-messenger with Benjamin. At its height the group had approximately 1,000 members living in its community and fielded a renowned baseball team. A group claiming to be the House of David maintains a Web site at http://www. israelitehouseofdavid.org.

House of Yahweh—Odessa, TX: See HOUSE OF YAHWEH.

House of Yahweh, Yisrayl Hawkins (aka Buffalo Bill Hawkins)—Abilene, TX: A SACRED NAME group founded in 1980 by Buffalo Bill Hawkins (who later changed his name to Yisrayl) after splintering from his brother's (Yaaqob's) earlier House of Yahweh in Odessa, Texas. Hawkins's teachings are a continually developing blend of YAHWEHISM, polygamy, and SABBATARIANISM. He claims that he and his brother, who died in 1991, are the two witnesses prophesied in Revelation 11, and it is only through following himself and his teachings that individuals can earn salvation (SALVATION BY WORKS). Hawkins promotes the doctrine of polygamy and encourages followers to pierce their ears as a sign of being a servant of Yahweh. Hundreds of his followers have legally changed their last names to Hawkins, according to published reports. Hawkins's teaching is strongly apocalyptic: he warns that the world is currently in the middle of the Great Tribulation and only by membership in the House of Yahweh can individuals survive the coming cataclysm. Hawkins set a date for the impending doomsday, declaring that a nuclear holocaust would occur on September 12, 2006 and plunge the world into a nuclear winter. The House of Yahweh uses Hawkins's *Book of Yahweh* as its Bible. The group publishes *The Prophetic Word*. Web site—http://www.yahweh.com. For further research, a four-page Watchman Fellowship Profile is available (see page 363). Web site—http://www.watchman.org/notebook.

Houston Church of Freethought: Congregation of ATHEISTS, AGNOSTICS, and other nonbelievers. Rejects traditional theism because the supernatural and faith are viewed as illogical, superstitious, and intolerant. The purpose for the Freethought church is to provide an unbelieving environment to meet the psychological and social needs of unbelievers. Web site—http://www.hcof.org. See ATHEISM; AGNOSTICISM.

Houston, Jean: Houston is a prominent NEW AGE spokesperson who promotes using PSYCHIC practices and CREATIVE VISUALIZATION to promote a global transformation in consciousness. Underlying all of Houston's teaching is PANTHEISM: All living things share, to some degree, the consciousness of all things which have ever lived. Houston's thinking has been strongly influenced by the studies in myth by JOSEPH CAMPBELL. She currently teaches courses in human development for major corporations and universities [in addition to her annual Mystery Schools], works with UNICEF as an advisor in human and cultural development, and creates programs in social artistry for the United Nations. Houston's publications include *The Varieties of Psychedelic Experience, The Possible Human,* and *The Hero and the Goddess.* Web site—http://www.jeanhouston.org. For further research, a four-page Watchman Fellowship Profile is available (see page 363). Web site—http://www.watchman.org/notebook.

Howard-Browne, Rodney: An evangelist from South Africa who founded Revival Ministries International and co-pastors, with his wife Adonica, The River at Tampa Bay Church in Florida. Browne, described as the "Holy Ghost Bartender," was instrumental in the spread and popularity of the HOLY LAUGHTER revival. See HOLY LAUGHTER; TORONTO BLESSING.

Hubbard, L. Ron: See CHURCH OF SCIENTOLOGY.

The Humanist: The bimonthly magazine of the AMERICAN HUMANIST ASSOCIATION, which has a circulation of about 15,000 subscribers and an international readership of approximately 30,000. Web site—http:// www. thehumanist.org. See AMERICAN HUMANIST ASSOCIATION.

Humanist Manifesto: See SECULAR HUMANISM.

Human Potential Movement (HPM): A diverse collection of training seminars and organizations that developed in the 1960s-70s based on the theory that human beings possess a largely untapped yet innate psychological or mental power. Properly awakened (through self-awareness seminars, group training, or other experiences), this power can unleash personal peace, happiness, empowerment, and enhanced abilities in all aspects of life. In extreme cases, participants were promised unlimited supernatural abilities or even god-like attributes. By the 1970s-80s, HPM courses were being marketed to businesses, including large corporations, as an enhancement for employee productivity. In most cases, the seminars and training were promoted as an aid to mental or physiological empowerment rather than as a spiritual or religious program. Pioneers in the field include EST, the ESALEN INSTITUTE, and the PACIFIC INSTITUTE.

Hunger Project: Founded in 1987 by WERNER ERHARD (founder of EST), folk singer JOHN DENVER, and Bob Fuller, Hunger Project focuses on eradicating hunger and misogyny through self-empowerment. Web site—http://www.thp.org.

Hypnosis: From the Greek words *hypnos* ("sleep") and *osis* ("condition"). Descended from MESMERISM, hypnosis refers to a wide array of verbal and nonverbal techniques used to induce an ALTERED STATE OF CONSCIOUSNESS. Induction techniques include VISUALIZATION, MEDITATION, and such methods as breath control and progressive relaxation. Some medical practitioners use hypnotherapy for the controversial goal of recovering forgotten or repressed memories. Hypnosis forms the basis of NEUROLINGUISTIC PROGRAMMING. Many critics oppose hypnosis on the basis of its OCCULT background, its inexplicable methodology, and the potential for unethical influence of the patient. For further research, a four-page Watchman Fellowship Profile is available (see page 363). Web site—http://www.watchman.org/notebook.

I

I AM Movement, Guy Ballard: Ballard claimed that, on Mount Shasta in 1930, one of the ASCENDED MASTERS, SAINT GERMAIN, gave him a magical drink that renewed his body. Ballard and his family then began recording messages from the ASCENDED MASTERS on three general themes: I AM as the creative name of God; experiencing in one's higher being the personal I AM presence; and the Violet Flame, which clears away disharmony and confusion.

I Ching: The *I Ching,* or *Book of Changes,* is an ancient Chinese manual for DIVINATION. The specific practice of divination involves casting the stalks of a yarrow plant or, in later times, coins; the results of this process are recorded as a series of six broken (corresponding to the YIN principle) or solid (corresponding to the YANG principle) parallel horizontal lines called a hexagram. The *I Ching* is a commentary on the possible hexagrams derived by this process, and is available online at http://www.sacred-texts.com/ich. See TAOISM.

Identity Movements: Similar to BRITISH ISRAELISM, the Identity movement maintains that the true identity of the ten lost tribes of Israel is the white Anglo-Saxon race. A number of independent churches and organizations (including some militant racist groups) make up the general movement. Most Identity groups deny the doctrine of the TRINITY. Some teach a form of the SERPENT SEED doctrine, which asserts that black people are descendants of Eve's alleged sexual relations with the serpent (Genesis 3) and therefore are not fully human. Conversely, some African-American cults maintain that Caucasians are descended from the serpent.

IFCA International: An association of churches formed in 1923 as the American Conference of Undenominational Churches in response to the growth of LIBERAL CHRISTIANITY in some denominations. In 1930 the name was changed to Independent Fundamental Churches of America and the current name was adopted in 1996. Web site—http://www.ifca. org. See FUNDAMENTALIST CHRISTIANITY.

Iglesia Ni Cristo, Felix Manalo: A significant pseudo-Christian group in the Philippines (Iglesia Ni Cristo is Tagalog for *Church of Christ*). Manalo (1886–1963) was raised in ROMAN CATHOLICISM, but as an adult joined a number of churches practicing EVANGELICAL CHRISTIANITY before joining the SEVENTH-DAY ADVENTIST CHURCH and THE CHURCH OF JESUS CHRIST OF LATTER-DAY SAINTS and then finally starting his own group. Iglesia Ni Cristo is staunchly anti-Trinitarian, maintaining that JESUS was simply given divine power by God. The group also teaches that true Christianity disappeared under the rule of Emperor Constantine in the fourth-century and did not reappear until Manalo began his work as the last messenger of God in 1914. For further research, a four-page Watchman Fellowship Profile is available (see page 363). Web site—http://www.watchman.org/notebook.

Imagery: See VISUALIZATION, GUIDED IMAGERY.

Independent Baptist Churches: Baptist churches that are not part of a denomination. Some participate in fellowships such as the BAPTIST BIBLE FELLOWSHIP INTERNATIONAL and the WORLD BAPTIST FELLOWSHIP. See BAPTIST CHURCHES; FUNDAMENTALIST CHRISTIANITY.

Independent Baptist Fellowship International (IBFI)—Fort Worth, TX: A fellowship of like-minded INDEPENDENT BAPTIST CHURCHES that supports missionaries and CHRISTIAN education. Web site—http://www.ibfi-nbbi.org. See BAPTIST CHURCHES; FUNDAMENTALIST CHRISTIANITY.

Independent Christian Churches: See THE RESTORATION MOVEMENT.

Independent Fundamental Churches of America: See IFCA INTERNATIONAL.

Infinity Institute International, Anne H. Spencer—Royal Oak, MI: A HOLISTIC HEALING organization that teaches HYPNOSIS and THERAPEUTIC TOUCH. Toward this end, the institute operates the International Medical and Dental Hypnotherapy Association. Web site—http://www.infinityinst.com.

Inner Circle Teachers of Light: See PROBERT, MARK; CHURCH OF E YADA DI SHI-ITE.

Inner Light Foundation, Betty Bethards—Petaluma, CA: A NEW AGE institution that offers courses in CHANNELING, NUMEROLOGY, PSYCHIC energy, and self-love. Bethards, who died in 2002, is best known for her book *Be Your Own Guru.* Web site—http://www.innerlight.org.

Inner Peace Movement, Francisco Coll—San Antonio, TX: Founded in 1964 by Coll, the movement is a NEW AGE institution that teaches people to engage in inner spiritual awareness. The foundation for the movement is PANTHEISM: There is no separation between each individual and the "all," a connection that can be experienced and confirmed through our feelings. Through the guidance of ANGELS and our spiritual gifts of prophecy, vision, intuition, and feeling, we can realize our unique purpose in life. Web site—http://www.innerpeacemovement.org.

Inner Space Center: See PROSPEROS.

Inner Visions Institute for Spiritual Development, IYANLA VANZANT—Silver Springs, MD: Network of spiritual and holistic practitioners founded in 1998 to empower understanding of the role each person plays in the divine order of life. The organization is spiritually pluralistic, incorporating a wide array of spiritual teachers and traditions to enable individuals to overcome emotional and spiritual barriers that prevent the experiencing of fulfillment. Courses include instruction in NEW AGE and Eastern religion practices such as Conscious Connected Breathing (REBIRTHING), APPLIED KINESIOLOGY, CHAKRA balancing, REIKI, and *A COURSE IN MIRACLES.* Web site—http://www.innervisionsworldwide.com.

Insight **magazine**—Washington, DC: Owned by the Unification Church. See HOLY SPIRIT ASSOCIATION FOR THE UNIFICATION OF WORLD CHRISTIANITY.

Insight Meditation Society, JACK KORNFIELD, JOSEPH GOLD- STEIN, and SHARON SALZBERG—Barre, MA: Founded in 1975, the organization's stated purpose, according to the FAQ section on its Web site, is "to provide an environment of spiritual refuge, conducive to the practice of BUDDHIST MEDITATION," particularly insight and loving-kindness meditations. The organization claims to have an international support base of 20,000 people and over 2,000 retreat participants annually. Web site—http://www.dharma.org/ims/index/htm. See SPIRIT ROCK MEDITATION CENTER.

Insight Transformational Seminars, John-Roger Hinkins: See CHURCH OF THE MOVEMENT OF SPIRITUAL INNER AWARENESS.

Institute for Bio-Spiritual Research—Coulterville, CA: Founded in 1975 by Peter Campbell and Edwin McMahon, the institute teaches "bio-spiritual focusing," which involves making decisions according to physical sensations rather than relying upon intellectual knowledge and understanding. See NEW AGE.

Institute for Family and Human Relations, Brad Brown—Los Gatos, CA: See KAIROS FOUNDATION.

Institute for Hypnosis: See FOUNDATION FOR HUMAN UNDER- STANDING.

Institute for the Advancement of Human Behavior—Portola Valley, CA: Offers workshops on a wide array of counseling situations. Approved by various medical, psychological, and social work boards for continuing edu-cation credit. One of the courses, Spirituality and Psychotherapy, teaches health practitioners to utilize spirituality to achieve rapid results (even for those who are adherents of ATHEISM and AGNOSTICISM). Web site—http://www.iahb.org.

Institute for the Study of American Religions: See MELTON, J. GORDON.

Institute for the Study of Human Knowledge, Robert Ornstein— Cambridge, MA: Founded in 1969 to study the link between mind and health. This institute researches the healing systems of NATIVE AMERICAN SPIRITUALITY and those of Eastern religions such as HINDUISM and BUDDHISM, MEDITATION, BIOFEEDBACK, and HYPNOSIS. Web site—http://www.ishkbooks.com. See HOLISTIC HEALTH.

Institute in Basic Life Principles: See GOTHARD, BILL.

Institute in Basic Youth Conflicts: See GOTHARD, BILL.

Institute of Divine Metaphysical Research, Henry Clifford Kinley— Springfield, OH: Kinley claimed to receive a vision in 1931 in which God revealed His plan for the future. Central to this plan is convincing the world that the non-Trinitarian God must be addressed by the name *Yahweh,* and the MESSIAH must be addressed by the name *Yahshua.* The Institute claims that Kinley made a wide array of accurate prophecies (such as the result of World War II, the assassination of John F. Kennedy, and Israel's Six-Day War), but the only verifiable prophecy is his FALSE PROPHECY that the world would end in 1996. Web site—http://www.idmr.net.

Institute of Judaic-Christian Research, Vendyl Jones—Arlington, TX: See VENDYL JONES RESEARCH INSTITUTES.

Institute of Mentalphysics, Edwin Dingle (1881–1972)—Joshua Tree, CA: Founded by Dingle in 1927, the institute teaches some of the basic principles and practices of HINDUISM as a way of awakening one's higher self. The institute operates the Joshua Tree Retreat Center and offers the *Lessons in Living* home study course. Web site—http://www.mentalphysicsretreat.com.

Institute of Noetic Sciences, Edgar Mitchell—Sausalito, CA: In 1971, while on the return flight from the moon aboard Apollo 14, Mitchell experienced a sense of the oneness of the universe. He created the institute in 1973 to expand the understanding of human potential by examining inner consciousness. By examining such phenomena as intuition, the institute hopes to build a global wisdom society. The institute publishes *Shift* magazine. Web site—http://www.noetic.org. See NEW AGE.

International Association for Near-Death Studies, Inc. (IANDS), John Audette—East Windsor Hill, CT: An organization founded in 1978 to promote near-death studies based on the early work of psychiatrists Elisabeth Kübler-Ross, MD, Raymond Moody, Jr., and George Ritchie. Web site—http://www.iands.org. See NEAR-DEATH EXPERIENCE (NDE).

International Association for Regression Research and Therapies, Inc. (IARRT): See ASSOCIATION FOR PAST-LIFE RESEARCH AND THERAPIES, INC.

International Association of Scientologists—West Sussex, England: The association promotes international unity among members of the CHURCH OF SCIENTOLOGY. Web site—http://www.iasmembership.org.

International Churches of Christ, Kip McKean—Los Angeles, CA: Formerly called the Boston Church of Christ, this worldwide splinter from the traditional CHURCHES OF CHRIST originally developed out of the controversial CROSSROADS CHURCH OF CHRIST campus ministry in Gainesville, Florida. Former members and critics allege that the church practices MIND CONTROL through such practices as SHEPHERDING. This behavior, combined with aggressive recruitment of students on college campuses, has resulted in the church being banned from many campuses across the country. The group claims to be the only true church, and teaches BAPTISMAL REGENERATION. McKean resigned as World Missions Evangelist in 2002, apologizing for the damage his arrogance had inflicted upon his family and members of the church and currently serves in the Portland, Oregon, congregation; other church leaders have issued similar apologies. The church publishes *Upside Down* magazine. For further research, a four-page Watchman Fellowship Profile is available (see page 363). Web site—http://www.watchman.org/notebook.

International Church of the Foursquare Gospel: See PENTECOSTAL MOVEMENT.

International Community of Christ, Church of the Second Advent, Douglas Eugene Savoy—Reno, NV: GENE SAVOY is an explorer who has traveled extensively in Peru (and in 1989 claimed to find evidence of Solomonic Israelites in Peru). Following the death of his son, Jamil (whom Savoy claimed to be a "second Christ"), in 1962, Savoy became an ordained minister and began developing an ESOTERIC theology in which JESUS and the first-century Christian church held to the allegedly mystical theology of the Essenes. This doctrine teaches that salvation is not by grace but through a secret process of spiritual rebirth taught by Jesus. This allegedly secret gospel of Jesus was never put into the New Testament writings. The Church of the Second Advent claims to have rediscovered this process through years of research and now makes it known to others. In conjunction with this theology, Savoy has developed Cosolargy, a mystical method of healing physical and spiritual maladies. The seminarial program of the church is the Jamilian University of the Ordained. Web site—http://www.communityofchrist.org.

International Congregation of Yahweh—Pocahontas, AR: Promotes the teachings of ARMSTRONGISM. The congregation publishes *Insight.* Web site—http://www.icyahweh.org.

International Cultic Studies Association (ICSA)—Bonita Springs, FL: The world's largest secular (nonreligious) organization that provides research and information on psychological influence, mind-control, and authoritarianism in cults and other alternative movements. The organization was founded in 1979 as the American Family Foundation (AFF). The group publishes the *Cultic Studies Review,* and Michael D. Langone serves as the executive director. Web site—http://www.icsahome.com.

International General Assembly of Spiritualists, Arthur Augustus Ford (1896–1971)—Norfolk, VA: Founded in 1936, the assembly is one of the largest associations of practitioners of SPIRITUALISM. The most recent statistics for it cite 250 congregations with a membership of 200,000 (164,000 in 1990). Ford claimed to have "realized" PSYCHIC abilities during World War I and became a MEDIUM for the spirit entity *Fletcher* in the early 1920s. He formed the International General Assembly of Spiritualists after breaking away from the NATIONAL SPIRITUALIST ASSOCIATION over his newly developed belief in REINCARNATION. Later he would also found SPIRITUAL FRONTIERS FELLOWSHIP.

International Institute of Sacred Knowledge: See COLE-WHITTAKER, TERRY.

International Meditation Society: See TRANSCENDENTAL MEDITATION.

International Metaphysical Association—New York, NY: The association was created in 1955 by independent followers of CHRISTIAN SCIENCE to disseminate the teachings of MARY BAKER EDDY through mass media.

International Nath Order, SHRI GURUDEV MAHENDRANATH—Seattle, WA: Founded in 1978 with the stated purpose of spiritual awakening, OCCULT attainment, and an enlightened social order based on a PAGAN past. Rooted in the occult and HINDUISM, its practices include MAGIC, YOGA, TANTRA, and MEDITATION. Since 1989 it has been under the leadership of SHRI KAPILANTH. Web site—http://www.nathorder.org. See AMOOKOS.

International Religious and Magical Order of Societe, La Couleuvre Noire: See TECHNICIANS OF THE SACRED.

International Society for Krishna Consciousness, A.C. Bhaktivendanta Swami Prabhupada (1896–1977): Commonly abbreviated as ISKCON, the organization was founded in 1966 by Prabhupada to emphasize devotion to the Hindu god KRISHNA. ISKCON is popularly known as the Hare Krishnas because of its repetition in the HARE KRISHNA MANTRA that forms the central spiritual discipline of the organization. Devotees practice vegetarianism and believe in REINCARNATION. ISKCON has suffered several legal and financial blows in recent years, losing millions of dollars to former members whose children had been physically abused in the organization's schools. ISKCON publishes *Back to Godhead* magazine. Web site—http://www.iskcon.com. For further research, a four-page Watchman Fellowship Profile is available (see page 363). Web site—http://www.watchman.org/notebook.

International Society of Divine Love, H.D. Prakashanand Saraswati—Austin, TX: See JAGADGURU KRIPALU PARISHAT.

International Success Institute: See CIRCLES OF LIFE.

Inward Bound Adventures—Washington, DC: Started in 1992, Inward Bound teaches HOLISTIC HEALING through MEDITATION, YOGA, and other disciplines to integrate the mind, body, and spirit. The primary activity of the group is its yoga trips, where participants immerse themselves in the Inward Bound program at scenic locales. Web site—http://www.inwardboundadventures.com.

Inward Healing Center: See HONOLULU CHURCH OF LIGHT.

Iridology: Invented by Ignatz von Péczely, a nineteenth-century Hungarian physician, iridology allegedly allows practitioners to diagnose diseases by reading the color patterns in the irises of the patient's eyes. Iridologists believe each bodily organ has a counterpart in the eye—thus, reading ocular color patterns provides insight into physical health. The practice is largely rejected by mainstream medical practitioners. See HOLISTIC HEALTH.

Isis Books and Gifts—Denver, CO: A NEW AGE distributor that provides resources for TAROT and WICCA. Web site—http://www.isisbooks.com. See NEO-PAGANISM.

ISKCON: See INTERNATIONAL SOCIETY FOR KRISHNA CONSCIOUSNESS.

Islam, Muhammad: Based on the teachings and life of Muhammad (A.D. 570–632) in Mecca and Medina, Saudi Arabia (then Persia), Islam is the second-largest world religion. Islam has recently become the third-largest religious body in America, with over six million adherents. Islam is composed of three major divisions—Sunni (the largest), Shi'ite, and Sufi. The Arabic word *Islam* means "submission to the will of God," and a person who submits is called a Muslim. The Koran (or QUR'AN), the TORAH, the Psalms of the Old Testament, and the Gospels of the New Testament are regarded as holy books. Only the Koran, however, is considered uncorrupted. Islam rejects the doctrine of the TRINITY as well as the deity of JESUS and His Sonship, claiming that Jesus was only a great prophet. Muhammad is considered to be the greatest prophet, and his coming was allegedly predicted by Christ. Islam is fiercely monotheistic. Salvation is sought through good works, which includes the observance of the Five Pillars: reciting "there is no God but ALLAH and Muhammad is his messenger," praying five times per day, fasting, giving alms (donations to the poor), and a pilgrimage to

Mecca. Historically, Islam experienced tremendous growth often by forced proselytism—unbelievers (infidels) were told to convert or die. While many Muslims exhibit tolerance towards other faiths, even today Islamic fundamentalism promotes *jihad* (holy war) against those of other religious and political views. However, some Muslims—particularly those in the West—in an attempt to separate themselves from extremists, reinterpret jihad to mean the internal struggle one experiences in trying to bring the self into submission to ALLAH/God. See MONOTHEISM; SUFISM; NATION OF ISLAM.

Israelite Nation Worldwide Ministries, Shadrock Porter—Toronto, Ontario: This group teaches that Adam was made from black soil and made in the image of God, and while all are made in the image of God, the likeness of God was given to the first man. They believe that the true Israelites are African Americans, and they blend the teachings of the New and Old Testaments, keeping many of the practices and cultures of the Old Testament Israelites. The King James Version of the Bible is the only one they use. Web site—http://www.israelitenation.com. See BLACK HEBREWS.

Isthmus Institute—Dallas, TX: A NEW AGE organization that studies possible convergences between science and religious thought. Much of its work focuses on environmentalism, asserting links between ecology and the earth as Mother. See GAIA.

J

Jagadguru Kripalu Parishat, Shree Kripaluji Maharaj—Austin, TX: A HINDU nonprofit religious organization formed to promote the teachings of its founder, who claims to be the fifth Jagadguru (divine presence descended to earth) in the last 5,000 years. There are five Ashrams—four in India and one in the United States, BARSANA DHAM. Web site—http://www.jkp.org.

Jainism, Mahavira: The origins of Jainism have been traced to the ancient civilizations of the Indus River Valley (approximately 3000 B.C.). The religion formally began in the late sixth-century B.C. when Mahavira—the last of 24 Tirthankaras (teachers who, while alive, attained all earthly knowledge)—attained enlightenment after 13 years of severe asceticism. Similar to its contemporary, HINDUISM, Jainism teaches that the soul is bound to this world by KARMA, which both accrues and is eventually overcome through REINCARNATION. Central to ridding oneself of karma is absolute nonviolence, which not only includes vegetarianism, but also the avoidance of accidentally killing insects. Currently there are approximately four million Jains, almost all of whom live in India.

Jakes, Thomas Dexter (T.D.): Popular PENTECOSTAL preacher who founded T.D. Jakes Ministries in 1994 and the Potter's House church in Dallas, Texas in 1996. He came to prominence with his sermon and subsequent *Woman, Thou Art Loosed!* book and conferences (this also became the basis for a film). Today he has a nationally syndicated television program and pastors a church with over 28,000 members. In 2005, *Time* magazine named him one of the 25 most influential evangelicals in America. His first pastorate was in 1979 at Greater Emmanuel Temple of Faith in West

Virginia. It was associated with Higher Ground Always Abounding Assemblies, a network of ONENESS PENTECOSTAL churches. Some critics believe that Jakes has not strayed far from his oneness roots, claiming his statement on the TRINITY is not clearly enough stated to distinguish it from oneness doctrine. Web sites—http://www.tdjakes.org and http://www. thepottershouse.org. See ONENESS PENTECOSTALISM.

The James Randi Educational Foundation, JAMES RANDI: A foundation begun by the former magician JAMES RANDI, who debunks and exposes fake PSYCHICS and faith healers. The foundation is best known for its still-unclaimed $1-million challenge offered to anyone who can document supernatural abilities. Web site—http://www.randi.org. See RANDI, JAMES.

Jamilian University of the Ordained—Reno, NV: Seminarial program of the INTERNATIONAL COMMUNITY OF CHRIST, CHURCH OF THE SECOND ADVENT. Web site—https://www.jamilian.org.

Jedi Religion: See STAR WARS.

Jeffs, Warren: Prophet and leader of the FUNDAMENTAL CHURCH OF JESUS CHRIST OF LATTER-DAY SAINTS (FLDS). He was placed on the FBI's Ten Most Wanted list in May 2006 for unlawful flight to avoid prosecution for sexual conduct with a minor, conspiracy to commit sexual conduct with a minor, and rape as an accomplice.

Jehovah's Witnesses: See WATCHTOWER BIBLE AND TRACT SOCIETY.

Jesus: Jesus of Nazareth founded the religious movement first known as "the Way," and later as CHRISTIANITY, in the first century. The four major historical sources for the life of Jesus are the Synoptic Gospels (Matthew, Mark, and Luke) and the Gospel of John. Three non-Judeo Christian sources, written in the 220s, attest to the existence of Jesus: writings by Pliny, Tacitus, and Suetonius. The Jewish historian Josephus, as well as the TALMUD, also refer to Jesus. Traditional Christians believe Jesus is the MESSIAH prophesied by the TANAKH (or TORAH, Prophets, and Writings of the Old Testament), and that He died to save humanity from sin and death. These Christians also believe that Jesus is the incarnate Son of God, the second person of the TRINITY, who is both fully human and fully divine. Other religious traditions, however, including some that claim to be Christian, see Jesus merely as a great teacher or as a divine being who was created by God. Some adherents of NEW AGE see Jesus as a human who realized His CHRIST CONSCIOUSNESS, but who is not uniquely God. See JESUS CHRIST; TRINITY; VIRGIN BIRTH.

Jesus Christ: The name and title of the founder of CHRISTIANITY. *JESUS* corresponds with the Hebrew name *Joshua,* which means "Jehovah is salvation," and *Christ* is derived from the Greek word *christos,* which means "anointed one" and the Greek rendering of the Hebrew word for *MESSIAH.* In the Gospels of Matthew, Mark, and Luke, Jesus is proclaimed as the Christ by Peter, and in the GOSPEL according to John, Andrew says this. The Acts of the APOSTLES describes the early Christians as preaching that Jesus is the Christ. As time progressed, this belief eventually became the confessional name Jesus Christ.

Jesusonian Foundation—Boulder, CO: Established in 1984 to promote the teachings of and to distribute *THE URANTIA BOOK.* Web sites—http://jesusonian.org and http://www.TruthBook.com.

Jesus Only: See ONENESS PENTECOSTALISM.

Jihad: Loosely translated as "holy war," *jihad* has many meanings in ISLAM. It refers to the inward spiritual struggle to attain perfect faith (commonly referred to as the greater jihad, particularly by MUSLIMS in the West), as well as the outward physical struggle to establish a just and holy society (commonly referred to as the lesser jihad, particularly by Muslims in the West). The term is commonly understood to refer to violent efforts to destroy individuals and groups who are declared to be threats to Islam and to forcibly convert people groups to the religion.

Jnama Yoga: See YOGA.

Johannine Daist Communion: The name used for a period in the mid-1980s for ADI DA.

John David—Coffs Harbour, New South Wales: A follower of OSHO until Osho's death in 1990, and later a follower of a Hindu GURU named Papaji,

John David claims to have been awakened and come close to enlightenment in the early 1990s. David gives seminars throughout Australia, Europe, and India. Web site—http://www.johndavid.org.

John-David Learning Institute, Dr. John David (1938–88)—Carlsbad, CA: Founded in 1984 and based on the research of its founder. David claimed that different sounds stimulate different parts of the brain and could be used to increase creativity, learning ability, and productivity, as well as decrease stress. He also claimed his products could be used to develop better health. Using sound to stimulate the left brain and right brain, these products are claimed to cause mind/brain expansion or whole-brain development. They are offered by a number of companies today that use similar techniques as David's and claim to be based upon or a continuation of his research. One, the WHOLE BRAIN LEARNING INSTITUTE, claims to be the appointed successor of David's work. See NEW AGE.

John-Roger: See MOVEMENT OF SPIRITUAL INNER AWARENESS. Web site—http://www.john-roger.org.

Jones, Jim: See PEOPLE'S TEMPLE CHRISTIAN CHURCH.

Jonestown: See PEOPLE'S TEMPLE CHRISTIAN CHURCH.

Jones, Vendyl: See VENDYL JONES RESEARCH INSTITUTES.

Joseph Plan Foundation, Tara Singh—Los Angeles, CA: Singh, a popular teacher of *A COURSE IN MIRACLES,* established the foundation in 1993 to promote the teachings of the course. Web site—http://www.josephplan. org.

Jouret, Luc: See ORDER OF THE SOLAR TEMPLE.

Joyner, Rick: Cofounder of MORNINGSTAR MINISTRIES and senior pastor of MorningStar Fellowship Church. Joyner is the author of over 30 books, including *The Final Quest, The Call,* and *The Torch and the Sword.* Critics have charged Joyner with FALSE PROPHECY and claimed that some of his teachings are similar to the HERESY of DOCETISM, which maintains that Jesus only appeared to be human. Joyner has also been criticized for his alleged support of KINGDOM NOW THEOLOGY, the

ASSOCIATION OF VINEYARD CHURCHES, and the KANSAS CITY PROPHETS. See MORNINGSTAR MINISTRIES.

Joy, W. Brugh: Teaches Heart Centered Transformation and Spiritual Enlightenment, which involves TOUCH THERAPY and ALTERED STATES OF CONSCIOUSNESS. Joy was, in the past, a licensed doctor of internal medicine. Web site—http://www.brughjoy.com. See HOLISTIC HEALING.

Judaism: World religion historically based on the call of Abram (Abraham) by God to forsake the idolatrous people in Ur of the Chaldeans and go with his descendants to inherit the land of Canaan (Genesis 12). Abraham's descendants were led by Moses and other prophets through centuries of trials, hardship, captivities, and slavery as recorded in the TORAH and the Prophets (Old Testament). Through times of extreme persecution, religious faithfulness, and infidelity, Abraham's descendants maintained a strong sense of national identity, identification with the Promised Land (Israel), and anticipation of a coming MESSIAH ("Anointed One"). Out of first-century Judaism, early CHRISTIANITY developed largely over the latter's belief that JESUS CHRIST was that promised Messiah. Today Judaism can be identified as a cultural, national, or religious concept. Modern religious beliefs can be generally classified as Orthodox (traditional, literal under-standing of Jewish scripture, history, and culture), Conservative (a middle position with a more moderate religious position), and Reform (liberal, nonliteral stance on scripture, often nonreligious or secular with emphasis on Jewish culture).

K

Kabat-Zinn, Jon: A faculty member in preventative and behavioral medicine at the University of Massachusetts Medical School, Kabat-Zinn is a leader in the developing field of mind/body medicine. Kabat-Zinn's emphasis is on using MEDITATION to enhance clinical, social, and physical performance. Web site—http://www.umassmed.edu/behavmed/faculty/kabat-zinn.cfm. See BUDDHISM.

Kabbalah (various spellings): *Kabbalah,* which means "what has been handed down," is a form of Jewish MYSTICISM allegedly given to Abraham and orally transmitted through the centuries until it was committed to writing in the twelfth-century *Sefer Bahir* (*Book of the Brilliant [Light]*). More influential is the *Sefer Zohar* (*Book of Splendor*), compiled in the thirteenth-century by Moses de Leon. At the heart of kabbalistic theology are the ten *sefirot,* or emanations, of God, similar in some respects to GNOSTICISM. For further research, a four-page Watchman Fellowship Profile is available (see page 363). Web site—http://www.watchman.org/notebook.

Kabbalah Centre, Philip Berg—Los Angeles, CA: A NEW AGE organization that claims to make the KABBALAH accessible to the general public. The center offers numerous courses and other resources to teach people to better their lives by acting in harmony with the laws of the universe. The center has been popularized by entertainment celebrities such as Madonna, Demi Moore, and Brittany Spears, who have openly embraced and promoted kabbalah teachings, wearing the center's special red string to ward off the evil eye, and drinking mineral water that has allegedly been purified and empowered by being in close proximity to the TORAH. The center is widely reviled by mainstream JUDAISM. Web site—http://www.kabbalah.com.

See KABBALAH. For further research, a four-page Watchman Fellowship Profile is available (see page 363). Web site—http://www.watchman.org/notebook.

Kairos Foundation, Roy Whitten and Brad Brown—Knoxville, TN: This nonprofit, formed in 1979, provides personal "life training" through its More to Life Weekends. Whitten, a former Episcopal minister, had previously served as a pastoral counselor at Brown's Institute for Family and Human Relations. Both men were interested in blending Eastern and Western spiritual thought and practices and combining these contemplative traditions with contemporary psychological tools. Web site—http://www.lifetraining.org. See NEW AGE.

Kalachandji's: A HARE KRISHNA temple in Dallas, Texas established by A.C. Bhaktivedanta Swami Prabhupada, founder of the INTERNATIONAL SOCIETY FOR KRISHNA CONSCIOUSNESS. The temple was acquired in 1971; the property also includes an award-winning vegetarian restaurant. Web site—http://www.kalachandjis.com.

Kansas City Prophets: A group of ministers connected with Kansas City Fellowship (begun in 1982, later called the Metro Christian Fellowship) who emphasize spiritual gifts such as visions, revelations, and prophecies. Leading figures associated with the movement in the early days include Bob Jones, Bill Hamon, John Paul Jackson, Mike Bickle, and Paul Cain. More traditional Christian critics have charged FALSE PROPHECY (Deuteronomy 18:20-22) and drawn parallels between the personal prophetic revelations and the COLD READING techniques of PSYCHICS. In 1989, the movement became affiliated with the ASSOCIATION OF VINEYARD CHURCHES until they withdrew in 1996. In 2004, the movement faced a serious setback when Rick Joyner published a call to repentance, charging that Paul Cain was an alcoholic and a practicing homosexual. Cain later confessed to both charges and sought restoration. See THIRD WAVE OF THE HOLY SPIRIT.

Karma: The Hindu principle of cause and effect. Representing neither good nor evil, all actions and events are balanced with corresponding actions and events in the past or future (including past and future lives through REINCARNATION). See HINDUISM; BUDDHISM.

Karma Yoga: A form of YOGA intended to open the individual to spiritual enlightenment. Some practitioners contrast karma yoga with HATHA YOGA, which, in North America, is commonly practiced exclusively as a form of physical exercise. See KARMA.

Keating, Thomas: While serving as the Abbott at St. Joseph's Abbey (1961–81), he and fellow Trappist monk BASIL PENNINGTON began to search for a MEDITATION technique that could be taught to young Roman Catholics who were being drawn to Eastern meditation techniques. Keating began to study eastern teachings and practices and invited eastern religion teachers to come to the abbey and provide retreats and training sessions for the monks. His studies and the books he authored would eventually become an important part of the present-day CENTERING PRAYER movement.

Keen, Sam: A prominent NEW AGE teacher, Keen received a Ph.D. in theology from Princeton University and briefly taught theology before becoming an observer and participant in the human potential movement of the 1960s. Keen asserts that reliance on GURUS or organized religion prevents the individual from developing self-knowledge by confronting the depths of our ignorance. Keen teaches that the process of answering questions about existence and meaning is the path to self-knowledge. He has written many books, including *Your Mythic Journey*, *Hymns to an Unknown God*, and *Learning to Fly*. Web site—http://www.samkeen.com.

Kerista Global Village—San Francisco, CA: Now defunct, Kerista was an intentional community dedicated to practicing "polyfidelity," in which all members of the community were permitted to engage in sexual activity without monogamous restraints.

Keyes, Ken: A popular NEW AGE teacher who taught the possibilities of human potential through higher consciousness. Keyes died in 1995. His most famous works are *Handbook to Higher Consciousness* and *The Hundredth Monkey*.

KidzVids International—Humble TX: A ministry with alleged ties to THE FAMILY (CHILDREN OF GOD) that produces religious videos for children. Web site—http://www.kidzvids.com. See THE FAMILY (CHILDREN OF GOD).

Kingdom Now Theology: A collection of beliefs concerning the end times that became popular among a small minority of leaders in the CHARISMATIC MOVEMENT in the latter half of the twentieth-century. The controversial doctrine holds that through the fall of Adam and Eve (Genesis 3), God lost ownership of the world to SATAN. In the last days, God is raising up a core group of followers ("overcomers") who are restoring supernatural powers and the lost offices APOSTLE and PROPHET to regain dominion over the world's laws, finances, and governments. This ministry of supernatural overcomers will help usher in the SECOND COMING of Christ. Elements of this doctrine have much in common with the earlier LATTER RAIN MOVEMENT.

King James Only (kjv Only): The belief among some PROTESTANT FUNDAMENTALISTS Christians in English-speaking countries that the King James Version (kjv) BIBLE translation of 1611 "authorized" or commissioned by King James of England is the only true and accurate English BIBLE. Some maintain that the King James translation was itself a work of special inspiration from God, resulting in an inerrant translation. Most, however, base their argument in large part on the underlying Greek text used in the kjv translation, the *Textus Receptus* (Received Text), a work of New Testament textural criticism compiled by Desiderius Erasmus in 1516. They distrust modern textural criticism that makes use of more recently discovered biblical manuscripts such as *Codex Sinaiticus,* a fourth-century manuscript discovered in 1859, which is significantly older than the manuscripts used by Erasmus. In virtually all cases, the 1769 edition of the King James translation (edited by Benjamin Blayney) is actually used rather than the 1611 original that included the Catholic APOCRYPHA. See BIBLE.

Kirpal Light Satsang—Kinderhook, NY: See KNOW THYSELF AS SOUL FOUNDATION.

Klassen, Frank—Fort David, TX: Publishes *The Overcomer* newsletter. See YAHWEHISM.

Knight, J.Z.: NEW AGE, channeler of a spirit entity called RAMTHA. See CHANNELING, ASCENDED MASTERS.

Knights of Columbus, Fr. Michael J. McGivney (1852–90): Named after the Italian explorer Christopher Columbus, this fraternal organization, founded in 1882, is made up of about 1.7 million Roman Catholic men. Called "the strong right arm of the Church," the movement has been criticized by some for its secret oaths and has been compared to a Catholic version of FREEMASONRY. The movement promotes a number of charitable and philanthropic works including life insurance, educational, and social welfare programs. Web site—http://www.knowthyselfassoul.org. See ROMAN CATHOLICISM.

Know Thyself as Soul Foundation, Sant Thakar Singh (1929–2005)— Umpqua, OR: Singh, a former practitioner of SIKHISM, became a devotee of Kirpal Singh, a Hindu scholar who strongly advocated listening through MEDITATION to "inner light and sound" as the manifestation of God. Central to this practice is satsang, meditating and learning in the presence of a living master who is the embodiment of truth. His successor is Sant Baljit Singh. Web site—http://www.knowthyselfassoul.org. See HINDUISM.

Koot Hoomi: ASCENDED MASTER also called Master KH, who allegedly contacted ALICE BAILEY. See BAILEY, ALICE; LUCIS TRUST; THEOSOPHY.

Koran: See QUR'AN.

Koresh, David: See BRANCH DAVIDIANS.

Kornfield, Jack: Author of several NEW AGE books, Kornfield trained in Buddhist monasteries in Thailand, India, and Burma. He has been teaching Eastern MEDITATION since 1974 and is a founding teacher of the INSIGHT MEDITATION SOCIETY AND SPIRIT ROCK MEDITATION CENTER.

Kosmon: See UNIVERSAL FAITHISTS OF KOSMON.

Krastman, Hank: See METAPHYSICAL UNION.

Krieger, Dolores: See TOUCH THERAPY.

Krishna: According to some Hindu sects, Krishna is the eighth or ninth incarnation of VISHNU and possibly the manifestation of the supreme

demigod/God incarnating as VISHNU. See INTERNATIONAL SO-
CIETY FOR KRISHNA CONSCIOUSNESS.

Krishnamurti Foundation of America—Ojai, CA: Jiddu Krishnamurti,
the eighth child in a middle-class Indian family, was adopted by ANNIE
BESANT, then leader of the THEOSOPHICAL SOCIETY, who in 1906
proclaimed him to be the world teacher for whom all people were waiting. In
1929, Krishnamurti rejected this role and began his work as an independent
teacher, emphasizing the importance of total negation of thought. Truth
is not understood through any philosophical or theological system, but
instead through observation of the content of one's mind. The foundation
operates a retreat and maintains an archive of Krishnamurti's teachings. Web
site—http://www.kfa.org. See THEOSOPHY; HINDUISM.

Kriya Yoga: See YOGA.

Kübler-Ross, Elisabeth: See NEAR-DEATH EXPERIENCE (NDE).

Kundalini: In Hindu thought, the kundalini energy is symbolized as a serpent coiled at the base of the spine. Through MEDITATION and YOGA
this latent energy is aroused, gradually ascending the CHAKRAS along the
spine. When it reaches the seventh Chakra at the crown of the head, the individual achieves complete union with the BRAHMA. See HINDUISM.

Kunz, Dora: See TOUCH THERAPY.

L

L'Abri: See SCHAEFFER, FRANCIS.

Lafferty, Ron: A self-proclaimed prophet who, with his brother Dan Lafferty, broke away from the CHURCH OF JESUS CHRIST OF LATTER-DAY SAINTS to practice a form of Mormon fundamentalism that included polygamy. In 1984, he received a "revelation" that Brenda Lafferty (the wife of his brother Alan) and her 15-month-old daughter were to be killed because she would not accept the doctrine of polygamy. The story of that crime is retold in Jon Krakauer's best-seller *Under the Banner of Heaven.*

Lakewood Church—Houston, TX: See OSTEEN, JOEL.

Laksmi: Also called *Lakshma,* Laksmi is one of KRISHNA's consorts. The term is also used by members of the INTERNATIONAL SOCIETY FOR KRISHNA CONSCIOUSNESS to refer to money.

Lamb, Markus: See DAYSTAR TELEVISION NETWORK.

Lamb, Joni: See DAYSTAR TELEVISION NETWORK.

Landmark Education: See EST.

Landmark Forum: See EST.

Laodicean Home Missionary, John Krewson—Fort Myers, FL: In operation from 1957–90, this was a splinter of the WATCHTOWER BIBLE AND TRACT SOCIETY.

Lao-Tzu: See TAOISM.

Latter Rain Movement: A development within a minority of believers in the PENTECOSTAL MOVEMENT based in part on a unique interpretation of Joel 2:23. In the last days, it is predicted that churches will abandon denominations and come together through the ministry of "overcomers" or MANIFESTED SONS OF GOD. This "latter rain" representing the new outpouring of the HOLY SPIRIT will be instrumental in making the world turn to Christianity and help usher in the SECOND COMING of Christ. Elements of this doctrine can be found in the teachings of WILLIAM BRANHAM, RICK JOYNER, C. PETER WAGNER, and PAUL CAIN. See KINGDOM NOW THEOLOGY.

LaVey, Magnus Anton Szandor (1930–97): Founder of the CHURCH OF SATAN.

Laya Yoga: See YOGA.

Laymen's Home Missionary Movement, Paul S.L. Johnson and Raymond Jolly—Chester Springs, PA: One of the oldest splinter groups from the WATCHTOWER BIBLE AND TRACT SOCIETY. The movement publishes *The Bible Standard and Herald of Christ's Kingdom* newsletter. Web site—http://www.biblestandard.com.

Lazaris: See PURSEL, JACH.

LDS: See CHURCH OF JESUS CHRIST OF LATTER-DAY SAINTS.

Lectorium Rosicrucianum—Bakersfield, CA: Formed in 1935 by Dutch members of the ROSICRUCIAN FELLOWSHIP, the group teaches people to awaken their CHRIST CONSCIOUSNESS. Web site—http://www.lectoriumrosicrucianum.org. See ROSICRUCIANISM.

Lee, Bo-In: See NEW LIFE HEALTH CENTER.

Lee, Witness (1905–97): Lee became a Christian at the age of 19, and in 1934 was appointed the director of the Shanghai Gospel Bookroom by WATCHMAN NEE. In 1949, Nee sent Lee to Taiwan, where Lee published Nee's writings through the Taiwan Gospel Bookroom. Lee moved to the

United States in 1962, where he started The LOCAL CHURCH. LIVING STREAM MINISTRY, the publishing arm of The Local Church, maintains a Web site about Lee at http://www.witnesslee.org.

Legalism: An informal term that refers to a system of belief and practice built upon the precept that salvation is dependent upon strict observance of religious laws or rituals. In legalistic religious systems, the leaders determine whether the followers are satisfactorily fulfilling their religious obligations; these leaders often punish, through such practices as SHUNNING and DISFELLOWSHIPPING, individuals whose efforts are deemed unsatisfactory. Legalistic systems frequently devolve into SPIRITUAL ABUSE. See SALVATION BY GRACE; SALVATION BY WORKS.

Legerdemain: From a French term that translates to "lightness of hand," a form of illusion performed by a MAGICIAN through sleight-of-hand, usually through the use of playing cards or coins. See MAGIC.

Lemuria: A legendary lost continent of the Indian Ocean that is said to be the location of the Garden of Eden. The theory of Lemuria was originally developed in the nineteenth-century by scientists who theorized that a now-lost land bridge must have existed to allow for movement of creatures between south Asia and Africa; the presence of Lemurs in both Africa and India led to the name *Lemuria*. Theosophists then theorized that Lemuria was inhabited by a 15-foot tall group of hermaphroditic psychics who fled to ATLANTIS when their continent was destroyed. See THEOSOPHY.

Lemurian Fellowship—Ramona, CA: Founded in 1936 by Robert D. Stelle, the fellowship claims to have its roots in the citizenship schools of the mythical lost continent of Mu, believed to have disappeared approximately 71,000 years ago. By recording and studying stories about the existence and disappearance of such areas as Mu, LEMURIA, and ATLANTIS, the fellowship has devised a master plan for the integration of a NEW AGE civilization. Web site—http://www.lemurianfellowship.org. See THEOSOPHY.

Lenz, Frederick: See ZEN MASTER RAMA.

Levitation: The OCCULT practice of suspending an object or oneself in midair using PSYCHIC power in such a way as to apparently suspend or supersede the law of gravity. Levitation of this sort has never been performed in a controlled environment, despite frequent claims of levitation by the MAHARASHI MAHESH YOGI and others. See TELEKINESIS.

Liberal Christianity: Generally, any movement within professing CHRISTIANITY that questions the accuracy or relevancy of BIBLE doctrine and history in favor of religious values and experience. More specifically, the influence of German rationalism on European (and later American) Christian doctrine that attempted to "demythologize" Christianity by forming a nonsupernatural understanding of biblical miracles, inspiration, and historical theology. The result is a rejection of the stated authorship and historical accuracy of biblical books and a denial of Christ's VIRGIN BIRTH, substitutionary atonement, resurrection, etc. Most influential in mainline Protestant denominations, liberalism receives its philosophical inspiration from the dialecticism of Immanuel Kant and religious thought from Friedrich Schleirmacher, Rudolph Bultmann, and Paul Tillich. See CHRISTIANITY; EVANGELICAL CHRISTIANITY; FUNDAMENTALIST CHRISTIANITY.

Liberation Theology: A movement that attempts to unite theology with social and religious principles for addressing oppression. It finds expressions among theologians from minority groups within numerous Christian denominations but it is best identified with the shift toward Marxism among Roman Catholic theologians and priests in Latin America. Influenced by the sociopolitical emphasis of the movement, JESUS and the BIBLE are defined and interpreted in light of a class struggle, with the GOSPEL seen as a radical call to activism (or even revolution) promoting political and social answers (usually in the form of classic Communism). See LIBERAL CHRISTIANITY; ROMAN CATHOLICISM.

Life Assurance Ministry, Dale Ratzlaf—Glendale, AZ: An APOLOGETICS ministry that defends the beliefs of EVANGELICAL CHRISTIANITY and critiques the theology, history, and truth-claims of the SEVENTH-DAY ADVENTIST CHURCH from a traditional Christian perspective. The organization publishes a free bimonthly periodical, *Proclamation!,* and is a member of EVANGELICAL MINISTRIES TO NEW RELIGIONS (EMNR). Web site—http://www.ratzlaf.com.

Life Energy Foundation, John Diamond—South Salem, NY: Adopts many teachings of Diamond's previous organization, the Cantillation Research

Foundation, a NEW AGE organization that teaches "All is God, All is Mother—All is Love." The foundation teaches that a person's general well being is dependent upon their Life Energy, a term coined by Diamond to refer to the innate healing power of the body. Web sites—http://www. lifeenergyfoundation.org and http://www.diamondcenter.net. See PANTHEISM; HOLISTIC HEALTH.

Life Training: See KAIROS FOUNDATION.

Life Understanding Foundation, Bill and Davina Cox—Santa Barbara, CA: A NEW AGE organization that offers information about DOWSING and PYRAMIDOLOGY. Web site—http://www.dowsing.com. See OCCULT.

Lifeways Foundation: The foundation teaches holistic ecology, which is rooted in a mixture of NATIVE AMERICAN SPIRITUALITY and popular psychology that attempts to bring all life to a Unified Being.

Lifton, Robert: Lifton studied Mao Tse-Tung's programs of THOUGHT REFORM or Chinese BRAINWASHING while doing research for military intelligence. His study focused on radical change in personality and belief systems of certain prisoners-of-war who were held and tortured in Chinese camps. This research was later expanded in his 1961 work *Thought Reform and the Psychology of Totalism,* in which he theorized that subtle elements of these BRAINWASHING techniques could also be found in other environments. He outlined eight criteria for thought reform, which he called: MILIEU CONTROL, MYSTICAL MANIPULATION, LOADING THE LANGUAGE, DOCTRINE OVER PERSON, SACRED SCIENCE, CULT OF CONFESSION, DEMAND FOR PURITY, and DISPENSING OF EVIDENCE. While some elements of these criteria could be found in virtually any group, Lifton warned that an environment of mind control or thought reform exists when all eight are found implemented in the extreme. See BRAINWASHING; MIND CONTROL.

Lion and Lamb Ministries, Monte W. Judah—Norman, OK: A Messianic Jewish ministry that emphasizes SABBATARIANISM and observance of Jewish holy days. Judah gives particular emphasis to the impending Great Tribulation, publishing an extensive time line detailing his understanding of biblical predictions concerning the last days. Judah falsely predicted that the abomination of desolation prophesied in the Bible would occur by March of 1997 and promised he would be "totally discredited" and "shut down" the ministry if circumstances proved him to be wrong. On March 23, 1997 he apologized for the false prediction but reneged on his vow to disband the movement. *Note: this group should not be confused with the Texas-based Lamb & Lion Ministries, a Christian organization led by David R. Reagan.* Web site—http://www.lionlamb.net. See FALSE PROPHECY.

Literary Criticism: Essentially a historical-critical method of textual analysis, literary criticism of the BIBLE attempts to discover underlying literary sources, stylistic variances, and literary genres, and deals with questions relating to the authorship, unity, and dates of biblical texts. Many scholars within LIBERAL CHRISTIANITY use this methodology to argue that the biblical books are composite texts compiled by an editor or editors different from the traditionally accredited authors. However, these conclusions are grounded more on the anti-ORTHODOX assumptions of these scholars than in the methodology of literary criticism itself; EVANGELICAL scholars have also used literary critical approaches in their research to argue for the essential unity and authenticity of scripture. See FORM CRITICISM.

Little Flock: Also called the Anointed Class, the Little Flock is the group of 144,000 JEHOVAH'S WITNESSES who have been selected by Jehovah to reign in heaven with JESUS. All other worthy Jehovah's Witnesses (the Great Crowd or Other Sheep) will live for eternity on a new paradise earth. See WATCHTOWER BIBLE AND TRACT SOCIETY.

Lively Stones Fellowship, Willard Fuller—Lloyd, FL: Fuller, a former Southern Baptist pastor, claims he was miraculously healed from an incurable disease in 1959. He now operates a ministry in which he performs miraculous healings, with an emphasis on filling decayed teeth. Fuller also combines CHRISTIANITY with Eastern religious concepts, teaching that the human soul is reincarnated into new physical bodies. Web site—http://www.willardfuller.com. See REINCARNATION.

Living Church of God, Roderick C. Meredith—Charlotte, NC: Meredith was one of the first evangelists ordained by HERBERT W. ARMSTRONG (in 1952), and he wrote many of the articles published in *The Plain Truth* and *Good News* magazines in the 1950s. In 1992, Meredith left the WORLD-WIDE CHURCH OF GOD to form the GLOBAL CHURCH OF GOD, and a subsequent power struggle within the Global Church prompted Meredith to start the Living Church of God in 1998. The church produces *THE WORLD TOMORROW* television program, publishes *Tomorrow's World* magazine, and numerous booklets. Web site—http://www.livingcog. org. See ARMSTRONGISM.

Living Stream Ministry—Anaheim, CA: The publishing arm of THE LOCAL CHURCH. Web site—http://www.lsm.org.

Living Waters, Lois Roden—Waco, TX: A defunct group that formed the basis for the BRANCH DAVIDIANS. Roden died in 1986.

Living Word Fellowship, John Robert Stevens: Beginning in 1949, Stevens received revelations that he should initiate a restoration of first-century Christianity. His movement, which was originally known as The Walk, emphasizes modern prophecies and revelations. Some critics allege that the group practices SPIRITUAL ABUSE through its emphasis on submission to the revelations given by church leaders. In addition to such writings by Roberts as *To Be a Christian,* the fellowship publishes the *Shiloh* newsletter. Web site—http://www.thelivingword.org. See PENTECOSTAL CHRISTIANITY.

Llewellyn New Times—St. Paul, MN: The longtime name of an OCCULT periodical published by LLEWELLYN WORLDWIDE. In the 1990s the periodical's name was changed to *New Worlds of Mind & Spirit.*

Llewellyn Worldwide—St. Paul, MN: Llewellyn is one of the premier publishers of OCCULT material. Started in 1901 by Llewellyn George as the Portland School of Astrology, the organization has grown into a substantial company that distributes information on a wide array of occult and ESOTERIC subjects. Llewellyn's consumer catalog, *New Worlds,* has a distribution of 200,000. Llewellyn publishes *FATE* magazine and the *Llewellyn Journal.* Web site—http://www.llewellyn.com.

L/L Research, Jim McCarty and Carla Lisbeth Rueckert McCarty—Louisville, KY: From 1981–84, the McCartys channeled Ra, who claimed to be a "group soul" that had evolved over hundreds of thousands of years from a population group on Venus. Their central book, *The Ra Material,* details the message of human evolution given in these CHANNELING sessions.

The McCartys also emphasize the GODDESS GAIA in their counseling and mediation. Web site—http://www.llresearch.org. See NEW AGE.

Loading the Language: One of eight criteria of Mind Control according to ROBERT LIFTON'S theory of THOUGHT REFORM. The process involves limiting or controlling the thought processes by regulating the language in such a way that communication constricts and limits rather than expands human understanding. This may include the use of thought-stopping cliches or artificially reducing complex issues to a false black-and-white dichotomy. See LIFTON, ROBERT; MIND CONTROL; BRAINWASHING.

The Local Church, Witness Lee—Anaheim, CA: The Local Church is a controversial movement begun by WITNESS LEE (1905-97), a disciple of the Chinese author and martyr Nee To-sheng, better known as WATCHMAN NEE (1903–72). Lee moved to America in 1962 and founded LIVING STREAM MINISTRY. Among issues drawing criticism from some evangelical Christians is The Local Church's use of the term *mingling* to describe the relationship between God and believers (i.e., Christians become both divine and human, like Jesus). Some evangelicals have also charged that the Local Church compromises the doctrine of the TRINITY by confusing the persons of the HOLY SPIRIT and the Son (as does the HERESY of MODALISM). The organization's exclusivity has also been criticized. According to Lee, each city should have only one church, and denominationalism is seen as of the devil. The end result of this position, according to critics, is that Lee-led local churches—usually called by the name of their cities (e.g., the Church in Anaheim or the Church in Chicago)—become the only true expressions of CHRIST. Thus, the group views Christian denominations as tools "utilized by Satan to set up his satanic system" (Witness Lee, *The Life Study of Genesis*, vol. 1 (Anaheim, CA: Living Stream Ministry, 1987), p. 464. The Local Church has also gained a negative reputation for threatening legal action to prevent unfavorable public evaluation of its movement—an action that goes against the injunction found in 1 Corinthians 6:1-8. The movement publishes *THE HOLY BIBLE RECOVERY VERSION*. Web site—http://www.localchurch.org. See: LEE, WITNESS; LIVING STREAM MINISTRY; NEE, WATCHMAN.

The Lodge: See FREEMASONRY.

The Lord's Recovery: See THE LOCAL CHURCH.

Lovecraft, H.P.: See CTHULHU MYTHOS.

Lucas, George: Highly successful filmmaker and creator of the STAR WARS saga. According to Lucas biographer Dale Pollock, Lucas was heavily influenced by seminal NEW AGE books such as *Tales of Power* by CARLOS CASTANEDA and *The Hero with a Thousand Faces* by JOSEPH CAMPBELL, who also wrote *The Power of Myth*. The latter's influence was verified by Lucas in a *Time* magazine interview with BILL MOYERS. See STAR WARS.

Lucifer: See SATAN.

Lucifer Trust: See ARCANE SCHOOL.

Lucis Trust: One of a number of organizations founded by ALICE BAILEY that promotes her contribution to the I AM and THEOSOPHY movements. Web site—http://www.alicebailey.org. See BAILEY, ALICE; ARCANE SCHOOL; THEOSOPHY.

Lumen Foundation—San Francisco, CA: Founded in 1984, the foundation works to promote Western OCCULT and ESOTERIC traditions. The foundation's primary activity was publishing *Gnosis* journal—while *Gnosis* has ceased publication, an anthology of articles was republished in *Hidden Wisdom*. Web site—http://www.lumen.org.

Lutheran Church—Missouri Synod (LCMS)—St. Louis, MO: A denomination of PROTESTANTISM based on LUTHERANISM that was formed by 12 pastors in 1847 as The Evangelical Lutheran Synod of Missouri, Ohio, and other States, which was shortened to the current name in 1947. The LCMS is the second-largest Lutheran denomination in the United States (about 2.5 million baptized members in over 6,000 congregations) and is considered somewhat more conservative theologically than the larger EVANGELICAL LUTHERAN CHURCH IN AMERICA (ELCA). Web site—http://www.lcms.org. See LUTHERANISM; REFORMATION; PROTESTANTISM.

Lutheranism: A movement within CHRISTIANITY based on the beliefs of the German monk Martin Luther, who was the catalyst for the REFORMATION in the early sixteenth-century, which helped birth PROTESTANTISM. The three largest international organizations of churches are the Lutheran World Federation, the International Lutheran Council, and the Confessional Evangelical Lutheran Conference. In the United States there are over 20 Lutheran denominations. The three largest are the EVANGELICAL LUTHERAN CHURCH IN AMERICA (ELCA), The LUTHERAN CHURCH—MISSOURI SYNOD (LCMS), and the WISCONSIN EVANGELICAL LUTHERAN SYNOD (WELS). See REFORMATION; PROTESTANTISM.

M

Mackey, Albert: Nineteenth-century scholar and author of some of the primary reference works on FREEMASONRY, including the *Encyclopedia of Freemasonry* and the *History of Freemasonry.*

MacLaine, Shirley: In 1983 MacLaine, a famous actress, published her autobiography *Out on a Limb.* The book, which described her experiences with ASTRAL PROJECTION, UFO encounters, and other NEW AGE events, established MacLaine as the preeminent NEW AGE celebrity in the 1980s. The theological significance of MacLaine's teachings is displayed in the 1986 television miniseries based on her autobiography. In a climactic scene, MacLaine's GURU convinces her to stand on a beach and shout toward the Pacific Ocean, "I am God!" MacLaine's books include *Out on a Limb, Dancing in the Light,* and *The Camino: A Journey of Spirit.* Web site—http://www.shirleymaclaine.com.

Mafu: See TORRES, PENNY.

Magic: There are three common usages of the term *magic:* 1) *Stage magic* refers to forms of entertainment involving performers (MAGICIANS) demonstrating various tricks or illusions using LEGERDEMAIN (sleight-of-hand), MENTALISM, misdirection, etc. This form of magic does not involve the OCCULT or any alleged supernatural power. Well-known practitioners include Harry Houdini, David Copperfield, Siegfried Fischbacher and Roy Horn (Siegfried & Roy), Criss Angel (the Mindfreak), and David Blaine ("the Street Magician"). 2) *Supernatural magic* refers to spiritual or religious practices involving the alleged ability to affect events supernaturally, influence people, or alter the future using PSYCHIC powers or SPELLS. Practitioners of such magic, including followers of WICCA, often separate this kind of magic into two basic categories: white magic (attempts to heal, help, or do good) and black magic (attempts to harm, attack, or destroy). Traditional Christians make no such distinction and view all forms of supernatural magic as spiritually harmful and biblically forbidden (Deuteronomy 18:9-14). 3) *Magick* refers to part of a philosophical system developed in the early twentieth-century by ALEISTER CROWLEY, who chose to use the archaic spelling (*k* on the end) to differentiate his practice from stage magic and illusion. Crowley defined the word *magick* as both a science and an art in which one causes transformation to happen in accord with one's true will (see THELEMA). More recently, the word *magick* (archaic spelling) has been used more generically as a category for all forms of supernatural magic besides stage magic/illusion. See MAGICK; OCCULT; DIVINATION; WICCA.

Magician: A practitioner of MAGIC. Today the term is more commonly used in reference to those who practice stage MAGIC.

Magick: An attempt to create a supernatural effect or gain hidden knowledge using OCCULT techniques. Common methodologies include rituals, SPELLS, and INCANTATIONS. Magick may also involve such practices as NECROMANCY, DIVINATION, or the use of psychotropic drugs. The archaic spelling of *magick* (with the *k* at the end) was first popularized by the famous occultist ALEISTER CROWLEY to differentiate his philosophical concept of magic from other forms. Eventually this archaic spelling became the preferred form used by many occultists and practitioners to reference any magic seen to be occult or supernatural in nature (i.e., not including stage magic or the performance of an illusionist). *Magick* is also often used to reference forms of ceremonial magic. Some variations of magick include Crowley's THELEMA magick (a causation in accord with one's "true will"), Hermetic magick (an occult philosophy attributed to the Greek god Hermes and the Egyptian god Thoth), alchemical magick (the transformation of base metals into gold), Goetic magick (the calling forth of some 72 demons), CHAOS MAGICK (involving techniques of an intense focus of the mind and ALTERED STATES), and WICCA (WITCHCRAFT). See MAGIC; OCCULT; CROWLEY, ALEISTER; HERMETICISM; WICCA.

Magic: The Gathering: A popular FANTASY ROLE-PLAYING card game in which players bring into play cards representing magical SPELLs; these spell cards are combined to defeat the combination played by an opponent. Critics allege the game contains strong OCCULT elements. Web site—http://www.magicthegathering.com.

Maharishi Ayur-Ved Foundation: Promotes teachings of MAHARISHI MAHESH YOGI.

Maharishi Mahesh Yogi: Founder of TRANSCENDENTAL MEDITATION.

Maharishi University of Management—Fairfield, IA: A fully accredited university that offers bachelor through doctoral-level degrees in numerous fields while also promising to enable students to experience a blissful level of consciousness. The school promotes the teachings and practices of TRANSCENDENTAL MEDITATION. Web site—http://www.mum.edu.

Mahavira: JAINISM.

Mahikari: The full name of the movement is Sekai Mahikari Bunmei Kyodan. The group claims to engage in the ancient Japanese practice of Mahikari-no-waza, in which the practitioner heals the follower with divine light that radiates from his or her palm. Web site—http://www.mahikari. org.

Malcolm X: Formerly Malcolm Little, Malcom X—who was murdered in 1965—remains the most famous member of the NATION OF ISLAM.

Mandara Spa: Part of STEINER LEISURE. Primarily located in cruise ships, luxury hotels, and resorts, these spas offer a variety of massage treatments, including AROMATHERAPY, Shiatsu (based on same principles as ACUPUNCTURE), REFLEXOLOGY, and AYURVEDIC treatments. See HOLISTIC HEALING. Web site—http://www.mandaraspa.com.

Manifested Sons of God: According to proponents of the controversial LATTER RAIN MOVEMENT, these believers are an elite group of end-time "overcomers" (sometimes known as Joel's Army) who have received the restored, lost powers of the early Christian leaders, including those of an APOSTLE and PROPHET. These overcomers have the HOLY SPIRIT without measure and will display virtually unlimited supernatural gifts and powers that will help bring forth the SECOND COMING of Christ. See LATTER RAIN MOVEMENT.

Manning, Brennan: Popular religious author and lecturer. A former Franciscan monk, he promotes CENTERING PRAYER, including the Eastern MEDITATION practices espoused by such centering proponents as THOMAS KEATING and BASIL PENNINGTON. Critics have also claimed that Manning fails to give a clear presentation of the GOSPEL in his writings because he is a UNIVERSALIST, a charge he has denied. One of his most widely read books is *The Ragamuffin Gospel.* Web site—http://brennanmanning.com.

Mantra: An Eastern MYSTICISM or NEW AGE term for a word or series of words that are continually repeated (either verbally or silently). The mantra is said to help one achieve an altered state of consciousness. Mantras are often recited during MEDITATION or relaxation exercises.

Marah—Madison, NJ: A provider of incense for AROMATHERAPY, as well as resources for MAGIC, GODDESS worship, and WICCA. Web site—http://members.aol.com/marahco.

Mark-Age—Elk Valley, TN: Originally started in Miami in 1960, Mark-Age is a NEW AGE company that promotes I AM teaching to assist individuals in developing their CHRIST CONSCIOUSNESS. Web site—http://www.thenewearth.org/markage.html.

Mark Probert's Educational Foundation—Palo Alto, CA: See CHURCH OF E YADA DI SHI-ITE.

Mark Probert's Kethra E'Da (Teachers of Light)—Palo Alto, CA: See CHURCH OF E YADA DI SHI-ITE.

Martindale, Craig: Former leader of THE WAY INTERNATIONAL. Martindale resigned in 2000 following allegations that he forced a member into a sexual relationship.

Martin, Water R. (1928–89): Well-known apologist who defended EVAN-GELICAL CHRISTIANITY from cults and heretical doctrine. Author of *The Kingdom of the Cults* and founder of the syndicated radio program

The Bible Answer Man and the CHRISTIAN RESEARCH INSTITUTE (CRI).

Mary's House of David, Mary Purnell—Benton Harbor, MI: Founded by the widow of Benjamin Purnell. See HOUSE OF DAVID.

Masonry: See FREEMASONRY.

Masterpath, Sri Gary Olsen—Temecula, CA: A system for realizing that the individual is God. The individual achieves this enlightenment by detaching the soul from the mind through the "divine science of light and sound," in which the soul listens to the "sound current" or "divine life stream" of God. Web site—http://www.masterpath.org. See NEW AGE; HINDUISM.

Masters, Roy: Founder of the FOUNDATION FOR HUMAN UNDERSTANDING.

Matagiri Sri Aurobindo Center, Inc.—Mount Tremper, NY: Founded in 1968, the Center is a Hindu retreat dedicated to promoting the teachings of Sri Aurobindo. Web site—http://www.matagiri.org. See HINDUISM.

Materialization: The alleged supernatural ability to create material objects or living beings out of nothing. Most stage MAGICIANS incorporate this into their MAGIC shows but readily admit it is an illusion rather than a supernatural act.

Maya: The Hindu principle that all is an illusion and that ultimately the physical world, contacted through the conscious mind and the five senses, does not represent reality. This philosophy is also taught by many practitioners of NEW AGE spirituality.

Maya Factor: The NEW AGE book on which the HARMONIC CONVERGENCE was based.

McDowell, Josh: Popular APOLOGIST who promotes EVANGELICAL CHRISTIANITY. Author of several Christian best-sellers, including *More than a Carpenter* and *Evidence That Demands a Verdict.* Affiliated with CAMPUS CRUSADE FOR CHRIST INTERNATIONAL. Web site—http://www.josh.org.

McKean, Kip: Founder and former leader of the INTERNATIONAL CHURCHES OF CHRIST.

Meditation: Meditation is a spiritual discipline—particularly in HINDUISM and BUDDHISM—in which the mind is detached from focus on objects and even from the process of thought itself. There are many disciplines associated with meditation in Eastern religions, including recitation of a MANTRA, YOGA, and controlled breathing. The result of such meditation is the total serenity of body and mind, and—in many traditions—an experience of the unity of all things; the goal of meditation is therefore enlightenment. This view of meditation is shared by practitioners of NEW AGE spirituality but is rejected by traditional CHRISTIANITY, in which meditation involves using all aspects of the mind to contemplate the attributes of God and the meaning of scriptural texts.

Medium: A medium is an intermediary between the physical world and the world of spirits. A medium enables contact and communication with the dead, usually through CHANNELING or conducting a SÉANCE. See NECROMANCY, OCCULT, SPIRITUALISM; MEDIUM (TV).

***Medium* (TV):** NBC's popular television drama staring Patricia Arquette and Jake Weber, which promotes PSYCHIC communication with the dead (NECROMANCY) and the OCCULT. Arquette plays the part of a real-life PSYCHIC, ALLISON DUBOIS, who lives in Phoenix, Arizona and serves as the research consultant for the show. Web site—http://www.nbc.com/Medium. See: DUBOIS, ALLISON; MEDIUM; PSYCHIC; NECROMANCY; OCCULT.

Megiddo Church, L.T. Nichols—Rochester, NY: Founded by Nichols in the last half of the nineteenth-century, Megiddo teaches that the ultimate hope for humanity is to live forever in God's paradisiacal kingdom on Earth. Megiddo is staunchly anti-Trinitarian, and the church publishes the *Megiddo Message*. Web site—http://www.megiddo.com.

Melton, J. Gordon: John Gordon Melton is a well-known scholar and researcher in the field of alternative spirituality and minority religions. He has authored over 25 books, including the 1,250-page *Encyclopedia of American Religions*. In 1969 he became the founding director of the Institute for the Study of American Religions at the University of California, Santa Barbara.

Some critics have questioned his objectivity, claiming that he has received funds from controversial groups such as the AUM SHINRIKYO and THE FAMILY (CHILDREN OF GOD). Pointing to his testimony and legal filings on behalf of groups like the CHURCH OF SCIENTOLOGY and the LOCAL CHURCH, some critics have labeled him a "cult apologist." Web site—http://www.americanreligion.org.

Menhir: Literally translated "long stone," a menhir is a stone set upright by an ancient culture as a memorial or monument. Menhirs are found throughout Great Britain and northern Europe. Arguably the most famous menhirs are those at STONEHENGE.

Meninger, William: A Trappist monk who, drawing upon a fourteenth-century book, *The Cloud of Unknowing* and the writings of the contemplatives Saint John of the Cross and Saint Teresa of Avila, helped pioneer the CENTERING PRAYER movement with THOMAS KEATING and BASIL PENNINGTON. Web site—http://www.contemplativeprayer.net.

Mennonite: A member of a Christian movement based on the teachings of the sixteenth-century Anabaptist leader Menno Simons (1496–1561), which developed out of the Radical Reformation. Radical reformers such as Felix Manz and Conrad Grebel believed that the REFORMATION, as led by Martin Luther and John Zwingli, was incomplete. They stressed additional beliefs and practices, including baptism for believers only and separation of church and state. They suffered intense persecution and are known for their historic commitment to pacificism. There are about 1.3 million worldwide in a variety of Mennonite sects. See REFORMATION.

Mentalism: A branch of stage MAGIC in which the practitioner is able to create the illusion that he or she can read minds or control others' thoughts.

Mental Telepathy: See TELEPATHY.

Meridians: Meridians are energy channels through which CHI flows. ACUPUNCTURE is used to clear blockages in the meridians.

Mesmerism, Franz Mesmer: An eighteenth-century movement begun in France by the Austrian doctor Franz Anton Mesmer, who believed that astrological influence on humans was based on a force or substance similar to magnetism. He first began treating patients with magnets or charged fluids but quickly modified his position, theorizing that cures were actually coming from an energy or mysterious "magnetic fluid" coming from the hands, voice, or nervous system of the practitioner. This invisible substance or magnetism was thought to be similar to electromagnetism and was dubbed "animal magnetism." Mesmer's pupils were later able to induce a "magnetic sleep" (TRANCE state or hypnotic condition) in their patients. The term *mesmerism* eventually became analogous with HYPNOSIS and was linked with both SPIRITUALISM and the MIND SCIENCE religions. See ALTERED STATES OF CONSCIOUSNESS; HYPNOSIS.

Messiah: Literally "anointed one" or CHRIST. The promised Savior of JUDAISM believed by CHRISTIANITY to be JESUS of Nazareth. See CHRIST.

Messianic Communities: See THE TWELVE TRIBES.

MEST: See CHURCH OF SCIENTOLOGY.

Metaphysical Union, Hank Krastman—Chatsworth, CA: Krastman, a legal specialist, believes that the Earth is hollow and is used by UFOs. He also writes on such OCCULT topics as PSYCHIC powers, ESP, and other phenomena. Krastman published *The Unexplained* magazine. Web site—http://home.earthlink.net/~krastman.

Metaphysics: Based on the Greek terms for "beyond the physical," metaphysics is the philosophical study of existence and knowledge; it addresses questions of "ultimate reality." In popular, modern usage, *metaphysics* has come to refer to the immaterial or spiritual, and therefore to experimentation with MAGIC, PSYCHIC phenomena, or the OCCULT.

Methodism: An expression of PROTESTANTISM with roots to an eighteenth-century movement within the CHURCH OF ENGLAND. This movement was led by John Wesley, and his methodological approach to BIBLE study led to the term *Methodism*. The movement began to grow in the United States beginning with the First Great Awakening (1730–40s) and subsequent revivals. A number of denominations today find their roots in Methodism, including the UNITED METHODIST CHURCH, the WESLEYAN CHURCH, the CHURCH OF THE NAZARENE, the AFRICAN METHODIST EPISCOPAL CHURCH, and the FREE METHODISTS. A number of Holiness Revivals during the mid-1800s were catalysts for the Wesleyan-Holiness movement that had a strong influence on the PENTECOSTAL MOVEMENT. In 2006, there were about 75 million Methodists worldwide.

Metro Christian Fellowship: See KANSAS CITY PROPHETS.

Metropolitan Community Church (MCC): See UNIVERSAL FELLOWSHIP OF METROPOLITAN COMMUNITY CHURCHES.

Meyer, Joyce: Popular WORD-FAITH televangelist and teacher and founder of Joyce Meyer Ministries. A popular conference speaker, Meyer is particularly helpful to women who have endured abuse or poor self-esteem, since she addresses those subjects from experience. However, she also includes the prosperity message in her teaching and holds to the controversial doctrine that Christians are actually "little gods." Critics also point out that one of her past pamphlets on salvation also included the "Jesus won His own salvation in hell" teaching popular with some Word-Faith teachers. Web site—http://www.joycemeyer.org. See WORD-FAITH MOVEMENT.

Midrash: In JUDAISM, a method of interpreting the TANAKH (Jewish Bible) and also the written commentaries that are produced through this method.

Midwest Christian Outreach, L.L. (Don) Veinot, Jr.—Wonder Lake, IL: An APOLOGETICS ministry founded in 1995 by Veinot and his wife, Joy, to promote evangelism and to defend EVANGELICAL CHRISTIANITY from heretical doctrines of religious cults and aberrant theology. Don Veinot has also served as president of EVANGELICAL MINISTRIES TO NEW RELIGIONS (EMNR). Publications include *The Midwest Christian Outreach Journal*. Web site—http://www.midwestoutreach.org.

Mike Warnke Ministries: See WARNKE, MIKE.

Milieu Control: One of eight criteria of MIND CONTROL according to ROBERT LIFTON'S theory of THOUGHT REFORM. Milieu control involves attempting to regulate human communication, relationships, and access to outside information and alternative viewpoints. See LIFTON, ROBERT; BRAINWASHING.

Miller, Monte Kim: See CONCERNED CHRISTIANS.

Miller, William: Miller (1782–1849) was a farmer and Baptist lay minister who predicted that JESUS would return in March 1843. When this date passed, Miller and his followers determined that they had miscalculated by one year. The failure of their prophecy that Christ would return on October 22, 1844 came to be known as the Great Disappointment. See SECOND ADVENT MOVEMENT.

Mind/Body Medical Institute, Herbert Benson—Cambridge, MA: Affiliated with Harvard Medical School, the institute was founded by Dr. Herbert Benson, an associate professor of medicine at Harvard, to research and train practitioners in HOLISTIC HEALING. Web site—http://www. mbmi.org/home.

Mind Control: Also referred to as thought control and BRAINWASHING. The mind control or THOUGHT REFORM model suggests that there are specific methods of deception that can be employed by abusive spiritual leaders that may result in a diminished capacity for critical thinking and suppression of autonomy in their followers. These methods are believed to involve an intense social influence conditioning program that may include a closed system of authoritarian control, manipulative group dynamics, a system of punishment and rewards, induced dissociation or TRANCE induction, information control, fraud, coercion, and DOUBLE BINDS. Depending on the number and intensity of undue influence elements and a person's own unique susceptibilities, one may experience a pseudopersonality change and marked debilitation, compliance, and servitude. The mind control model should not be interpreted to mean that the subject is not responsible for the consequences of his or her decisions and actions, nor is it justification for holding individuals against their will or for conducting forcible, involuntary deprogramming. While evangelicals are lacking consensus on the nature, extent, or, in some cases, even existence of mind control, the BIBLE warns against seducers, deceivers, and exploiters who employ methods that can bring about spiritual harm or personal abuse. See LIFTON, ROBERT.

Mind Power System: Developed by Jose Silva, the system involves a method of "dynamic MEDITATION" in which the practitioner can rapidly reach a mental level producing alpha brain waves. The practitioner then engages in VISUALIZATION to create circumstances favorable to achieving one's goals. Finally, the practitioner is able to use sleep to achieve deeper levels of consciousness. Web site—http://www.mindpowersystem.com.

Mind Science: A generic, general classification of religious groups that hold to the belief in the inherent divinity of man and that the mind or thoughts are energy forms that can create or alter reality. The term is most often used in reference to the American religions formed in the latter half of the nineteenth-century that deny the actuality of sin, sickness, or death and promote health though mental practices. See NEW THOUGHT; PANTHEISM; FIRST CHURCH OF CHRIST, SCIENTIST; RELIGIOUS SCIENCE; NEW AGE.

Miracle Distribution Center—Fullerton, CA: The center promotes *A COURSE IN MIRACLES* and publishes *The Holy Encounter* newsletter. Web site—http://www.miraclecenter.org.

MISA, John-Roger Hinkins: See CHURCH OF THE MOVEMENT OF SPIRITUAL INNER AWARENESS.

Mishnah: Religious texts used in JUDAISM that were compiled from oral law passed down by rabbis and written in Hebrew.

Mitchell, David Bryan: Kidnapper of Elizabeth Smart in 2002, Mitchell (aka Immanuel David Isaiah) is a former member of the CHURCH OF JESUS CHRIST OF LATTER-DAY SAINTS (LDS). After leaving the LDS church, he began to practice a form of Mormon fundamentalism, claiming to be God's prophet and called to practice polygamy. Mitchell said he received a revelation from God that he was to take Smart as one of his plural wives. Smart was found alive in March of 2003. Mitchell and his wife, Wanda Ileen Barzee, were arrested but the courts found Mitchell mentally incompetent to stand trial.

Mo Letters: Messages written from Moses David Berg to members of THE FAMILY (CHILDREN OF GOD).

Modalism: Also called patripassianism, modalistic MONARCHIANISM, SABELLIANISM, JESUS ONLY, and Oneness. Modalism is a second- and third-century HERESY that denies the doctrine of the Trinity, teaching there is only one person in the Godhead. While the doctrine of the trinity teaches there are three distinct persons in the Godhead, modalism maintains that one person (usually the Father) has manifested Himself at different times under different names (Jesus/Spirit) or modes. Thus, Father, Son, and Holy Ghost are three names for the same person. Originally taught in various forms by Noetus, Praxeas, and Sabellius, modified forms of this doctrine can be found in the teachings of WILLIAM BRANHAM, some APOSTOLIC CHURCHES, and the UNITED PENTECOSTAL CHURCH. See TRINITY; MONARCHIANISM; BRANHAM, WILLIAM; ONENESS PENTECOSTALISM.

Mohammad: Founder of ISLAM.

Moksha: A Sanskrit term that means "release" or "liberation" and refers to the process of being released from the karmic cycle of birth and death (REINCARNATION) and becoming one with the impersonal God-force which is the true self (or ATMAN). The term is used with various shades of meaning in HINDUISM, JAINISM, BUDDHISM and some forms of YOGA. See REINCARNATION; SAMSARA; KARMA.

Moltzan, Toni: NEW AGE author. She claims to be a CHANNELER for the GREAT WHITE BROTHERHOOD (of the Order of Melchizedek) and that the ASCENDED MASTER Azreal is her SPIRIT GUIDE. See A COURSE IN LIGHT; AZ REALITY PUBLISHERS.

Monarchianism: A rejection of the doctrine of the TRINITY found sporadically throughout early Christian history. Monarchianism is the belief that, because God's nature is one, He cannot exist eternally in three persons. The two most common forms of monarchianism are DYNAMIC MONARCHIANISM and MODALISM.

Monotheism: The belief in the existence of one and only one true God, in contrast to ATHEISM (the belief in no God), POLYTHEISM (the belief in more than one true God), and PANTHEISM (the belief that all is God). The three largest monotheistic religions are JUDAISM, CHRISTIANITY, and ISLAM.

Monroe Institute, Robert Monroe—Faber, VA: Begun by Monroe in 1956 to determine the feasibility of learning during sleep, the institute allegedly discovered, in 1958, the phenomenon now known as an OUT-OF-BODY EXPERIENCE. The Institute now studies OBEs and has developed the Hemi-Sync technology to influence brainwaves and generate ALTERED STATES OF CONSCIOUSNESS. Web site—http://www.monroeinstitute. org (now defunct).

Moonies: A popular albeit derogatory nickname for members of the HOLY SPIRIT ASSOCIATION FOR THE UNIFICATION OF WORLD CHRISTIANITY.

Moon, Sun Myung: Founder of the HOLY SPIRIT ASSOCIATION FOR THE UNIFICATION OF WORLD CHRISTIANITY.

Moravian Church: A denomination of PROTESTANTISM that developed out of the leadership of a number of reformers in Bohemia and Moravia (present-day Czech Republic), including Jon Hess (1369–1415), who protested many of the practices and doctrines of ROMAN CATHOLICISM. Catholic officials found Hess guilty of heretical beliefs and burned him at the stake. His reformation, which predated Luther's PROTESTANT REFORMATION by over 100 years, did not die with him. The Moravian Church was officially organized in 1457 as *Unitas Fratrum* (Unity of Brethren) in Kunvald about 100 miles east of Prague. The Moravian Church in America is in full communion with the Evangelical LUTHERAN CHURCH IN AMERICA and the UNITED METHODIST CHURCH. Web site—http://www.moravian.org.

More to Life Weekend: See KAIROS FOUNDATION.

Mormonism: See THE CHURCH OF JESUS CHRIST OF LATTER-DAY SAINTS.

Mormonism Researched Ministry, Bill McKeever—Draper, UT: An APOLOGETICS ministry founded in 1979 that defends the beliefs of EVANGELICAL CHRISTIANITY and critiques the theology, history, and truth claims of the CHURCH OF JESUS CHRIST OF LATTER-DAY SAINTS from a traditional Christian perspective. The organization publishes a free newsletter and is a member of EVANGELICAL MINISTRIES TO NEW RELIGIONS (EMNR). Web site—http://www.mrm.org.

MorningStar Ministries, Rick and Julie Joyner—Fort Mill, SC: Founded in 1985, the ministry publishes the *MorningStar Journal,* maintains a school of ministry, and a local congregation, MorningStar Fellowship. The ministry is headquartered on a portion of the Heritage Village property once owned by Jim Bakker's PTL. The ministry is not affiliated with Morning Star International, now renamed EVERY NATION CHURCHES. Web site—http://www.morningstarministries.org. See JOYNER, RICK

Moses de Leon: Thirteenth-century compiler of the KABBALAH.

Mother Ruth: See SCIENCE OF MAN.

Movement for the Restoration of the Ten Commandments of God, Joseph Kibweteere—Kanunga, Uganda: Founded in 1987 in Uganda, Africa by a former ROMAN CATHOLIC who claimed to have tape-recorded conversations with the VIRGIN MARY, who warned him that the world would end on December 31, 1999. Members were encouraged to make sacrificial donations to the church and fully commit themselves to the Ten Commandments in preparation for the end. When the date proved to be a FALSE PROPHECY the movement faced a crisis, with many members demanding answers and, in some cases, refunds. Kibweteere, the movement's founder, initially explained that the Virgin Mary had extended the Armageddon date to March 17, 2000. However, when the new date arrived and the congregation gathered in a building to pray, the worshipers were locked inside and the building was burned to the ground in a gruesome suicide or murder that killed at least 330, of whom 78 were children. Some estimated the total body count was closer to 600. Mass graves containing hundreds of bodies of other members, apparently murdered weeks before the fire, brought the death toll estimates as high as 1,000, placing the tragedy on the same level as that of JONESTOWN.

Movement of Spiritual Inner Awareness (MSIA), Roger "John-Roger" Hinkins—Los Angeles, CA: Hinkins, who was raised in a MORMON family, claims he awoke from a nine-day coma in 1963 to find another spiritual personality, named John, had merged with him. He then took the name John-Roger and began exploring different spiritual teachings, including ECKANKAR. In 1968 he began giving spiritual seminars in homes and this led to the establishment of the Church of the Movement of Spiritual Awareness in 1971. This NEW AGE group teaches what John-Roger calls Soul Transcendence: awareness of oneself as a soul and as one with God (PANTHEISM). Beliefs and practices include CHRIST CONSCIOUS-NESS, REINCARNATION, GUIDED IMAGERY, MEDITATION, and CHANNELING. Web site—http://www.msia.org.

Moyers, Bill: Moyers is a longtime journalist—and former Baptist—known for his exploration of NEW AGE themes on public television. Moyers has hosted many documentaries on the Public Broadcasting Service, including *The Power of Myth* with JOSEPH CAMPBELL, *The Wisdom of Faith* with Huston Smith, and *Genesis: A Living Conversation.*

Muhammad: Founder of ISLAM.

Muhammad, Elijah: First leader of the NATION OF ISLAM.

Murray, Arnold: Founder of the SHEPHERD'S CHAPEL.

Murray O'Hair, Madalyn (1919–95): Founder of AMERICAN ATHEIST, INC., who was best known for her 1960 lawsuit (*Murray v. Curlett*) that ultimately determined Bible reading in public schools to be unconstitutional. The suit was filed on behalf of her son, William J. Murray, who later became a Baptist minister and author of the book *My Life Without God.* O'Hair and two of her other children disappeared in 1995. In 2001, their dismembered bodies were unearthed on a Texas ranch. David Roland Waters, former office manager for American Atheist, Inc., had kidnapped and murdered them. See AMERICAN ATHEISTS, INC.

Muscle Testing: See APPLIED KINESIOLOGY.

Music Square Church: See ALAMO CHRISTIAN FOUNDATION.

Muslim: A follower of ISLAM.

Mysteria Products Company—Fort Worth, TX: Mail-order house established in 1959 that offers OCCULT and MAGIC products. See DORENE PUBLISHING.

Mystical Manipulation: One of eight criteria of MIND CONTROL according to ROBERT LIFTON'S theory of THOUGHT REFORM. A group dynamic involving contrived, manipulated behavior designed to appear spontaneous, which produces feelings or actions that are misinterpreted as spiritual phenomena. See LIFTON, ROBERT; BRAINWASHING.

Mysticism: The use of intuition and deep personal experience in the religious pursuit of union with God, contact with the divine, or the innate knowledge of ultimate truth and reality. In many cases, such insights are gained through ALTERED STATES OF CONSCIOUSNESS by initiation into clandestine ceremonies or by receiving access to secret knowledge. Many religions have mystical sects or offshoots. For example, KABBALAH is a mystical, ESOTERIC system within Hasidic JUDAISM, the Whirling Dervishes of SUFISM attempt to blend mysticism with ISLAM, and GNOSTICISM provides a mystical interpretation of early CHRISTIANITY.

N

Narconon—Los Angeles, CA: Not to be confused with Narcotics Anonymous, Narconon is an organization affiliated with the CHURCH OF SCIENTOLOGY. Started in 1966, Narconon is a program for ending drug addictions that utilizes total withdrawal, massive infusions of vitamins and sauna treatment, and counseling based on the principles of Scientology. While Narconon claims a 70-percent success rate in treating patients with drug addictions, many physicians have criticized the program as being medically unsound. Web site—http://www.narconon.org.

National Association of Free Will Baptists—Antioch, TN: A denomination of EVANGELICAL CHRISTIANITY that forms the largest body of Free Will Baptist Churches in the United States, with 2,400 churches in 42 states and 14 countries. Web site—http://nafwb.net. See FREE WILL BAPTISTS.

National Baptist Convention, USA—Nashville, TN: A denomination of PROTESTANTISM with over 7.5 million members in over 30,000 congregations. The nation's oldest and largest African American religious convention. Web site—http://www.nationalbaptist.com. See BAPTIST CHURCHES.

National Council for Geocosmic Research—Brewster, MA: Founded in 1971, the council engages in the formal study of ASTROLOGY to determine correspondences between celestial movements and events on Earth. The council publishes *Geocosmic Journal*. Web site—http://www. geocosmic.org.

National Council of Churches (NCC)—New York, NY: A religious association organized in 1950 and comprised of about 35 denominations of PROTESTANTISM, ANGLICAN, and ORTHODOX CHURCHES. Members in the NCC tend toward LIBERAL CHRISTIANITY and have drawn criticism from some within EVANGELICAL CHRISTIANITY and FUNDAMENTALIST CHRISTIANITY for their left-wing stand on theological and political issues. Web site—http://www.ncccusa.org.

National Institute for Clinical Application of Behavioral Medicine—Mansfield Center, CT: Founded in 1987, the institute works to integrate traditional medical practices with HYPNOSIS, GUIDED IMAGERY, VISUALIZATION, and NEURO-LINGUISTIC PROGRAMMING. In addition to its professional development courses in HOLISTIC HEALING, the institute sponsors a conference on the relationship between psychology and health. Web site—http://www.nicabm.com.

National Spiritual Science Center, Alice Wellstood Tindall—Washington, DC: Established in 1941 as the First Spiritual Science Church. Due to illness, Tindall retired in 1969 and her appointed successors, Henry and Diane Nagorka, changed the name to the National Spiritual Science Center. This NEW AGE organization is based on the tenets of PANTHEISM. Beliefs and practices include REINCARNATION, MEDITATION, PSYCHIC Readings, and CHANNELING. Web site—http://www.nsscdc.org.

National Spiritualist Association of Churches—Cassadaga, FL: Formed in 1893 to promote worship services and education on SPIRITUALISM, the association promotes DIVINATION and spiritual healing for individuals and society. The role of MEDIUM is central to the life of Spiritualist congregations. The association has over 50 churches in 27 states. Web site—http://www.nsac.org.

Nation of Islam, Elijah Muhammad: A sect of ISLAM that originated in America and is composed of black Americans. Followers, sometimes called Black Muslims, believe that ALLAH (God) appeared in 1930 to the last great prophet Elijah Muhammad in the person of Wallace D. Fard. Elijah Muhammad borrowed many beliefs from traditional ISLAM and introduced some important differences—most notably the focus on black oppression and equating SATAN and evil with the white race. MALCOLM X became a notable leader of the movement in the 1960s, and the focus on black supremacy and militancy escalated. Malcolm X later converted to traditional ISLAM and rejected radical black supremacy and was subsequently murdered. The current leader of the Nation of Islam is Louis Farrakhan. Web site—http://www.noi.org. See ISLAM. For further research, a four-page Watchman Fellowship Profile is available (see page 363). Web site—http://www.watchman.org/notebook.

Nation of Yahweh, Yahweh ben Yahweh, aka Hulon Mitchell, Jr.—Miami, FL: Founded in 1979, the Nation of Yahweh claims that blacks are the chosen people of God and Mitchell is Yahweh ben Yahweh (literally, "God, the Son of God"), their MESSIAH. In 1992, Mitchell and six followers were convicted of racketeering and conspiracy to commit murder; Mitchell was paroled in 2001. Originally based in Miami, the group has moved to Montreal. Web site—http://www.yahwehbenyahweh.com. See IDENTITY MOVEMENT; SERPENT SEED; YAHWEHISM.

Native American Spirituality: The religious beliefs, practices, and rituals associated with Native Americans. Early Native American beliefs, though diverse, often shared common religious ideas. Many believed in a Great Spirit, that nature in all of its forms possessed spirits, and that all life was interconnected. Seasons and moons often were viewed as marking times of evocation for spirits and prosperity. Many NEW AGE practitioners, seeing parallels with popular NEW AGE beliefs, have been promoting a revival of Native American spirituality.

Natural Law Party: Political party started by MAHARISHI MAHESH YOGI. Critics allege it existed to promote the Maharishi's religious movement at taxpayers' expense through campaign matching funds provided for political candidates in the United States. One of the platform planks of the party was pursuing permanent peace using "MEDITATION technologies." In 2004, the Natural Law Party was dissolved, and its 2000 presidential candidate, Dr. John Hagelin, founded a political think tank and "complementary government" called the UNITED STATES PEACE GOVERNMENT. Web site—http://www.natural-law.org. See TRANSCENDENTAL MEDITATION.

Nature's Sunshine, Gene and Kristine Hughes—Provo, UT: Produces herbal remedies that promote weight loss, hair and body care, and

AROMATHERAPY. Web site—http://www.naturessunshine.com. See HOLISTIC HEALING.

Near-Death Experience (NDE): The phenomena reported by some survivors who almost died or were declared clinically dead before being resuscitated. While accounts are quite diverse, some common elements of NDE stories include feelings of peace and well-being and the sensation of being drawn toward a bright light. The best-known pioneer in near-death studies was Elisabeth Kübler-Ross, MD (1926–2004), who wrote *On Death and Dying*. While some have tried to use accounts of NDE to develop doctrines on the afterlife or corroborate their pre-existing beliefs, many physiological and psychological factors may account for the phenomena. See INTERNATIONAL ASSOCIATION FOR NEAR-DEATH STUDIES (IANDS).

Necromancy: The practice of obtaining information—particularly about the future—through communication with spirits of the dead. See OCCULT; DIVINATION; SPIRITUALISM.

Necronomicon: See CTHULHU MYTHOS.

Nee, Watchman: Nee, born Nee Shu-tsu in 1903, took the name Nee To-sheng ("watchman's rattle") after his 1920 conversion to CHRISTIANITY because he considered himself a watchman commissioned to raise an alarm in the night. In 1936, Nee experienced a revelation to start local churches in various parts of China. He was imprisoned in 1952 and remained in prison until he died in 1972. Nee was a close friend of WITNESS LEE, whom he sent to Taiwan in 1949 to continue their evangelistic work; this work led to the formation of THE LOCAL CHURCH. Nee wrote many books, most notably *The Normal Christian Life*. LIVING STREAM MINISTRY maintains a Web site about Nee at http://www.watchmannee.org.

Neo-Orthodox Christianity: A theological movement within PROTES-TANTISM that was a reaction against LIBERAL CHRISTIANITY and is associated with such theologians as Karl Barth and Emil Brunner. Neo-orthodox theologians emphasized God's transcendence; God's self-revelation in JESUS, in the BIBLE, and in sermons; and in the sinfulness of humanity. Many scholars within EVANGELICAL CHRISTIANITY disagree with the neo-orthodox hermeneutic, which maintains that Scripture becomes the Word of God when it is heard and accepted by the Christian, thereby emphasizing the existential (and subjective) encounter rather than the absolute, propositional truth in revelation.

Neo-Pagan/Neo-Paganism: Neo-paganism refers to a modern movement, begun in the nineteenth-century, to revive extinct (predominantly European) pagan religions. Particularly influential in the early phase of the revival was Sir James George Frazer's *The Golden Bough,* published in 1900. Arguably the largest and most successful neo-pagan movement is WICCA. See PAGANISM.

Neuro-Linguistic Programming: A general methodology developed in 1975 by Richard Bandler and Dr. John Grinder that allegedly enables practitioners to read random eye movements and other visual cues during conversation or counseling to "program" a client's behavior and restructure his or her core beliefs. Called "software for the brain," NLP is supposed to be faster and more powerful than traditional clinical counseling and can work without the subject's conscious knowledge. The founders have been heavily involved with other NEW AGE practices, and the early experiments were conducted on individuals involved in such alternative practices as HYPNOSIS and Gestalt therapy. NLP failed scientific tests conducted by the U.S. Army.

New Age: See the "Some Christian Definitions" section of the introduction.

New Age Church of Being—Middletown, CA: See HEART CONSCIOUS-NESS CHURCH.

New Age Church of Truth, Gilbert and June Holloway—Deming, NM: First established in south Florida, the church was relocated to Deming in 1966 as part of CHRIST LIGHT COMMUNITY. June claimed to be a spiritual healer. The Gilberts also gave PSYCHIC readings.

New Age Community Church, Dr. John Rodgers—Phoenix, AZ: A group of five NEW AGE churches in Arizona. The group teaches PANTHEISM and engages in an extremely wide array of practices borrowed from many different traditions. They accept as scripture the BIBLE, the Bhagavad-Gita, and *A COURSE IN MIRACLES.* The church runs a small seminary program at its mother church in Phoenix. Web site—http://www.aznewage.com/motherchurch.htm.

New Age Journal—Brighton, MA: see *BODY & SOUL.*

New Age Medicine: See HOLISTIC HEALTH.

New Age Music: While there is music composed to promote NEW AGE philosophy or facilitate ALTERED STATES OF CONSCIOUSNESS and MEDITATION, much of the music sold as such is not explicitly New Age in doctrine. Some light jazz, instrumental, electronic, ambient, folk, and even religious choral music has been labeled (or relabeled) New Age simply as a marketing category.

The New Apostolic Order in Messiah: See THE TWELVE TRIBES.

Newbrough, John: See *OAHSPE.*

New Apostolic Reformation: This movement, promoted by C. Peter Wagner and developed out of the CHARISMATIC MOVEMENT, attempts to restore the "lost offices" of APOSTLE and PROPHET to the modern church. See THIRD WAVE OF THE HOLY SPIRIT.

New Church: See SWEDENBORG FOUNDATION.

New Dimensions Foundation—San Francisco, CA: Started in 1973 to promulgate NEW AGE teachings through the mass media, the foundation operates the New Dimensions World Broadcasting Network. Web site—http://www.newdimensions.org.

New England Institute of Religious Research, Robert T. Pardon—Lakeville, MA: An APOLOGETICS ministry that defends the beliefs of EVANGELICAL CHRISTIANITY. The institute was founded in 1991 as a mission outreach to provide churches, secular organizations, and interested individuals with current information on new religious movements and cultic organizations. The organization runs Meadow Haven, a service that can provide temporary housing in certain extreme situations when someone leaving a cult or abusive group has no alternative shelter. The institute is a member of EVANGELICAL MINISTRIES TO NEW RELIGIONS (EMNR). Web site—http://www.neirr.org.

New Life Clinic—Baltimore, MD: A small NEW AGE group that meets at Mount Washington United Methodist Church. Founded by Ambrose and Olga Worrell, who began their PSYCHIC work in the 1930s after seeing the spirit of Olga's sister holding the spirits of their dead twin sons. Olga began healing people in 1950, and in 1957 they were invited to hold services at Mount Washington. There were approximately 300 people attending services at the time of Olga's death in 1985; the group currently numbers 20-30 people.

New Life Foundation, Vernon Howard—Pine, AZ: Howard, who died in 1992, taught that humans are trapped in the "psychic sleep" of an illusory self-image. The purpose in life is to rid ourselves of this self-image and evolve into a higher being. The foundation conducts classes in Arizona, California, and Colorado. Web site—http://www.anewlife.org.

New Life Health Center, Professor Bo-In Lee—Jamaica Plain, MA: Founded in 1987 by Lee, a Korean trained in YOGA, the martial arts, and ZEN BUDDHIST MEDITATION. The center uses Eastern medical practices such as ACUPUNCTURE, Kyun Hyun Tape (to restore energy flow), YOGA, and Moxibustion (an oriental healing treatment that uses heat to focus healing energy). Web site—http://www.anewlife.com. See HOLISTIC HEALTH.

Newman Centers: Educational organization that promotes ROMAN CATHOLICISM on college and university campuses. Named after the former ANGLICAN John Henry Newman (1801–90), who converted to Catholicism and became a cardinal in 1879. Web site—http://www.catholic. net/RCC/Indices/subs/OtherNC.html.

New Thought: In 1838, PHINEAS PARKHURST QUIMBY began to study MESMERISM. This study, combined with viewing the beneficial effects of placebos on some patients, convinced Quimby that the mind has the ability to heal the body. Among the patients and students who formalized Quimby's teachings were Warren Felt Evans, Julious and Annetta Seabury Dresser (who founded the New Thought movement itself), and MARY BAKER EDDY (who founded the FIRST CHURCH OF CHRIST, SCIENTIST). The MIND SCIENCE and RELIGIOUS SCIENCE movements developed from New Thought.

New Wiccan Church International—Sacramento, CA: Established in 1973 as an international association of individual members of various traditions of

WICCA with an emphasis on British Traditional Wicca (BTW). Members practice WITCHCRAFT and recognize the gods of nature—in particular, the "Great Goddess and her Consort, the Horned God." For over 25 years this group published the now-defunct *Red Garters International.* Web site—http://www.newwiccanchurch.org. See WICCA.

New World Translation: The official BIBLE translation of the WATCH-TOWER BIBLE AND TRACT SOCIETY. Key verses have been inaccurately rendered especially to obscure the deity of Christ, and the name *Jehovah* has been inserted into New Testament passages. Competent Bible scholars have universally rejected this translation as inaccurate.

Nicene Creed: See COUNCIL OF NICEA.

Nichiren Shoshu of America (NSA): Organized in the United States in 1960. Later it would also be known as Nichiren Shoshu Academy and Nichirenshoshu Sokagakkai of America. Web site—http://www.nst.org. See SOKA GAKKAI INTERNATIONAL. For further research, a four-page Watchman Fellowship Profile is available (see page 363). Web site—http://www.watchman.org/notebook.

Nightingale-Conant—Chicago, IL: Publishes books and audiotapes on personal growth, business, positive mental attitude, and self-help. A significant portion of their material contains NEW AGE themes. Nightingale-Conant also publishes *AdvantEdge* magazine. Web site—http://www.nightingale.com.

Nirvana: While nirvana has roots in HINDUISM, the concept of nirvana is far more fully developed in BUDDHISM. Sanskrit for "to extinguish," the Buddhist understanding of achieving nirvana involves extinguishing all of one's earthly attachments (including such emotions as hatred and desire). By achieving nirvana, the individual can escape the cycle of SAMSARA (REINCARNATION); this escape is called *parinirvana.*

Niscience, Ann Ree Colton—Glendale, CA: Niscience combines CHRISTIANITY with NEW AGE concepts. The organization exhorts individuals to follow the ethical example of JESUS, but also teaches followers to engage in MEDITATION that will expand the horizons of their souls—most notably, KUNDALINI energy and the CHAKRAS—and open their lives to the guidance of ANGELS. Web site—http://www.niscience.org.

Nizhoni School of Global Consciousness, Chris Griscom—Galisteo, NM: The school teaches participants to clear KARMA from previous lifetimes so as to release healing on a higher cellular level. Web site—http://www. nizhonischool.com. See NEW AGE; REINCARNATION.

NLP: See NEURO-LINGUISTIC PROGRAMMING.

Noahides: See B'NEI NOACH.

Nondenominational Churches: A reference to independent and autonomous Christian churches that are not officially united or legally aligned with any denomination (formal organization of like-minded churches). In the United States, many nondenominational churches have roots in the CHARISMATIC MOVEMENT.

Northeast Kingdom Community Church: See THE TWELVE TRIBES.

North Texas Church of Freethought: Congregation of atheists, agnostics, and other nonbelievers. Rejects traditional theism because the supernatural and faith are viewed as illogical, superstitious, and intolerant. The purpose for the Freethought church is to provide an unbelieving environment to meet the psychological and social needs of unbelievers. Web site—http://www. churchoffreethought.org. See ATHEISM; AGNOSTICISM.

Nubian Nation of Moors: See ANCIENT MYSTIC ORDER OF MAL-CHIZEDEK.

Numerology: Numerology is the study of the alleged mystical correspondence between numbers and both living and nonliving objects. Numerology was considered an essential aspect of mathematics by Pythagorus, but discarded by later mathematicians. In its most basic form, numerology can be as simple as considering certain numbers to be unlucky (e.g., 13). In some practices of DIVINATION, however, numbers are assigned to letters to determine hidden meanings. See OCCULT.

Nuwaubians: See ANCIENT MYSTIC ORDER OF MALCHIZE-DEK.

O

OAHSPE, John B. Newbrough: *OAHSPE* (translated as "sky, earth, spirit") is a 921-page "scripture" written in 1881 by John B. Newbrough, a PSY-CHIC and practitioner of SPIRITUALISM who was allegedly gifted in ESP. Newbrough claimed to create *OAHSPE* from ANGELS who held their hands over his head, casting light from their hands onto his hands, and dictating their message to him. Newbrough first published the book in 1882; it was republished in 1883 and republished and revised several additional times by Kosmon Press. *OAHSPE* is the central text of the UNIVERSAL FAITHISTS OF KOSMON, who do not consider it to be literally true, but instead inspirational in its ethics and spirituality. *OAHSPE* is available online at http://www.sacred-texts.com/oah.

Occult: From the Latin word for "hidden." See the "Some Christian Definitions" section of the introduction.

Odinism: Modern Odinism is a revival of the worship of the gods of Norse mythology. Odin (*Woden* in Anglo-Saxon England and *Wotan* in Germany) was the chief or supreme god of the Norse pantheon. He was the patron god of the nobility and of poets, and determined the fates of warriors and armies in battle. As an initiate of MAGIC and hidden lore, he gained use of the RUNES and passed these on to humanity. Norse legends predict that Odin will lead the forces of good against the forces of evil at Ragnarok, the apocalyptic day of doom, in which both sides will be annihilated. Some Odinist groups are white supremacists and maintain a DUALISM between the world of light (Caucasians) and the world of dark (non-Caucasians). See NEO-PAGANISM.

O'Hair, Madalyn: See MURRAY O'HAIR, MADALYN.

Olcott Memorial Library, Henry S.—Wheaton, IL: The national library for the THEOSOPHICAL SOCIETY. Web site—http://www.theosophical. org/resources/library.

Old Catholic Church: A movement of churches broke away from ROMAN CATHOLICISM beginning in the 1870s due to their rejection of the doctrine of papal infallibility as adopted by the First Vatican Council (1869–70). Some European Old Catholic Churches are part of the Union of Utrecht, but most churches are independent—especially in the United States. Doctrines vary widely among independent churches, with some holding to more traditional Catholic faith and practice while others share more in common with NEW AGE spirituality.

Old German Baptist Brethren Church: A movement of Anabaptist PROT-ESTANTISM that traces its history to Schwarzenau, Germany in 1708. See THE BRETHREN, ALEXANDER MACK.

Omega Institute for Holistic Studies—Hudson River Valley, NY: Inspired by the writings of Teilhard de Chardin, the institute was established in 1977 to promote HOLISTIC HEALTH and alternative spiritualities. The institute offers workshops and conferences on many subjects, including YOGA, MEDITATION, feminist spirituality, and PSYCHIC practices. Web site—http://www.eomega.org. See NEW AGE.

Oneness Pentecostalism: Also referred to as JESUS ONLY, the Oneness Pentecostal movement began in 1913 when R.E. McAlister concluded a worship service by baptizing individuals in the name of Jesus alone (rather than in the name of the Father, Son, and HOLY SPIRIT, as is traditionally practiced in CHRISTIANITY). Frank Ewart actively promoted the move-ment, promulgating McAlister's message that Acts 2:38 provides a biblical basis for Jesus Only baptism. Unlike traditional Pentecostals, Oneness fol-lowers deny the doctrine of the TRINITY in favor of MODALISM. Most Oneness Pentecostal organizations also teach that practicing GLOSSO-LALIA and maintaining various moral standards are necessary for salvation. Oneness Pentecostal beliefs are also being promoted in the CHRISTIAN market through musicians, such as PHILLIPS, CRAIG, AND DEAN. Some have also charged former Oneness Pentecostal preacher T.D. JAKES with continuing to promote Oneness Pentacostalism and criticize his re-fusal to make a clear statement on the doctrine of the TRINITY. Similarly, the popular author Tommy Tenney has a background in Oneness Penta-costalism (his father is still a Oneness minister) and has drawn criticism for not clearly confessing the doctrine of the Trinity. The largest Oneness Pentecostal organization is the UNITED PENTECOSTAL CHURCH INTERNATIONAL. See SALVATION BY WORKS. For further research, a four-page Watchman Fellowship Profile is available (see page 363). Web site—http://www.watchman.org/notebook.

One to Grow On, Trenna Sutphen—Malibu, CA: One to Grow On pro-vides tapes with subliminal messages for children. See SUTPHEN, DICK AND TARA.

Operating Thetan: See CHURCH OF SCIENTOLOGY.

Oprah: See WINFREY, OPRAH.

Opus Dei: Latin for "the Work of God." A very conservative lay organization of ROMAN CATHOLICISM founded in Spain in 1928 by Fr. Josemaría Escrivá de Balaguer. Web site—http://www.opusdei.org. See ROMAN CATHOLICISM.

Order of the Cross, J. Todd Ferrier—London: A former Congregationalist pastor, Ferrier left his church in 1903 to found the Order of the Cross, teaching that walking the "Mystic Way" of nonviolence and vegetarianism would lead to achieving one's CHRIST CONSCIOUSNESS. All literature published by the group is claimed to have been received through visions and mystical experiences. Web site—http://www.orderofthecross.org.

Order of the Solar Temple, Luc Jouret and Joseph Di Mambro: Founded in 1984 by Jouret as the International Chivalric Order Solar Tradition, and in-corporated into Di Mambro's Foundation Golden Way, the order combines CHRISTIANITY with NEW AGE concepts. Jouret, who believed himself to be the CHRIST, taught that he was a leader of the medieval Order of the Knights Templar, that his daughter, Emanuelle, was the "cosmic child," and that he would lead his people—after their deaths—to live on a planet that revolves around Sirius. In October 1994, 54 members committed suicide or were murdered (including a three-month-old infant who was believed to be the Antichrist). Another 16 members committed suicide in November 1995, and eight members attempted suicide in March 1997. Several hundred members are believed to remain in communities around the world. For further research, a four-page Watchman Fellowship Profile is available (see page 363). Web site—http://www.watchman.org/notebook.

Order of the Star: See KRISHNAMURTI FOUNDATION OF AMERICA.

Ordo Templi Astarte (OTA)—Silverado, CA: Founded in 1970 by Carroll "Poke" Runyon, the OTA is affiliated with the Church of the Hermetic Sciences. The OTA claims to conjure a good-natured spirit name Vassago, who prophesies through a "Dark Mirror." The OTA follows in the tradition of the ORDO TEMPLI ORIENTIS. They publish *The 7th Ray* journal. Web site—http://members.aol.com/CHSOTA. See OCCULT.

Ordo Templi Orientis: Drawing from the FREEMASONRY and ROSICRUCIANISM movements of the eighteenth and nineteenth centuries, the OTO was founded by Carl Kellner and Theodor Reuss in 1895. The OTO grew in popularity following ALEISTER CROWLEY's initiation in 1910 (and his 1912 charter to establish the order in the United Kingdom). Under Crowley, the OTO began to teach his Law of THELEMA, "Do as Thou Wilt." The OTO now practices a mixture of the OCCULT, GNOSTICISM, and Rosicrucianism. Web site—http://www.oto-usa.org. See ABBEY OF THELEMA; CROWLEY, ALEISTER; GOLDEN DAWN.

Orr, Leonard: See REBIRTHING INTERNATIONAL.

Orthodox Christianity: In a PROTESTANTISM context, Orthodox CHRISTIANITY refers to traditional forms of Protestantism (such as maintained by EVANGELICAL CHRISTIANITY and FUNDAMENTALIST CHRISTIANITY), particularly as opposed to LIBERAL CHRISTIANITY. Orthodoxy in this context includes belief in the TRINITY, the authority of the BIBLE, and SALVATION BY GRACE through faith. In its general context, Orthodox Christianity refers to the Orthodox Church (popularly known in the West as the Eastern Orthodox Church), because of the Great Schism of A.D. 1054 dividing the Eastern and Western Churches over the issues of papal authority and the procession of the HOLY SPIRIT. See ORTHODOX CHURCH.

Orthodox Church: Popularly known in the West as the Eastern Orthodox Church. In A.D. 1054, a major spilt called the Great Schism occurred, dividing the "One Holy Catholic, and Apostolic Church" between the East and the West. The Western Church, headed by the Pope in Rome at the Basilica of St. John Lateran, became known as ROMAN CATHOLICISM. The four eastern patriarchs (of Constantinople, Alexandria, Antioch, and Jerusalem) led the Eastern Church, which had its headquarters in Constantinople (modern-day Istanbul, Turkey). The major issues causing the division were the extent of papal authority (the patriarch of Rome) and the procession of the HOLY SPIRIT. The latter, also called the *Filioque* Controversy, debated the question of whether the HOLY SPIRIT proceeded eternally from God the Father *only* (the Eastern view) or proceeded from *both* the Father and the Son (Latin *filioque*="and the son"), which was the Western position. The Orthodox Church today includes the Eastern Orthodox Church (such as the Orthodox Church of Constantinople, the Cypriot Orthodox Church, The Greek Orthodox Church, and the Russian Orthodox Church) and the Oriental Orthodoxy (such as the Coptic Church, the Armenian Apostolic Church, etc.). A 2001 survey conducted by Pew Research Center suggested that about one percent of the U.S. population belonged to an Orthodox Church.

Osho: A former philosophy professor, the Bhagwan Shree Rajneesh became a religious teacher in India in 1966. In 1981, the Bhagwan and his followers took over the town of Antelope, Oregon, renaming it Rajneeshpuram. After allegations of poisoning and wire fraud, the Bhagwan pleaded guilty to wire fraud in 1985 and was deported to his native India. Although the Bhagwan (or Osho, as he renamed himself) died in 1990, many followers still practice his unique form of Hindu philosophy and system of sexual YOGA to gain enlightenment. See HINDUISM.

Osteen, Joel: Pastor of Lakewood Church in Houston, Texas since the death of his father John Osteen in 1999. Lakewood, which was founded by Joel's father, has over 35,000 people in attendance each week. Osteen is widely recognized as a gifted communicator and is also a best-selling author. Though not as overtly WORD-FAITH in his preaching as his father, critics maintain that he still holds to and teaches the prosperity message, though somewhat toned down to reach a broader audience. Web site—http://www.joelosteen.com. See WORD-FAITH MOVEMENT.

Ouija Board: A game of SPIRITUALISM and DIVINATION, consisting of a board on which are printed the letters of the alphabet and such words as *yes* and *no,* and a pointer. The users ask a question that is allegedly answered by a visitor from the spirit world, who guides the pointer (held by the users) to spell out the answer. The movement of the pointer is generally attributed to ideomotor action (physical responses to subconscious impulses); some Christian critics of the practice, however, state that there is the possibility for demonic influence. See OCCULT.

Our Lady of Enchantment, Sabrina—Cobb, CA: Sabrina operates an online seminary for practitioners of WICCA, claiming 25,000 students. She also runs a church and gift shop in Cobb. Web site—http://members. aol.com/LadyS1366/oloe.html.

Out-of-Body Experience (OBE): See ASTRAL PROJECTION.

P

Pacific Institute, Louis Tice—Seattle, WA: Founded in 1971, the institute teaches that humans have unlimited potential for growth and creativity, and that changes in belief are necessary to unleash this potential in high-performance individuals. A key component of The Pacific Institute Process is VISUALIZATION: We can create things we see as desirable. Web site—http://www.pac-inst.com. See NEW AGE; HUMAN POTENTIAL MOVEMENT.

Paganism: *Paganism* has historically been used as a generic term to describe primitive non-Christian religions and superstitions. More recently, *paganism* is used as an umbrella term referring to WICCA and WITCHCRAFT, ceremonial MAGIC, nature worship, POLYTHEISM (particularly GOD-DESS worship), and ancient mythologies (Celt, Norse, Egyptian, Greek, and Roman). See OCCULT; NEO-PAGANISM.

Pagan Spiritual Alliance, Selena Fox—Mount Horeb, WI: See CIRCLE SANCTUARY.

Pagels, Elaine (b. 1943): Professor of religion at Princeton University and author of numerous books. The best known is her 1979 best-seller *The Gnostic Gospels,* which was a product of her earlier studies at Harvard on the Nag Hammadi Library, a collection of gnostic writings discovered in 1945. Her 1995 book *The Gnostic Paul* presents the case that the apostle Paul was actually a Gnostic and that several New Testament books attributed to him (e.g., 1 and 2 Timothy and Titus) are forgeries. Her 2003 work, *Beyond Belief: The Secret GOSPEL OF THOMAS,* contrasts that GNOSTIC GOSPEL with the Gospel of John. See GNOSTIC GOSPELS.

Palm Reading: A popular term for chiromancy, this OCCULT practice of DIVINATION involves reading the shape, lines, or markings on the palm of the hand.

Pan African Orthodox Christian Church, Jaramogi Abebe Agyeman— Detroit, MI: Albert B. Cleage, Jr., a Congregationalist pastor in the 1950–60s, became disillusioned with the achievements of the Civil Rights movement. In 1967, Cleage launched the Black Christian National movement, which reinterpreted JESUS' teachings for impoverished African-Americans; in 1968 he published *The Black Messiah* to promote his teachings. In 1972 Cleage formed the Pan African Orthodox Christian Church and changed his name to Jaramogi Abebe Agyeman, which is Swahili for "liberator, holy man, savior of the nation." The Pan African Church works to return African-Americans to the alleged African roots of CHRISTIANITY and Jesus. The main centers of this organization are the Shrines of the Black Madonna in Detroit, Michigan, Houston, Texas, and Atlanta, Georgia. Web site—http://www.shrinebookstore.com.

Pan-American Indian Association: The association is a NEW AGE organization that promotes NATIVE AMERICAN SPIRITUALITY. The association is not affiliated with any Native American tribe and is not recognized by the Bureau of Indian Affairs. The association operates the Loving Hands Institute of Healing Arts in Fortuna, California. Web site—http://www.lovinghandsinstitute.com.

Panentheism: Panentheism maintains that the divine is in all things and unifies all things, but ultimately transcends all things. Therefore, while the universe is a part or aspect of God (or the GODDESS), it is not equivalent to God or the entirety of God's being.

Pantheism: The belief that the universe is God—there is no separation or distinction between creator and creation. Everything is therefore equally and indivisibly divine, thereby inspiring the popular phrase, "All is God, and God is all." Pantheism is the foundational theistic concept of HINDUISM and BUDDHISM, and is one of the most prevalent beliefs in the NEW AGE.

Papa Jim's Botanica—San Antonio, TX: Founded in 1979 when spirits told Papa Jim that people were unable to obtain the products mandated by the spirits, Papa Jim's Botanica is a retailer in items for the OCCULT and HOLISTIC HEALTH. Jim retired in 2001, but regularly visits the store. See CESAR.

Paranormal: Observable phenomena that allegedly cannot be explained by science or the known laws of physics.

Parapsychology: Literally "beyond psychology," parapsychology is the study of PSYCHIC phenomena (e.g., ESP) that appear to be outside the natural laws understood by the scientific community. The Society for Psychical Research was founded in 1882. J.B. Rhine, one of the foremost parapsychological researchers in the 1920–30s, created the *Journal of Parapsychology* in 1937 and the Parapsychological Association in 1957. The Rhine Research Center at Duke University is one of the most significant and active scientific organizations studying parapsychology. Web site—http://www.rhine.org.

Past Life Regression: A NEW AGE practice, usually achieved through HYPNOSIS, which allows a person to discover and—at least emotionally—re-experience his or her past lives. Inherent in the practice is belief in REINCARNATION. An organization called the International Board for Regression Therapies attempts to establish ethical standards and professional credentials for the practice. Web site—http://www.ibrt.org.

Pastoral Bible Institute—Milwaukee, WI: A splinter of the WATCHTOWER BIBLE AND TRACT SOCIETY. Publishes *The Herald of Christ's Kingdom.* Web site—http://www.heraldmag.org. See BIBLE STUDENTS.

Path of Light, LaUna Huffines—Ashland, OR: NEW AGE group that teaches MEDITATION and receiving guidance from ANGELS. Publishes the *Path of Light* newsletter. Web site—http://www.pathoflight.com.

Patrick, Ted: Patrick is arguably the most famous practitioner of DEPROGRAMMING. Patrick was convicted three times of kidnapping and false imprisonment.

Patripassianism: See MODALISM.

Patterns in the Cults: There are four characteristics often found in CULTS: *Add* to the BIBLE new scriptures, *subtract* from JESUS, *multiply* the requirements of salvation, and *divide* their followers' loyalties. For more, see "Some General Definitions" and "Some Christian Definitions" sections of the introduction of this book. For further research, a four-page Watchman Fellowship Profile is available (see page 363). Web site—http://www. watchman.org/notebook.

Paulk, Bishop Earl: Longtime WORD-FAITH pastor of Chapel Hill Harvester Church in Decatur, Georgia. For over a decade, Paulk has been embroiled in allegations of sexual misconduct by former church members who were kept somewhat out of the public eye until litigation was filed against him in 2005. Web site—http://www.col.tv. See WORD-FAITH MOVEMENT.

Peace Pole: Poles on which the message "May peace prevail on earth" is printed in different languages on each of its sides. The purpose of the poles is to remind individuals to visualize world peace. Web site—http://www. worldpeace.org/activities.html. See VISUALIZATION; NEW AGE.

Peacevision—Houston, TX: In 1985, Carmel Temple (which supports Peacevision) began distributing blue-and-white bumper stickers which read "Visualize World Peace." Web site—http://www.peacevision.org.

Peale, Norman Vincent: Peale, who died in 1993, was a popular writer and promoter of the belief in the power of positive thinking. His philosophy was particularly popularized through the interfaith magazine *Guideposts.* Peale's views of CHRISTIANITY were heavily influenced by his mentor, Ernest Holmes, and often reflected the philosophies of NEW THOUGHT, UNITY SCHOOL OF CHRISTIANITY, and RELIGIOUS SCIENCE. The Web site for *Guideposts* is http://www.guideposts.com.

Pearl of Great Price: One of the scriptures or Standard Works of THE CHURCH OF JESUS CHRIST OF LATTER-DAY SAINTS. Most of the book, including the controversial Book of Abraham, was purportedly translated by the LDS prophet JOSEPH SMITH, JR. in 1835 in Kirtland, Ohio, from Egyptian documents purchased along with some mummies. At that time, prior to the discovery and decoding of the Rosetta Stone, no one could translate Egyptian hieroglyphics or hieratic writing. Nevertheless,

Smith claimed that with God's help he was able to translate the papyri documents into a text that was later canonized as part of the LDS scriptures. In 1967, some of the original documents that were translated by Joseph Smith were rediscovered in the Metropolitan Museum of Art in New York and were donated to the LDS church. The church subsequently authenticated them and published photographs of the documents in their magazine *The Improvement Era*. All modern Egyptologists who have translated the texts concur that the documents were actually part of the Egyptian *Book of the Dead* and that Smith's translation found in the Pearl of Great Price had nothing in common with the Egyptian documents. See CHURCH OF JESUS CHRIST OF LATTER-DAY SAINTS.

Peck, M. Scott: Peck, a former lieutenant colonel and psychiatrist in the Army, was baptized by a Methodist minister in 1980 after some years in which he studied and practiced BUDDHISM. Peck's books are a combination of Christian and Eastern religious concepts. While he affirms his belief in a transcendent deity, the god described by Peck is a hermaphroditic combination of male and female attributes. Peck describes the BIBLE as being somewhat unreliable due to deletions and accretions that have occurred in the text. He also rejects the biblical concept of a bodily resurrection. It should be noted that while he is complimentary of NEW AGE spirituality, Peck explicitly denies being involved in the New Age. Peck's books include *The Road Less Traveled, People of the Lie: The Hope for Healing Human Evil,* and *In Heaven as on Earth: A Vision of the Afterlife.* Web site—http://www.mscottpeck.com.

Pelley, William D.: Pelley was an author highly influenced by NEW THOUGHT. He was an associate of MARY BAKER EDDY (founder of the FIRST CHURCH OF CHRIST, SCIENTIST) and influenced Guy and Edna Ballard's I AM philosophy. Pelley has been accused of being anti-Semitic.

Pennington, Basil: Trappist monk who studied contemplative MEDITATION methods, including those of Eastern religions, with THOMAS KEATING. He was a pioneer in the CENTERING PRAYER movement and in addition to speaking at retreats and lectures, he wrote several books on the subject.

Pentagram: The five-pointed, star-shaped OCCULT symbol used in ceremonial MAGIC. Practitioners of WICCA and NEO-PAGANISM orient the star with one point upwards, and the points are often claimed to represent earth, air, water, fire, and spirit. Practitioners of SATANISM invert the star to form a goat's head, or a sign of SATAN.

Pentecostal Assemblies of the World (PAW)—Indianapolis, IN: PAW is the oldest of the APOSTOLIC CHURCHES. Like many Apostolic Churches, PAW teaches ONENESS PENTECOSTALISM and SALVATION BY WORKS. Web site—http://www.pawinc.org.

Pentecostal Churches of Apostolic Faith: A denomination of approximately 25,000 that teaches ONENESS PENTECOSTALISM.

Pentecostal Free-Will Baptist Church: See PENTECOSTAL MOVEMENT.

Pentecostal Movement: A development within PROTESTANTISM beginning in the early twentieth-century with an emphasis on the gifts of the HOLY SPIRIT, such as SPEAKING IN TONGUES. Named after the biblical events of the day of Pentecost recorded in Acts 2, the movement had its beginnings in 1901 when Agnes Ozman began to speak in tongues during a prayer meeting at Bethel Bible College in Topeka, Kansas. The Topeka outpouring was followed by the Azuza Street Revival of 1906 led by William J. Seymour in Los Angeles, California. CHRISTIAN denominations that developed out of the Pentecostal movement—such as the ASSEMBLIES OF GOD, the International Church of the Foursquare Gospel, CHURCH OF GOD (CLEVELAND, TN), and the Pentecostal Free-Will Baptist Church—are commonly considered to be expressions of ORTHODOX CHRISTIANITY within Protestantism. However, controversy among early Pentecostal leaders surrounding the proper formula for water baptism led to a schism. Some argued that one must be baptized in Jesus' name only—not in the name of the Father, Son, and Holy Ghost. Many of these JESUS ONLY proponents, as they came to be known, eventually begin to deny the doctrine of the TRINITY and teach MODALISM and SALVATION BY WORKS. By 1915 they began to break away from orthodox Pentecostal ranks to form rival oneness Pentecostal churches, including the PENTECOSTAL ASSEMBLIES OF THE WORLD (PAW) and THE

UNITED PENTECOSTAL CHURCH, INTERNATIONAL (UPC). See ONENESS PENTECOSTALISM.

People's Temple Christian Church, Jim Jones—Jonestown, Guyana: Jones established the People's Temple in Indianapolis, Indiana, in the 1950s as an interracial outreach to the socioeconomically marginalized people of the city. Jones eventually incorporated socialism into his teaching, claiming that communalism was the essence of the Christian lifestyle. His claims that he could cure such ailments as cancer and heart disease provoked a government investigation, prompting Jones to move his community to California. A magazine's 1977 investigation of alleged illegal activities led Jones to move his community to Jonestown, an agricultural commune in Guyana. Growing increasingly paranoid as his dependence on prescription drugs increased and as authorities in the United States investigated possible human rights violations, Jones led his group to commit mass suicide and murder in 1978, which resulted in 914 deaths.

Perry, Troy D.: Homosexual activist and church founder who authored the autobiography *The Lord Is My Shepherd and He Knows I'm Gay,* and a sequel titled *Don't Be Afraid Anymore.* Web site—http://www.revtroyperry. org. See UNIVERSAL FELLOWSHIP OF METROPOLITAN COMMUNITY CHURCHES.

Personal Freedom Outreach (PFO), M. Kurt Goedelman—St. Louis, MO: An APOLOGETICS ministry founded in 1975 to promote evangelism and to defend EVANGELICAL CHRISTIANITY from the heretical doctrines of religious cults and aberrant theology. Publications include *The Quarterly Journal.* Web site—http://www.pfo.org.

Peyote: Peyote is a small, spineless, globe-shaped cactus that is the source of mescal buttons. Mescal buttons are so named because they contain mescaline, a hallucinogenic agent. These buttons were traditionally used by Native Americans of the American southwest to induce visions and are used by modern practitioners of NATIVE AMERICAN SPIRITUALITY to induce ALTERED STATES OF CONSCIOUSNESS.

Peyote Way Church of God—Willcox, AZ: The church traces its roots as an institution to Jonathan Koshiway, a former missionary for the COMMUNITY OF CHRIST who established a peyote church in 1914. Peyote

Way itself was established in 1966. Peyote Way is a blend between NATIVE AMERICAN SPIRITUALITY and MORMONISM: The group follows JOSEPH SMITH, JR.'s "Word of Wisdom," but interprets Smith's call to reopen the windows of heaven as an exhortation to ingest hallucinogens. Web site—http://www.peyoteway.org. See THE CHURCH OF JESUS CHRIST OF LATTER-DAY SAINTS.

Phanes Press—Grand Rapids, MI: In Greek mythology, Phanes was the "Revealer" hatched from the egg that was the source of the universe. Phanes Press publishes an extensive array of books on OCCULT and NEW AGE subjects. Web site—http://www.phanes.com.

Philadelphia Church of God, Gerald Flurry—Edmond, OK: Continues the teachings of ARMSTRONGISM. Flurry formed the PCG in 1989 after being fired from his position as a minister in the WORLDWIDE CHURCH OF GOD. In his most significant books, *Malachi's Message to God's Church Today* and *Who Is that Prophet?*, Flurry claims that the Old Testament prophesied that HERBERT W. ARMSTRONG would be God's chosen prophet, that the WCG would turn apostate, and that Flurry is God's successor for Armstrong. The PCG operates the unaccredited four-year Imperial College. The church publishes *The Philadelphia Trumpet* magazine and produces *The Key of David* television program. Web site—http://www.pcog.org. For further research, a four-page Watchman Fellowship Profile is available (see page 363). Web site—http://www.watchman.org/notebook.

Philadelphia Congregations of Yahweh, William Scampton—Myerstown, PA: A SACRED NAME organization that uses its own *Family of Yah Edition* of the BIBLE. The organization publishes the *Yahweh's Watchmen* magazine. Web site—http://www.homestead.com/pcoy. See also YAHWEHISM

Phillips, Craig, and Dean: A contemporary CHRISTIAN music group featuring Randy Phillips, Shawn Craig, and Dan Dean. The group has drawn controversy from some EVANGELICAL CHRISTIANITY critics because all three vocalists are ONENESS PENTECOSTALISM ministers—a faith that denies the doctrine of the TRINITY and teaches JESUS ONLY theology. Web site:—http://www.phillipscraiganddean.com. See ONENESS PENTECOSTALISM.

Philosophical Research Society, Manly P. Hall—Los Angeles, CA: Hall, who died in 1990, was dedicated to the study of the Western mystery religions, particularly as presented in FREEMASONRY and ROSICRUCIANISM. The society extends Hall's research to the study of the philosophy of consciousness, utilizing the work of scholars in many religious traditions and philosophical disciplines. The society operates the University of Philosophical Research. Society Web site—http://www.prs.org. University Web site—http://www.uprs.edu.

Pike, Albert: Pike, a brigadier general in the Confederate Army, was one of the most famous leaders of FREEMASONRY in the United States. Pike died in 1890.

Plantard, Pierre: See PRIORY OF SION.

Plural Covenant: See DUAL COVENANT.

Plymouth Brethren: An early nineteenth-century movement of EVANGELICAL CHRISTIANITY that developed in Ireland and spread to England. The group does not view itself as a denomination and eschews any formal name. The name given them, however, is traced to the assembly of believers (brothers) who were in Plymouth, England. Important early leaders include the dispensationalist John Nelson Darby (1800–82) and George Müller (1805–98), the well-known British evangelist and builder of orphanages. The movement has experienced numerous schisms that basically fall into two categories: the Open Brethren recognize and cooperate with other Christian churches, whereas the Closed Brethren do not support the events and meetings of other Christians and usually enforce the disciplinary actions against churches in fellowship with other groups. They are not historically connected with THE BRETHREN, ALEXANDER MACK or THE BRETHREN, JIM ROBERTS.

Poltergeist: German for "rattling ghost" or "noisy spirit," *poltergeist* is a term applied to a wide array of site- and person-specific supernatural phenomena. These phenomena can include variations in temperature, anomalous sounds, or the unexplained movement of physical objects. The activity of poltergeists is commonly attributed to a traumatic—and usually violent—event at that location or to the spirit of an individual who has experienced such trauma. See GHOST; DEMON; SPIRITUALISM; NECROMANCY; OCCULT.

Polytheism: The belief in a multitude of distinct gods. A polytheistic system is different from both PANTHEISM (because it asserts the existence of distinct gods, as opposed to an impersonal God identical with the universe) and MONTHEISM (because it asserts the existence of more than one true God). Most of the world's mythological systems have been polytheistic (e.g., Greco-Roman, Norse, Egyptian, Babylonian, Assyrian, etc.). THE CHURCH OF JESUS CHRIST OF LATTER-DAY SAINTS adheres to a variation of polytheism called *henotheism:* Mormons assert that there are many gods (in fact, LDS males hope to become gods), but there is only one God whom we—the children of this God—are to worship.

Popoff, Peter: Controversial televangelist and faith healer whose fake "word of knowledge" manifestations of the HOLY SPIRIT were exposed by JAMES RANDI in 1987. At his huge crusades, Popoff claimed to receive personal information from God about participants—information that he would reveal publicly with great fanfare. RANDI discovered that undercover ministry employees had subtly acquired information from audience members before the event and that Popoff's wife was reading the information into a radio linked to a small receiver in Popoff's ear (see WARM READING). The subsequent exposure on NBC's *Tonight Show* led to a sharp drop in contributions, forcing the ministry into bankruptcy. Popoff eventually returned to television and rebounded, however, with his ministry raising over $16 million in 2004 and Popoff receiving over a half a million dollars in personal compensation. Web site—http://www.peterpopoff.org.

Positive Confession: See WORD-FAITH MOVEMENT.

Potter's House: See THE DOOR CHRISTIAN FELLOWSHIP CHURCHES. *Note: This is not the Dallas church of which T.D. Jakes is pastor* (see next entry).

Potter's House Church—Dallas, TX: See JAKES, T.D.

Power for Abundant Living: The main recruitment and initial indoctrination course (and book by the same title) for potential members of THE WAY INTERNATIONAL.

Power of Myth: See CAMPBELL, JOSEPH.

Prana: See CHI.

Precognition: The ability to predict or experience a future event using supernatural or unknown means in a manner similar to EXTRASENSORY PERCEPTION.

Presbyterian Church (USA) (PCUSA)—Louisville, KY: A denomination of PROTESTANTISM based on PRESBYTERIANISM that was formed in 1983 by the union of the Presbyterian Church in the U.S. (PCUS), known as the southern branch, and the United Presbyterian Church in the U.S.A. (UPCUSA), known as the northern branch. PCUSA is the largest Presbyterian denomination in the United States (about 2.4 million members in 11,000 congregations) and is considered much more liberal and progressive (theologically and socially) than other Presbyterian denominations such as the PRESBYTERIAN CHURCH IN AMERICA (PCA). Web site—http://www.pcusa.org. See PRESBYTERIANISM; REFORMATION; PROTESTANTISM.

Presbyterian Church in America (PCA)—Lawrenceville, GA: A denomination of PROTESTANTISM based on PRESBYTERIANISM that was formed in 1973 in reaction to what was viewed as LIBERAL CHRISTIANITY in the Presbyterian Church in the U.S. denomination—including rejection of essential doctrines such as the deity of CHRIST and the inerrancy and authority of the BIBLE. The PCA is the second-largest Presbyterian denomination in the United States (over 306,000 members in 1,450 congregations as of 2000) and is considered much more conservative theologically than the larger PRESBYTERIAN CHURCH (USA). Web site—http://www.pcanet.org. See PRESBYTERIANISM; REFORMATION; PROTESTANTISM.

Presbyterianism: A form of PROTESTANTISM based on the theology of the French-born Swiss reformer John Calvin (1509–64) and his student John Knox (1505–72), who helped spread the REFORMATION to Scotland. The name is taken from Greek word *presbyteros* ("elder") because their churches are governed by elders rather than bishops (Episcopalian) or church members (Congregational). The doctrinal roots of Presbyterianism are found in Reformed theology (Calvinism), which has been summarized by the popular acronym TULIP: Total Depravity, Unconditional Election, Limited Atonement, Irresistible Grace, and Perseverance of the Saints. In the

United States, there are nearly a dozen different Presbyterian denominations including the PRESBYTERIAN CHURCH (USA), PRESBYTERIAN CHURCH IN AMERICA (PCA), the Cumberland Presbyterian Church, the Associate Reformed Presbyterian Church (ARP Synod), the Orthodox Presbyterian Church, the Evangelical Presbyterian Church, the Reformed Presbyterian Church, the Bible Presbyterian Church, and the Reformed Presbyterian Church in the United States (RPCUS). See REFORMATION; PROTESTANTISM.

Price, Frederick K.C.: Popular WORD-FAITH teacher and pastor/founder of Crenshaw Christian Center in Los Angeles, California. The church claims over 17,000 members. Price also operates a nationally syndicated radio and television ministry, the Ever Increasing Faith Ministries. Web site—http:// www.crenshawchristiancenter.net. See WORD-FAITH MOVEMENT.

Prieuàe de Sion: See PRIORY OF SION.

Priory of Sion (Prieuàe de Sion): A secret society claimed to have originated over 1,000 years ago in association with the Crusades and central to many popular CONSPIRACY THEORIES, especially those built around the HOLY GRAIL. It was an important component of the *DA VINCI CODE* and was critical to the research claimed in *HOLY BLOOD, HOLY GRAIL*. However, the Priory depicted in the *Da Vinci Code* and *Holy Blood, Holy Grail* has been proven to be the elaborate ruse developed in the 1950s by a group under the leadership of PIERRE PLANTARD, a Frenchman who planted forged documents in hopes of establishing himself as the true heir to the throne of France.

Probert, Mark: One of the earlier individuals involved in CHANNELING, Probert channeled the Kethra E Da, or the INNER CIRCLE TEACHERS OF LIGHT and their leader, Yada di Shi'te, from 1948 until his death in 1969.

Process Church of the Final Judgment, Robert de Grimston: Robert and Mary Anne de Grimston met in the CHURCH OF SCIENTOLOGY, but left Scientology in 1963 because they did not believe the church was effective in identifying compulsive goals. They then formed a company called Compulsion Analysis, which soon became The Process. The close interpersonal relationships formed between the members of The Process and the de Grimstons led the group to separate from society and, for a period of time, to live in central America before settling in the United States. Internal problems led to Robert de Grimston being removed from leadership in 1974; Mary Anne and the Council of Masters continued The Process, but it gradually diminished as splintering occurred in the late 1970s and through the 1980s. The Process maintained that there were four dichotomous Gods: Jehovah and Lucifer, and Christ and Satan. Through The Process, Christ and Satan are united. In 1993, the Society of Processians declared the old Process teachings obsolete, destroyed the church's archives, and dissolved the church.

Process Theology: Built on the philosophy of Alfred North Whitehead and furthered by the work of Charles Hartshorne, process theology holds that reality is *becoming* rather than *being*—that is, in process rather than static. Hartshorne's neoclassical theism is in effect similar to PANENTHEISM: Even though God is socially unsurpassable and therefore has a transcendent self-identity, He also includes the world within Himself. God is therefore in process as evolving along with creation into future possibilities.

Progressive National Baptist Convention (PNBC)—Washington, DC: A Christian denomination of PROTESTANTISM that split in 1961 from the larger NATIONAL BAPTIST CONVENTION, USA. The convention, with an estimated two million members, was the denominational home of Dr. Martin Luther King and has had a history of focusing on civil rights and social justice. Web site—http://pnbc.org. See BAPTIST CHURCHES.

Project Starlight International (PSI), Ray Stanford—Austin, TX. Operates a research facility intended to make contact with and confirm the existence of UFOs and extraterrestrials. Founded in Arizona in 1964, it was relocated to Texas in 1967 and eventually became a research subsidiary of the Association for the Understanding of Man. Some of their materials are preserved at http://www.nicap.org/madar/psi.htm.

Project X: See JAMILIAN UNIVERSITY OF THE ORDAINED.

Prophet: One who claims to speak for God or announce future events on behalf of God. Biblical prophets, including Isaiah, Ezekiel, Daniel, etc., authored a large portion of the Old Testament. The BIBLE is replete with warnings about false prophets (Jeremiah 14:14; Matthew 24:24). Biblical tests for discerning true prophets from false, include a theological test (if the prophet leads you after a false god—Deuteronomy 13:1-5) and a chronological test (if the prophet's prediction fails to come to pass at the predicted time—Deuteronomy 18:20-22). See FALSE PROPHECY.

Prophet, Mark and Elizabeth Clare: See CHURCH UNIVERSAL AND TRIUMPHANT. Personal Web site for Elizabeth Clare Prophet—http://www.ecprophet.info.

Prosperity Doctrine: See WORD-FAITH MOVEMENT.

Prosperos, Kenneth Wayne "Thane" Walker—Culver City, CA: Founded in Florida in 1956 by Thane, who claimed to have been a student of George Gurdjieff, founder of the FOURTH WAY. The influence of the fourth way is prevalent in this NEW THOUGHT school. Prosperos is named after the MAGICIAN in Shakespeare's comedy *The Tempest*. Web site—http://www.theprosperos.org.

Prosveta U.S.A., Omraam Mikhaël Aïvanhov (Mikael Ivanov)—North Hatley, Quebec: Mikhael Ivanov claimed to have experienced spiritual ecstasy in 1915 and bathed in the light that suffuses all things. In 1917 he met Peter Deunov, who introduced him to the teachings of the GREAT WHITE BROTHERHOOD. Ivanov received the name Omraam Mikhaël Aïvanhov in 1958 during a trip to India. He died in 1986. His teachings blend traditional HINDUISM—particularly an emphasis on YOGA—with elements common to THEOSOPHY. Prosveta publishes and promotes Aïvanhov's teachings. Web site—http://www.prosveta-usa.com.

Protestantism: Often used generically of all non-Roman Catholic or Orthodox Christian churches, the term more specifically refers to the movement that originated in the sixteenth-century REFORMATION. Martin Luther, Ulrich Zwingli, John Calvin, and others led efforts to correct, reform, or "protest" the errors in doctrine and practice that they saw in medieval ROMAN CATHOLICISM. The sixteenth-century Protestants saw their main doctrinal differences with Roman Catholicism to include *soli Deo gloria* (God's wisdom and glory as opposed to church/papal sovereignty); *sola scriptura* (the authority of the BIBLE over official papal interpretation and tradition); and *sola gratia* (eternal life received from God as a free gift by grace through faith in the imputed righteousness of CHRIST rather than by works, rituals, or sacraments). See REFORMATION; SALVATION BY GRACE.

Protestant Reformation: See REFORMATION.

PROUT: An acronym for Progressive Utilization Theory, a HINDU-based spiritual program that enables life forms to progress from animals to divinity. PROUT is promoted by ANANDA MARGA, who hopes to establish, through practice of the Theory, a single world government and religion. Proutist Universal, ANANDA MARGA's formal organization for promoting PROUT, publishes *Prout Journal* and *Global Times*. Web site for Proutist Universal—http://www.prout.org.

Psionics: See FIRST UNIVERSAL CHURCH OF GOD-REALIZATION.

Psychic: A person with alleged supernatural powers (e.g., ESP, CLAIRVOYANCE, DIVINATION) who gains hidden knowledge apart from the five senses; the term also refers to the supernatural powers themselves. Psychic practices can be traced back to ancient times and were condemned in the Old Testament (Deuteronomy 18:9-13). Modern interest in psychics and psychic abilities began with the eighteenth-century studies in MESMERISM and grew with the rise of SPIRITUALISM in the nineteenth century and the popularity of HELENA PETROVNA BLAVATSKY. Such twentieth-century psychics as JEANE DIXON and Arthur Ford (of the SPIRITUAL FRONTIERS PROJECT) rekindled interest in psychic abilities. The craze grew to the point that psychic hotlines became a staple of the pay-per-minute phone services. While many psychics have been exposed as faking their supernatural abilities, the BIBLE indicates that some psychic powers can be attributed to real evil spirits known as DEMONS (Acts 16:16-18). Some of the deceptive techniques used by psychics to feign supernatural powers include COLD READING, WARM READING, and HOT READING. See OCCULT; DIVINATION; NECROMANCY. For further research, a four-page Watchman Fellowship Profile is available (see page 363). Web site—http://www.watchman.org/notebook.

Psychic Healing: Psychic healing—also commonly called spiritual healing—involves balancing healing energy through physical touch or the practitioner moving his or her hand over the patient. The concept is rooted in HINDUISM, where CHI flows—or is blocked from flowing—through the CHAKRAS. One of the most popular forms of psychic healing is REIKI, although healing with CRYSTALS remains popular among NEW AGE adherents. See HOLISTIC HEALING.

Psychokinesis: See TELEKINESIS.

Puranas: A class of 18 scriptural texts (with an additional 18 supplemental texts called *Upa Puranas*) that contain the creation myths (as well as other legends) of HINDUISM. Included in the Puranas are the Laws of Manu, which are the basis for the caste system that continues to influence Indian culture.

Pursel, Jach: Since 1974, Pursel has channeled a disembodied energy named Lazaris, who claims that all religions are channeled. The focus of the *Lazaris Material* (a substantial body of writings and recordings channeled by Lazaris through Pursel) is to guide humanity back to the "All That Is." Web site—http://www.lazaris.com. See CHANNELING; NEW AGE.

Pyramidology: The study of the ancient Egyptian and/or Central American Mayan pyramids, which are believed to possess keys to hidden mystic knowledge or secret spiritual messages. Some teachers, particularly in the nineteenth-century, believed that the dimensions of the pyramids held the keys to understanding biblical prophecies (e.g., prophetic dating was predicated on the assumption one inch in the dimensions of the Great Pyramid equals one solar year). Pyramidology can be seen in such diverse groups and belief systems as THEOSOPHY, the writings of CHARLES TAZE RUSSELL (founder of the WATCHTOWER BIBLE AND TRACT SOCIETY), and Edgar Cayce (of the FOUNDATION FOR RESEARCH AND ENLIGHTENMENT). See PYRAMID POWER. For further research, a four-page Watchman Fellowship Profile is available (see page 363). Web site—http://www.watchman.org/notebook.

Pyramid Power: The NEW AGE belief that ancient pyramids or the geometric shape of a pyramid generates or directs OCCULT power or energy. Some individuals and groups also believe that pyramids are related to extraterrestrials and are used as message transmitters or landing beacons for UFOs. See PYRAMIDOLOGY. For further research, a four-page Watchman Fellowship Profile is available (see page 363). Web site—http://www.watchman.org/notebook.

Q

Quakers: See RELIGIOUS SOCIETY OF FRIENDS.

Qabalah: See KABBALAH.

Qabbalah: See KABBALAH.

Quartus Foundation, John and Jan Price—Boerne, TX: Quartus is a NEW AGE foundation that initiated the now-annual Global Healing Day on December 31, 1986. On this day participants are asked to engage in a "global mind link" and visualize peace. The Prices conduct workshops on ANGELS and experiencing spiritual joy. Web site—http://www.quartus.org.

Questhaven Retreat: See CHRISTWARD MINISTRY.

Quimby, Phineas P.: A nineteenth-century New England practitioner of MESMERISM whose theories influenced NEW THOUGHT. A Web site about Quimby is at http://www.ppquimby.com.

Qur'an: Sometimes spelled *Koran* and, in Arabic, literally means "the recitation." This is the central scripture of all branches of ISLAM, containing 114 *surah* (chapters) and 6,236 *ayat* (verses). It is believed by MUSLIMS that ALLAH (God) delivered the text of the Qur'an to the Prophet MUHAMMAD through the ANGEL Gabriel. See ISLAM.

R

Radical Feminism: Feminism—an umbrella term for a wide array of social and political ideologies and movements focusing primarily on the experiences of women in Western societies—is rooted in the concept of social, political, and economic equality between genders. Feminism, as a movement, is generally understood to have begun in the nineteenth-century, and can be traced as an organized movement to the first women's rights conference in Seneca Falls, New York, in 1848. Many commentators recognize three waves in the feminist movement: the first wave—largely represented by the suffrage movement—focused on the basic (and particularly political) status of women in society; the second wave—which occurred in the 1960–70s—expanded upon the first wave by focusing on issues of feminine identity (and particularly self-identity); the third wave—comprised of modern feminists—is further exploring concepts of identity, as well as workplace equality and reproductive issues. Radical feminism is an outgrowth of second-wave feminism and considers patriarchy—i.e., a male-dominated society—as the oppressive source of social problems. While united in their opposition to so-called patriarchal systems, radical feminists differ in their emphases and specific platforms. Some radical feminists call for a complete separation of genders in society, others call for redefining or erasing the social constructs of gender (and even of relationship), while still others see feminism as only one movement (along with racial and economic movements) in a larger impetus toward human liberation. While radical feminism has had its greatest influence in LIBERAL CHRISTIANITY and some NEW AGE beliefs, it has also become a foundational philosophy (through GODDESS worship) for much of NEO-PAGANISM, as well as WICCA.

Rael: French journalist Claude Vorilhon, the leader of THE RAELIAN RELIGION.

The Raelian Religion, Rael: On December 13, 1973, a four-foot-tall alien who claimed to be from the alien race that created all life on Earth allegedly contacted French journalist Claude Vorilhon. This alien exhorted Vorilhon to create an embassy to which these aliens could return. The alien gave Vorilhon the name *Rael,* and began giving Rael commentaries on the Bible. Rael claims that two years later, he was taken by spaceship to the aliens' planet. According to Rael, who is addressed by Raelians as Our Beloved Prophet, all the prophets and teachers of the world's religions were members of this alien race who endeavored to gradually increase humanity's understanding of our existence as atoms that are part of the "huge atom." Raelians believe that their adherence to Rael's teachings is monitored by a computer that will determine their eligibility, after death, to be recreated or cloned from their current cells. In 2002, Clonaid, a Raelian organization, announced that they had successfully cloned a seven-pound baby girl—named *Eve*—as the first step in the process of cloning that will eventually lead to human immortality; this claim is largely disbelieved by the scientific community. Rael leads numerous seminars and has written many books, including *The Message Given by Extra-Terrestrials.* Web site—http://www.rael.org. See NEW AGE; UFO. For further research, a four-page Watchman Fellowship Profile is available (see page 363). Web site—http://www.watchman.org/notebook.

Rainbow Family of Living Light: From an initial gathering in July 1972, in Aspen, Colorado, the Rainbow Family of Living Light has grown into a national, informal group of individuals who practice a self-identified hippie lifestyle and come together in an annual gathering every July 1-7 (as well as assorted regional gatherings). The early movement was heavily influenced by Eastern and NEW AGE religious philosophies, although some current participants claim that religious philosophies have been increasingly de-emphasized since the 1980s. Unofficial Web site—http://www.welcomehome.org.

Rainbow Miracle Sharing Center, Brian Cordova and Jim Cunningham— Dallas, TX: A study group for *A COURSE IN MIRACLES* that focuses on gay and lesbian issues.

Raja Yoga: See YOGA.

Ram Dass: Born in 1931, Richard Alpert studied human motivation and personality development at Stanford University and served on the psychology faculties of Stanford, the University of California at Berkeley, and Harvard. Alpert's early 1960s research into LSD and other psychotropic drugs with such individuals as Timothy Leary resulted in his dismissal from Harvard in 1963. In 1968, Alpert traveled to India and studied under GURU Neem Karoli Baba, who gave Alpert the name *Ram Dass* (meaning "servant of God"). A preeminent NEW AGE teacher, Ram Dass incorporates HINDUISM (particularly YOGA), BUDDHISM, SUFISM, and ESOTERIC JUDAISM into his teachings and practices. His most famous book, published in 1971, is *Be Here Now,* and he has since published many other works, including *Journey of Awakening* and *Still Here: Embracing Aging, Changing and Dying.* Web site—http://www.ramdasstapes.org.

Ramtha: Ramtha is a 35,000-year-old spirit warrior who is allegedly channeled by J.Z. KNIGHT. See CHANNELING.

Randi, James (b. 1928): A skeptic and former MAGICIAN/illusionist (stage name "The Amazing Randi") who now debunks and exposes fake PSYCHICS (such as URI GELLER) and fraudulent faith healers (such as PETER POPOFF). He was a prominent member of the COMMITTEE FOR SCIENTIFIC INVESTIGATION OF CLAIMS OF THE PARANORMAL (CSICOP) before forming the JAMES RANDI EDUCATIONAL FOUNDATION.

Rastafarianism, Marcus Garvey: Garvey (1887–1940) promoted the Universal Negro Improvement Association in the 1920s, encouraging African-Americans to return to their rightful homeland in Africa. In the late 1920s Garvey took his message to Jamaica, where he proclaimed that the soon-coming coronation of a king would portend the salvation of African-Americans. In 1930, Prince Ras Tafari Makonnen was crowned as emperor of Ethiopia and took the name Haile Selassie ("power of the Trinity"). This coronation was understood by many to be a fulfillment of Garvey's prophecy, and Rastafarians began to worship Selassie (even though he himself was a Copt, and Garvey did not support Selassie). Selassie visited Jamaica on April 21, 1966 (this day is celebrated as Grounation Day in Rastafarianism), convincing the Rastafarians that they should not seek to move to Ethiopia until they had freed their people in Jamaica from their problems. Selassie's death in 1975 provoked a crisis of faith in the movement, with responses ranging from believing that his death was a media fabrication to believing that Selassie had overthrown death. In the 1970s, Rastafarianism became far more visible and popular outside Jamaica with the popularity of Bob Marley and the spread of the musical form known as reggae. It should be noted that many of the more visible aspects of Rastafarianism, such as dreadlocks and objects painted with the Rasta colors of red, green, and gold, have lost much of their meaning as reggae has become more accepted within secular culture. For further research, a four-page Watchman Fellowship Profile is available (see page 363). Web site—http://www.watchman.org/notebook.

RavenWolf, Silver (b. 1956): Pen name for Jenine E. Trayer, a Pennsylvania author who has written 18 books on the subject of WICCA since 1990, including *Teen Witch, Solitary Witch, To Ride a Silver Broomstick, To Light a Sacred Flame, To Stir a Magick Cauldron, American Folk Magick, Angels: Companions in Magick.* RavenWolf has been the source of some controversy within the Wiccan communities, as some have charged her with falsifying or inflating her Wiccan credentials and background. Some Wiccans have also criticized her works targeting teens as being age-inappropriate without parental consent. Web site—http://www.silverravenwolf.com. See WICCA.

Ray, Sondra: Ray, with LEONARD ORR, was one of the developers of REBIRTHING. Ray now operates SACRED RENEWAL MINISTRIES.

REACH, Inc., Bishop Luke Edwards—Meridian, MS and Emelle, AL: Edwards, the son of Alabama sharecroppers, began his work in Michigan, but eventually moved to Alabama. Edwards formed REACH, Inc. (REACH is an acronym for Research, Education, and Community Hope) as a church welfare venture in which church members' food stamps were used as seed money to form such communal ventures as meat processing and peanut brittle sales. A commune in Emelle, known as Holyland, was formed in 1978. The group has faced extensive legal problems: In 1990 the organization was cited for over 100 violations of child labor laws; in 1991 a former secretary won a $650,000 judgment against Edwards in a suit alleging sexual misconduct and mind control; in 1993 Holyland was investigated by child protection authorities; four children died in a 1998 dormitory fire (another dormitory burned in 1999); and a deacon was tried and acquitted of child abuse in 2000. REACH has also been criticized for soliciting donations outside retail stores to assist abused children; the money is instead pooled with all other income and used for a variety of purposes, of which—according to critics—abused children constitutes only a minimal part. The group's theology is generally consistent with ONENESS PENTECOSTALISM. For further research, a four-page Watchman Fellowship Profile is available (see page 363). Web site—http://www.watchman.org/notebook.

Rebirthing: Begun in 1973 by LEONARD ORR, rebirthing is a process of connected conscious breathing in which the patient's personality is reborn through transcending (some say integrating) an experience that had previously been repressed. Rebirthing practitioners claim that all people have experienced, and repressed, an exceptionally traumatic experience: birth. According to Rebirthers, each person, as a baby being born, worries about the trauma of birth, the effects of the birth on the mother, and even the violent intent of the obstetrician performing the delivery. By "experiencing rebirth," the process allegedly enables the individual to transcend the self-limitations that were instilled by this trauma. The process initially involved the patient being submerged in—and then rising from—a hot tub that simulated the womb; it has since developed into "dry rebirthing," in which the patient simply curls into a fetal position (although some Rebirthers also swaddle their patients in blankets). Rebirthing has been controversially used to treat "attachment disorder," where adopted children do not develop loving relationships with their adoptive parents; according to news reports, at least four children have died undergoing rebirthing. The U.S. House of Representatives condemned the practice in 2002, and Colorado—where two therapists were sentenced to 16 years in prison for suffocating a ten-year-old girl during rebirthing—has banned the practice.

Rebirthing Breathwork International (RBI), Leonard Orr—Orr is coauthor with Sondra Ray of *Rebirthing in the New Age,* which helped develop and popularize the NEW AGE practice of REBIRTHING. RBI publishes a quarterly newsletter, *The Conscious Connection.* Web site—http://www. rebirthingbreathwork.com.

Recovered Memory Therapy (RMT): A mental health treatment and theory popular in the 1980s and 1990s that attempted to help patients recall painful events (usually involving some form of abuse) that had been subconsciously repressed or blocked in a reaction to the pain associated with the incident. Opponents have been critical of RMT methodologies, some of which allegedly can induce ALTERED STATES OF CONSCIOUSNESS similar to HYPNOSIS, making the "planting" of memories possible. RMT was used in many cases to recover suppressed memories of alleged victims of SATANIC RITUAL ABUSE (SRA). In virtually every case, however, law enforcement agencies and investigators were unable to corroborate any of the crimes reported by RMT patients. In addition to SRA memories, RMT-like techniques can be used to "recover" memories of past lives (RE-INCARNATION "therapy") and to recall the alleged suppressed memories of UNIDENTIFIED FLYING OBJECTS (UFO) abductees. See FALSE MEMORY SYNDROME.

Recovery Version: See HOLY BIBLE RECOVERY VERSION.

Redfield, James: Redfield is author of *THE CELESTINE PROPHECY,* a bestselling NEW AGE novel, as well as the sequels *The Tenth Insight* and *The Secret of Shambhala: In Search of the Eleventh Insight.* He also wrote the nonfiction *God and the Evolving Universe* and workbooks based on his novels. With his wife, Salle Merrill Redfield, Redfield publishes *The Celestine Journal.* Web site—http://www.celestinevision.com. See NEW AGE.

Reese, Della: Popular singer, actress, and television personality who starred in the hit series *Touched by an Angel.* She is the founder and pastor of UNDERSTANDING PRINCIPLES FOR BETTER LIVING, a NEW THOUGHT church.

Reflexology: Reflexology is an ancient medical practice based upon the theory that there are reflexes in the hands and feet that correspond with every part of the body; applying pressure to these areas stimulates circulation and muscular health. While some practitioners approach reflexology according to modern medical understandings regarding the nervous system and muscular functions, others base their work on Eastern religious principles, believing that reflexology opens blocked MERIDIANS and thereby permits the full flow of CHI. The Association of Reflexologists maintains a Web site at http://www.aor.org.uk. See HOLISTIC HEALTH.

Reformation: The Reformation refers generally to a series of related movements in sixteenth-century European CHRISTIANITY that resulted in the formation of religious groups distinct from—and frequently in opposition to—the Roman Catholic Church. The roots of the Reformation can be found in three sociopolitical and religious developments: the fifteenth-century religious works of John Wyclif and Jan Hus; the Renaissance interest in classical sources that sparked the critical biblical scholarship of such individuals as Lorenzo Valla and Johann Reuchlin as well as the individualistic humanism of such scholars as Desiderius Erasmus; and the growing power of political states in Europe. In 1517, a German protest against the sale of indulgences inspired Martin Luther, an Augustinian monk, to attempt a reform of 95 perceived problems within ROMAN CATHOLICISM. In 1519 Luther openly disagreed with several elements of Roman Catholic doctrine—disagreements that became fully realized in his emphasis on SALVATION BY GRACE and explicit rejection of SALVATION BY WORKS—and was excommunicated in 1520. Luther's emphases were accepted and expanded by such Reformation leaders as Philip Melanchthon, Martin Bucer, Ulrich Zwingli, and most notably John Calvin, whose teachings were instrumental for the Reformation in Switzerland, France, and some sections of England and Scotland (England officially became a Protestant country as the result of conflict between Henry VIII and Rome over an annulment of Henry's marriage to Katherine of Aragon).

The doctrinal issues at the heart of Reformation theology included a rejection of papal authority, a rejection of the Roman Catholic sacramental system (although there were serious disagreements between many Reformers over such issues as the Eucharist), a rejection of the intermediary role of the church in salvation, and an emphasis on independent biblical translation and interpretation. Leaders of the Radical Reformation, which rejected both ROMAN CATHOLICISM and mainstream PROTESTANTISM, took these emphases further. There were three general groups of Radical Reformers: Anabaptists, such as MENNONITE founder Menno Simmons and Balthasar Hübmaier, who rejected such common Reformation practices as paedobaptism; Spiritualists, such as Caspar Schwenkfeld, who rejected all sacraments and ordinances in favor of the "inner witness of the Spirit"; and evangelical Rationalists, such as Michael Servetus, who emphasized the use of reason alongside Scripture.

Reformed Churches: An association of Christian denominations and churches of PROTESTANTISM that identify with the Reformed theology of PRESBYTERIANISM and the Swiss reformer John Calvin. For an unofficial list of reformed churches, see the Web site—http://reformed.net/church/orgs.html. See REFORMATION.

Refuge Ministries International, Jeff and Liz Harshbarger—Aiken, SC: An APOLOGETICS ministry that defends the beliefs of EVANGELICAL

CHRISTIANITY and provides outreach and biblical counseling to those involved in the OCCULT and SATANISM. Jeff Harshbarger is author of the book *From Darkness to Light.* The group is a member of EVANGELICAL MINISTRIES TO NEW RELIGIONS (EMNR). Web site—http://www. refugeministries.cc.

Reiki: *Reiki,* which means "universal life energy," is a process of healing a person by moving one's hand over (but not on) his or her body, thereby manipulating CHI and clearing blocked CHAKRAS. The philosophy behind Reiki was developed in 1914 when Mikao Usui, the founder of the practice, allegedly experienced CHI entering his crown chakra while standing under a waterfall in Japan; Usui was subsequently able to miraculously heal individuals without any reduction in his personal energy level. The practice was brought to Hawaii in 1937–38 by Reiki master Hawayo Takata. See HOLISTIC HEALTH; NEW AGE.

Reincarnation: While many shamanistic religions maintain a belief in some form of reincarnation, the concept as it is commonly understood is rooted in HINDUISM (and specifically Hinduism after the ninth-century B.C., because the concept is not found in the thirteenth-to-tenth-century *VEDAS*). The underlying principle of reincarnation is that some essential part of a person transmigrates into another body following the death of the previous body. BUDDHISM differs from Hinduism in that, while Hinduism maintains that the *ATMAN* (impersonal self) transmigrates from body to body, Buddhism maintains that there is no self (not even an impersonal one), and therefore a new collection of psycho-physical components that makes up a person simply forms at each rebirth. The goal in both religions is freedom from rebirth by eradicating KARMA, which is the cause of rebirth. A significant difference between Eastern concepts of reincarnation, and the concept popular in NEW AGE spirituality, is that in Eastern religions transmigration can occur between all life forms (and even inanimate objects), whereas many New Age devotees believe that transmigration occurs only from one human body to another.

Religious Science: A NEW THOUGHT system of belief rooted in the teaching of Ernest Holmes. In 1927 Holmes wrote *Science of Mind,* in which he synthesized the teachings of the major world religions to form the perspective that humans are divine and must develop their CHRIST

CONSCIOUSNESS. See MIND SCIENCE; RELIGIOUS SCIENCE IN-TERNATIONAL; UNITED CHURCH OF RELIGIOUS SCIENCE.

Religious Science International: A NEW THOUGHT organization which, along with the UNITED CHURCH OF RELIGIOUS SCIENCE, is rooted in the teachings of Ernest Holmes. Religious Science teaches MIND SCI-ENCE, claiming that humans are divine and have unlimited potential. Its teachings are similar to those of the CHURCH OF CHRIST, SCIENTIST. Publishes *Creative Thought*. Web site—http://www.rsintl.org.

Religious Society of Friends, George Fox: A seventeenth-century movement begun by George Fox in England. Also called *Quakers* because they were said to "quake" before the Lord. An important distinctive is their emphasis on MYSTICISM and the presence of God within every person, called the "Inner Light," which can be heard by anyone who learns to be silent and actively listen. RICHARD FOSTER, a leader in the CENTERING/CON-TEMPLATIVE PRAYER movement, is a prominent Quaker. Friends are known for their Christian pacifism (antiwar sentiments) and many, if not most, Quakers hold to some form of UNIVERSALISM. The movement lacks a hierarchical structure or a paid ministry, but there are two basic traditions within Quakerism: the unprogrammed tradition (meetings that begin in silence and have no sermon or structured order of service) and the programmed tradition (meetings that include hymns, readings from Scripture, and a sermon). There are three major organizations of Quakers in the United States: Friends General Conference with 32,000 members, Friends United Meeting with about 45,000 members, and Evangelical Friends International with an estimated 30,000 members.

Remnant Fellowship Church, Gwen Shamblin—Brentwood, TN: This church developed out of a popular faith-based diet program, the WEIGH DOWN WORKSHOP by GWEN SHAMBLIN, cofounder of the church. The movement has drawn criticism concerning its rejection of the GOSPEL of grace, teaching of SALVATION BY WORKS, and denying the doctrine of the TRINITY. There are about 130 churches in 130 cities (although many may have only a few members meeting through live webcasts from the main location). Membership in 2005 was estimated at 1,100, with almost 500 members at the main church in Brentwood, Tennessee. Web site—http://www.remnantfellowship.org. See SHAMBLIN, GWEN; WEIGH DOWN WORKSHOP.

Remnant of YHWH, Mark Deacon—Abilene, TX: A splinter of the HOUSE OF YAHWEH, the Remnant of YHWH teaches a blend of YAHWEHISM and SABBATARIANISM. The group places a strong emphasis on SACRED NAME ideology, proclaiming that Hebrew is the language of heaven and rejecting such non-Hebraic consonants as *J*. The group produces a shortwave radio program, *Babylon Is Fallen*. Web site—http://www.remnantofyhwh.com.

Reorganized Church of Jesus Christ of Latter-Day Saints (RLDS), Joseph Smith, III—Independence, MO: The original name of the COMMUNITY OF CHRIST.

Restoration Branches: Groups who have broken away from the COMMUNITY OF CHRIST as a result of changes in the Community's theology and stand on social issues. The Branches tend to adhere to traditional Community of Christ understandings of Latter-day Saint doctrine, scripture, and the prophet. The Conference of Restoration Elders, a voluntary and nonauthoritative association of Restoration Branches, maintains a Web site at http://www.eldersconference.org. A collection of Restoration resources, including a directory of Restoration Branches, can be found at http://www.centerplace.org.

The Restoration Movement: A movement in the early nineteenth-century led by Alexander Campbell, Walter Scott, and Barton W. Stone. This movement attempted to restore a more primitive form of CHRISTIANITY that would eliminate man-made creeds and unite all Christian churches by replacing denominations with unity. The movement eventually fragmented, but there are a number of churches that have roots in the Restoration Movement, including the Disciples of Christ (Christian Church), Independent Christian Churches, CHURCHES OF CHRIST (noninstrumental), and the INTERNATIONAL CHURCHES OF CHRIST (which broke away from the previous group). For controversy concerning the latter two, see CHURCHES OF CHRIST; INTERNATIONAL CHURCHES OF CHRIST.

Restored Church of God, David C. Pack—Wadsworth, OH: The Restored Church of God is one of the groups that developed from the dissolution of the GLOBAL CHURCH OF GOD. Pack started the Restored Church in 1999 with the stated intent of republishing HERBERT W. ARMSTRONG's writings; he changed this plan, however, and has since engaged in rewriting the works himself. The church publishes *The Real Truth* and *Ambassador Youth* magazines, and produces *The World to Come* radio program and an extensive number of booklets. Web site—http://www.restoredcog.org. See ARMSTRONGISM.

Reverend Ike, aka Frederick Eikerenkoetter: Eikerenkoetter began his work more than 50 years ago at the age of 14. His message is that "the Presence of God-in-you is your Unlimited Resource of Good." People can achieve wealth, health, and happiness through VISUALIZATION and creating a self-image of what he or she desires. This process of thinking about oneself as possessing the presence of God and the ability to create one's reality is variously referred to by Eikerenkoetter as "Thinkonomics" and the "Science of Living." Eikerenkoetter teaches these principles at the Christ United Church in New York City and at his Science of Living Institute. Web site—http://www.revike.org. See PANTHEISM.

Rhema Bible Church/Training Center—Tulsa, OK: See HAGIN, KEN-NETH.

Right Knowledge: See ANCIENT MYSTIC ORDER OF MAL-CHIZEDEK.

Right Way: See CHEN TAO.

The Road Less Traveled: See PECK, M. SCOTT

Robbins, Anthony (Tony): Born in 1960, Robbins is one of the most popular motivational speakers in the world, having sold over 50 million books and being named one of the "Top 50 Business Intellectuals in the World." The thrust of Robbins's message involves overcoming and eradicating self-created barriers that prevent success and happiness. Critics note two areas of concern with Robbins's teachings. First, Robbins incorporates a wide array of religious teachers and resources into his work, including DEEPAK CHOPRA, MARIANNE WILLIAMSON, *A COURSE IN MIRACLES,* Moses, and JESUS CHRIST. Second, APOLOGIST Ron Rhodes notes that Robbins relies on NEURO-LINGUISTIC PROGRAMMING to alter a student's thought processes (as well as the physiological response to those thoughts). Robbins's works include *Robbins Results Coaching* courses, as well as such books as *Awaken the Giant Within* and *Unlimited Power.* Web site—http://www.anthonyrobbins.com.

Roberts, Jane: Roberts, arguably one of the most famous practitioners of CHANNELING, first contacted a spirit entity named Seth in 1963 while playing with a OUIJA BOARD with her husband, Robert Butts. Roberts soon began to channel Seth on a regular basis, with Butts serving as the secretary for the messages communicated by Seth. Seth's messages covered a wide array of popular NEW AGE topics, including ASTRAL PROJECTION, ASTROLOGY, PYRAMIDOLOGY, MEDITATION, and UFOs. Roberts died due to complications from rheumatoid arthritis in September, 1984.

Robertson, Pat: Influential Christian leader, televangelist, and former U.S. presidential candidate who founded the CHRISTIAN BROADCASTING NETWORK (CBN), Regent University, and the American Center for Law and Justice (ACLJ). Web site—http://www.patrobertson.com.

Rocky Mountain Institute for Yoga and Ayurveda—Boulder, CO: The institute is an educational organization that teaches a number of Yogic traditions, as well as TANTRA and AYURVEDA. The institute offers a 500-plus-hour course in the practice and teaching of YOGA, a 750-plus-hour Ayurveda and YOGA therapy program, and many courses in practicing yoga as part of a healthy lifestyle. Web site—http://www.rmiya.org. See HINDUISM; HOLISTIC HEALTH.

Rocky Mountain Research Institute—Boise, ID: This institute provides academic research on unexplained phenomena and awareness of activity with other dimensions.

RoHun Therapy: Patricia Hayes—founder of DELPHI UNIVERSITY AND SPIRITUAL CENTER—developed RoHun in the early 1980s following 20 years of work in METAPHYSICS. RoHun is presented as a spiritual and psychological therapy in which energy blocks in the CHAKRAS are cleared, thereby enabling the practitioner and patient to clear away negative emotions and traumas and allow the free flow of energy. The primary training center for RoHun practitioners is The RoHun Institute at Delphi University. The RoHun Institute offers a directory of practitioners at http://www.delphi-center.com/healing/rohundir.htm. See NEW AGE.

Roman Catholicism: The Roman Catholic church is one of 24 *sui juris* churches, all of whom are in communion under the authority of the bishop of Rome. The bishop of Rome, commonly referred to as the Pope (from the Greek *pappas,* meaning "father"), is understood by Roman Catholics to be the Vicar of Christ, the head of the universal church on earth; this claim is disputed by both ORTHODOX CHRISTIANITY and PROTESTANTISM, and in fact was one of the bases for the Great Schism between East and West in the eleventh through thirteenth centuries, and the REFORMATION in the sixteenth-century. The spirituality of Roman Catholicism is rooted in seven sacraments: baptism, confession, the Eucharist, confirmation, matrimony, holy orders (including the episcopate, clerical ranks, and monastics), and anointing of the sick and dying. While Roman Catholicism and Protestantism hold in common many central doctrines, Protestantism was founded in protest against two central aspects of Roman Catholicism (in addition to the authority of the Pope): the Roman Catholic understanding of salvation (including the sacramental system, the concept of purgatory for the expiation of sins before entering heaven, and the role of good works), and the role of the church in interpreting Scripture and establishing doctrine (as contrasted with the Protestant principle of *sola scriptura*—Scripture as the sole religious authority). It should be noted that Roman Catholicism is not homogenous: Due to its size (over one billion adherents) and global organization, there are numerous movements and ideologies within the Roman Catholic church. For example, Roman Catholic clergy and laity have been leaders in LIBERATION THEOLOGY in Central and South America. Clergy in other areas have combined Roman Catholicism with native SPIRITISM or the NEW AGE (as exemplified by the defrocked Dominican priest MATTHEW FOX). Furthermore, since the 1960s, a small CHARISMATIC MOVEMENT has developed within the Roman Catholic church. Web site—http://www.vatican.va. See SALVATION BY GRACE; SALVATION BY WORKS; GOSPEL.

Rosary: In ROMAN CATHOLICISM, a set of prayer beads used in conjunction with a repetitive system of prayer and MEDITATION in which practitioners recite the Lord's Prayer and the Hail Mary prayer (taken from the angel Gabriel's salutation to the VIRGIN MARY in Luke 8:1). A recitation of both prayers is called a *decade* and is counted off using the beads. A full rosary involves 20 decades. On rare occasions, some churches in PROTESTANTISM will use the rosary for prayer or liturgical purposes, including ANGLICAN CHURCHES and some congregations of the EVANGELICAL LUTHERAN CHURCH IN AMERICA.

Rosicrucian Fellowship, Max Heindel—Oceanside, CA: In 1907, Max Heindel allegedly received initiation and instruction in ROSICRUCIANISM with the provision that he retain the secret of the Mystery Teachings; through this refusal he passed the final test of his teachers and was then commissioned to teach the world about Rosicrucianism. Heindel launched the Rosicrucian Fellowship in Seattle, Washington, in 1909, and moved the fellowship to "Mount Ecclesia" in Oceanside in 1911. The primary message of the fellowship, outlined in Heindel's *The Rosicrucian Cosmo-Conception,* is that through physical and mental evolution (specifically through REINCARNATION), all life will attain perfection. This perfection is attainable because JESUS surrendered his physical body to the CHRIST spirit, which, after the crucifixion, was released into the earth and became the Earth spirit; this spirit indwells every living thing. The fellowship publishes *Rays from the Rose Cross* magazine, and their main textbook is *The Rosicrucian Cosmo-Conception,* which is available on their Web site at http://www.rosicrucian. com. See ROSICRUCIANISM; OCCULT.

Rosicrucianism, Christian Rosenkreutz: The term *Rosicrucian* is rooted in the words *rosae* ("rose") and *crucis* ("cross"). According to Rosicrucian legend, Rosicrucianism was started by a German nobleman named Christian Rosenkreutz, who studied under OCCULT masters in Palestine in 1407. Rosenkreutz and a small group of adepts—according to many sources, no more than eight—allegedly studied the mysterious forces of nature and prepared their findings and teachings for the benefit of humanity. Many scholars believe, however, that seventeenth-century references to Rosicrucians are in fact referring to a small number of isolated societal reformers who used the sciences—particularly ALCHEMY—as a vehicle for expressing their opinions. The publication of the "Rosicrucian manifestos"—*The Fama Fraternitas of the Meritorious Order of the Rosy Cross* (1614), *The Confession of the Rosicrucian Fraternity* (1615), and *The Chymical Marriage of Christian Rosenkreuz* (1616)—generated widespread interest throughout Europe in the mysterious Rosicrucians. Rosicrucianism is generally believed to have been brought to North America by Pascal Beverly Randolph, who started the Fraternitas Rosae Crucis in the nineteenth-century. The doctrines of Rosicrucianism can vary between groups, but generally incorporate alchemy, the occult, GNOSTICISM, and elements of ancient Egyptian religion.

Rosicrucian Order (AMORC), Harvey Spencer Lewis—San Jose, CA: Started in 1915 by Lewis, the AMORC is one of the most visible Rosicrucian groups. Lewis's active involvement in Egyptian archaeology—especially the 1921 excavation of Tell el-Armana—led to his opening the 2,000-artifact Rosicrucian Egyptian Oriental Museum (now Rosicrucian Egyptian Museum) in 1928. Lewis's son constructed and opened the current facility in Rosicrucian Park in 1966. Lewis assisted in starting the now-defunct Fédération Universelle des Ordres et Sociétés Initiatiques in 1934 as an attempt to gather all mystical societies into one organization. The AMORC offers a 62-month correspondence program in which the initiate studies *Master Monographs* to learn the secrets for physical and spiritual progression. The AMORC publishes numerous books by Lewis and other leaders, as well as the *Rosicrucian Digest.* Web site—http://www.rosicrucian.org. See ROSICRUCIANISM; OCCULT.

Rowan Tree Church, Paul Beyerl—Kirkland, WA: Founded in 1979 by Beyerl, the church combines the beliefs and practices of WICCA with the mythology in the fiction of J.R.R. Tolkien. Beyerl's "Tradition of Lothloriën" is an Earth-focused religion that celebrates nature as sacred and incorporates Wiccan ritual in its practice to heal nature and all life. Beyerl claims to have borrowed from BUDDHISM the concept of the novice, who are guided in their study and practice to grow in knowledge and ability in the tradition. His novices learn GUIDED MEDITATION as part of their "Attributes and Abilities." The church publishes *The Unicorn* and *RTNews* newsletters. Web site—http://www.therowantreechurch.org.

Rune: An ancient Scandinavian magical alphabet of 24 symbols. Runes are used by some modern practitioners for divining the future, performing MAGIC, or evoking Norse deities. See DIVINATION.

Russell, Charles Taze: Founder of the WATCHTOWER BIBLE AND TRACT SOCIETY.

Russian Orthodox Church: See ORTHODOX CHURCH.

S

Sabbatarianism: Generally the view that one day of the week is to be reserved for religious observance as prescribed by the Old Testament Sabbath laws of the BIBLE. As used in this reference guide, Sabbatarianism generally refers to an extreme form of the belief in which salvation is conditional upon keeping the Sabbath laws. Breaking the laws results in losing eternal life. In most cases, the Jewish Sabbath (Saturday) must be observed by refraining from work, sports, and travel from sundown Friday evening to sundown Saturday evening. The belief is often accompanied by the observance of the dietary laws and religious festivals prescribed in the Old Testament. See LEGALISM; SALVATION BY GRACE; SALVATION BY WORKS; GOSPEL; SPIRITUAL ABUSE.

Sabellianism: In the early third century, Sabellius of Rome developed a sophisticated form of MODALISM, teaching the existence of a divine monad (*Huiopator*), which, by a process of expansion, successively revealed itself as the Creating and Lawgiving Father, the Redeeming Son, and the grace-giving Spirit. These were three different modes of the same divine person. The indivisibility of God therefore means that the Son did not exist before the incarnation and, because the Father and Son are one, the Father suffered with the Son in His passion and death (this belief is known as *patripassianism*). Sabellius was excommunicated by Pope Callistus I in A.D. 220, and Sabellianism was condemned by a synod in Rome in 262.

Sabin, Robert A.: Sabin, the pastor emeritus of Apostolic Bible Church in St. Paul, Minnesota, is one of the foremost teachers of ONENESS PENTE-COSTALISM.

The Sacred Mushroom and the Cross, **John Allegro:** Allegro (1923–88) was a renowned scholar of Hebrew and Semitic languages who, in 1953, was one of the scholars chosen to reconstruct and translate the Dead Sea Scrolls. In 1956, Allegro published *The Dead Sea Scrolls,* one of the most famous and influential books about the scrolls. Angered by the restriction of the public from the scrolls, as well as the delay in publication of his transcription of the copper scroll, Allegro published his own version in 1960, *The Mysterious Copper Scroll.* Allegro's continuation in publishing the status and contents of the scrolls eventually resulted in his access to the scrolls being removed by the scroll committee. Allegro also lost his faith during this process and, in 1970, published *The Sacred Mushroom and the Cross,* in which he alleged that "Jesus" was a New Testament code for a psychedelic mushroom that induced hallucinations when received in sacramental communion.

Sacred Name: Sacred Name theology is based on one of two doctrinal points (depending upon the emphasis of the teacher): either the belief that the name of God is too sacred to speak (and/or fully write), or the belief that God must be addressed by a single, special name (either Yahweh, Jehovah, Yah, or Yahvah, etc.). In the latter case, whichever name is believed to be true, all other terms or names for God are considered incorrect or references to false deities. Salvation, it is believed, depends on referring to God by His correct name. Arguably the earliest Sacred Name publication is Alexander McWhorter's *The Memorial Name, or Yahweh-Christ,* published in 1857. The Sacred Name movement began in earnest, however, in the CHURCH OF GOD (SEVENTH DAY) in the late 1930s when Clarence O. Dodd, one of the founders of the movement, began to teach Sacred Name ideology; he became particularly influential after leaving the church and starting publication of *The Faith* magazine in 1937. Numerous other Sacred Name groups also started in the late 1930s. Most—but not all—Sacred Name groups also practice SABBATARIANISM. See YAHWEHISM.

Sacred Renewal Ministries, Sondra Ray—Marina Del Ray, CA: Ray is a NEW AGE teacher who trains students to open their energy centers in order to achieve CHRIST CONSCIOUSNESS. Ray also promotes the GODDESS, claiming that the Divine Mother is the source of all knowledge, and that devotion to her produces regeneration and renewal. Web site—http://www.sondraray.com.

Sacred Science: One of eight criteria of MIND CONTROL according to ROBERT LIFTON's theory of THOUGHT REFORM. According to Lifton, a group promoting sacred science considers that their doctrines and beliefs are sacred and beyond question. Therefore, no alternative viewpoint is allowed to exist, and open consideration of alternative ideas and free discussion are quashed. See BRAINWASHING.

Sadhana Society—Prescott, AZ: The society is a 60-acre NEW AGE retreat center located approximately 20 miles west of Prescott. The society teaches PANTHEISM, focusing on the unity of God, humanity, and the universe.

SageWoman Magazine—Point Arena, CA: *SageWoman* celebrates the GODDESS within each woman, featuring articles on the sacred aspects of female life (such as the menstrual cycle and childbearing) and WITCHCRAFT. Web site—http://www.sagewoman.com. See NEW AGE.

Saint Germain: The Comte de Saint Germain is one of the most notable of the ASCENDED MASTERS and a member of the GREAT WHITE BROTHERHOOD. Little is known about the life of the real Saint Germain. He is widely believed to be the son of the widow of Charles II of Spain, born approximately 1690. In the 1750s he reportedly spent time in the court of Louis XV of France, but was forced to flee to England in 1760 after a debacle in foreign affairs. It is claimed that he traveled to Russia, and even took part in a conspiracy that resulted in the ascension to the throne of Catherine the Great in 1762. It 1774, Saint Germain allegedly entered the court of Louis XVI and Marie Antoinette. He reportedly died in Germany on February 27, 1784, although followers of THEOSOPHY and the I AM MOVEMENT claim he traveled to the Himalayas. ANNIE BESANT of the ARCANE SCHOOL claimed to have met Saint Germain in 1896 (possibly in a vision), while Guy Ballard claimed to have met him on Mount Shasta in 1930. Followers of the I AM Movement believe Saint Germain now releases the violet flame that burns the KARMA that ties the soul to the body and prevents release into the realm of light.

Saint Germain Foundation—Schaumburg, IL: The foundation is an organization of the I AM MOVEMENT and traces its founding to Guy Ballard's encounter with SAINT GERMAIN in 1930. The foundation is parent to 300 local groups with the names "I AM" Sanctuary, "I AM" Temple, "I

AM" Study Group, or "I AM" Reading Room. The foundation operates the Saint Germain Press, which publishes Godfre Ray King's 1934 work *Unveiled Mysteries* and other publications promoting I AM teachings. Web site—http://www.saintgermainfoundation.org.

Saint John Coltrane African Orthodox Church, Franzo Wayne King—San Francisco, CA: Also known as Saint John Will-I-Am Coltrane African Orthodox Church, the church attempts to achieve one mind through the music of jazz saxophonist John Coltrane. The church, which claims to be a part of ORTHODOX CHRISTIANITY through the Patriarch of Antioch, was founded by King, who received his ordination to bishop from the AFRICAN ORTHODOX CHURCH. The church sponsors a women's monastic group called the Sisters of Compassion. Produces the *UPLIFT* radio program. Web site—http://www.saintjohncoltrane.com. See RASTAFARIANISM.

Saint John's Retreat Center: Developed in 1996 as part of the WHITE EAGLE CENTER FOR THE AMERICAS. Web site—http://www.whiteaglelodge.org.

Sai Organization: See SATHYA SAI BABA.

Salvation by Grace: The REFORMATION slogan *sola gratia*—"grace alone"—states one of the central doctrines of CHRISTIANITY: eternal life with God depends not upon the goodness of the individual, but instead upon the goodness of God. Salvation therefore cannot be earned through any prescribed regimen of activities and observances—i.e., "works"—but instead, is entirely a gift of our gracious God. See SALVATION BY WORKS; GOSPEL.

Salvation by Works: In contrast to the doctrine of SALVATION BY GRACE, the concept of salvation by works refers to the belief that an individual's faithfulness to a prescribed regimen of activities and observances will determine—either partially or fully—whether an individual qualifies for eternal life with God. See GOSPEL; LEGALISM.

Salzberg, Sharon: Exposed to BUDDHISM in a university philosophy course, she went to India in 1970 as part of an independent study program and spent the next few years in intensive study under Buddhist teachers. In

1974 she began teaching insight meditation in the United States. Salzberg is a cofounder of INSIGHT MEDITATION SOCIETY and serves as a contributing editor for OPRAH WINFREY'S *O, The Oprah Magazine*. Web site—http://www.sharonsalzberg.com.

Samhain: Pronounced *"Sah-ween,"* Samhain was a new-year celebration observed on November 1 by the pre-Christian CELTS. It was believed by the Celtic DRUIDS that the dead would cause panic and destruction among the living unless appeased with an offering. See HALLOWEEN.

Samsara: A Sanskrit term that means "the running around," this refers to the repeated cycles of birth, misery, and death in conjunction with RE-INCARNATION. The term is used with various shades of meaning in HINDUISM, JAINISM, BUDDHISM, and some forms of YOGA. See REINCARNATION; MOKSHA; KARMA.

Sankirtan: In traditional HINDUISM, sankirtan is a religious chant or MANTRA continually repeated to draw practitioners into an ever-closer state of God-consciousness. The INTERNATIONAL SOCIETY OF KRISHNA CONSCIOUSNESS has added to sankirtan the practice of distributing literature, which is said to contribute to the salvation of both the devotee and the recipient.

Santeria: Santeria, a religion of the Cuban Yoruba slaves from West Africa, developed in the sixteenth-century as the native Yoruba religion was blended with ROMAN CATHOLICISM. In Santeria the supreme deity is Olodumare, the spiritual source of all life. His emissaries to the world are the Orisha, the guardians over nature and every aspect of human life. Beneath these in the Santeria hierarchy are humans, human ancestors, and other elements of creation. Animal sacrifice to the Orisha—the most controversial (in North America) element of Santeria—is necessary for human well-being. See CHURCH OF THE LUKUMI BABALU AYE.

Saraydarian Institute: See AQUARIAN EDUCATIONAL GROUP.

Satan: Lucifer (or "morning star" [Isaiah 14:12]) was an angelic creature who led a multitude of ANGELS in rebellion against God. This rebellion failed. Lucifer fell and became Satan, the Devil, leading with him rebellious angels who became DEMONS (Isaiah 14:12-14). The BIBLE depicts Satan as causing the fall of humanity (Genesis 3), and his central goal is to thwart the plans of God (2 Corinthians 4:4) by continuing to tempt and mislead humanity (Revelation 12:10). The BIBLE prophesies that ultimately, Satan will fail, and he and the demons will be punished for all eternity (Matthew 25:41, Revelation 20:10).

Satanic Ritual Abuse: The theory of Satanic Ritual Abuse (SRA) is that a widespread network of individuals engage in ritualistic physical, emotional, and SPIRITUAL ABUSE on unwilling victims in the worship or service of SATAN. In the 1980s, widespread reports of horrific satanic abuse were reported in the media, and the reports included physical (including murder and cannibalism), emotional, sexual, and spiritual abuse. Two of the individuals who claimed to be victims of SRA, MIKE WARNKE and LAUREN STRATFORD, were prominent in evangelical Christian circles. Despite the large number of claims of SRA, no conclusive evidence has been found in these cases (including the cases of Warnke and Stratford, both of whom were disproved after extensive investigation). The lack of evidence for widespread SRA does not in itself prove that satanic abuse never occurs—it does demonstrate, however, that Christians must be highly discerning regarding the truthfulness or falsity of all religious claims.

Satanism: The term *Satanism* is unfortunately misused by many Christians who apply the term indiscriminately to any number of OCCULT or NEO-PAGAN groups, including those who deny the existence of SATAN (such as WICCA). In reality, there are only two types of Satanists: material Satanists, who do not believe in the existence of Satan but nonetheless engage in Satanic ritualism for entertainment or to mock CHRISTIANITY (the foremost example of material Satanism is the CHURCH OF SATAN); and religious Satanists, who believe in the existence of both the Christian God and Satan, and who choose to worship Satan (Robert M. Bowman adds a third category—mystical Satanists, who believe they can tap an impersonal spiritual power).

The Satan Seller: See WARNKE, MIKE.

Satan's Underground: See STRATFORD, LAUREN.

Savoy, Gene: Head bishop of the INTERNATIONAL COMMUNITY OF CHRIST, CHURCH OF THE SECOND ADVENT since

1971 and president of the JAMILIAN UNIVERSITY OF THE OR-DAINED. Founder of the AMERICAN COSMIC SOLAR RESEARCH CENTER.

Schaeffer, Francis (1912–84): Influential Christian philosopher and APOL-OGIST of EVANGELICAL CHRISTIANITY. Schaeffer and his wife Edith founded L'Abri community in Switzerland in 1955, which began when the couple opened their home for visitors who wished to discuss philosophy and spirituality. L'Abri (French="shelter") continued to grow after Schaeffer's death in 1984, spreading to the United States and six other countries. Schaeffer is author of several best-selling books, including *How Should We Then Live?* (which was also made into a video series). Web site—http://www.labri.org.

Scholarly & Historical Information Exchange for Latter-Day Saints (SHIELDS), Doug Marshall and Doug Yancey: The name SHIELDS was first used as part of an informal APOLOGETICS effort by Doug Marshall and Doug Yancey to defend the CHURCH OF JESUS CHRIST OF LATTER-DAY SAINTS (LDS) against online critics. Marshall (who is no longer associated with the LDS church) and Yancey allowed others to use the moniker in defense of LDS doctrines and practices. There is no formal organization, but a Web site has been in operation since 1997. Web site—http://www.shields-research.org. See FOUNDATION FOR ANCIENT RESEARCH AND MORMON STUDIES (FARMS); FOUNDATION FOR APOLOGETIC INFORMATION RESEARCH (FAIR).

School for Esoteric Studies—Asheville, NC: Rooted in the teachings of ALICE BAILEY, the school trains students to facilitate the progress of their higher self by recognizing and channeling the energies in their environment. Web site—http://www.esotericstudies.net. See ARCANE SCHOOL.

School of Ageless Wisdom—Arlington, TX: The school promotes the teachings of ALICE BAILEY, Agni Yoga, and a specialized form of ASTROLOGY called *Astrochemistry.* Web site—http://www.unol.org/saw. See AGNI YOGA SOCIETY; ARCANE SCHOOL.

School of Natural Order, Vitvan—Baker, NV: Vitvan, aka Ralph M. deBit (1883–1964), blended GNOSTICISM and an interest in semantics to expand self-awareness that each person is part of a large universal energy. Vitvan further claimed that Jesus attained the CHRIST CONSCIOUSNESS that was taught by the Egyptian and Greek mystery religions; he further taught that 1950–2050 is the transitional period between the Piscean and Aquarian ages (the Aquarian age being marked by a universal rise in consciousness). Vitvan started the school in 1946 to share his teachings. The school publishes numerous books by Vitvan and his followers, as well as the bimonthly newsletter *Resonance*. Web site—http://www.sno.org. See NEW AGE.

Science and Health with Key to the Scriptures: First published by MARY BAKER EDDY in 1875, *Science and Health with Key to the Scriptures* is the central text of THE CHURCH OF CHRIST, SCIENTIST.

Science of Living Institute: See REVEREND IKE.

Scientology: See CHURCH OF SCIENTOLOGY.

Séance: A séance (derived from the old French verb *seoir,* "to sit") is an OCCULT ritual in which a MEDIUM leads a group of observers, called *sitters,* in an alleged contact with the spirit world; usually this is an attempt to communicate with the dead. See NECROMANCY; SPIRITUALISM.

Search and Prove, Jerry Gross—St. Paul Park, MN: Gross teaches individuals how to engage in ASTRAL PROGRESSION. Web site—http://members.aol.com/rgross6162. See NEW AGE.

Second Advent Movement: The Second Advent Movement (also commonly called the Great Second Advent Movement) was an early-mid nineteenth-century movement begun by WILLIAM MILLER. Miller read in Daniel 8:14 (which prophesies the restoration of the temple in Jerusalem) that, after 2,300 days, the sanctuary would be cleansed. Miller believed two things about this prophecy: it refers to the SECOND COMING of JESUS CHRIST, and—based on Miller's belief that each day in the prophecy refers to one year, and that the prophetic period began in 457 B.C.—the second coming would occur between March 21, 1843 and March 21, 1844. When the second coming did not occur during this period, a follower of Miller theorized that the second coming would then occur on October 22, 1844. The subsequent failure of this prophecy resulted in what is called the Great Disappointment. Despite this, small groups of followers either revised their chronologies and dates (e.g., the WATCHTOWER BIBLE AND

TRACT SOCIETY), or revised their theology to believe that an unseen event occurred in heaven in 1844 (e.g., the SEVENTH-DAY ADVENTIST CHURCH). See FALSE PROPHECY.

Second Coming: A central hope of CHRISTIANITY is the return to Earth of JESUS CHRIST (Acts 1:11). The doctrine of the second coming is frequently expressed in the New Testament in the word *parousia,* which literally means "being by," and also means "presence, coming, or arrival" (see 1 Thessalonians 3:13; 4:15; 2 Thessalonians 2:8). Christians are exhorted to continually await the return of Christ, but are also warned that no one knows the date on which this will occur (Matthew 24:42). Despite this warning, many groups and individuals have erroneously attempted to prophesy the date of the second coming. See FALSE PROPHECY; SECOND ADVENT MOVEMENT.

The Secret Doctrine: The seminal 1888 book by HELENA P. BLAVATSKY. Subtitled *The Synthesis of Science, Religion, and Philosophy,* Blavatsky's book is one of the most influential works of THEOSOPHY. The THEOSOPH-ICAL SOCIETY has placed the book online at http://www.theosociety.org/pasadena/sd/sd-hp.htm.

Secrets, **Norma Cox**—Marshal, AR: Until Cox ceased publication in 1996 due to failing health, *Secrets* was a popular newsletter proclaiming that pagan alien gods called "Watchers"—residing both in the hollow core of the Earth and UFOs—were concealing the truths of the universe from Caucasian Americans. Cox taught a highly modified version of BRITISH ISRAELISM in which the legitimate biblical Israelites were Aryans, and Jews are simply Canaanites who pretend to be Israelites. Cox also denounced all forms of organized CHRISTIANITY as sun worshippers.

Secular Humanism: A belief system of values and ethics that excludes existence of a personal God, gods, or any power or authority higher than humans. The worldview and values have been articulated through the last century in a series of essays: the *Humanist Manifesto I* (1933), *Humanist Manifesto II* (1973), and *Humanism and Its Aspirations* (2003, aka *Humanist Manifesto III*). See ATHEISM; AGNOSTICISM.

Seeing Beyond, **Bonnie Coleen**—Scotts Valley, CA: Presented as "personal growth talk radio," *Seeing Beyond* is a radio program on which Coleen interviews guests who teach a wide variety of NEW AGE ideologies and practices. Two notable focuses for Coleen are ASTROLOGY and TAROT. Web site—http://seeingbeyond.com.

Sekai Mahikari Bunmei Kyodan: See MAHIKARI.

Self-Realization Fellowship, Paramahansa Yogananda—Los Angeles, CA: Mukunda Lal Ghosh (1893–1952) became a follower of Swami Sri Yukteswar Giri in 1915 and received the name *Yogananda* ("bliss—*ananda*—through divine union—*yoga*"). Yogananda started the fellowship after receiving an enthusiastic reception to his presentation on the science of religion at the 1920 International Congress of Religious Liberals. The focus of Yogananda's teachings is practicing KRIYA YOGA and MEDITATION in order to achieve a realization of the practitioner's oneness with the divine. Instruction in these practices is offered through the correspondence program *Self-Realization Fellowship Lessons.* The fellowship also operates temples and over 500 meditation centers in 54 countries. Yogananda's most famous book is his 1946 *Autobiography of a Yogi;* the fellowship also publishes, in addition to many books and recordings, *Self-Realization* magazine. Web site—http://www.yogananda-srf.org. See HINDUISM.

Self-Revelation Church of Absolute Monism, Swami Premananda—Washington, DC: The church traces its roots to PARAMAHANSA YOGANANDA, who consecrated Premananda a swami in 1941. Premananda was actively involved in FREEMASONRY, and according to the church attained high degrees within the Lodge. The philosophy of Absolute Monism is derived from the Vedic doctrine of PANTHEISM. The goal of life is to realize that the soul is identical with the God of the universe. The church's Golden Lotus Temple was built in 1952. Web site—http://www. self-revelationchurch.org. See HINDUISM.

Serpent Seed: The Serpent Seed doctrine is based on an interpretation of Genesis 3 that Eve's sin in the Garden of Eden involved sexual intercourse with the serpent (SATAN). The result of this alleged intercourse was Cain, whose descendants are believed by various religious groups to be the ethnic, political, or religious group against which they are particularly biased. Adherents of the IDENTITY MOVEMENTS therefore often maintain that Jews or Africans and African-Americans are descendants of Cain (and therefore of Satan); adherents of the NATION OF YAHWEH believe these descendants are Caucasians; adherents of the HOLY SPIRIT ASSOCIATION FOR THE UNIFICATION OF WORLD CHRISTIANITY believe they are communists; followers of BRANHAMISM believe they are all people who are unsaved, etc.

Seth: See ROBERTS, JANE.

The 7 Habits of Highly Effective People: A self-help book used primarily by people who are pursuing success in business. See COVEY, STEPHEN.

Sevenoaks Pathwork Center—Madison, VA: Founded by Donovan and Susan Thesenga in 1972, the center is a 130-acre NEW AGE retreat facility that teaches awareness of the fact that God is inside each person. The foundation for the center's Pathwork is "Core Energetics," developed in a series of 258 lectures by Eva Broch Pierrakos between 1957 and 1979, which equips practitioners to fully realize their potential through self-love, self-awareness, and self-transformation. This process is accomplished by reverting evil—which is simply a distortion of positive energy—back to its original, healthful current. Web site—http://www.sevenoakspathwork.org.

Seventh-day Adventist Church (SDA)—Washington, DC: The Seventh-day Adventist (SDA) church is the largest group to come from the SECOND ADVENT MOVEMENT. On the morning after the Great Disappointment, Hiram Edson experienced a vision of Jesus standing before the altar of heaven; Edson concluded that this meant WILLIAM MILLER was right in determining the date of 1844, but that JESUS—instead of returning to Earth—moved into the heavenly sanctuary mentioned in Hebrews 8:1-2. This revision of Miller's teaching—particularly as published by Joseph Bates in 1846 and 1849—greatly influenced James and Ellen G. White (1827–1915). To this theology the Whites added SABBATARIANISM, and the SDA church was officially organized in 1863. The person and writings of ELLEN G. WHITE—the "Messenger" who held the "spirit of prophecy"—are central to SDA theology; her works, however, have been widely criticized by non-SDA scholars for plagiarizing from the writings of other contemporary Christians. One of the SDA church's most distinctive teachings concerns the Investigative Judgment, in which Jesus is believed to be currently reviewing the cases of individuals in order to deem their worthiness of eternal life; the conclusion of this judgment will be followed by the SECOND COMING. Closely related to these doctrines is the fact that the SDA church believes it is the "remnant church," the only organization maintaining and proclaiming true CHRISTIANITY in its entirety. (It should be noted that, at the same time, the SDA church affirms the existence of true Christians who are nonetheless not ADVENTISTS.) While some SDA hold a more evangelical theology, many traditionalists within the movement believe that worship on Sunday will be the "mark" of "the beast" (Revelation 13:16-17). Many also deny SALVATION BY GRACE through faith in Christ alone, believing instead that personal salvation in Christ depends on faith plus keeping the Sabbath and an Old Testament dietary law of no shellfish or pork (or in some cases no meat at all). Because of these doctrines and the diversity within the movement, there is widespread disagreement regarding whether the SDA church should be considered part of EVANGELICAL CHRISTIANITY. Among White's most popular and influential writings are *The Great Controversy* and *The Desire of the Ages;* the SDA church also publishes *Adventist Review* journal and operates Adventist Television Network and Adventist World Radio. Web site—http://www.adventist.org. See SECOND ADVENT MOVEMENT. For further research, a four-page Watchman Fellowship Profile is available (see page 363). Web site—http://www.watchman.org/notebook.

Shaman: A shaman is a MEDIUM between the physical and spiritual worlds. Shamans usually function as religious and often medical leaders in their communities. Outsiders and skeptics sometimes use the term *witch doctor.* See SHAMANISM.

Shamanic Journeys, Nicki Scully—Eugene, OR: Scully combines SHAMANISM, METAPHYSICS, ALCHEMY, and claims about Egyptian mystery religions into a system for spiritual healing. In addition to classes and seminars in these subjects, Scully offers trips to sacred locations in Egypt, Greece, and Peru. Web site—http://www.shamanicjourneys.com. See NEW AGE.

Shamanism: Shamanism is based on the belief that spirits move through and affect the physical world. The SHAMAN interacts with the spirits or forces that control all aspects of life (e.g., weather, physical health, etc.) in an attempt to influence these for the benefit of the community. The shaman typically enters an ecstatic TRANCE in order to communicate with beings in the spirit world; these ALTERED STATES OF CONSCIOUSNESS frequently involve some form of ASTRAL PROJECTION. These ecstatic states are believed to be a necessary condition for the shaman to obtain and dispense wisdom and healing to the community. See DIVINATION; OCCULT; SPIRITISM.

Shambhala International, Chögyam Trungpa Rinpoche—Halifax, Nova Scotia, Canada: Shambhala is the name of a mythical kingdom that allegedly existed in central Asia. The residents of this kingdom were believed to be profoundly wise and compassionate; some NEW AGE versions of the legend also attribute supernatural powers to these individuals. The myth of Shambhala exists primarily within TIBETAN BUDDHISM and has been particularly promoted in the West by Chögyam Trungpa Rinpoche and his Shambhala International community. There are currently over 150 Shambhala meditation centers teaching the beliefs and practices of TIBETAN BUDDHISM. Web site—http://www.shambhala.org.

Shambhala Publications—Boston, MA: Founded in 1969 as an outgrowth of the Shambhala Booksellers bookstore in Berkeley, California, Shambhala Publications publishes works that cover a wide range of perspectives rooted in Eastern religions, from classical works of BUDDHISM to modern NEW AGE philosophies and practices. Web site—http://www.shambhala.com.

Shamblin, Gwen: Registered dietitian and controversial author of the bestselling book *The Weigh Down Diet,* which helped launch a popular faith-based diet and weight-loss program, THE WEIGH DOWN WORKSHOP, and a 12-week weight-loss seminar, Exodus Out of Egypt. Shamblin's popular workshop, which had been used in 17,000 CHRISTIAN churches, drew criticism when she began publicly to deny the doctrine of the TRINITY and SALVATION BY GRACE. She cofounded a church in harmony with her beliefs, REMNANT FELLOWSHIP CHURCH. Web site—http://www. wdworkshop.com/gwen_bio.asp. See WEIGH DOWN WORKSHOP; REMNANT FELLOWSHIP.

Shared Heart Foundation, Joyce and Berry Vissell—Aptos, CA: Engaged in counseling since 1973, the Vissells promote the theory that interpersonal relationships are a vehicle to fully realizing an individual's oneness with all the world. Love given to a spouse or partner is therefore a gift given to all the world. Web site—http://www.sharedheart.org. See NEW AGE.

Share International, Benjamin Crème—London: In 1959, Creme was contacted by one of the Masters of Wisdom (analogous to the GREAT WHITE BROTHERHOOD), and told that CHRIST would return in 20 years. This return allegedly occurred in 1978 when a being named Maitreya began appearing in London's Indian-Pakistani community. The Maitreya—the current incarnation of Christ—is head of the Masters of Wisdom, and is teaching humanity that all must adhere to the laws of KARMA and REINCARNATION. Maitreya and Creme's teachings are largely influenced by THEOSOPHY. Creme predicted that Christ would reveal himself between April and June of 1982. In addition to numerous books, Share publishes the periodicals *Share International* and *Emergence Quarterly.* Web site—http://www.shareintl.org. See NEW AGE. For further research, a four-page Watchman Fellowship Profile is available (see page 363). Web site—http://www.watchman.org/notebook.

Shepherding: Also frequently called *discipleship,* shepherding is a process intended to stimulate guidance and discipline. The process involves requiring almost every member of a group to submit to the oversight of a senior or more advanced member. Frequently, the only individual who is not accountable to this shepherding is the leader of the group. While usually intended as loving pastoral guidance, shepherding can degenerate to SPIRITUAL ABUSE: The shepherd controls every aspect of the submitting member's life and can enact strict punishment if the shepherd's orders are not faithfully—and unquestioningly—followed. It must be noted that shepherding differs from simple pastoral counseling or from the sacrament of confession practiced in ORTHODOX CHRISTIANITY and ROMAN CATHOLICISM.

Shepherding Movement: A radical accountability movement formed by five leaders from south Florida within the CHARISMATIC MOVEMENT (Bob Mumford, Derek Prince, Charles Simpson, Don Basham, and Ern Baxter). Known as the Fort Lauderdale Five, they developed a system in which all believers were to voluntarily submit themselves to the "covering" or spiritual authority of "shepherds." Ultimately, a widespread chain-of-command network of cell groups was formed that indirectly linked back to the five leaders. Because of the heavy emphasis on obedience to one's shepherd, the movement drew criticism from outsiders, who alleged that the system fostered SPIRITUAL ABUSE. One of the most influential critics was PAT ROBERTSON of CBN. Eventually, most of the leaders abandoned the movement and Bob Mumford offered a public apology for the doctrine in 1990. Charles Simpson's Covenant Movement continues to promote some of these concepts. See SHEPHERDING.

Shepherd's Chapel, Arnold Murray—Gravette, AR: Murray is the founding pastor of The Shepherd's Chapel, and more notably, host of *The Shepherd's Chapel* television program. Murray's history is largely unknown; what little that has been told—such as his claims to have attended Biola University and to have received a PhD from an individual named Roy Gillespie—have been disproved by researchers. Murray denies the TRINITY and instead teaches MODALISM. He further teaches that humans pre-existed during the rebellion in heaven: those who served God are predestined to salvation, while those who served SATAN are cursed with free will and the opportunity to choose to serve God or Satan in this lifetime. Murray promotes a version of the SERPENT SEED doctrine in which the Jewish people (called *Kenites*) are the descendants of Cain; Anglo-Saxons, however—in a modification of BRITISH ISRAELISM—are not only the true Israelites, but also the descendants of Adam. Web site—http://www.shepherdschapel.com. For further research, a four-page Watchman Fellowship Profile is available (see page 363). Web site—http://www.watchman.org/notebook.

SHIELDS: See SCHOLARLY & HISTORICAL INFORMATION EXCHANGE FOR LATTER-DAY SAINTS.

Shintoism: Shintoism—also called *kami no michi,* "way of the gods"—is the indigenous religious tradition of Japan. Shinto has no central, all-powerful deity; instead, the kami are the powers of nature (as well as, according to some, the earliest ancestors of the Japanese and the souls of the dead). Shinto itself is a diverse set of rituals for purification, honoring kami, and celebrating seasons. There are four main forms of Shinto: *Koshitsu Shinto* (the Shinto of the Imperial House, or rituals performed by the emperor); *Jinja Shinto* (Shinto of the Shrines); *Kyoha Shinto* (Sectarian Shinto, referring to the rituals—and occasionally deities—of the 13 ancient sects of Shinto); and *Minzoku Shinto* (Folk Shinto, which is an unorganized Shinto of local, rural practices). Shinto is rooted in four affirmations: family, love of nature, physical cleanliness, and worship of the kami (called *matsuri*). The most famous Shinto place of worship is the Ise Shrine, at which Amaterasu (the sun goddess, and ancestor of the emperor) is worshipped. While Shinto has no authoritative canon of scripture, early Shinto mythology can be found in the eighth-century *Kojiki* ("Records of Ancient Matters") and *Nihon Shoki* ("Chronicles of Japan").

Shiva: The destroyer and third member of the triad of Hindu demigods/gods including BRAHMA and VISHNU. See HINDUISM.

Shri Gurudev Mahendranath: See INTERNATIONAL NATH ORDER.

Shri Kapilanth: See INTERNATIONAL NATH ORDER

Shrine of the Master Church, Russell and Dorothy Flexer—Sarasota, FL: The Flexers moved to Tampa in 1946 and established the Shrine of the Master Church the following year. In 1949 they established a second church in Sarasota. The church's practices and teachings include MEDITATION, spirit communication, MEDIUMSHIP, vibrational healing energies, and that you create your life through your thoughts. The Flexers also formed the CHURCH OF METAPHYSICAL CHRISTIANITY in Sarasota. See NEW AGE.

Shriners of North America—Tampa, FL: The Shrine of North America was founded in 1872 by 13 practitioners of FREEMASONRY to provide entertainment for lodge members. The Shrine operates 191 chapters, as well as 22 famous Shriners Hospitals for Children (particularly children suffering orthopedic problems, burns, and spinal cord injuries). Web site—http://www.shrinershq.org/index.html.

Shunning: Commonly called *disfellowshipping,* shunning is an effective technique of control used by the WATCHTOWER BIBLE AND TRACT SOCIETY and other groups to instill discipline, punish, or maintain idealistic purity. Current, faithful members isolate members who disagree on dogma or do not maintain the group's behavioral expectations. This shunning includes, in most cases, even family members or friends, who are not allowed to communicate or interact with those being shunned. The faithful members who violate the rule and communicate with the dissident can themselves be shunned. See MILIEU CONTROL; MIND CONTROL.

Siddha Yoga Dham of America, Swami Muktananda Paramahansa—South Fallsburg, NY: Siddha Yoga was founded by Muktananda in 1962. Based in HINDUISM, Siddha Yoga is a form of Kashmir Shaivism, in which the ultimate goal is union with SHIVA (central to this union is KUNDALINI). While Muktananda was popular with many celebrities until his death in 1982, Siddha Yoga has been accused by a number of former members of extensive sexual abuse.

Siegel, Bernie: Siegel teaches that MEDITATION and CREATIVE VISU-ALIZATION will lead to greater physical and emotional health. In 1978, Siegel started Exceptional Cancer Patients, in which both individual and group therapy utilized patients' dreams and artwork in a process of "Care-frontation" to promote personal change. Following his 1986 publication of *Love, Medicine, and Miracles,* Siegel went public with his teaching theories about the mind/body connection and healing. Siegel has also published *Peace, Love, and Healing* and *Meditations for Enhancing Your Immune System.* See HOLISTIC HEALTH; NEW AGE.

Sikhism, Nanak: Sikhism—which exists primarily in the Punjab district of India, although it has spread with Punjabi emigration following the inde-pendence of Pakistan in 1947—is a blending of the Bhakti movement of HINDUISM and ISLAM (specifically SUFISM). The religion was started by Sri Guru Nanak Dev Ji (1469–1538), who received a revelation of both MONOTHEISM and the unity of humanity. Until 1708, a succession of nine GURUS—believed to be the REINCARNATION of Nanak—led the Sikhs; following the tenth, the function of guru passed to the followers and to the holy text, the *Guru Granth.* Sikhs believe in a single God who can be known through MEDITATION. They also teach that through reincarna-tion, humans become purified and united with God. The *Guru Granth* is online at http://www.sikhs.org/english/frame.html.

Silva Method, Jose Silva: Created in 1966 by Jose Silva, students of the Silva Method learn to use the power of their minds to relax, increase physical and emotional health and efficiency, and develop natural abilities in CLAIRVOY-ANCE. Web site—http://www.silvamethod.com. See NEW AGE.

Singer, David: Singer promotes the teachings and practices of the CHURCH OF SCIENTOLOGY as a means to increase one's personal success. Web site—http://www.our-home.org/drdavidsinger.

Singh, Sant Thakar: See KNOW THYSELF AS SOUL FOUNDA-TION.

Skeptical Enquirer: See COMMITTEE FOR THE SCIENTIFIC INVES-TIGATION OF CLAIMS OF THE PARANORMAL.

The Sleeping Prophet: See CAYCE, EDGAR.

Smith, David J.: Founder of the CHURCH OF GOD EVANGELISTIC ASSOCIATION.

Smith, Jr., Joseph: Founder of THE CHURCH OF JESUS CHRIST OF LATTER-DAY SAINTS.

Societas Rosicruciana in America—New York, NY: Founded in 1909 by George Winslow Plummer, the Societas—also known as the Society of Rosicrucians, Inc. and the MOST HOLY ORDER OF THE RUBY ROSE AND GOLDEN CROSS—teaches ROSICRUCIANISM. Web site—http://www.sria.org.

Society for Organizational Learning—Boston, MA: An affiliate of the Massachusetts Institute of Technology, the SOL researches and promotes learning organizations that facilitate institutional evolution and the re-thinking of conventional and reactionary beliefs. Web site—http://learning.mit.edu. See SECULAR HUMANISM.

Society of Novus Spiritus, Sylvia Browne—Campbell, CA: A church founded in 1986 by the popular PSYCHIC Sylvia Browne. This church promotes a form of gnostic Christianity with "no fear, no guilt, no sin, no hell, and no Satan." Beliefs include REINCARNATION and "God the Female." Web site—http://www.novus.org. See BROWN, SYLVIA; PSYCHIC; GNOSTICISM.

Society of Pragmatic Mysticism, Mildred Mann—New York, NY: Mann (1904–71) taught METAPHYSICS as understood by adherents of NEW THOUGHT. Mann taught that each person is a divine spirit in whom can be found the presence of God. Because of this divinity and presence, each person can live a life of expectancy and gratitude: Ask God for the things you need and want, expect those things with an attitude of thankfulness, and you will receive everything you desire. Web site—http://websyte. com/alan/socpm.htm.

Soka Gakkai, International (SGI), Daisakqu Ikeda—Santa Monica, CA: Originally formed in 1975 as an affiliate of Nichiren Shoshu of America. In the early 1990s the group split from Nichiren Shoshu due to a growing distrust among the leadership of the two groups that culminated with Ikeda's excommunication from Nichiren Shoshu in 1992. After the split it became a global umbrella for Soka Gakkai organizations. SGI promotes enlightenment though gongyo. This involves kneeling before a gohonzon (black wooden box containing passages from the *Lotus Sutra*), quoting this scripture, and chanting the daimoku (pronounced *nam-myoho-renge-kyo*). Compared with other forms of BUDDHISM, this sect is very aggressive in its missionary efforts. It has affiliated organizations or adherents in more than 190 countries, with an estimated membership of 100,000–300,000 in the United States. This sect allegedly practices mind control, authoritarianism, and desires world power. See BUDDHISM.

Soka Gakkai, Tsunesaburo Makiguchi (1871–1944) **and Josei Toda** (1900– 58)—Tokyo, Japan: Founded in 1930 as Soka Kyoiku Gakkai by two educators to serve as a lay Buddhist organization dedicated to educational reform. It was renamed Soka Gakkai after World War II with an expanded purpose to reach all people, not just educators. It is based on Nichiren Shoshu BUDDHISM, which follows the teachings of a thirteenth-century Japanese fisherman, Nichiren Daishonin, who taught that the true interpretations of Buddha's teachings were recorded in the *Lotus Sutra*. Makiguchi later became convinced that all who practiced Nichiren Shoshu would have the potential within to attain Buddhahood, including women. Soka Gakkai claims to have over 10 million members in Japan. Web site—http://sokagakkai.info. See SOKA GAKKAI INTERNATIONAL.

Solar Temple: See ORDER OF THE SOLAR TEMPLE.

Sons of Noah: See B'NEI NOACH.

Sophia: Sophia was the ancient Greek goddess of wisdom. Sophia is utilized in CHRISTIANITY: in the Septuagint translation of the Old Testament, *sophia* is the translation of *hokmah,* the personification of God the creator and guide (Job 28:20-28; Proverbs 8:22-32); in the New Testament, JESUS

CHRIST is called the *"sophia* of God" (1 Corinthians 1:24; cf. Colossians 1:15-20); and in theology, *sophiology* is a theology centered on the concept of wisdom. GNOSTICISM held to a concept of Æon Wisdom—Sophia or Achamoth. Sophia frequently appears in NEO-PAGANISM as a GODDESS or expression of the divine feminine.

Sophia Divinity School, Herman Adrian Spruit—Santa Fe, NM: Established in 1958 to train those seeking the priesthood in the Church of Antioch or other independent Catholic/Orthodox institutions. See CATHOLIC APOSTOLIC CHURCH OF ANTIOCH. Web site—http://www. churchofantioch.org/sophia.html.

The Sophia of Jesus Christ (aka *The Wisdom of Jesus Christ): one of the GNOSTIC GOSPELS discovered in Nag Hammadi, Egypt, in 1945. The manuscript is a fourth-century A.D. document written in Coptic on papyrus (although the original may date to the third century A.D.). The book, considered to be an example of New Testament APOCRYPHA, purports to contain CHRIST's answers to 13 questions posed by His APOSTLEs after His resurrection.

Soul Mates: Soul mates are believed to be individuals with whom one had a loving, intimate relationship (e.g., marriage or a domestic partnership) in a previous lifetime.

Soul Sleep: *Psychopannychy*—a Greek term translated as "soul sleep"—is the doctrine that human souls sleep or cease conscious existence between death and resurrection. This doctrine is usually (but not always) a doctrine associated with groups descended from the SECOND ADVENT MOVEMENT. See SEVENTH-DAY ADVENTISM; WATCHTOWER BIBLE AND TRACT SOCIETY.

Southern Baptist Convention (SBC)—Nashville, TN: The largest denomination of PROTESTANTISM in the United States, consisting of 16 million members in autonomous, cooperating churches that collaborate for missions and educational purposes. The SBC was formed in 1845 when it split from the Northern Baptist Convention (now AMERICAN BAPTIST CHURCHES USA) over the issue of slavery. Operates the International Missions Board, the North American Mission Board, six seminaries, and

LifeWay Christian Resources. Web site—http://www.sbc.net. See BAPTIST CHURCHES; EVANGELICAL CHRISTIANITY.

Southern Dharma Retreat Center—Hot Springs, NC: Founded in 1978, the center offers MEDITATION retreats based primarily in BUDDHISM, but also has retreats based on other traditions. Web site—http://www.southerndharma.org.

Spangler, David: Spangler has been one of the foremost NEW AGE writers and speakers since the 1970s and early 1980s. Spangler taught at the FINDHORN community and OMEGA INSTITUTE, and has since served as an individual writer and retreat leader. Among Spangler's books are *Revelation: The Birth of a New Age, Emergence: The Rebirth of the Sacred,* and *Everyday Miracles.*

Speaking in Tongues: See GLOSSOLALIA.

Spell: In MAGICK, a ritual used to enact a spiritual or supernatural effect. Spells can be cast many different ways, including through incantations, ceremonies, or potions (drinkable concoctions). See MAGIC; OCCULT.

Spiral Dynamics, Don Edward Beck—Denton, TX: The central teaching of the National Values Center (started by Beck), spiral dynamics is an elaboration upon the teachings of Clare W. Graves. Graves (and now Beck) attempted to merge biology, psychology, and sociology into a single discipline oriented around the endless evolutionary potential of human nature. Beck unsuccessfully attempted to persuade the Grapevine-Colleyville (Texas) school district to utilize his program (for $100,000) in the area schools. Beck offers Spiral Dynamics learning courses. Web site—http://www.spiraldynamics.com.

Spirit Guide: In SPIRITUALISM and some NEW AGE beliefs, a deceased person or ASCENDED MASTER who chooses to remain in a disembodied, nonphysical state while making contact with and providing spiritual teachings to humans through CHANNELING, SÉANCES, or GUIDED IMAGERY. See NECROMANCY; SPIRITUALISM.

Spiritism: The belief that geological locations, flora, and fauna are (or at least may be) inhabited by spirits. Contact with these spirits usually necessitates the intervention of a SHAMAN, although in some forms of spiritism, any individual has the potential for interaction with spirits. The practice is related to—although distinct from—SPIRITUALISM. See SHAMANISM.

Spirit of Prophecy Evangelical Ministries, Rick and Andy Hall—Las Vegas, NV: Founded in 1984 by Rick Hall, the ministry is dedicated to receiving and teaching prophetic revelations. The ministry erroneously prophesied that the SECOND COMING of CHRIST would occur in 1998. Andy Hall—Rick Hall's son—joined as the co-pastor of Spirit of Prophecy Christian Fellowship in 1995, and now—in addition to their prophetic work—they offer weddings in many Nevada locations (including skydiving and jet-skiing weddings). The ministry publishes the *Insights into Prophecy* newsletter. Web site—http://www.spiritofprophecy.org. See FALSE PROPHECY.

Spirit Rock Meditation Center, JACK KORNFIELD—Woodacre, CA: Formed in 1996 as an offshoot of the INSIGHT MEDITATION SOCIETY, the center offers silent meditation retreats, classes, trainings, and dharma study rooted in BUDDHA's teachings in the Pali discourses. Web site—http://spiritrock.org.

Spiritual Abuse: Spiritual abuse is the infliction of psychological, spiritual, or physical damage or mistreatment on someone seeking spiritual or religious help or guidance. This injury can occur when someone in a pastoral or clerical position or office exercises an improper and unhealthy control of his or her followers. There are five characteristics of spiritually abusive leaders: they are authoritarian, averse to criticism, image conscious, perfectionistic, and unbalanced. See LEGALISM. For further research, a four-page Watchman Fellowship Profile is available (see page 363). Web site—http://www.watchman.org/notebook.

Spiritual Counterfeits Project—Berkeley, CA: An APOLOGETICS ministry formed in 1973 to defend EVANGELICAL CHRISTIANITY and to explain and confront the teachings of CULTS, the OCCULT, and NEW AGE spirituality. Tal Brooke, a former disciple of SATHYA SAI BABA and author of *Avatar of the Night,* serves as president and chairman. They publish the *SPC Journal* and a newsletter. Web site—http://www.scp-inc.org.

Spiritual Emergence Network—San Francisco, CA: Affiliated with the CALIFORNIA INSTITUTE OF INTEGRAL STUDIES, the network is now a call-in information and referral service through which people undergoing spiritual crises can receive guidance and assistance. The network specializes in ALTERED STATES OF CONSCIOUSNESS, PSYCHIC events, KUNDALINI, SHAMANISM, and other spiritual practices and ideologies. The network changed its name to the Center for Psychological and Spiritual Health in 2002, and ceased clinical practice in 2003 after the loss of funding. Web site—http://www.cpsh.org. See NEW AGE.

Spiritual Frontiers Fellowship International, Arthur Augustus Ford (1896–1971)—Philadelphia, PA: The SFFI was founded in 1956 by Arthur Ford, a well-known PSYCHIC who blended Eastern and Western religious traditions to develop a greater understanding of ALTERED STATES OF CONSCIOUSNESS and MYSTICISM. A central belief of the SFFI is that all life—both on this planet and in all possible universes—is interconnected. Joseph Fitch, Elizabeth Fenske, and Martin Ebon are well-known leaders in the fellowship, which is affiliated with the ACADEMY OF RELIGION AND PSYCHICAL RESEARCH. Web site—http://www.spiritualfrontiers. org. See NEW AGE; PSYCHICS.

Spiritualism: Spiritualism is the practice of contacting and communicating with the spirits of the dead (usually through the intermediary work of a MEDIUM). Some scholars trace the development of modern spiritualism to the work of Emmanuel Swedenborg. More often, the practice is traced to Catherine and Margaretta Fox, who, beginning in 1848, developed a method of communicating with a spirit in their home—initially claimed to be that of Charles Rosna, who had murdered the previous resident of the house—by rapping in specific sequences to indicate yes, no, or the letters of the alphabet. Hundreds of people visited the home to witness the phenomenon, and the Fox sisters eventually became prominent and toured the United States. Spiritualism is predicated on two central beliefs: the eternality of the spirit or soul, and the potential (and, generally, the benefit) of contacting individuals in the spirit world. See NECROMANCY; OCCULT; SWEDENBORG FOUNDATION.

Spring Hill Media Group, Robert and Judith Gass: The Gasses founded Spring Hill to create music that expands human consciousness. In addition to NEW AGE MUSIC, the group also produces works of world and classical music. One of the most notable musicians on the Spring Hill roster is Don Campbell, who pioneered the Mozart Effect theory, which maintains that listening to classical music—and particularly Wolfgang Amadeus Mozart—will enhance the listener's intelligence and mental ability. Web site—http://www.springhillmedia.com.

Stafford, Greg: An APOLOGIST for the doctrines of the WATCHTOWER BIBLE AND TRACT SOCIETY and founder of Elihu Books and Media. He is the author of *Jehovah's Witnesses Defended: An Answer to Scholars and Critics*. This is highly unusual, as the Watchtower Society frowns on any individual Jehovah's Witnesses who attempt to write or publish religious books. Stafford has also been involved with public debates with APOLO-GISTs representing EVANGELICAL CHRISTIANITY in several forms. Eventually he acknowledged that some of the apologists' criticisms were valid, stating, "So it was that I found some criticisms against JEHOVAH'S WITNESSES justified; so it was that I found them too dangerous to stay near." His last public defense of Watchtower theology was in December of 2003 when he debated Christian apologist James White of Alpha and Omega Ministries. In July of 2006, Stafford announced that he was going to take "another look" at the JEHOVAH'S WITNESSES by meeting with the elders and returning to the congregation on a limited basis. Web site—http://www.elihubooks.com. See WATCHTOWER BIBLE AND TRACT SOCIETY.

Stanford, Ray: Founder of the ASSOCIATION FOR THE UNDER-STANDING OF MAN and PROJECT STARLIGHT INTER-NATIONAL. He is a UFO researcher and PSYCHIC/MEDIUM who CHANNELS voices referred to collectively as the "Brothers." However, he does not claim these to be the GREAT WHITE BROTHERHOOD.

Star Center for the Americas—Montgomery, TX: See CHURCH OF THE WHITE EAGLE LODGE.

Star's Edge International—Altamonte, Springs, FL: An organization dedicated to the development of enlightened belief systems that will help usher in world peace. Promotes the Butterfly Enlightenment Project and AVATAR, a nine-day seminar for human empowerment taught by licensed Avatar Masters to more than 50,000 students in 65 countries. Publishes *Avatar Journal*. Web site—http://www.avatarepc.com.

Star Wars: A series of six science fiction motion pictures created by GEORGE LUCAS. Known for their use of special effects and the struggle of good against evil, the films also contain religious themes borrowed from HINDUISM, CHRISTIANITY, and BUDDHISM. "The Force," an important element in all six films, contains the key concept of YIN AND YANG found in TAOISM. The films contain many activities associated with PSYCHIC or OCCULT practice, including TELEKINESIS, LEVITATION, CLAIRVOYANCE, EXTRASENSORY PERCEPTION, and PRECOGNITION; some characters return after death as SPIRIT GUIDES. Some of the religious themes and occult elements visually presented in the movies are explained in Terry Brook's authorized novel *Star Wars: The Phantom Menace,* based on the Lucas screenplay. The Jedi knights are explicitly called a "theological and philosophical" order. The counsel of 12 meets in the Jedi temple, a "colossal pyramid with multiple spires" where "the whole order [is] engaged in contemplation and study of the Force." In 2001, over half a million people identified their religion as "Jedi" in official government censuses taken in Great Britain, Australia, New Zealand, and Canada. The census results—part cultural phenomena and part colossal prank—now list Jedi as the fourth-largest religion in Great Britain, while JUDAISM ranks fifth. Web site—http://www.starwars.com. For further research, a four-page Watchman Fellowship Profile is available (see page 363). Web site—http://www.watchman.org/notebook.

Steiner Education Group, Inc.: Part of STEINER LEISURE. Provides training and certification in various forms of massage and AROMATHERAPY. Offers Associate of Science degrees in massage, advanced therapy, and skin care. Acquired the FLORIDA COLLEGE OF NATURAL HEALTH in 1999 and the VIRGINIA SCHOOL OF MASSAGE and BALTIMORE SCHOOL OF MASSAGE in 2000. Web site—http://www.steinered.com. See HOLISTIC HEALING.

Steiner Leisure, Herman Steiner—London: Largest spa provider in the world. Grew out of a hair salon operated by Herman Steiner, which offered a line of grooming products developed in 1901 by his father, Henry. In the 1950s the company began operating salons on cruise ships, and in the 1960s it began offering massage. It now operates spas on over 100 cruise ships in addition to a number of land-based facilities under the names ELEMIS SPA and MANDARA SPA. Web site—http://www.steinerleisure.com. See STEINER EDUCATION GROUP, HOLISTIC HEALING.

Steiner, Rudolph: See ANTHROSOPHICAL SOCIETY.

Stelle Group, Richard Kieninger—Stelle, IL: See ADELPHI ORGANI-ZATION.

Sterling, Fred (Kahu): See HONOLULU CHURCH OF LIGHT.

Sterling Management System—Glendale, CA: Sterling provides resources for practice management in the following fields: CPAs, dentists, orthodontists, chiropractors, podiatrists, physical therapists, veterinarians, and optometrists. Sterling's systems are based upon the teachings and practices of the CHURCH OF SCIENTOLOGY. In addition to seminars and workshops, Sterling offers background and effectiveness analyses for hiring and training staff in accordance with the principles of Hubbard Management Technology. In addition to the primary Web site at http://www.sterling-management.com, Sterling also maintains the Web site http://www.sterlingcpa.net.

Stonehenge: Circular cluster of upright stones called *menhirs* (long stones) located on Salisbury Plain, which is approximately 80 miles west of London, England. The prevalent theory of Stonehenge's origin is that the site is an ancient DRUID temple. Other individuals believe Stonehenge was created by extraterrestrials. Some NEW AGE followers, practitioners of NEO-PAGANISM, and others believe that the site has mystical powers or energy. Official Web site—http://www.english-heritage.org.uk/stonehenge.

Stratford, Lauren (1941–2002): The pen name of Laurel Rose Willson, who wrote the autobiography *Satan's Underground,* which purported to be the true story of her life as a victim of SATANIC RITUAL ABUSE (SRA). The book told amazing tales of satanic crime involving child pornography, baby breeding for human sacrifice, and snuff films. The CHRISTIAN magazine *Cornerstone* conducted a detailed investigation and, in 1999, published a lengthy article documenting the book to be a hoax. Later Willson (whose name by this time had been legally changed to Lauren Stratford) assumed the identity of a Jewish Holocaust survivor, Laura Grabowski, claiming that she recognized another survivor, Binjamin Wilkomirski, from the concentration camps. Stratford allegedly received thousands of dollars in donations intended for Holocaust survivors until the deception was exposed with the help of Wilkomirski (whose real name is Bruno Grosjean), who had also fabricated his story of being a Jewish Holocaust survivor. Web site:—http://www.cornerstonemag.com/features/iss117/lauren.htm.

Strieber, Whitley: In the late 1970s-early 1980s Strieber was a successful author of such horror novels as *The Hunger* and *Wolfen*. In 1987, Strieber published *Communion: A True Story*, in which he describes his alleged abduction by a UFO in 1985. Strieber claims that the extraterrestrials took him to distant planets during the night; he and his family can now see extraterrestrials. Strieber has since written several books about abductions, including *Transformation: The Breakthrough* and *Breakthrough: The Next Step*, and produces the *Dreamland* radio program. Web site—http://www.unknowncountry.com.

Strobel, Lee: A well-known APOLOGIST who defends EVANGELICAL CHRISTIANITY and is the author of almost 20 best-sellers, including *The Case for Christ*, *The Case for Faith*, and *The Case for a Creator*. Strobel was also the executive producer and host of the television program *Faith Under Fire* on PAX TV. Strobel, the former legal editor for the *Chicago Tribune*, was an atheist who converted to Christianity in 1981. Web site—http://www.leestrobel.com.

Students' International Meditation Society: The society promotes TRAN-SCENDENTAL MEDITATION among school students.

Subliminal Messages: *Subliminal* is a combination of two words: *sub* ("below"), and *liminal* ("the lowest level at which a physical sensation is detectable"). In its strictest definition, subliminal phenomena are audio-visual impressions that are below conscious perception but can be received and processed by the subconscious mind. Claims regarding the use of subliminal messages in advertising prompted the Federal Communications Commission in 1974 to ban subliminal broadcasting. The primary concern regarding subliminal messages is that, through bypassing the conscious (and therefore cognitive) mind, subliminal messages could affect an individual's thoughts and behavior without that person's knowledge or consent. Some practitioners of HOLISTIC HEALTH, however, use subliminal messages in audio recordings to assist patients in overcoming such ingrained habits as smoking, overeating, or engaging in thought processes that foster low self-esteem. See HYPNOSIS.

Sufism: Sufism—or *tasawwuf,* referring to purity (literally, wool over purity)—began in the eighth-century as an Islamic movement of ascetic withdrawal from the world, the goal of which is union with God. In addition to asceticism and MEDITATION, Sufism involves the recitation of specific names combined with rhythmic movements (the most notable practitioners being the Whirling Dervishes). Many exemplary poets—most famously, Jalal al-din Rumi (1207–73), founder of the Dervishes—have advocated an "ISLAM of the heart," an ecstatic union with God. Sufism has become increasingly popular in the West as elements of the movement have been incorporated by practitioners of NEW AGE spirituality. See ISLAM.

Summit Lighthouse: Founded in 1958 by MARK PROPHET, Summit Lighthouse is the umbrella organization of the CHURCH UNIVERSAL AND TRIUMPHANT. Web site—http://www.tsl.org.

Summit University: Founded in 1971 by MARK PROPHET, the university is the educational arm of SUMMIT LIGHTHOUSE. Web site—http://www.tsl.org/AboutUs/SummitUniversity.asp. See CHURCH UNIVERSAL AND TRIUMPHANT.

Summum—Salt Lake City, UT: In 1975, Claude Rex Nowell began a series of encounters with extraterrestrials he calls the Summa Individuals. These individuals—allegedly referenced in ancient Egyptian hieroglyphs as *Neter*—work to guide others in the paths of spiritual evolution. Nowell—who in 1980 changed his name to Summum Bonum Amon Ra—founded Summum ("the sum total of all creation") to promote the Summum philosophy: psychokinesis, correspondence, vibration, opposition, rhythm, cause and effect, and gender. Through MEDITATION, sacerdotal worship inside a pyramid, and mummification, individuals can make spiritual progress. Web site—http://www.summum.us.

Sundoor, Peggy Dylan—Twain Harte, CA: Dylan began offering motivational and leadership training in 1976. Her seminars combine firewalking, NATIVE AMERICAN SPIRITUALITY, and SHAMANISM to assist individuals in realizing their human potential. Web site—http://www.sundoor.com. See NEW AGE.

Sunstone: A magazine for "free and frank exchange" of Mormon history, culture, and experience. Published by Latter-day Saints through Sunstone

Educational Foundation, the publication is not owned by the CHURCH OF JESUS CHRIST OF LATTER-DAY SAINTS and has occasionally drawn criticism from church officials for addressing controversial issues and questioning some LDS dogma. The foundation also hosts annual symposia. Web site—http://www.sunstoneonline.com.

Superet Light Center, Josephine C. Trust—Los Angeles, CA: Trust—called Mother Trust by her followers—taught that the religion of JESUS was the "Superet Science" in which vibrations of energy and color form the inner AURA that dictates health and happiness. Web site—http://superet.com/Introduction/gby20.html. See NEW AGE.

Sutphen, Dick and Tara: In the 1970s, Dick Sutphen began undergoing HYPNOSIS to better understand how to use persuasion in advertising. He began experimenting in other metaphysical activities, and in 1976 began selling hypnosis audiocassettes. He and Tara now engage in an extensive array of NEW AGE and OCCULT practices, including CHANNELING, AUTOMATIC WRITING, PALMISTRY, and ASTROLOGY. Their works include *Finding Your Answers Within* and *The Oracle Within*. Web site—http://www.dicksutphen.com.

Sweat Lodge: Native American tribes throughout North and Central America have used sweat lodges as a means for both spiritual purification and treating physical illnesses. There are three general methods for heating sweat lodges: hot rocks (used by tribes in the American Southwest), fire chambers filled with burning wood, and a system of heating ducts (believed to have originated with the Mayans). While still a vital practice of NATIVE AMERICAN SPIRITUALITY, many NEW AGE practitioners have also adopted the practice of frequenting sweat lodges.

Swedenborg Foundation, Emanuel Swedenborg—New York, NY: Swedenborg (1688–1772) was a successful geologist and scientist who began to independently study theology by opening his consciousness to "inner influences." At the age of 55, he was contacted by a spirit being who claimed to be JESUS CHRIST. Through continued spiritual encounters, Swedenborg developed a theology in which God appeared in different modes as Father, Son, and HOLY SPIRIT; humans progress to become ANGELS; and the BIBLE is interpreted according to correspondences of literal and mystical meanings. He further taught that the New Jerusalem, or New Church, is necessary to replace the corrupt modern churches. The Swedenborg Foundation, founded in 1849, publishes and distributes Swedenborg's writings. The New Church—or Church of the New Jerusalem—was founded in 1798. The New Church publishes *Chrysalis*. Web site for the Swedenborg Foundation—http://www.swedenborg.com. The Web site for the New Church is http://www.newchurch.org. See MODALISM; SPIRITUALISM. For further research, a four-page Watchman Fellowship Profile is available (see page 363). Web site—http://www.watchman.org/notebook.

SYDA: See SIDDHA YOGA DHAM OF AMERICA.

Synchronicity Foundation, Charles Cannon—Faber, VA: Cannon—called Master Charles by his followers—studied HINDUISM and TANTRA under Paramahamsa Muktananda. Cannon trains individuals to live the Synchronicity Paradigm, in which the individual—through a holistic lifestyle and MEDITATION—acknowledges a state of actualized wholeness that is unity with the one consciousness. Web site—http://www.synchronicity.org. See SIDDHA YOGA DHAM OF AMERICA; NEW AGE; PANTHEISM.

T

Taff, Signe Quinn—Sedona, AZ: Taff began studying ASTROLOGY at the age of 17, eventually combining her interests in astrology and acting to host the cable television program *Astrology with Signe Quinn Taff.* Web site—http://www.signe-astrology.com.

Taj Mahal—Agra, India: The Taj Mahal is a seventeenth-century mausoleum and mosque complex built by Shah Jehan in memory of his wife, Mumtaz Mahal. Some practitioners of NEW AGE spirituality believe the complex is a site of mystical power. An online tour of the Taj Mahal is available at http://www.taj-mahal.net. See ISLAM.

Talisman: A talisman is an object believed to be imbued with supernatural powers that are capable of warding off evil or attracting desired objects or circumstances. Talismans are frequently associated with the practice of the OCCULT or MAGIC. See AMULET.

Talmud: In JUDAISM a written record of rabbinic insights concerning Jewish law and history consisting of the MISHNAH (derived from the oral law) along with related commentary.

Tanakh (Tanach): Considered scripture by JUDAISM, the Tanakh is comprised of the 40 books of the Hebrew BIBLE based on the three Hebrew letters representing the three main divisions: 1) TORAH ("Instruction"—first 5 books), 2) Nevi'im ("Prophets"—24 books), and 3) Ketuvim ("Hagiographa" or "Writings"—11 books). See JUDAISM.

Tantra: A diverse practice found in a number of Eastern religions, such as HINDUISM and BUDDHISM and some of the modern NEW AGE streams. The focus of Tantra is to expand one's spiritual awareness and to connect with the divine. Common aspects are VISUALIZATION, MEDITATION, and use of a MANTRA. One form popularized in the West includes tantric sex, in which spiritual advancement is achieved or enhanced through the practice of ritualistic sex. This sometimes involves visualizing participation by a deity.

Taoism, Lao-tzu: A Chinese philosophy that teaches there is no personal God—all is the impersonal Tao (similar to the impersonal God-force of Hindu PANTHEISM). The Tao is composed of conflicting opposites (YIN AND YANG) that should be balanced or harmonized through YOGA, MEDITATION, etc. to promote spiritual wholeness. According to ancient legend, Taoism founder Lao-tzu wrote *Tao Te Ching* ("The Way and Its Power") about 550 B.C. His teaching was developed and spread in the third century B.C. by Chuang-Tzu, whose writings inspired the *Tao Tsang,* 1,200 volumes of Taoist scripture. See YIN AND YANG.

Tao Te Ching: The *Tao Te Ching*—translated "The Way and Its Power"—is the classic work of TAOISM, written by Lao Tsu in the sixth-century B.C.

Tao Tsang: The *Tao Tsang* is the canon of Taoist writings. The *Tao Tsang* was originally printed by the emperors of the Sung dynasty (960–1279) and numbered over 5,000 volumes. After the reign of the Mongols from 127–1368, however, only 1,000 volumes remain. See TAOISM.

Tara Center, Benjamin Creme: See SHARE INTERNATIONAL.

Tarot Cards/Tarot: Tarot cards are used for the practice of DIVINATION. The original Tarot deck dates to the fifteenth-century; the cards were initially used for a complex card game and had no OCCULT meaning. The modern deck, however, contains 78 cards—56 cards are divided into four suits, while 22 cards contain specific symbolism (such as Fool, Strength, Death, etc.; these are therefore called the Major Arcana). Divination is practiced by reading the pattern in which the cards are placed. One of the most popular Tarot decks is the Rider-Waite Tarot, which was designed by A.E. Waite (a prominent member of the GOLDEN DAWN).

Teachers of Light: See CHURCH OF E YADA DI SHI-ITE.

Technicians of the Sacred—Burbank, CA: Formed in 1983 by Courtney Willis, the Technicians promote the practice of VOODOO and Neo-African religious systems. The Technicians claim to be related to the pre-ALEISTER CROWLEY ORDO TEMPLI ORIENTIS. Web site—http://www.tech niciansofthesacred.com. See OCCULT.

Telekinesis: From the Greek words *tele* ("distant") and *kinesis* ("movement"), this is the OCCULT practice of supernaturally moving an object or person using alleged mystical or PSYCHIC power to apparently suspend or super-sede the laws of physics. Also known as *psychokinesis* ("mind movement").

Telepathy: From the Greek words *tele* ("distant") and *patheia* ("feeling"), this is the OCCULT practice of supernaturally transferring mental thoughts or ideas from one person to another using alleged mystical or PSYCHIC power of the mind. Also known as *mental telepathy,* the term is sometimes used to describe the planting of thoughts in the mind of another, as well as receiving thoughts from someone as a form of mind reading. Similar to ESP. See EXTRASENSORY PERCEPTION (ESP).

***Templar Revelation,* Lynn Pickett and Clive Prince:** Published in 1997, this book was popularized by its inclusion in *The DA VINCI CODE* as one of the evidentiary records that Jesus was married to Mary Magdalene and they were priests of the Egyptian goddess Isis and were determined to restore GODDESS worship to the Jews. In their CONSPIRACY THEORY, the authors maintain that for almost 2000 years CHRISTIANITY has tried to cover up and destroy this information. The truth continues to be known and guarded, however, by a secret society, the PRIORY OF SION. This secret also survives through such means as symbols and popular artwork such as Leonardo da Vinci's painting *The Last Supper,* which allegedly depicts Mary Magdalene as the HOLY GRAIL seated beside Jesus. This is also a central component of *The Da Vinci Code.*

Temple of Danann, Michael Ragan—Hanover, IN: Founded in 1979, the temple is reconstructing the beliefs and practices of ancient, pre-Christian CELTICISM. Ragan, a former practitioner of WICCA, differentiates between his Irish Reconstructionism and modern Wicca and NEO-PAGANISM by claiming that his religion is a restoration of a pre-existing tradition, whereas Wicca and neo-paganism are modern syntheses of varied traditions. Web site—http://www.danann.org.

Temple of Kriya Yoga, Goswami Kriyananda—Chicago, IL: Claiming to be descended from the work of PARAMAHANSA YOGANANDA, the temple teaches a variety of YOGA practices as well as MEDITATION and ASTROLOGY. A unique focus of the temple is "Kriyology," which is said to be the inner, ESOTERIC tradition of KRIYA YOGA, and is beneficial for restoring energy and health, and for enabling the individual to transcend self-limitations. Web site—http://www.yogakriya.org. See SELF-REALIZATION FELLOWSHIP; NEW AGE.

Temple of Set, Michael Aquino: Aquino joined the CHURCH OF SATAN in 1969—and was made a priest in 1970—but left to form the Temple of Set in 1975 over a disagreement with ANTON LAVEY over the function and theology of the church (Aquino believed SATAN is a literal being: the Egyptian god Set). In 1986, temple member Gary Hambright, along with Aquino and his wife, were accused of child molestation. No charges were brought against Aquino and his wife, and the case against Hambright was dismissed. In 1994 and 1997, Aquino sued critics who accused him of pedophilia; the first case was settled out of court, and the second was dismissed. Aquino resigned as high priest in 1996. Web site—http://www.xeper.org. See SATANISM. For further research, a four-page Watchman Fellowship Profile is available (see page 363). Web site—http://www.watchman.org/notebook.

Temple of the Golden Rose: Opened in 1982 as part of the WHITE EAGLE CENTER FOR THE AMERICAS.

Temple of the People, William H. Dower—Halcyon, CA: Founded in 1898 by William Dower and Francia La Due, the temple builds upon the teachings of HELENA BLAVATSKY. The temple's principles are rooted in PANTHEISM: By realizing the oneness of humanity and nature and with the help of REINCARNATION and KARMA (which the temple calls "hope and responsibility"), humanity can continually progress. The temple also emphasizes the importance of NATIVE AMERICAN SPIRITUALITY. The temple publishes the quarterly *Temple Artisan*. Web site—http://www.templeofthepeople.org. See THEOSOPHY.

Temple of the Presence, Monroe and Carolyn Shearer—Tuscon, AZ: The Shearers came together in 1993 and claim to have been sponsored by the ASCENDED MASTERS to form the temple in 1995. The teachings of the temple are heavily influenced by the I AM MOVEMENT, and channeled messages from the Ascended Masters are read on the Temple's *Perpetual Voice* broadcast. CULT expert Steve Hassan states that the temple is a splinter group of the CHURCH UNIVERSAL AND TRIUMPHANT. Web site—http://templeofthepresence.org. See CHANNELING; NEW AGE.

Terra Nova Center of the Brigade of Light, Inc.: See BRIGADE OF LIGHT.

Thelema: From the Greek term meaning "to will or to purpose," a key principle of the MAGICK of ALEISTER CROWLEY applied to the GOLDEN DAWN orders. Thelema emphasizes the sovereignty and power of one's true will, higher purpose, or destiny: "Do what thou wilt shall be the whole of the Law." Thelema also contains elements of sexual MAGICK. See CROWLEY, ALEISTER; GOLDEN DAWN; MAGICK.

Thelemic Order of the Golden Dawn, David Cherubim—Los Angeles, CA: Founded in 1990 in the tradition of ALEISTER CROWLEY and the ORDER OF THE GOLDEN DAWN. Brian Goldstein became leader after Cherubim's departure. Web site—http://www.thelemicgoldendawn.org. See CROWLEY, ALEISTER; ORDER OF THE GOLDEN DAWN.

Theosophical Society in America—Wheaton, IL: Founded in 1875 by HELENA PETROVNA BLAVATSKY and Henry Steel Olcott, the society is the oldest organization of THEOSOPHY. The society publishes the works of Blavatsky and other theosophists through Quest Books (an imprint of Theosophical Publishing House) and publishes *Quest Magazine*. Web site—http://www.theosophical.org.

Theosophical Society, International—Pasadena, CA: Founded in 1895 by W.Q. Judge after a debate between Judge and HELENA BLAVATSKY and Henry Steel Olcott over the authorship of a series of letters, the society was the American section of the Theosophical Society until the 1895 split. The Society operates Theosophical University Press and publishes *Sunrise Magazine*. Web site—http://www.theosociety.org. See THEOSOPHY; THEOSOPHICAL SOCIETY IN AMERICA.

Theosophy Company: See UNITED LODGE OF THEOSOPHISTS.

Theosophy, Helena Petrovna Blavatsky: *Theosophy*—which literally means "God wisdom"—is claimed to be the "divine wisdom" that is the inner, mystical truth found in all cultures, and the primary goal is universal brotherhood. Theosophy as an organized religious system began in 1874 when HELENA PETROVNA BLAVATSKY and Henry Steel Olcott met and formed the Miracle Club to promote Blavatsky's teachings and activities. In 1877, Blavatsky published the two-volume *Isis Unveiled,* and in 1888—one year after Blavatsky and Olcott moved to India—she came out with *The Secret Doctrine* (the most influential Theosophical book). Blavatsky died in 1891. *The Secret Doctrine* reveals the three foundational beliefs of Theosophy: There is an omnipresent, omnipotent, omniscient power that is the truth sought by all humanity; because the power is unlimited, humanity is unlimited; and everything is a part of this unlimited power. All humanity is on a pilgrimage, an evolution achieved through REINCARNATION; this evolution is guided by the GREAT WHITE BROTHERHOOD. Many groups, such as the ARCANE SCHOOL and I AM MOVEMENT, have their roots in Theosophy. For further research, a four-page Watchman Fellowship Profile is available (see page 363). Web site—http://www.watchman. org/notebook.

Therapeutic Touch: Therapeutic Touch was developed by Dolores Krieger in 1975. Krieger, a nurse, based her practice on the work of biochemist Bernard Grad and PSYCHIC healer Dora Van Gelder Kunz; the basis for the practice, however, can be found in THEOSOPHY. The process consists of four steps: *centering,* in which the patient enters a relaxed state through MEDITATION; *assessment,* in which the practitioner moves his or her hands several inches above the patient's body, searching for an imbalance in the patient's energy field (a tingling sensation or pressure in the practitioner's hands indicates a point of imbalance); *unruffling,* in which the practitioner moves his or her hands in a circular motion over the patient's body to either redistribute the energy flow or remove excess energy; and *modulation,* in which the practitioner's hands hover over an area of imbalance (some believe this channels CHI to the area, while others believe it simply redistributes the patient's energy to the area). Therapeutic Touch is similar to REIKI. The Nurse-Healers Professional Associates International, the official organization for Therapeutic Touch founded in 1977 by Krieger, has a Web site at http://www.therapeutic-touch.org. See HOLISTIC HEALTH. For further research, a four-page Watchman Fellowship Profile is available (see page 363). Web site—http://www.watchman.org/notebook.

Thieme, Robert B.: See BERACHAH CHURCH.

Third Eye: Called *ajna* in Sanskrit, the third eye is the sixth CHAKRA, which is located in the center of the forehead. See CHAKRAS.

Third Wave of the HOLY SPIRIT: A phrase coined by C. Peter Wagner, who also wrote a book by the same title to describe neo-Charismatic or post-Charismatic manifestation and ministry that began in the 1980s. According to Wagner, the first wave was the PENTECOSTAL MOVEMENT begun in the early 1900s, and the second wave was the CHARISMATIC MOVEMENT of the 1960s. Wagner's third wave began in the 1980s and was marked by a fresh outpouring of manifestations, including a return of apostolic signs and wonders, gifts, an emphasis on EXORCISM (DELIVERANCE MINISTRIES), power evangelism (demonstrating the GOSPEL to the lost by miracles), the ASSOCIATION OF VINEYARD CHURCHES, and revivals such as the TORONTO BLESSING.

Thought Reform: See BRAINWASHING; LIFTON, ROBERT; MIND CONTROL.

3HO: See HEALTHY, HAPPY, AND HOLY.

Thunder-Horse Ranch: See BLUE STAR, INC.

Tibetan Buddhism: While BUDDHISM arrived in Tibet as early as A.D. 173, it was not until the reign of Songtsen Gampo in the seventh-century that the religion took hold in the region. The most important event in Tibetan Buddhism was the arrival of Padmasambhava—more popularly known as Guru Rinpoche—in 777; Padmasambhava merged Buddhism with the local Bön religion to form the distinctive Buddhism of Tibet. Tibetan Buddhism has five main schools—arguably the most famous is the *Geluk,* which is headed by the DALAI LAMA (the lamas who lead these schools are believed to be REINCARNATIONs of the founders of each lineage). Like other schools of TANTRA, Tibetan Buddhism incorporates rituals and objects—such as *mandalas* (religious diagrams made with colored sand), *dorjes* (an eight-pronged object representing compassion), and *phurpas* (a dagger symbolically used to kill demons)—in its practice. See BUDDHISM; DALAI LAMA; REINCARNATION.

Tilton, Robert (b. 1946): Controversial televangelist in the WORD-FAITH MOVEMENT and host of the television program *Success-N-Life,* which once aired in over 200 TV markets nationwide. In 1991, an ABC *Primetime Live* segment featuring Diane Sawyer brought devastating scandal to his TV program and his church, the Word of Faith Family church in Farmer's Branch (a Dallas suburb), which he co-pastored with his wife Marte. The documentary made a number of allegations, including the claim that prayer requests mailed to Tilton's church in Texas were actually routed to Oklahoma, where the checks were removed and the requests destroyed. Tilton unsuccessfully sued ABC and the ministry quickly declined. Tilton eventually left Word of Faith Family Church (which later dissolved) and divorced his wife Marte. He was briefly married to televangelist Leigh Valentine (1994–96) before moving to Fort Lauderdale, Florida to relaunch *Success-N-Life* on the Black Entertainment Television (BET) network. Web site—http://www. successinlife.tv. See WORD-FAITH MOVEMENT.

Time Line Therapy: See ADVANCED NEURO DYNAMICS.

Timothean Religion, Timothy Allen Campbell—Fraser, MI: An Internet-based religious group that meets in the "I Saw God in Person" and "Timothean Religion" chat rooms. Campbell claims to have seen God in Torrance, California, in 1985, and says that God was accompanied by John the Baptist. Campbell teaches that JESUS is not the MESSIAH, and that SATAN is a group of people opposed to the truth as interpreted by Timotheans. While the group reads the scriptures of all world religions, their central text is Campbell's *The Gospel of Timothy.* Web site—http://members. aol.com/GoTimothy/myhomepage/business.html.

TM: The popular acronym for TRANSCENDENTAL MEDITATION.

Tolle, Eckhart: NEW AGE author and teacher best known for his 1998 book *The Power of Now,* which is based on his years of study of Eastern religions and visits to BUDDHIST monasteries. He emphasizes Eastern beliefs, including enlightenment. See BUDDHISM; REINCARNATION; MEDITATION. Web site—http://www.eckharttolle.com.

Tongues: See GLOSSOLALIA.

Torah: The first five books of the Hebrew BIBLE and the Christian Bible (Genesis, Exodus, Leviticus, Numbers, and Deuteronomy). Also called *Chumash,* meaning "the five," "the five books of Moses," or "the Pentateuch." See TANAKH; BIBLE; JUDAISM.

Toronto Blessing: A revival that began in 1994 in Toronto, Canada, at the Airport Vineyard Fellowship (now named Toronto Airport Christian Fellowship), which is pastored by John and Carol Arnott. The blessing was marked by unusual spiritual outbreaks in which worshipers broke out in HOLY LAUGHTER and mimicked animal noises. *Charisma* magazine reported, "Worshipers are overcome by laughing, weeping, groaning, shaking, falling and, to the chagrin of some, noise-making that has been described as 'a cross between a jungle and a farmyard.' But of greater significance are the reports of changed lives: healings, restored relationships and increased fervor for God" (August 1994, p. 22). The revival quickly spread to other churches when hundreds of ministers began visiting Airport Vineyard Fellowship to receive the anointing. Earlier manifestations of the holy laughter accompanied the ministry of RODNEY HOWARD-BROWNE, a South African evangelist whose Louisville, Kentucky-based ministry was also a major catalyst for the phenomena. By late 1995, John Wimber and other leaders in the ASSOCIATION OF VINEYARD CHURCHES took exception to some of the more unusual animal-like behavior (such as barking like dogs and roaring like lions) and forced the Arnotts' church out of the association. The church changed its name to Toronto Airport Christian Fellowship and continued to promote the phenomena, although its popularity has diminished since the late 1990s.

Torres, Penny: Torres claims to channel Mafu, a leper in first century Pompeii. See CHANNELING; NEW AGE.

Touch for Health: See THERAPEUTIC TOUCH.

Touch Therapy: See THERAPEUTIC TOUCH.

Trance: A trance is an ALTERED STATE OF CONSCIOUSNESS involving the minimizing of mental activity and conscious thought by blocking physical stimuli and awareness of physical surroundings in order to maintain some level of consciousness while going into a deep sleep-like state, allegedly facilitating spiritual well-being and awareness. Similar to HYPNOSIS, the state is often employed by MEDIUMS and is viewed as necessary for serving as a channel for disembodied beings. See CHANNELING.

Trance Channeling: See CHANNELING.

Transcendental Meditation, Maharishi Mahesh Yogi: Rooted in HINDUISM, Transcendental Meditation—popularly abbreviated as TM—was developed by the Maharishi in 1955 as a means to achieve "serenity without drugs." As in traditional PANTHEISM, the focus of TM is the realization that the individual is in fact the impersonal God—this realization is achieved in large part through the recitation of a MANTRA given by the TM teacher to the student. TM, which was popularized in the 1960s by such celebrities as the BEATLES, has largely been presented in North America as a nonreligious system that reduces stress and improves physical health and mental abilities; critics and many researchers have noted, however, that the tests cited by TM are unreliable, and many other tests have determined that TM practitioners frequently suffer from depression and tension. There are numerous TM programs and institutions, including the Maharishi University of Management, Maharishi Vedic City (an incorporated community near Fairfield, Iowa), and the NATURAL LAW PARTY (a political organization). Web site—http://www.tm.org. For further research, a four-page Watchman Fellowship Profile is available (see page 363). Web site—http://www.watchman.org/notebook.

Treat, Casey: Popular WORD-FAITH teacher and pastor/founder of Christian Faith Center in Seattle, Washington. Treat established the church in 1980 with 30 people and now has over 8,000 in attendance. He and his wife, Wendy, were ordained to the ministry by FREDERICK K.C. PRICE. Web site—http://casey.iactivesite.com. See WORD-FAITH MOVEMENT.

Tree of Life Foundation—Patagonia, AZ: Teaches people to live with the Sevenfold Peace—peace with the body, mind, family, humanity, culture, living planet, and divine presence. Clergy in the foundation's ESSENE ORDER OF LIGHT attempt to heal all of nature through such practices as REIKI and YOGA and the spirituality of the KABBALAH. Also operates the Tree of Life Rejuvenation Center and the Tree of Life Health Center.

All Tree of Life property is owned by an organization called Patlanco. Web site—http://www.treeoflife.nu. See NEW AGE.

"Trick or Treat": A phrase uttered by children in exchange for candy and other treats on HALLOWEEN. The implication in the phrase is that if the child does not receive a treat, he or she will perform a trick or prank upon the householder from whom the child is attempting to solicit the treat. In reality, however, the phrase is largely an entertainment ritual devoid of any threat.

Trinitarianism: See TRINITY.

Trinity: The doctrine that the one true God eternally exists as three distinct persons—the Father, Son, and HOLY SPIRIT. These three are co-equal, co-eternal, and one in essence. Critics of the doctrine point out that the term *Trinity* is extrabiblical. While this is true, the term accurately designates God's self-revelation in the BIBLE. The New Testament clearly states—in accordance with the Old Testament (e.g., Deuteronomy 6:4)—that there is only one God (Galatians 3:20). At the same time, JESUS proclaims Himself to be divine (John 8:58). The apostle John states that, as the Son or Word, Jesus is God (John 1:1). And the HOLY SPIRIT is also proved to be God (John 14–16). Furthermore, Trinitarian formulas are given in several Scripture passages (Matthew 28:19; 2 Corinthians 13:14; 1 Peter 1:2). See GOD; MONOTHEISM; COUNCIL OF NICEA.

Trinity Broadcasting Network (TBN)—Santa Ana, CA: See CROUCH, PAUL AND JAN.

Tritheism: A form of POLYTHEISM, tritheism maintains the existence of a divine triad, or three separate and distinct gods; in a HERESY of CHRISTIANITY, tritheism maintains that the Father, Son, and HOLY SPIRIT are separate gods. Critics of the doctrine of the TRINITY frequently confuse that doctrine with tritheism.

Triumph Prophetic Ministries Church of God, William Dankenbring—Altadena, CA: Dankenbring, a former writer for *Plain Truth* and *Good News* magazines, started Triumph Publishing Company in 1974. In 1987, following the death of HERBERT W. ARMSTRONG, Dankenbring started the Triumph Prophetic Ministries Church of God. With a number of revisions (such as changing the dates on which such biblical feasts as

Passover and Trumpets are celebrated), Dankenbring promulgates the teachings of ARMSTRONGISM with a strong emphasis on prophetic speculation. Dankenbring publishes *Prophecy Flash* magazine. Web site— http://www.triumphpro.com.

Triumph Publishing: See TRIUMPH PROPHETIC MINISTRIES CHURCH OF GOD.

True and Living Church of Jesus Christ of Saints of the Last Days, Jim Harmston—Manti, UT: Harmston was a member of THE CHURCH OF JESUS CHRIST OF LATTER-DAY SAINTS. He claims that in 1990, he was given the keys to the priesthood by Elohim, Jehovah, Adam, and JESUS. Believing the LDS church to be in APOSTASY (particularly for its failure to retain the practice of polygamy), Harmston and approximately 30 followers left in 1992 to start the Council of High Priests (later the True and Living Church [TLC]). In addition to restoring the practice of polygamy and using the 1830 BOOK OF MORMON, the TLC has added such doctrines as "multiple mortal probations" (i.e., REINCARNATION), "rescuing" (in which a woman is taken from her legal husband and religiously married to a member of the TLC), and the "true order of prayer," which enables members to communicate with individuals in the spirit world. In preparation for the end times, the TLC ceased proselytism and contact with the media on April 15, 1999. In 2002, a jury ordered the TLC to return $300,000 in contributions to two former members who alleged that Harmston defrauded them and reneged on such promises as producing a physical appearance by JESUS CHRIST. The TLC publishes the *Manti Times and Seasons*. For further research, a four-page Watchman Fellowship Profile is available (see page 363). Web site—http://www.watchman.org/notebook.

True Mother and True Father: Titles assumed by Rev. SUN MYUNG MOON and his wife. See HOLY SPIRIT ASSOCIATION FOR THE UNIFICATION OF WORLD CHRISTIANITY.

Truth Forum: See HOMESTEAD HERITAGE.

Tucson Tabernacle—Tucson, AZ: The tabernacle promotes the teachings of BRANHAMISM. Web site—http://www.tucsontabernacle.org.

The Twelve Tribes, Elbert Spriggs: Founded in 1972 as the Church in Island Pond (other names: Messianic Communities, The Vine Community Church, The New Apostolic Order in Messiah, and Northeast Kingdom Community Church). Spriggs's movement is seen as a restoration of the 12 tribes of Israel in the Old Testament under JESUS CHRIST. It functions as a COMMUNAL SOCIETY that practices SABBATARIANISM and teaches that for believers, CHRIST's death does not forgive intentional sins—only unintentional ones. In 2001, membership was estimated at 2,500 to 3,000 in 27 locations. Members operate many COMMON GROUND CAFEs in a number of communities in the United States and internationally. Web site—http://www.twelvetribes.com. For further research, a four-page Watchman Fellowship Profile is available (see page 363). Web site—http://www.watchman.org/notebook.

Twin Cities Church of God—Maple Grove, MN: An independent group focused on SABBATARIANISM. Many members were formerly with the CHURCH OF GOD, INTERNATIONAL. Web site—http://www.mtn.org/tccg.

Two by Twos: See COONEYITES.

U

UFO: See UNIDENTIFIED FLYING OBJECTS.

UFO's A New World, Karen Lyster: Studies UNIDENTIFIED FLYING OBJECTS (UFOs), UFO sightings, CROP CIRCLES, UFO abductions, abduction stories, cattle mutilations, alien implants, NEW AGE predictions, etc. Advocates the GNOSTIC GOSPELS and REINCARNATION. Web site—http://www.karenlyster.com.

Unarius Academy of Science, Ernest and Ruth Norman—El Cajon, CA: The Normans started the academy in 1947 to promote UNARIUS—an acronym for Universal Articulate Interdimensional Understanding of Science—which they claim is the basis for the galactic intelligence of advanced persons. The primary practice of Unarius is a psychotherapy based on REINCARNATION, in which the patient learns to avoid the negative experiences of previous lifetimes. The Normans predicted that UFOs will bring spirit brothers and sisters to Earth; these spirit beings will teach humanity to transcend warlike behavior (Charles Louis Spiegel, Ruth Norman's successor as director of Unarius, erroneously predicted that this would occur in 2001). Ernest died in 1971; Ruth, who claimed to be the reincarnation of the archangel Uriel, died in 1993. The Normans wrote a number of books, and Unarius publishes *Unarius Light: A Journal of Logic and Reason* and produces the *Unarius Science of Life* cable TV program. Web site—http://www.unarius.org. See NEW AGE; PSYCHIC.

Understanding Inc., Daniel Fry—Tonopah, AZ: On July 4, 1949 or 1950 (at various points Fry gave both dates), Daniel Fry—who was an engineer at the White Sands Proving Grounds—was allegedly visited by an extraterrestrial named A-lan, who, speaking in American slang, took Fry into his UFO and traveled to New York and back. Later contacts revealed that A-lan was a member of a previous Earth civilization that had emigrated to space. Fry first published his story in 1954 in *The White Sands Incident* and started Understanding as a quasi-religious group based upon his UFO theories. Fry underwent a lie-detector test on live television to verify his truthfulness regarding his claims, and failed the test. Fry died in 1992. A Web site dedicated to his life and teachings is at http://www.danielfry.com.

Understanding Principles for Better Living, DELLA REESE—West Hollywood, CA: A NEW THOUGHT church that is part of the UNIVERSAL FOUNDATION FOR BETTER LIVING. Web site—http://www.up church.org.

Unidentified Flying Objects (UFOs): Unknown craft or airborne objects thought by some to be alien spaceships. Sightings of UFOs were reported as early as the eighteenth-century, and several sightings in 1944 and 1946 were reported in Europe. The modern UFO movement, however, began on June 24, 1947, when pilot Kenneth Arnold reported seeing nine objects flying over western Washington; in the same year, a crash near Roswell, New Mexico, is widely believed by CONSPIRACY THEORISTS to have been a UFO (according the U.S. Air Force in 1995, the crash was a cluster of weather balloons). In 1954, the U.S. Air Force began Project Blue Book to study UFO reports; with the exception of a 1964 encounter it labeled "unexplained," the project attributes all UFO reports to such natural phenomena as electrical storms and swamp gas (the project concluded in 1969). Interest in UFOs skyrocketed in the mid-1980s with the publication of WHITLEY STRIEBER's abduction novel, *Communion,* and Steven Spielberg's popular movie *Close Encounters of the Third Kind.* The title of Spielberg's 1977 blockbuster was based on the three categories of alien "close encounters" (CE) developed by Josef Allen Hynek: CE1—UFO seen nearby but no physical contact; CE2—UFO creates physical evidence; CE3—UFO occupants are seen by humans. As noted in the description of the Project Blue study, there are varying theories regarding UFOs: some attribute their appearance to natural phenomena; some believe that UFOs carry extraterrestrials—either physical or nonphysical beings—that engage in telepathic (i.e., PSYCHIC) communication with contactees; and some Christians have theorized that some UFO phenomena may actually be DEMONS intent upon deceiving humanity.

Unification Church: See HOLY SPIRIT ASSOCIATION FOR THE UNIFICATION OF WORLD CHRISTIANITY.

Unitarianism: Unitarianism is the strict monotheistic belief that, because God is one, He cannot exist in three persons. The doctrine is rooted in the fourth-century teachings of ARIUS, who taught that the Word (JESUS) was created in time, and therefore did not share in the divine essence of the Father. Modern Unitarianism is generally understood to have begun with the anti-Trinitarianism of Faustus Socinus (1539–1604). While some scholars attribute Joseph Priestly with establishing the first Unitarian church in North America in 1794, other scholars state that Unitarianism first appeared in New England in the early eighteenth century, and by 1750 was widely accepted by Congregationalist ministers. Individuals in the Transcendentalist movement, such as Ralph Waldo Emerson and Theodore Parker, eventually removed all concept of the supernatural from Unitarianism, making it increasingly humanistic. See MONARCHIANISM; TRINITY; UNITARIAN-UNIVERSALIST.

Unitarian Universalist Association—Boston, MA: The Unitarian Universalist Association was formed in 1961 by a merger of the American Unitarian Association and the Universalist Church of America. The association is strongly pluralistic, with ATHEISM, humanism, NEO-PAGANISM, LIBERAL CHRISTIANITY, JUDAISM, and BUDDHISM being among many faith traditions synthesized within the movement. Web site—http://www.uua.org. See UNITARIANISM; UNIVERSALISM.

United Church of Christ: A mainline Christian denomination of PROTESTANTISM formed in 1957 by the union of the Evangelical and Reformed Church and the Congregational Christian Churches. There are about 1.3 million members in independent churches located mostly in the United States. Web site—http://www.ucc.org.

United Church of God—Birmingham—Birmingham, AL: A SABBATARIAN organization. Through its United Christian Ministries, the church publishes *The UCM Newsletter* and *Christian Beacon*.

United Church of Religious Science: A NEW THOUGHT organization which, along with RELIGIOUS SCIENCE INTERNATIONAL, is rooted in the teachings of Ernest Holmes. The church teaches MIND SCIENCE, claiming that humans are divine and have unlimited potential. Its teachings are similar to those of the CHURCH OF CHRIST, SCIENTIST. Publishes *Science of Mind.* Web site—http://www.religiousscience.org.

United Lodge of Theosophists—New York, NY: Founded in 1909, the primary purpose of the lodge is to achieve union among the various groups teaching THEOSOPHY. The lodge operates 25 local lodges and a small number of study groups. Web site—http://www.ult.org.

United Methodist Church: A denomination of PROTESTANTISM that was formed from a merger between the Evangelical United Brethren Church and the Methodist Church in 1968. The church is generally more liberal and progressive (in doctrine and on social issues) than other churches with roots in METHODISM. In 2004 there were 8.6 million members in the United States. Web site—http://www.umc.org. See METHODISM.

United Pentecostal Church International (UPC)—Hazelwood, MO: Rooted in the revival that occurred in Topeka, Kansas, in 1901, as well as a controversy within Pentecostal denominations in 1915–16, the UPC is the largest of the groups practicing ONENESS PENTECOSTALISM. The UPC itself was formed in 1945 when the Pentecostal Church, Incorporated, merged with the Pentecostal Assemblies of Jesus Christ. Some UPC musicians and songwriters—particularly (Randy) PHILLIPS, (Shawn) CRAIG, AND (Dan) DEAN—are extremely popular among many followers of EVANGELICAL CHRISTIANITY. The UPC publishes *The Pentecostal Herald* magazine. Web site—http://www.upci.org.

United Research, James and Diana Goure—Black Mountain, NC: Based on a prayer group they started in 1970, the Goures founded United Research in 1976 to promote James's theory of effective prayer, which entails realizing that each individual is a "Light Being" who radiates light everywhere and to everyone. This prayer is allegedly effective in cleansing the seven energy centers of the body. United Research opened the Light Center, a two-story geodesic dome, in 1979. The group publishes the *UR Light* newsletter. Web site—http://www.urlight.org. See NEW AGE; CHAKRAS; MEDITATION; PSYCHIC.

United States Peace Government, Dr. John Hagelin—Maharishi Vedic City, IA: When the NATURAL LAW PARTY (NLP) dissolved in 2004, the

NLP's presidential candidate in the 2000 election, Dr. John Hagelin, formed a new organization to bring Maharishi Mahesh Yogi's teachings into the political sphere. The USPG is a political think-tank and a "complementary government" which addresses national problems by raising consciousness, lowering stress, and creating peace through TRANSCENDENTAL MEDITATION. The USPG has its own president and state governors, with its own national capital and USPG capitol buildings in each state capital city. Web site—http://www.uspeacegovernment.org.

Unity School of Christianity, Charles and Myrtle Fillmore—Lee's Summit, MO: The impetus for this school occurred in 1886 when, after attending a NEW THOUGHT lecture, Myrtle Fillmore was allegedly healed from a lingering illness. The movement was started in 1889 with the first publication of *Modern Thought* (later *Unity*) magazine; the Unity School of Christianity itself started in 1914. Unity, like other new thought groups, teaches PANTHEISM: All things are a manifestation of the one spirit. Each person has within him or her the CHRIST, and the purpose of life is to fully unite ourselves with the one divine mind. Because the one spirit or divine mind includes all things, sickness and suffering are simply an illusion. Unity publishes the monthly *Daily Word* devotional booklet. Web site—http://www.unityworldhq.org. See FIRST CHURCH OF CHRIST, SCIENTIST; NEW AGE; CHRIST CONSCIOUSNESS.

Unity Village: The headquarters for the UNITY SCHOOL OF CHRISTIANITY in Lee's Summit, Missouri.

Universal Faithists of Kosmon, George Morley: A small group that uses *OAHSPE* as their central text. Notably, the Faithists generally do not consider *OAHSPE* to be literally true, but instead are inspired by its ethical principles.

Universal Fellowship of Metropolitan Community Churches (UFMCC), Troy Perry—Abilene, TX: An organization of independent churches of predominately homosexual ministers and members that promote the spirituality and rights of gay, lesbian, bisexual, and transgender people. Founded in 1968 by Rev. Troy D. Perry, author of *The Lord Is My Shepherd and He Knows I'm Gay,* the UFMCC has over 300 churches with 43,000 members in 22 countries. The organization's title is usually shortened to Metropolitan Community Church (MCC). In 2005, Perry retired as moderator of

UFMCC. The Rev. Dr. Cindi Love currently serves as executive director. Web site—http://www.mccchurch.org.

Universal Foundation for Better Living, Johnnie Colemon—Miami Gardens, FL: Founded in 1974. See CHRIST UNIVERSAL TEMPLE. Web site—http://www.ufbl.org.

Universalism: Universalism—from the Greek term *apokatastasis*, or "restoration"—is the belief that God will ultimately bestow salvation upon all individuals. The belief, in a Christian context, is based upon an interpretation of biblical passages such as 1 Corinthians 15:24-28 and 2 Peter 3:13 which understands such phrases as God being "all in all" to refer to a restoration of every individual to life with God. The foremost advocate of universalism in early CHRISTIANITY was Origen; the doctrine largely disappeared after the fourth-century, but was revived by some Anabaptists during the Radical REFORMATION. While some universalist sects developed from seventeenth-century Puritanism—most notably the Philadelphians—the first organized universalist movement did not appear until approximately 1759 in England. The first universalist congregation in North America was started by John Murray in Gloucester, Massachusetts, in 1779. Hosea Ballou, an early nineteenth-century teacher, changed the previous universalist understanding of the effects of the crucifixion from a substitutionary position (which maintained that JESUS died in place of humanity) to a moral position (which maintained that Jesus died on behalf, but not in the place of humanity). In the twentieth-century, universalism was widened to accept universal concepts from all religions. See UNITARIANISM; UNITARIAN UNIVERSALIST ASSOCIATION; LIBERAL CHRISTIANITY; SALVATION.

Universalist: See UNIVERSALISM.

Universal Life Church, Kirby Hensley—Modesto, CA: Hensley founded the Universal Life Church in 1962 under the principle that every person should be allowed to choose his or her religion, and that his church should provide a forum for freely practicing all faiths without criticism or repression. The church teaches eternal progression through REINCARNATION. One of the central focuses of the church is a free ordination service—the church claims to have ordained 20 million ministers since 1959. Web site—http://www.ulc.org.

Universal Spiritualist Association—Chesterfield, IN: Founded in 1956 by Clifford Bias, the association promotes the practice of SPIRITUALISM, claiming that humanity can be guided through CHANNELING. One of the primary activities of the association is the College of Religious Education (C.O.R.E.), which provides distance learning in SPIRITUALISM. Web site—http://www.spiritualism.org.

Universist Foundation, Dr. Ford Vox: An organization that promotes a diverse philosophy loosely shared by people searching for the ultimate meaning of life while maintaining the belief that there is no ultimate source of truth outside of the self. The organization, originally called Universist Movement, celebrates personal human freedom, reason, and experience while maintaining a purely relativistic view of ethics and morals. In 2006, Universist Movement was dissolved and replaced by the Universist Foundation. Vox, who conducts interviews with major media and presents lectures on the subject, claims over one million adherents to Universism as of 2006. Web sites—http://www.universist.org and http://www.deism.org.

The University of Metaphysical Sciences, Christine Breese—Arcata, CA: Provides training in all areas of METAPHYSICS, offering unaccredited bachelor's, master's, and doctoral degrees. Courses include study in Native America traditions, wizards, WITCHCRAFT, SHAMANISM, HYPNOSIS, MANTRAS, ESP, DIVINATION, dreams, ASTROLOGY, CHAKRAS, AURAS, and *A COURSE IN MIRACLES,* among others. Web site—http://www.umsonline.org.

The University of Metaphysics, Paul Leon Masters—Advertised as the only "real University of Metaphysics," the online school offers accelerated degrees in METAPHYSICS, holistic life coaching, pastoral counseling psychology, transpersonal counseling, and more. In operation for almost 50 years, the school is part of the International Metaphysical Ministry and connected with the University of Sedona, which offers higher-consciousness education. There is no connection with the UNIVERSITY OF METAPHYSICS operated by Reverend Joan. Web site—http://www.metaphysics.com.

The University of Metaphysics, Reverend Joan—Bellflower, CA: Reverend Joan is a PSYCHIC who engages in the OCCULT, ASTROLOGY, NUMEROLOGY, DIVINATION, CLAIRVOYANCE, and uses TAROT CARDS. Joan claims to have helped police solve a murder using psychic powers. She became embroiled in controversy in 1986 after unsuccessfully suing the Bellflower school district and a local cult awareness ministry for terminating a lecture series she was delivering to high school students in school facilities. Not affiliated with the UNIVERSITY OF METAPHYSICS operated by Paul Leon Masters.

Upanishads: The 108 Upanishads comprise the *Vendanta,* the end of the *VEDAS.* See HINDUISM.

Upper Triad Association—Madison, NC: Established in 1974, the association studies the ways in which Eastern and Western religious traditions can contribute to spiritual growth. The foundational belief systems of the association are METAPHYSICS and THEOSOPHY. From this foundation the association sees seven "rays" into which an array of religious traditions can be placed: purpose, consciousness, truth and reality, KARMA, knowledge, religion, and manifestation. Web site—http://www.uppertriad.org. See NEW AGE.

The URANTIA Book: William Sadler, a psychotherapist who treated a "sleeping subject" who engaged in AUTOMATIC WRITING, noted that the writings were dictated by an order of extraterrestrial beings. In 1924, a being named Machiventa Melchizedek from the celestial Melchizedek school requested that Sadler form a "Contact Commission" for the further writings, which eventually formed *The URANTIA Book.* The first 118 pages were published in 1934; by the time the messages ceased coming in 1955, the book totaled 2,097 pages. The cosmology of *The URANTIA Book* is extensive: The cosmos are divided into five concentric rings, with a Trinity of Trinities (the most important Trinity is the existential Paradise Trinity consisting of the Universal Father, the Eternal Son and the Infinite Spirit). *The URANTIA Book* claims that JESUS traveled to Rome as a tutor for the sons of a wealthy Indian merchant, and that upon His death He underwent "the Morontia Transit," in which His resurrected form and personality were initiated into the morontia world (the next level of existence). Sin is avoided simply by choosing good; humanity must, over the course of many lifetimes on many planets, emulate the example of love and faith in God shown by Jesus. Since 2001 the book has been part of the public domain (see URANTIA FOUNDATION). *The URANTIA Book* is available online at http://www.urantia.org/detail.html. For further research, a four-page Watchman Fellowship Profile is available (see page 363). Web site—http://www.watchman.org/notebook.

URANTIA Book Fellowship—Chicago, IL: The fellowship promotes study groups on *THE URANTIA BOOK.* Web site—http://www.urantiabook.org.

URANTIA Brotherhood—Chicago, IL: The brotherhood—originally called the Fifth Epochal Fellowship—was established in 1955 as a fraternal organization for studying and enacting the teachings of *THE URANTIA BOOK.* The URANTIA FOUNDATION disenfranchised the brotherhood in 1990, and threatened the brotherhood with a lawsuit (the threat was dropped in 1996). In 1997, the brotherhood and fellowship agreed to jointly translate *The URANTIA Book* into foreign languages.

URANTIA Foundation—Chicago, IL: Established in 1950 to promote and distribute *THE URANTIA BOOK.* The foundation claimed that it held the sole copyright to *The Urantia Book* and vigorously defended that right, causing numerous disputes with other Urantia organizations, particularly URANTIA BOOK FELLOWSHIP. In 2000 a suit was filed in a federal court against the URANTIA FOUNDATION, maintaining that the foundation's copyright renewal of *The Urantia Book* filed in 1983 was invalid. In 2001 a jury ruled the copyright claimed by the foundation was invalid and that the book was part of the public domain. This decision was appealed all the way to the U.S. Supreme Court without being overturned. Web site—http://www.urantia.org.

Urshan, Andrew: One of the early teachers of ONENESS PENTECOSTALISM.

Utah Lighthouse Ministry, Jerald and Sandra Tanner—Salt Lake City, UT: An APOLOGETICS ministry that defends the beliefs of EVANGELICAL CHRISTIANITY and analyzes the theology, history, and truth claims of the CHURCH OF JESUS CHRIST OF LATTER-DAY SAINTS. Originally founded as the Modern Microfilm Co. in 1983, the organization became a nonprofit ministry under its current name. Sandra Tanner and her late husband, Jerald (1938-2006), are seen as pioneers in the field and have authored over 40 books including *Mormonism—Shadow or Reality?* Web site—http://www.utlm.org.

Uversa Press—New York, NY: Publishing subsidiary of the URANTIA BOOK FELLOWSHIP. Web site—http://www.uversapress.com.

V

Van Praagh, James: Well-known PSYCHIC and author of several popular books including *Heaven and Earth: Making the Psychic Connection, Talking to Heaven: A Medium's Message of Life After Death,* and *Reaching to Heaven.* Praagh has made several appearances on *Larry King Live* and is the co-executive producer of the hit CBS drama *GHOST WHISPERER,* which stars Jennifer Love Hewitt. Web site—http://www.vanpraagh.com. See PSYCHIC; GHOST WHISPERER.

Vanzant, Iyanla: NEW AGE author and lecturer. Founded INNER VISIONS INSTITUTE FOR SPIRITUAL DEVELOPMENT. Teaches universal or spiritual law, a blending of Western and Eastern religious beliefs and practices to empower others. At one point she appeared regularly on OPRAH as an empowerment expert.

Vedas: The primary texts of HINDUISM consist of ancient hymns and rituals. There are four Vedas: the Rig Veda, Sama Veda, Yajur Veda, and Atharva Veda. The Rig Veda, the oldest of the four, was composed approximately 1500 B.C., and written sometime after 300 B.C. The Vedas are online at http://www.sacred-texts.com/hin/.

Vendyl Jones Research Institutes—Arlington, TX: In 1956, Jones decided that the early Christians had altered the text of the New Testament to remove all traces of JUDAISM. Jones eventually abandoned CHRISTIANITY and changed the name of his organization from the Institute of Judaic-Christian Research to Vendyl Jones Research Institutes. His primary work today is advancing the B'NEI NOACH. Jones is said to have claimed that the movie character Indiana Jones is based on him, though his Web site denies the assertion. Web site—http://www.vendyljones.org.il.

Vine Community Church: See THE TWELVE TRIBES.

Vineyard Church Movement: See ASSOCIATION OF VINEYARD CHURCHES.

Virgin Birth: The doctrine of the virgin birth of JESUS refers to the Christian belief that Jesus was miraculously conceived in the womb of the VIRGIN MARY by the power of the HOLY SPIRIT without sexual intercourse or fertilization by sperm from a human male. The doctrine is based upon the accounts in Matthew 1:18,22-25 and Luke 1:26-38, and is viewed by followers of CHRISTIANITY as the fulfillment of a prophecy in Isaiah 7:14.

Virginia School of Massage: Part of the STEINER EDUCATION GROUP. In addition to offering training in more traditional types of massages such as sports and medical, this school teaches Eastern massage techniques, including Shiatsu, REFLEXOLOGY, and AROMATHERAPY. See STEINER EDUCATION GROUP; HOLISTIC HEALING.

Virgin Mary: The mother of JESUS CHRIST, who miraculously conceived the Son of God while still a virgin apart from sexual contact with any man. ROMAN CATHOLICISM holds to the perpetual virginity of Mary. Most Protestants believe that Christ was Mary's firstborn son (Matthew 1:24-25), and that after the birth of Christ, Mary had other children naturally with her husband Joseph (Mark 6:3). Recently there has been a controversial movement among many Catholics to elevate Mary officially to a position of Co-Redemptrix (co-redeemer with Christ) and Mediatrix (mediator) of grace with Christ (see 1 Timothy 2:5). There has been much excitement and controversy generated over alleged Marian apparitions (supernatural appearances of the Virgin Mary), which some critics, including many Christians, have dismissed as hallucinations fueled by superstitions or hoaxes. See VIRGIN BIRTH.

Vishnu: The preserver and second member of the triad of Hindu gods, including BRAHMA and SHIVA. See HINDUISM.

Vision Quest: In many traditions of NATIVE AMERICAN SPIRITU-ALITY, the vision quest was a rite of passage for a male in which he withdrew from his camp for a solitary vigil of fasting and prayer in order to gain—usually through a dream—a sign or indication of the identity of his spiritual guardian; this dream was then interpreted by the tribal SHAMAN. The interpretation of the vision then provided purpose and direction in the male's life. Some NEW AGE practitioners engage in heavily modified vision quests to provide a renewed sense of purpose in life.

Visualization: In its most basic sense, visualization simply involves generating a mental image of an object or circumstance; any act of memory can therefore be understood as an act of basic visualization. Among many NEW AGE practitioners, however, visualization—in this sense, frequently called creative visualization—involves the manipulation or creation of reality through intently meditating upon an object or goal. This activity is usually based upon the belief that the individual is part of the one divine, creative energy and consciousness; the individual therefore possesses the ability to utilize and manipulate this energy to generate a desired outcome. See PANTHEISM.

Voodoo: The popular name for Vodoun (also Vodou and Vodun), which, like SANTERIA, is a religion of the Yoruba people of west Africa. Vodoun developed in Haiti in the nineteenth-century, where the lack of a solid Christian infrastructure enabled the slaves to practice their native religion. A pantheon of gods is worshipped in Vodoun, foremost among these the unknowable Olorun (a lesser god, Obatala, was responsible for the creation of Earth and all life). A large number of minor spirits rule over such things as emotions, natural forces, or specific locations. Priests make offerings (both simple gifts such as food, and more significant gifts such as animal sacrifices) to spirits in exchange for their assistance. This relationship is symbiotic—the spirits require food, and humans require the assistance of the spirits. See ZOMBIE. For further research, a four-page Watchman Fellowship Profile is available (see page 363). Web site—http://www.watchman.org/notebook.

Vorilhon, Claude: Now known as Rael, Vorilhon is the founder and leader of THE RAELIAN RELIGION.

W

Wagner, C. Peter: See THIRD WAVE OF THE HOLY SPIRIT.

Waldorf Schools: An association of primary and secondary schools based on the teachings of RUDOLF STEINER. According to the theory of Waldorf Education, humanity is a tripartite being: spirit, soul, and body. These three aspects of people unfold in the developmental stages of early childhood, middle childhood, and adolescence. The curricula in Waldorf schools therefore is holistic and arts-based, emphasizing natural (i.e., non-electronic) activities that promote creativity and independent thinking and brings together the spirit, soul, and body. Some parents of Waldorf students have objected to what they claim is a tendency by the schools to downplay or obscure their reliance upon Steiner's teachings. The Association of Waldorf Schools of North America publishes *Renewal* journal. Web site—http://www.awsna.org. See ANTHROPOSOPHICAL SOCIETY.

Walker, J. Lamah: Walker, the stepson of Gilbert Holloway, is an ordained minister in the NEW AGE CHURCH OF TRUTH and a medicine man in the Bear Clan. He is the author of several books and operates the Age of Reality Web site. Web site—http://www.theageofreality.net. See NEW AGE; SHAMANISM.

Warm Reading: A technique sometimes used by PSYCHICS in order to appear to gain supernatural OCCULT knowledge about their clients. The technique involves doing research on the clients prior to the psychic reading (including Internet searches, covertly contacting associates, or hiring private investigators). Thus, the psychic can appear to have a supernatural knowledge of the client's past. See COLD READING; HOT READING.

Warnke, Mike (b. 1946): A CHRISTIAN speaker and comedian whose popular 1973 autobiography, *The Satan Seller,* revealed his secret life as a high priest in SATANISM. The book and his personal testimony painted a shocking picture of a huge, well-financed, worldwide network of Satanists involved in all kinds of crimes including drug trafficking, SATANIC RITUAL ABUSE (SRA), and murder. The book became a Christian best-seller and was instrumental in shaping Christian understanding of the OCCULT and Satanism. An in-depth investigation by *Cornerstone* magazine published in 1992, however, exposed Warnke's entire story as a hoax perpetrated on an undiscerning Christian audience. (See *Cornerstone* article, "Selling Satan," at http://www.cornerstonemag.com/features/iss098/sellingsatan.htm.) Web site—www.mikewarnke.org.

Watchman Fellowship, Inc., David Henke—Arlington, TX: Watchman Fellowship was incorporated in 1979 as an EVANGELICAL CHRISTIAN discernment ministry focusing on APOLOGETICS and evangelism in the field of new religious movements, CULTS, the OCCULT, and NEW AGE spirituality. James K. Walker (author and editor of this book) currently serves as president of the ministry, which has offices in seven states and employs two full-time missionaries in Eastern Europe. The ministry is a member of EVANGELICAL MINISTRIES TO NEW RELIGIONS (EMNR). Web site—http://www.watchman.org.

Watchtower: The flagship publication of the WATCHTOWER BIBLE AND TRACT SOCIETY.

Watchtower Bible and Tract Society, Charles Taze Russell—Brooklyn, NY: Russell was greatly influenced by some of the descendants of the SECOND ADVENT MOVEMENT. When, however, he disagreed with the ADVENTISTS and decided that the SECOND COMING would be an invisible event, he left and later founded Zion's Watch Tower in 1879. In 1886, Russell began writing *The Divine Plan of the Ages,* which became the first in his six-volume set *Studies in the Scriptures* (Russell's successor, Joseph "Judge" Rutherford, wrote a seventh volume). Russell died in 1916; his replacement by Rutherford led to a split between those who followed the teachings of Russell (these individuals founded the BIBLE STUDENTS movement) and the followers of Rutherford. It was under Rutherford's presidency, in 1931, that the group—at that time called the International Bible Students—adopted the name Jehovah's Witnesses. Jehovah's Witnesses adamantly reject the doctrine of the TRINITY: they believe Jehovah (the Father) is God; JESUS—who before His incarnation was Michael-the Archangel—is Jehovah's first work of creation; and the HOLY SPIRIT is the impersonal active force or energy of Jehovah. Jehovah's Witnesses further believe that only 144,000 individuals (the LITTLE FLOCK) will go to heaven after death; other faithful Witnesses (the Great Crowd) will live upon a renewed paradise earth. The society enforces a strong form of LEGALISM, in which all the requirements of the society must be followed unquestioningly. Such requirements include staunch separatism from governmental involvement and from all other religions. The Watchtower Society erroneously predicted the APOCALYPSE would occur in 1914, 1918, 1925, and 1975. The Society publishes *Watchtower* and *Awake!* magazines, as well as at least one new book or booklet each year. Web site—http://www.watchtower.org. See FALSE PROPHECY. For further research, a four-page Watchman Fellowship Profile is available (see page 363). Web site—http://www.watchman.org/notebook.

Way Corps: The training program for leaders in THE WAY INTERNATIONAL.

The Way International, Victor Paul Wierwille—New Knoxville, OH: The initial activity that resulted in The Way International was Wierwille's *Vesper Chimes* radio program, which began in 1942. Wierwille, at the time a pastor in what became the United Church of Christ, claimed that God spoke to him and promised to teach him the Word of God as it had not been taught since the first century. The Way was formally started in 1967 on Wierwille's family farm, and within 20 years over 100,000 people had taken The Way's introductory course, *The Power for Abundant Living* (which has been replaced by *The Way of Abundance and Power*). The Way teaches MONARCHIANISM, claiming that only the Father is God; JESUS did not exist before His incarnation, and was only a perfect man rather than divine. Wierwille also created a distinction in the HOLY SPIRIT: HOLY SPIRIT (capitalized) is another name for God the Father, while HOLY SPIRIT (uncapitalized) is a reference to God's impersonal force. The Way has experienced a steady decline in the number of followers since Wierwille's death in 1985, and the Rock of Ages—The Way's highly popular Christian music festival—has been discontinued. L. Craig Martindale, Wierwille's appointed successor, resigned in 2000 after admitting to an extramarital affair that resulted in a $2 million lawsuit. Estimates of The Way membership in that year were between 3,000-5,000 (from a peak of nearly 100,000 in 1982). The Way operates American Christian Press and publishes *The Way Magazine*. Web site—http://www.theway.com. See LEGALISM. For further research, a four-page Watchman Fellowship Profile is available (see page 363). Web site—http://www.watchman.org/notebook.

Weigh Down Workshop: This is the controversial faith-based diet and weight-loss program developed by GWEN SHAMBLIN based on her popular book *The Weigh Down Diet*. The program encourages people to eat only when they feel real, physical hunger and not to use food to try to fill spiritual or emotional needs. Overeating is viewed as gluttony, which is equivalent to the sin of idolatry. The program was very popular in the 1990s and was used in some 17,000 CHRISTIAN churches. Doctrinal controversy developed, however, when Shamblin publicly denied the doctrines of the TRINITY and of SALVATION BY GRACE through faith in CHRIST alone. When her questionable beliefs were publicized, thousands of churches dropped the program and her publisher, Thomas Nelson, cancelled publication of an upcoming book. Shamblin helped form a new church called REMNANT FELLOWSHIP, which is in alignment with her beliefs. Web site—http://www.weighdown.com. See SHAMBLIN, GWEN; REMNANT FELLOWSHIP. For further research, a four-page Watchman Fellowship Profile is available (see page 363). Web site—http://www. watchman.org/notebook.

Weil, Andrew: Weil, a graduate of Harvard Medical School, is one of the most popular advocates of HOLISTIC HEALTH. Such books as *Spontaneous Healing* and *Optimum Health* teach that mind, body, and spirit must be in balance for optimum health. Weil promotes such practices as GUIDED IMAGERY (i.e., VISUALIZATION), ACUPUNCTURE (which Weil recommends for clearing MERIDIANS), and HYPNOSIS as methods of spiritual healing. In addition to his writings, Weil also offers a personal line of vitamins and supplements. Web site—http://www.drweil. com. See NEW AGE.

Wellspring Retreat and Resource Center, Paul R. Martin—Albany, OH: A residential treatment facility that provides licensed counseling and mental health care for the victims of SPIRITUAL ABUSE and for those experiencing the debilitating effects of past involvement with cultic organizations or abusive groups. The center is staffed by followers of EVANGELICAL

CHRISTIANITY but it provides treatment and recovery from a secular mental health perspective. Web site—http://wellspringretreat.org.

Wesleyan Church—Fishers, IN: A denomination of PROTESTANTISM with roots in METHODISM. The church was formed in 1968 by the merger of several like-minded groups. In 2006, there were 5,000 churches in 80 countries with almost 400,000 constituents. Web site—http://www.wesleyan.org. See METHODISM; EVANGELICAL CHRISTIANITY.

Whidbey Institute for Earth, Spirit, and the Human Nature, Fritz and Vivienne Hull—Clinton, WA: A NEW AGE organization that grew out of a meeting in 1993 primarily consisting of the Hulls and fellow members of the CHINOOK LEARNING CENTER. The Whidbey Institute continues the core commitments of the Chinook Learning Center, which was absorbed into Whidbey in 1995. Web site—http://www.whidbeyinstitute.org. See NATIVE AMERICAN SPIRITUALITY; MEDITATION.

Whirling Dervishes: see SUFISM.

White Dove International, Stuart Wilde—Denver, CO: Wilde, a NEW AGE teacher, presents books and seminars that teach participants an eclectic array of methods to realize the potential of their infinite self. Web site—http://www.whitedoveinternational.com.

White Eagle: See CHURCH OF THE WHITE EAGLE LODGE.

White Eagle Center for the Americas—Montgomery TX: American headquarters for the WHITE EAGLE LODGE. The group operates the Temple of the Golden Rose and St. John's Retreat Center in Montgomery, Texas, as well as White Eagle Lodges in numerous cities around the world. Publishes *On Eagle's Wings.* Web site—http://www.whiteaglelodge.org.

White Eagle Lodge, Grace ("Minesta," d. 1979) and Ivan (d. 1979) Cooke—Hampshire, England: Grace was a MEDIUM for the spirit teacher White Eagle, who was also believed to be a symbol of John, the beloved disciple of Jesus. White Eagle allegedly gave Grace the name by which she was more commonly known, Minesta. Founded in 1936, the church teaches that all religions lead to truth. According to the church, God is both a male and female spirit, and Jesus achieved his higher spiritual state by realizing his CHRIST CONSCIOUSNESS. Humans escape the cycle of cause-and-effect (i.e., KARMA) and REINCARNATION through developing their inner light. The church's teachings are influenced by ROSICRUCIANISM and the NEW AGE belief in the GREAT WHITE BROTHERHOOD. The group operates St. John's Retreat Center in Montgomery, Texas, as well as White Eagle Lodges in numerous cities around the world. Publishes *On Eagle's Wings*. Web site—http://www.whiteagle.org.

White, Ellen G: The "Messenger" of the SEVENTH-DAY ADVENTIST CHURCH.

White, Walter: See FOLLOWERS OF CHRIST CHURCH.

Whitney, Michael: Patriarch of the AMERICAN TEMPLE.

Whole Brain Learning Institute (WBLI), Deborah DeBerry—Chandler, AZ: Founded in 1989 as a continuation of the work of the JOHN-DAVID LEARNING INSTITUTE. DeBerry was a training consultant for the John-David Learning Institute from the mid 1980s until the death of its founder in 1988. She said that she formed the WBLI in order to fulfill the request of her mentor, John-David, who left his work in her hands. Web site—http://www.brainspeak.com. See NEW AGE.

Wicca: The modern Wiccan movement was started by Gerald B. Gardner in 1951 after British laws against WITCHCRAFT were repealed (Gardner claimed to have been initiated into the craft in 1939, and published a novel about witchcraft, *The Craft*, in 1949). While Gardnerian and Alexandrian (named after Alexander Sanders, a student of Gardner) Wicca were brought to North America in the 1960s and 1970s, a prevalent tradition in the United States is Dianic Wicca (which focuses on the Greek goddess, Diana, and GODDESS worship). Wiccan spirituality is a polarity between goddess and God: the triple goddess (Maiden, Mother, and Crone) is the emanating source of nature, while the God is both the source of the fertility through which the goddess gives life as well as the bringer of death. Wiccans follow three laws: the Rede, "An Ye Harm None, Do What Ye Will"; the threefold law, in which the deeds committed by a person will return threefold (similar to the concept of KARMA); and REINCARNATION. Wiccan rituals are performed in a circle that contains the energy generated by the rituals until that energy is released in the Cone of Power, thereby accomplishing the purpose for which the rituals were performed. See WITCHCRAFT. For further research, a four-page Watchman Fellowship Profile is available (see page 363). Web site—http://www.watchman.org/notebook.

Williamson, Marianne: Williamson, who began lecturing professionally in 1983, is one of the foremost teachers of *A COURSE IN MIRACLES.* The concept that we are already in heaven and need only to realize our divinity is found throughout Williamson's work: fully realizing ourselves will enable us to fully love, forgive, and experience grace in our lives. Williamson's seminal book is *A Return to Love: Reflections on the Principles of a Course in Miracles;* other best-sellers include *Everyday Grace: Having Hope, Finding Forgiveness, and Making Miracles* and *Illuminata: A Return to Prayer.* Web site—http://www.marianne.com. See NEW AGE.

Willson, Laurel: See STRATFORD, LAUREN.

Wimber, John: See ASSOCIATION OF VINEYARD CHURCHES.

Winfrey, Oprah: Host of the long-running and popular *Oprah Winfrey Show.* During the mid 1990s the show became a sympathetic venue for NEW AGE teachers to promote their teachings and books, giving many their first big boost of popularity. Some of those include MARILYN FERGUSON, MARIANNE WILLIAMSON, DEEPAK CHOPRA, GARY ZUKAV, IYANLA VANZANT, ECKHART TOLLE, SHIRLEY MACLAINE, SOPHY BURNHAM, and ERIC BUTTERWORTH. Concerning Butterworth, Winfrey said, "This book [*Discover the Power Within*] changed my perspective on life and religion." Oprah made it clear that these were more than just talk-show guests; these were people who had influenced her through their writings, views, and teachings. While Winfrey has denied being New Age and rarely discusses her personal spirituality, she has, on occasion, made statements on her show, in interviews, and in her writings that indicate she has adopted many of the beliefs of her New Age guests: a view of God akin to pantheism (all is God, God is not a personal being, God is a universal force); Jesus is merely a great teacher (like many others); salvation takes many forms through many lives (reincarnation); all religions lead to the same truth (no absolute truth). In a 2002 *Christianity Today* interview, her former pastor in Chicago, Jeremiah Wright of Trinity United Church of Christ, expressed his views on this, stating, "She has broken with the [traditional faith].... She now has this sort of 'God is everywhere, God is in me, I don't need to go to church, I don't need to be a part of a body of believers, I can meditate, I can do positive thinking' spirituality. It's a strange gospel. It has nothing to do with the church JESUS CHRIST founded." Web site—http://www.oprah.com. For further research, a four-page Watchman Fellowship Profile is available (see page 363). Web site—http://www.watchman.org/notebook.

Wisconsin Evangelical Lutheran Synod (WELS), Milwaukee, WI: A denomination of PROTESTANTISM based on LUTHERANISM that was formed in 1950 out of the German Evangelical Ministerium of Wisconsin. The synod was in fellowship with THE LUTHERAN CHURCH–MISSOURI SYNOD (LCMS) from 1871 until 1961, when they withdrew over doctrinal issues pertaining to church fellowship. WELS is the third-largest Lutheran denomination in the United States (about 400,000 baptized members in over 1,200 congregations) and is known for its doctrinal conservatism. Web site—http://www.wels.net. See LUTHERANISM; REFORMATION; PROTESTANTISM.

WISE International—Los Angeles, CA: An acronym for World Institute of Scientology Enterprises, WISE applies the teachings of L. Ron Hubbard—specifically Hubbard Management Technology—to personal and business management. The institute offers a range of membership options, from an individual membership (for executives and employees) to a CEO's circle membership (for executives who desire to promote Hubbard Management Technology to people and organizations with whom they are in communication). WISE publishes *Prosperity* magazine. Web site—http://www.wise.org. See CHURCH OF SCIENTOLOGY.

Wise Woman Center, Susun Weed—Woodstock, NY: Weed specializes in HOLISTIC HEALTH, particularly as it applies to women. She claims to be a high priestess in Dianic WICCA, among other spiritual affiliations. Her "Wise Woman Way" involves pursuing wholeness through herbal medicines, SHAMANISM, GODDESS worship, and elements of NEO-PAGANISM. Web site—http://www.susunweed.com.

Witchcraft: The roots of European witchcraft are largely unknown. Claims by some advocates to a craft descended from ancient matriarchal societies are unfounded and have been discredited by scholars. The meaning of *witchcraft*—commonly simply called *the craft*—is varied according to the practitioner. In general, witchcraft is an experiential religion in which rituals and the celebration of seasonal festivals are intended to enhance an individual's self-awareness and increase the power that person has to influence his or her destiny without outside influence. The most prevalent form of modern witchcraft is WICCA. For further research, a four-page Watchman Fellowship Profile is available (see page 363). Web site—http://www.watchman.org/notebook.

Witch Doctor: See SHAMAN.

Witches' Voice, Wren Walker and Fritz Jung—Tampa, FL: A nonprofit organization founded in 1997 that provides an extensive and significant online resource for widely diverse practitioners of WICCA and PAGANISM. Web site—http://www.witchvox.com. See WICCA.

Women's Federation for World Peace, Hak Ja Han Moon—New York, NY: Founded in 1992 by Rev. SUN MYUNG MOON, this organization is affiliated with the United Nations. Web site—http://www.wfwp.org. See HOLY SPIRIT ASSOCIATION FOR THE UNIFICATION OF WORLD CHRISTIANITY.

Word-Faith Movement: Word-Faith—frequently called Word of Faith or name-it-and-claim-it—is the belief that Christians have within themselves the supernatural power to create reality by speaking the word. This movement is often presented as an answer to the lack of life and miracles in some Christian churches. In its fully developed form, however, it differs from traditional Christian views of faith and miracles in several important ways. While not all Word-Faith teachers believe exactly alike on all issues, there are some common elements found among many of them, especially among the popular Word-Faith tele-preachers/evangelists. These include: 1) The believer's faith itself (independent of God's direct action or will) contains the power to bring desired results—usually pertaining to health and financial prosperity. 2) Believers are little gods or divine beings who possess all or some of the distinctive attributes of God. 3) As little gods, believers can therefore emulate God, who spoke all things into existence. This means words are containers of power. Whatever one speaks will occur, be it negative or positive. Therefore, one should only speak positive or faith-filled words. Those who believe this tend to also believe it is a spiritual law that applies to both the believer and the nonbeliever. 4) In taking man's sins upon Himself, Jesus died as a sinner in need of redemption and had to obtain His own redemption in hell. In contrast to the Word-Faith theology, traditional Christian theology teaches that God is uniquely different from humans, who are limited and finite. Historically, Christians have viewed the potential or presence of supernatural health, wealth, and miracles as very real and valid aspects of Christian life. They are viewed, however, as answers to prayer and acts of God contingent on His sovereign will. Many within the movement recognize Kenneth Hagin, Jr. as one of the fathers of the movement, even referring to him as Dad Hagin. Other popular Word-Faith teachers include KENNETH AND GLORIA COPELAND, CHARLES CAPPS, CREFLO DOLLAR, FREDERICK K.C. PRICE, PAUL AND JAN CROUCH, CASEY TREAT, MARILYN HICKEY, JESSE DUPLANTIS, and EARL PAULK. Many critics also include JOYCE MEYER and JOEL OSTEEN among the Word-Faith teachers, though their message (particularly OSTEEN'S) may not be as overtly Word-Faith. For further research, a four-page Watchman Fellowship Profile is available (see page 363). Web site—http://www.watchman.org/notebook.

Words of Jesus Ministry, Keith and Lettie Siddens—Albany, MO: Siddens, a member of the CHURCH OF GOD (SEVENTH DAY), formed the ministry to market his books and tracts on SABBATARIANISM.

World Baptist Fellowship (WBF)—Arlington, TX: A fellowship of like-minded INDEPENDENT BAPTIST CHURCHES that supports missionaries and CHRISTIAN education. Web site—http://www.wbfi.net. See BAPTIST CHURCHES; FUNDAMENTALIST CHRISTIANITY.

World Changers Church—College Park (Atlanta), GA: See DOLLAR, CREFLO.

World Church of the Creator, Matt Hale—East Peoria, IL: A racist group founded in 1973 as the WORLD CHURCH OF THE CREATOR and reestablished as the World Church in 1996 by Hale following the 1993 suicide of original founder Klassen. The church teaches "Creativity," a doctrine which maintains, based on Darwin's theory of natural selection, that the white race is genetically superior to nonwhite "mud" races and therefore is the only race worthy of survival. Creativity mandates that whites take over the world through RAHOWA, an acronym for "racial holy war." While the group officially denounces violence, a member beat a black man in 1996, and in 1999 member Benjamin Smith killed two people—and wounded nine others—during a shooting spree. The church republishes Klassen's *Building a Whiter and Brighter World, The White Man's Bible* and *Nature's Eternal Religion,* and publishes the newsletter *The Struggle.* Web site—http://www.creatorforum.com.

World Council of Churches: The World Council of Churches (WCC) was formed in 1948 by representatives of 147 Christian churches to promote ecumenical cooperation and unity; the WCC currently consists of 340 churches and denominations. Most of the member churches and denominations are proponents of LIBERAL CHRISTIANITY; in 1998, the member churches of ORTHODOX CHRISTIANITY raised significant objections to the worship practices, public statements, and decision-making of the WCC. Web site—http://www.wcc-coe.org.

WorldPeace, John: WorldPeace claims that world peace can be achieved after all humans are one with God, whom he also calls the Infinite Potential. On his old Web site, in addition to publishing his NEW AGE teachings, WorldPeace also advertised his services as an attorney in Houston, Texas. Web site—http://www.statebaroftexass.com. See PANTHEISM.

The World Tomorrow: Originally a radio and television program produced by HERBERT W. ARMSTRONG, *The World Tomorrow* is now a television program produced by the LIVING CHURCH OF GOD. Web site— http://www.livingcog.org/cgi-bin/tw/telecast/tw-telecast.cgi?action=view_ telecast_h.

Worldwide Church of God, Herbert W. Armstrong—Pasadena, CA: Under the leadership of its founder, HERBERT W. ARMSTRONG, this church rejected the essential doctrines of EVANGELICAL CHRISTIANITY and denied the doctrine of the TRINITY, the full deity of Jesus, and the personality of the HOLY SPIRIT. The church epitomized the somewhat eclectic set of beliefs and practices that became known as ARMSTRONGISM. Beginning in the early 1990s, under the leadership of Armstrong's successors, Joseph W. Tkach and his son, Joseph Tkach, Jr., this group has undergone remarkable doctrinal transformation. They now hold to a traditional evangelical position on the nature of God and the GOSPEL, teaching the doctrine of the TRINITY and SALVATION BY GRACE through faith. The church is now an expression of evangelical

Christianity and is a member of the National Association of Evangelicals (NAE). A large percentage of its membership has left to join splinter groups that still teach classic Armstrongism. Through its Plain Truth Ministries, the church publishes *The Plain Truth* magazine and produces *Plain Truth Radio.* Web site—http://www.wcg.org.

Worrall, Olga: See NEW LIFE CLINIC.

Y

Yahweh ben Yahweh: Founder of the NATION OF YAHWEH.

Yahwehism: Yahwehism is a SACRED NAME movement that insists upon the use—and very specific pronunciation—of the Tetragrammaton (the required pronunciation can vary between groups). Followers of Yahwehism are generally SABBATARIAN, requiring an adherence to the dietary laws and festivals of the Old Testament. The movement includes a large number of groups with various names; it should be noted, however, that some individuals and groups that incorporate the name *Yahweh*—such as YAHWEH BEN YAHWEH—are not followers of Yahwehism.

Yahweh's Assembly in Messiah, David Barnard—Rocheport, MO: The assembly practices YAHWEHISM. Though headquartered in Rocheport, groups meet in six additional locations in Pennsylvania, Alabama, Indiana, Oklahoma, Texas, and Michigan. The assembly publishes *The Master Key, Unlocking Bible Truth* magazine. Web site—http://www.yaim.org.

Yi King: See I CHING.

Yin and Yang: A fundamental concept of TAOISM is harmony and unity: the word *tao* signifies a way of life that is in harmony with the natural laws of the universe (as well as the principle that governs those laws). Directly related to this are the concepts of *yin* and *yang:* in order to achieve harmony, yin and yang must be in balance. Yin and yang represent the necessary polarity in every object. The yin is the feminine, negative, and passive force in the universe; night and water are part of the yin. Yang is the masculine, positive, and active force in the universe; day and the sun are part of the yang.

In traditional Chinese medicine, the body is viewed as a whole: Therefore (in a simplification of the concept), the interior and front of the body, and below the waist, belong to the yin; and the exterior and back of the body, and above the waist, belong to the yang. An imbalance between yin and yang is the source of physical ailments. These ailments are treated through readjustment—e.g., cold symptoms are therefore treated with heat. An imbalance between yin and yang further leads to a blockage or imbalance in the flow of CHI; many NEW AGE medical techniques are intended to balance and restore the flow of CHI. See ACUPUNCTURE; HOLISTIC HEALTH; TOUCH THERAPY.

Yoga: The word *yoga* is taken from the Sanskrit word that means "union." HINDUISM teaches that through yoga, the individual moves beyond the "surface mind" of life in the body to fully realize the union of oneself with all selfs in the one spirit. There are five main paths of yoga: 1) BHAKTI YOGA (the path of devotion to a GURU), 2) HATHA YOGA (the path of the body; commonly used in North America for physical exercise); 3) KARMA YOGA (the path of selfless action); 4) Jnana Yoga (the path of transcendental knowledge); 5) Raja Yoga (the path of stillness through MEDITATION). To these paths are added such practices as TANTRA or Kriya Yoga (union with Shakti through the rising of the KUNDALINI); MANTRA Yoga (the path of transformative sound); and Laya Yoga (the path of dissolution). All the paths of yoga are based upon the Eastern concept of PANTHEISM.

Yoga Journal—Berkeley, CA: The most popular periodical on the practices of YOGA. Web site—http://www.yogajournal.com.

Yogananda, Paramahansa: See SELF-REALIZATION FELLOWSHIP.

Yoga Research Foundation, Jyotirmayananda—Miami, FL: Swami Jyotir-mayananda moved to Puerto Rico in 1962 after working as a professor of religion at the Yoga Vedanta Forest Academy in India; he then moved to Miami in 1969. Jyotirmayananda teaches a YOGA practice called Integral Yoga; the goal of this practice goes beyond self-realization to achieve an innate happiness. Web site—http://www.yrf.org.

Yoga Research Society—Philadelphia, PA: In 1924, Swami Kuvalayananda began applying a scientific approach to the study of YOGA. Under the direction of Vijayendra Pratap, the society works to integrate yoga into Western medical theories and practices. The society hosts seminars and workshops that teach medical practitioners how to utilize such practices as yoga and AYURVEDIC MEDICINE, as well as general courses on yoga. Web site—http://www.yogaresearchsociety.com.

Yogi: A master or teacher of YOGA.

York, Malachi Z.: Founder of the ANCIENT MYSTIC ORDER OF MALCHIZEDEK.

Your Choice—Warren, MI: A magazine that promotes SABBATARIANISM. Web site—http://www.biblestudy.org/ychoice/main.html.

Z

Zacharias, Ravi: A popular philosopher, APOLOGIST, and evangelist who promotes EVANGELICAL CHRISTIANITY, Zacharias is Visiting Professor at Wycliffe Hall, Oxford University and author of a number of best-selling books, including *Can Man Live Without God?*, *The Lotus and the Cross: Jesus Talks with Buddha,* and *Light in the Shadow of Jihad.* He is also the general editor of the current edition of *The Kingdom of the Cults* written by the late WALTER MARTIN. His organization, Ravi Zacharias International Ministries (RZIM), is headquartered in Norcross, Georgia, with staff in six countries. Web site—http://www.rzim.org.

Zen Buddhism: Zen is a branch of Mahayana BUDDHISM believed to have been brought to China by Bodhidharma approximately 526 B.C. Zen was brought to Japan in the seventh-century, but did not flourish until the twelfth-thirteenth centuries with the founding of the Rinzai school (founded by Eisai in 1191) and the Soto school (founded by Dogan before 1253). Practitioners of Zen seek *satori* (sudden illumination enabling bliss and harmony), which cannot be explained but only experienced. Techniques for achieving satori include *zazen* (sitting MEDITATION techniques) and the employment of *koans,* a riddle or paradoxical statement that embodies a realized principle. *Koans* (which number about 1,700) are not designed to have cognitive answers, but be realized in experience.

Zen Master Rama: *Zen Master Rama* was the pseudonym of Frederick P. Lenz (1950–98), a software designer who was believed by many followers to be the incarnation of VISHNU. In the 1970s, Lenz was a student of SRI CHINMOY, but in 1980 started his own organization. Lenz taught that enlightenment could be achieved through a process of MEDITATION called *Tantric Zen;* many former followers accused Lenz of sexual and drug abuse. In the mid-1990s Lenz authored the best-selling NEW AGE books *Surfing the Himalayas* and *Snowboarding to Nirvana,* in which a snowboarder studies under a Buddhist monk and learns the secrets of other dimensions. Lenz committed suicide in 1998. Web site—http://www.fredericklenzfoun dation.org. See SPIRITUAL ABUSE.

Zendik Farm, Wulf and Arol Aendik—Mill Spring, NC: Zendik Farm was started in 1969 as a sanctuary for artists, in accordance with the Aendiks' belief that humans are biologically inclined toward COMMUNAL LIVING. The farm promotes the "Genius Potential Principle": every individual has interests that can lead them to artistic genius. Zendik promotes a new religious movement called *Creavolution,* in which—by accepting that the individual is part of the one creative energy of the universe—the person will fully evolve with the creative universe. Zendik produces *The Zendik Perspective* television program. Web site—http://www.zendik.org. See PANTHEISM.

Zodiac: The zodiac is an imaginary celestial band, centered on an elliptic, which encompasses the paths of all the planets (excluding Pluto). The zodiac is divided into 12 constellations or signs, and each sign is believed to influence the energy of the planets. See ASTROLOGY.

Zohar: A group of books central to KABBALAH. The Zohar is reputed to be the second-century work of Simeon ben Yohai, but was compiled in thirteenth-century Spain by Moses ben Shem-Tov de Leon. See JUDAISM.

Zombie: According to VOODOO beliefs, the bodies of the dead can be reanimated into a TRANCE-like state by a SHAMAN to do his bidding. Some have hypothesized that a powerful drug may be used to simulate death and to control the victim. A botanist, Dr. Wade Davis, presented a pharmacological case for zombies in his popular book *The Serpent and the Rainbow,* which was also adapted into a motion picture. See VOODOO.

Zoroastrianism, Zarathushtra: Zoroastrianism is generally understood by historians to have begun about 1500–1000 B.C. in Persia. Founded by Zarathushtra (*Zoroaster* in Greek), the MONOTHEISTIC religion overcame the native POLYTHEISM and became the state religion until A.D. 650, when Islamic invaders took over the area and persecuted the Zoroastrians (a small number fled to India and now constitute the majority of Zoroastrian membership). Zoroastrian cosmology is dualistic: Ahura Mazda, the supreme God, is in continual conflict with Angra Mainyu, the spirit of evil. This conflict will involve the entire universe until the end of time, when goodness will prevail and evil will be destroyed (some Zoroastrians understand this conflict to be an internal, ethical battle within the human conscience). Zoroastrian worship is centered in prayer and ceremony; central to this ceremony is the sacred fire that represents God. In some Zoroastrian practices, *haoma,* a hallucinogenic, is used to reach the divine power. The Zoroastrian life follows the path of good thoughts, good words, and good deeds. The Zoroastrian sacred text is the Avesta, which contains the Gathas, or five hymns allegedly written by Zarathushtra.

Zukav, Gary: Author of best-seller *Seat of the Soul,* which clarifies many of his NEW AGE views. He teaches that all must become part of the Universal Human, or citizens of the universe, a living, conscious entity that is intelligent and feeling. This occurs as humans become multisensory, trusting the intuition of the soul rather than the five physical senses, thus increasing their awareness of the universe. As this is done, the body and personality will evolve through future lives, or REINCARNATION. Zukav believes the physical body and the personality are temporal but the soul is immortal. He says this evolution takes place through the power of intention and the rate at which it takes place is dependent upon the degree to which the intentions of one's personality are brought into agreement with those of the soul during each life. According to Zukav, intention determines whether negative or positive KARMA is created. The ultimate goal is to attain "authentic power": the personality brought under the energy of the soul. OPRAH WINFREY is a fan of Zukav's and has had him as a guest on her show numerous times. She includes *Seat of the Soul* as one of her favorite books, stating on her Web site, "We are held responsible for every action, thought and feeling, which is to say, for our every intention." Web site—www.zukav.com.

Zygon International, Dane Spotts—Redmond, WA: Zygon International claimed that its "Learning Machine" and "SuperMind" would enable users to expand their mental abilities, and change their thought processes and behaviors. It also made similarly extravagant claims for its "Fat Burner Pills" and "Day and Night Eyes." Under a 1996 settlement with the Federal Trade Commission, Zygon agreed to pay up to $195,000 in refunds to consumers.

Notes

1. "Top Twenty Religions in the United States, 2001" (with updated 2004 estimates). Accessed July 2006 at http://www.adherents.com/rel_USA.html#Pew_branches.

2. "The Religious and Other Beliefs of Americans 2003."Accessed August 2006 at http://www.harrisinteractive.com/harris_poll/index.asp?PID=359.

3. Top Ten Organized Religions in the United States, 2001" (with updated 2004 estimates). Accessed August 2006 at http://www.adherents.com/rel_USA.html#Pew_branches.

4. "Statistics: 2005 Report of Jehovah's Witnesses Worldwide." Accessed August 2006 at http://www.watchtower.org/statistics/worldwide_report.htm.

5. "The Missionary Program." Accessed August 2006 at http://www.lds.org/newsroom/page/0,15606,4037-1---6-168,00.html.

6. "Key Facts and Figures." Accessed August 2006 at http://www.lds.org/newsroom/page/0,15606,4034-1---10-168,00.html.

7. "Largest denominational families in the U.S., 2001." Accessed July 2006 at http://www.adherents.com/rel_USA.html#Pew_branches.

8. "Statistics: 2005 Report of Jehovah's Witnesses Worldwide."

9. *The Concise Evangelical Dictionary of Theology*, s.v. "Cults."

10. "Cultic Studies: Information about Cults and Psychological Manipulation." Accessed August 2006 at http://www.csj.org.

11. This general meaning is also reflected in the third basic definition for *cult* listed in *Merriam-Webster's Collegiate Dictionary*, Eleventh Edition: "3: a religion regarded as unorthodox or spurious; *also*: its body of adherents."

12. Thomas Keating, *Open Mind, Open Heart* (Rockport, MA: Element, 1992), p. 29.

About Watchman Fellowship

Watchman Fellowship, founded in 1979, is one of America's largest Christian discernment ministries and provides research, education, and outreach for individuals involved with new religious movements, cults, and the occult. With offices in seven states and missionaries in Eastern Europe, we maintain a research library of over 50,000 cataloged resources (including files, books, periodicals, and media) and an award-winning Web site, www.watchman.org. Teaching in hundreds of churches, colleges, and universities annually, we help tens of thousands to understand biblical Christianity as contrasted to new religious movements, cults, the occult, and New Age spirituality. We are recognized by the media as trusted experts and have been interviewed on *Nightline, World News Tonight, The NewsHour with Jim Lehrer,* and *USA Today.* For contact information, visit www.watchman.org.

To learn more about books by Harvest House Publishers
or to read sample chapters, log on to our website:

www.harvesthousepublishers.com

HARVEST HOUSE PUBLISHERS

EUGENE, OREGON